Genocide Denials and the Law

Genocide Denials and the Law

LUDOVIC HENNEBEL THOMAS HOCHMANN

OXFORD
UNIVERSITY PRESS

OXFORD
UNIVERSITY PRESS

Oxford University Press, Inc., publishes works that further Oxford University's objective of excellence in research, scholarship, and education.

Oxford New York
Auckland Cape Town Dar es Salaam Hong Kong Karachi Kuala Lumpur Madrid Melbourne
Mexico City Nairobi New Delhi Shanghai Taipei Toronto

With offices in
Argentina Austria Brazil Chile Czech Republic France Greece Guatemala Hungary Italy
Japan Poland Portugal Singapore South Korea Switzerland Thailand Turkey Ukraine
Vietnam

Published by Oxford University Press, Inc.
198 Madison Avenue, New York, New York 10016

Library of Congress Cataloging-in-Publication Data

Genocide denials and the law / edited by Ludovic Hennebel, Thomas Hochmann.
p. cm.
Includes bibliographical references and index.
ISBN 978-0-19-973892-2 ((hardback) : alk. paper)
1. Genocide. 2. Criminal liability (International law)
3. Holocaust denial. I. Hennebel, Ludovic. II. Hochmann, Thomas.
K5´302.G36 2011
345′.0251--dc22 2010038786

1 2 3 4 5 6 7 8 9

Printed in the United States of America on acid-free paper

Note to Readers

This publication is designed to provide accurate and authoritative information in regard to the subject matter covered. It is based upon sources believed to be accurate and reliable and is intended to be current as of the time it was written. It is sold with the understanding that the publisher is not engaged in rendering legal, accounting, or other professional services. If legal advice or other expert assistance is required, the services of a competent professional person should be sought. Also, to confirm that the information has not been affected or changed by recent developments, traditional legal research techniques should be used, including checking primary sources where appropriate.

(Based on the Declaration of Principles jointly adopted by a Committee of the American Bar Association and a Committee of Publishers and Associations.)

Contents

Contributors

Lawrence Douglas: James J. Grossfeld Professor of Law, Jurisprudence and Social Thought at Amherst College. He is the author of four books including, *The Memory of Judgment* (Yale University Press, 2001).

David Fraser: Professor of Law and Social Theory at the University of Nottingham. He is the author of *Law After Auschwitz: Towards A Jurisprudence of the Holocaust* (Carolina Academic Press, 2005) and *The Fragility of Law: Constitutional Patriotism and the Jews of Belgium 1940–45* (Routledge, 2009), as well as several articles on Nazi law and legality and works on Holocaust Denial.

Emanuela Fronza: Professor of International Criminal Law, Researcher in Criminal Law, University of Trento (Italy), Faculty of Law. She is a Fellow of the Alexander von Humboldt Foundation at the University of Berlin, Faculty of Law. She is the author of several publications in the field of International Criminal Law, Criminal Law and Comparative Criminal Law, including: (Amati et al.) "Introduction to International Criminal Law" (Giuffré, Milan, 2005; II. edition 2010); she also co-authored (Delmas Marty et al.) the book, Le crime contre l´humanité" (Puf, Paris, 2009).

Ludovic Hennebel: Fellow at the National Fund for Scientific Research (Belgium); Member of the Perelman Center for Legal Philosophy at the Law School of the Université Libre de Bruxelles; Global Fellow at New York University (Law School, Center for Human Rights and Global Justice, B.A.E.F. Fellow 2007–2008); Faculty Director of the Magna Carta Institute. He is the author of a number of publications on international human rights law and global justice including a monograph on the American Convention on Human Rights (Bruylant, 2007) and a monograph on the International Covenant on Civil and Political Rights (Bruylant, 2007), published in French with Bruylant Publishers.

Thomas Hochmann: Research Fellow at the University of Paris Panthéon-Sorbonne where he taught public law. He won several awards for his PhD research (supervised by Professor O. Pfersmann) on Holocaust denial and freedom of speech, including a scholarship from the Fondation pour la Mémoire de la Shoah (2006) and the prize of the City of Paris for researches on anti-Semitism and xenophobia (2010). He is the author of a number of publications on human rights, freedom of speech, and comparative constitutional law in peer-reviewed journals and edited volumes.

Martin Imbleau: Lawyer (Quebec Bar, Canada). He is an independent researcher, mainly on the interplay between massive human rights violations and the establishment of historical truth. He is the author of a number of publications on human rights law and freedom of speech, notably La négation du génocide nazi, Liberté d'expression ou crime raciste? (Holocaust Denial: free speech or racist crime?, L'Harmattan, 2003) and articles in The Encyclopedia of Genocide and Crimes Against Humanity (Macmillan, 2004).

Robert A. Kahn: Associate Professor of Law at the University of Saint Thomas (Minnesota). He is the author of *Holocaust Denial and the Law: A Comparative Study* (Palgrave-MacMillan, 2004).

Kenneth Lasson: Professor of Law at the University of Baltimore. He has written and lectured widely on freedom of expression and religion, as well as Holocaust denial. He is the author of ten books (most recently *Trembling in the Ivory Tower: Excesses in the Pursuit of Truth and Tenure* [2003]) and numerous law review articles concerning civil liberties and international human rights.

Laurent Pech: *Jean Monnet* Lecturer in EU Public Law at the School of Law, National University of Ireland (Galway). He is the author of *Freedom of Expression and its Limitation. Lessons from the United States with regard to European case-law* (in French, L.G.D.J., 2003). He recently published *Fondement du droit de la presse et des médias* in B. Beignier et al. (eds), *Traité de droit de la presse et des medias* (Paris: LexisNexis, 2009), p. 69 and *Liberté d'expression: Aperçus de droit comparé* in *Juris-Classeur Communication* (Paris: LexisNexis, 2010), no. 1250.

Preface

"IRVING: CONSIGNED TO HISTORY as a racist liar," read the headline in *The Guardian* on April 12, 2000, after the famous decision by Justice Charles Gray in the libel suit against Deborah Lipstadt was released. I can still recall the excitement that morning, when I first saw it on a newsstand at the Vienna airport. The headline was provocative, almost as if *The Guardian* was inviting Irving to file another claim in court, against it this time, but I don't believe he ever did. The idea that he was "consigned to history" is rich in significance. The suggestion, finally, is that "history" triumphed over falsehood. In this case, at any rate, the marketplace of ideas seems to have worked.

My own views on this complex issue have evolved over the years. They may change in the future, too. Sometimes, I find myself sharing the opinion of the last persuasive person with whom I have spoken, my perspective tilting in one direction or another. I find myself torn between the militant anti-racism of punishing denial and a latent libertarianism that bristles at any attempt to muzzle expression. I think that at various times in my life, I have argued for both extremes on these issues. Now, I find myself somewhere in the middle. My preferable compass, international human rights law, seems to have two needles that point in opposite directions.

Nearly two decades ago, when I was teaching in Canada, the *Zundel* and *Keegstra* trials were on the docket of the Supreme Court. At about the same time, *Faurisson* was adjudicated by the United Nations Human Rights Committee. Both the Supreme Court of Canada and the Human Rights Committee seemed divided. There was a visible rupture in *Keegstra*, with four justices opting for what might be called the "European" approach to hate speech, while the minority of three judges preferred the "American" approach. In *Zundel*, the Court shifted ever so slightly the other way. It was a quintessentially Canadian standoff.

At the Human Rights Committee, the disagreement may have been more subtle. Thomas Buergenthal recused himself on the basis of his own personal involvement in the fact of Auschwitz, where he had been imprisoned as a boy. I never found this explanation for recusal to be very convincing. I would have thought a survivor would be a particularly appropriate person to assess the behavior of Faurisson. I've since wondered whether Judge Buergenthal might also have been of two minds, pulled between his inevitable hatred of anti-Semitism and the strong commitment to free speech that he would have absorbed as one of America's greatest human rights experts. I would love to read the decision that he never wrote. There was also a nuanced individual opinion signed, amongst others, by another Jewish member of the Committee, David Kretzmer. One can imagine the surprise of Faurisson himself, whose perverse world view probably made him fear a Jewish conspiracy. As it turned out, the Jewish members of the Committee were probably among those most uncomfortable with the French anti-denial legislation.

The legacy of the prosecutions of *Zundel, Keegstra,* and *Faurisson* seems shrouded in ambiguity, whereas it is the Irving trial, launched by the famous revisionist himself, which seems to have cleared the air. Since then, one has the impression that the storm of Holocaust denial may have passed or at least subsided. The big exception is Ahmadinejad's famous conference in Tehran. Iran's demagogic president muddles the distinction between anti-Semitism and harsh criticism of Israel. His opponents seize on the point and suggest that anti-Semitism is somehow linked to the important struggle for the rights of the Palestinians. Thus, the memory of one of history's greatest atrocities, the attempted extinction of European Jews, gets reduced to a debating ploy by both Ahmadinejad and his detractors.

But if denial was once a vehicle for anti-Semites, the concept has spread to other historical issues. The other two great genocides of the twentieth century, of the Armenians in the Ottoman Empire in 1915 and of the Rwandan Tutsi in 1994, have their own deniers. The Armenian diaspora has campaigned for legislation and declarations acknowledging the Armenian genocide, in some places with considerable success, in others with failure. Debates about historical events of nearly a century ago feature on parliamentary agendas in Brussels, Washington, and elsewhere. Increasingly, legal regulations seem to frame our view of history. Truth has become a matter for legislators, a strange situation given the reputation of many politicians.

Often, there is confusion between the factual underpinning and its legal qualification. The term "genocide" has become such a loaded label that those who may disagree on its application to specific facts find themselves called "deniers," even if there is little or no disagreement about the reality of the events themselves. Thus, some who speak of crimes against humanity in Bosnia or Darfur or Cambodia but who resist the term "genocide" may find themselves described as "deniers." And what of disputing whether the Ukrainian famine of the 1930s, whose cause may have been a combination of the natural and artificial, should be branded as genocide? Or the argument as to whether the bombing of Hiroshima and Nagasaki was "genocide" or a lawful act of war?

There is a lot of abuse of language, and it is not just the racists who are responsible. Well-meaning activists for groups of victims sometimes indulge in their own forms of hyperbole. This can poison both historical and legal debate. At what point does legitimate discussion about the appropriate terminology to describe historic atrocities start to merge with vulgar racism? Law doesn't have to provide absolute clarity, but it should aspire to a norm with some degree of predictability, so that sincere academic discussion can be clearly demarcated from hate propaganda.

The European Parliament made a stab at this in its recent Framework Directive. It requires Member States to enact legislation addressed at punishment of "publicly condoning, denying or grossly trivializing crimes of genocide, crimes against humanity and war crimes . . . carried out in a manner likely to incite to violence or hatred" against groups defined by race, color, religion, descent, or national or ethnic origin. Thus, denial is linked to incitement, which becomes the real test. It is presented as a form of incitement, although an inchoate one in the sense that the law can intervene before the result.

The "likely to incite" phrase seems calculated to make this context specific. For example, it would appear unlikely that an Irish historian or legal academic who disputed elements of the great famine who be "likely to incite" violence or hatred, although this remark might well have been less unequivocal a few decades ago, at the height of the "troubles" and if the denial were made in one of the conflict zones of Northern Ireland.

The objective approach by which denial is "likely to incite" seems preferable to the subjectivity of other legislative models, such as the Additional Protocol on the Convention on Cybercrime. The latter makes the test whether denial "is committed with the intent to incite hatred, discrimination or violence." The focus is on the individual intent, rather than on the environment and the probability of consequences. We may make more progress in dealing with racism by focusing on the potential for results. The more obvious the danger of violence and persecution, the more such encroachments on freedom of expression can find some justification. Where these threats are absent or very remote, it is much harder to allow the law to intervene, even in situations where the intent is an ugly one.

In the final words of their introduction, Ludovic Hennebel and Thomas Hochmann invite the readers to "decide for themselves." There will be some, however, including myself, who are buffeted by conflicting values and who find they are unable to draw a clear line. Maybe that's because there isn't one.

Professor William Schabas OC MRIA
Galway, January 25, 2010

Introduction
Questioning the Criminalization of Denials

-Ludovic Hennebel & Thomas Hochmann

FOR HISTORIANS, DENIAL OF GENOCIDE (or of any other crime against humanity) does not raise any serious issue. Indeed, they can demonstrate easily the absurdity of the deniers' arguments. Furthermore, historians can take denial as a subject of inquiry.[1] They can wonder whether it is preferable to expose the denier for what he is in a debate, or rather to avoid such direct confrontation, given the fact that deniers understand better than anybody else Schopenhauer's *Art of Controversy* and its leitmotiv that the "discovery of objective truth must be separated from the art of winning acceptance for propositions; for objective truth is an entirely different matter."[2] It seems fair to say that one of Schopenhauer's stratagems to win this acceptance seems to have been written for deniers:

> This is chiefly practicable in a dispute between scholars in the presence of the unlearned. If you have no argument *ad rem*, and none either *ad hominem*, you can make one *ad auditores*; that is to say, you can start some invalid objection, which, however, only an expert sees to be invalid. . . . To show that your objection is an idle one, would require a long explanation on the part of your opponent, and a reference to the principles of the branch of knowledge in question, or to the elements of the matter which you are discussing; and people are not disposed to listen to it.[3]

---

1. See, for instance, DEBORAH LIPSTADT, DENYING THE HOLOCAUST: THE GROWING ASSAULT ON TRUTH AND MEMORY (New York: Free Press, 1993); FLORENT BRAYARD, COMMENT L'IDÉE VINT À M. RASSINIER, NAISSANCE DU RÉVISIONNISME (Paris: Fayard, 1996); VALÉRIE IGOUNET, HISTOIRE DU NÉGATIONNISME EN FRANCE (Paris: Seuil, 2000).

2. ARTHUR SCHOPENHAUER, THE ART OF CONTROVERSY (London: Swan Sonnenschein & Co., 1990), 7 (Die Kunst, Recht zu behalten, 1831.)

3. *Id.* at 42.

Furthermore, because the deniers' contributions are void to the historical inquiry, most historians have concluded that although demonstrating the deniers' falsehood is a task worth undertaking, it is preferable not to honor the deniers with a debate; or to put it in a widely quoted formula: "there can be no question of any discussion with [the negationists]."[4]

Denial is much more problematic for the legal scholar since denial prohibition currently may be the most controversial issue related to the freedom of expression in Europe, especially since the 2008 adoption of the European Union Framework Decision on combating racism and xenophobia. The present book aims at offering a legal analysis of such a limit on free speech along with some legal-political reflections on its legitimacy.

In this general introduction to the book, some clarification must be made concerning the title. Although it refers to "Genocide Denials," the present volume includes the study of denial of other crimes against humanity. Most of the existing statutes only target the denial of the Holocaust and other crimes against humanity committed by the Nazis and their accomplices. For a long time, only Switzerland and Spain had adopted a broader approach; the former for every crime against humanity and the latter for every genocide.[5] Things may change however, due to the European Union's Framework Decision, which includes the denial of any genocide, crime against humanity, or war crime. One should nevertheless be aware that the Framework Decision contains other stipulations restricting its scope; indeed, it seems only to require the Member States to target "aggravated denial."[6]

---

4. Pierre Vidal-Naquet, *Qui sont les assassins de la mémoire?* (1981), *in* Pierre Vidal-Naquet, Les Assassins de la Mémoire 206 (Paris: La découverte, 2005)

5. The Spanish statute was found to be unconstitutional by the Tribunal Constitucional in 2007. See in this volume the contributions of Emmanuela Fronza and Laurent Pech.

6. According to Article 1, the denial must be "directed against a group of persons or a member of such a group defined by reference to race, colour, religion, descent or national or ethnic origin." (The English and the French versions of the Decision do not allow understanding whether this requirement applies to the expression of denial or to the denied crime, but the German and Italian versions do not leave any doubt.) The denial must also be "likely to incite to violence or hatred against such a group or a member of such a group." Furthermore, Article 1, paragraph 2 allows limiting the punishment of denial to the cases where it is "threatening, abusive or insulting."

"Denial,"[7] indeed, describes many types of expression.[8] Under its purest form, denial is an expression contesting the existence of a crime or a characteristic feature of a crime.[9] Examples include statements such as "the Holocaust did not happen," and "no gas chambers were used to kill anybody under the Third Reich." The German legal scholarship[10] called this kind of denial *einfache Auschwitzleugnung*, which can be translated as "bare denial." But there exists also a kind of expression called *qualifizierte Auschwitzleugnung* or "aggravated denial." In this case, a group of individuals is targeted explicitly. An example is the "usual" claim that "Jews invented the myth of the Holocaust to exploit Germany financially." Furthermore, some expressions are closely related to denial. More often than not, the statutes forbidding the denial of a crime against humanity also target its approval, justification, and minimization.[11]

It seems that these various expressions can be located on a continuum stretching from "hate speech" to "bare denial." Aggravated denial is indeed a kind of hate speech, a hostile expression targeting a group of individuals for some reasons such as origin, nationality, color, or "race." Justification, approval, or qualitative minimization of a crime against humanity, while not necessarily targeting anyone explicitly, can be linked quite easily to the expression of hate and possibly also to the infliction of harm toward victims of crimes alleged to have been legitimate. Bare denial and quantitative minimization—considered literally—do not appear to target anybody; rather, they seem to act only as general statements about a historical event without drawing any conclusions.

Of these kinds of speech, the most striking issue arises with bare denial and quantitative minimization. The well-examined path of "hate speech"

---

7. The French word for Denial is *Négationnisme*. In German, Holocaust Denial is referred to as *Auschwitzleugnung*, although a number of authors keep on resorting to the confusing term of *Auschwitzlüge* (Auschwitz Lie).

8. *See* Gérard Cohen-Jonathan, *Négationnisme et droits de l'homme -Droit international et européen (la sentence du Comité des droits de l'homme, Faurisson c. France)*, 32 REVUE TRIMESTRIELLE DES DROITS DE L'HOMME 571 (1997).

9. CAROLE VIVANT, L'HISTORIEN SAISI PAR LE DROIT. CONTRIBUTION À L'ÉTUDE DES DROITS DE L'HISTOIRE 417 (Paris: Dalloz, 2007).

10. See, for instance, the major German study on the topic: THOMAS WANDRES, DIE STRAFBARKEIT DES AUSCHWITZ-LEUGNENS 96–9 (Berlin: Duncker & Humblot, 2000).

11. For an overview of the statutes, please refer in this volume to the contribution of Martin Imbleau.

is certainly relevant to any study of genocide denial,[12] but one must acknowledge that "bare denial" confronts the regulation of freedom of expression with some new questions and casts a new light on some more classical "hate speech regulation" problems. Some of these questions are merely legal, while others pertain more broadly to the political or philosophical reflection about the limitation of expression. This introduction (1) presents the main legal issues raised by the prohibition of denial, (2) offers some deeper analysis of the relationship between freedom of speech and denial in international law, and (3) inquires about the existence of an international obligation to criminalize denial under international human rights law. Last, (4) it confronts the main political and moral arguments *pro* or *contra* the prohibition of denials.

1. Prohibiting Denials: Legal Issues

The first question that arises whenever one studies the constitutionality of a norm forbidding a type of behavior is whether the behavior is covered by the Constitution, i.e., whether it belongs to the domain of protection (*Schutzbereich*) of some of the guarantee of the right. In some legal systems, denial is precluded from any protection at this very first step. The European Court of Human Rights considers Holocaust denial to "run counter to the fundamental values of the Convention, as expressed in its Preamble, namely justice and peace"[13] and thus is excluded from any protection by the Convention, in accordance to Article 17. In Austria, the *Verbotsgesetz* (Prohibition Act), a norm with constitutional rank, forbids any expression favorable to the Nazi ideology, including the denial of crimes committed in its name.[14] One can also wonder whether some treaties are arguing for genocide denial as an internationally uncovered expression.

More tangentially, the German Constitutional Court ruled that as a false statement of fact dealing with a notorious historical event, "bare" Holocaust

---

12. See the recently published and excellent collection of essays gathered in EXTREME SPEECH AND DEMOCRACY, (Ivan Hare & James Weinstein eds., New York: Oxford University Press, 2009). On the relationship between "bare" denial and hate speech, see the contribution of Robert Kahn in this volume.

13. Garaudy v. France (dec.), no. 65831/01, 2003. See *infra*.

14. See Felix Müller, DAS VERBOTSGESETZIM SPANNUNGSVERHÄLTNIS ZUR MEINUNGSFREIHEIT (Vienna: Verlag Österreich, 2005).

denial, did not belong to the domain of protection of the freedom of expression.[15] One could wonder whether the almost proverbial sentence of the Supreme Court of the United States in *Gertz v. Robert Welch, Inc.*, stating that "there is no constitutional value in false statements of fact,"[16] could be understood as denial as an expression uncovered by the First Amendment. However, one should not forget the subsequent observation that the "First Amendment requires that we protect some falsehood in order to protect speech that matters."[17] The First Amendment does cover false statements of facts: they can be suppressed only in some circumstances, such as defamation, and even then only under certain conditions, such as proving the speaker's "actual malice" or at least negligence.[18]

To say that an expression is covered by the protection of free speech does not lead to any conclusion regarding its effective protection. Indeed, in most legal systems, the norm that guarantees the freedom of expression entails some possibilities to restrict it under certain conditions, such as for the protection of individual rights or collective interests.

There are two main ways to forbid an expression, both of which can apply to denial. First, a lawmaker can target an expression that has some consequences and provokes some harm. These harmful effects may pertain to individuals (for instance, seeing denial as harming victims and survivors of the denied crime and/or their descendants). A lawmaker may also wish to counter a more general and indirect consequence, like the threat to democracy perceived in a whitewashing of National Socialism. The organ applying these kinds of norms will have to establish whether the targeted consequence did occur.

In Germany for instance, Holocaust deniers can be convicted with the offenses of insult or defamation, since the courts consider this expression to be an attack on the "personality," that is, the "self-conception" (*Selbstverständnis*) of Jews living today in the country.[19] In the United States,

---

15. BVerfGE 90, 241, 249. See in this volume the contribution of Laurent Pech.

16. 418 U.S. 323 (1974), 340.

17. *Id.*, 341.

18. *See* New York Times Co. v. Sullivan, 376 U.S. 254 (1964), 279; Gertz v. Robert Welch, Inc., 418 U.S. 323 (1974), 347.

19. This reasoning of a 1979 decision of the civil chamber of the Federal Court of Justice was afterwards adopted by both criminal and constitutional jurisprudence. In 1985, a statute was voted that suppressed the requirement of a request to prosecute for a lawsuit based on insult if the person targeted was persecuted as a member of a group under the National

given the unconstitutionality of group libel regulation after *New York Times v. Sullivan*[20] and *R.A.V. v. City of St. Paul*,[21] Holocaust denial cannot be prosecuted as a defamation of "the Jews." Nevertheless, it is fair to say that the case—which seems insignificant for practical purposes—of an aggravated denial targeting a specific individual can be punished in the United States: "X is a liar because the Holocaust did not happen" may give rise to liability.[22]

The European Union Framework Decision requiring the prohibition of denial allows the Member States to include such a "consequential requirement" in their statutes. One should wait and see how this international instrument will be implemented, but it is possible to already observe that most of the statutes specifically targeting denial did not choose this path. Germany seems to link the prohibition of denial with some consequences since its statute requires that the speech be able to "disturb the public peace." But the definition of "public peace" shows how toothless this requirement is. It is generally understood by German scholars and judges to be "the condition of general security as well as general trust in the further existence of safe conditions and the sense of security within the population."[23] One must thus agree that such a "public peace" is automatically "disturbed" whenever a criminal act is committed.[24]

Socialist or another authoritarian regime and if the insult is connected to this persecution. A very widespread extrapolation and mistake in the English and French speaking scholarship persists in arguing that this statute forbade Holocaust denial. The article usually cited to support this claim did not make it. *See* Eric Stein, ***History against Free Speech: The New German Law against the "Auschwitz"—and Other—Lies"***, 85 MICH. L. REV. 277 (1986). It seems that the French Parliament was also persuaded that Germany forbade Holocaust denial in 1985 and intended to follow this example while voting the Gayssot Act in 1990. See Jean Stengers, ***Quelques libres propos sur « Faurisson, Roques et Cie »***, CAHIERS-BIJDRAGEN, Centre de recherches et d'études historiques de la seconde guerre mondiale, no. 29, May 12, 1989. No earlier than 1994 did Germany pass a law forbidding Holocaust denial.

20. 376 U.S. 254 (1964).

21. 505 U.S. 377 (1992).

22. The Supreme Court ruled explicitly that "X is a liar" can be a defamatory statement. Milkovich v. Lorain Journal, 497 U.S. 1 (1990), 19.

23. See Tatjana Hörnle, *Offensive Behavior and German Penal Law*, 5 BUFF. CRIM. L. REV. 255 (2001), 256.

24. See Andreas Stegbauer, *Anmerkung*, JURISTISCHE RUNDSCHAU (2003), 75. It seems therefore that the "public peace" clause is nothing but a way to comply with the constitutional requirement that a statute limiting expression be "general," i.e., that it does not target an opinion as such but aims at protecting some interest. However, the Constitutional Court seemed recently to adopt a more demanding conception of the public peace, defining its

Therefore, the German statute corresponds much more to the second manner of forbidding an expression and is similar to most of the other European statutes forbidding denial that target a meaning without requiring the judge to verify that it has caused some harmful consequences. The prohibition of denial seems therefore to be very "un-American" because one of the most characteristic features of the First Amendment is precisely that "[w]henever the fundamental rights of free speech and assembly are alleged to have been invaded, it must remain open to a defendant to present the issue whether there actually did exist at the time a clear danger; [and] whether the danger, if any, was imminent."[25] The legislative estimation is "merely a rebuttable presumption that these conditions have been satisfied."[26] In Europe and Canada, the rational legislative estimation that racist speech or genocide denial is likely to have some harmful consequences is sufficient to justify speech regulation, and thus a mere meaning can be prohibited without requiring that its empirical consequences be verified in each case. American judges, to the contrary, "are compelled to examine for [themselves] the statements in issue and the circumstances under which they were made to see whether or not they do carry a threat of clear and present danger."[27] In the words of one contributor to this volume: "While Americans, post-Brandenburg, debate about the impact of the words on an audience, Europeans debate the meaning of the words themselves."[28] European statutes forbidding genocide denial generally do not require the judge applying it to establish that the speech caused any harm to anybody or threatened anything. As a result, since the mens rea of an offense is linked with its actus reus, these statutes, lacking a specific provision, also do not require evidence that the denier intended to inflict any harm.[29]

Of course, the fact that the lawmaker did not make harmful effects of denial a part of the offense does not mean that it did not want to avoid such consequences. From a legal point of view, the judge controlling the

---

threat as the danger of the commission of an illegal act. See BVerfG (2009), *Wunsiedel*, 1 BvR 2150/08, par. 77–78.

25. Whitney v. California, 274 U.S. 357 (1927), 378–79 (Brandeis, conc.)

26. *Id.*, 379.

27. Pennekamp v. Florida, 328 U.S. 331 (1946), 335. See especially Brandenburg v. Ohio, 395 U.S. 444 (1969), 447.

28. See in this volume the contribution of Robert Kahn.

29. See in this volume the contribution of Thomas Hochmann.

conformity of the statute with a superior norm will be competent to identify which possibility to limit the freedom of expression the statute concretizes, a task that in some cases can amount to identifying which consequences one can attribute to denial.

The International Human Rights Law regime regarding freedom of expression helps to understand the dialectic between denial and free speech. The posture of international human rights law regarding genocide denials can be analyzed through two main questions. First, the criminalization of genocide denial questions the compatibility of such limitations to freedom of speech with human rights standards. It questions whether and under what conditions States may or may not, under international human rights law, criminalize genocide denials. Second, international human rights law may impose some positive obligations born by the States to criminalize some behaviors that affect the full enjoyment of the rights and liberties protected at the international level. It is therefore critical to solve the question of whether or not the States have a positive obligation under international human rights law to criminalize denials.

2. Denial as Speech

Deniers claim the protection of their freedom of expression. That is why the chapters of this book refer extensively to the moral foundations and the legal arrangements related to free speech. This freedom is one of the key human rights protected in all the major human rights treaties as well as in most of the world's domestic constitutions. At the international and regional levels, the protection of freedom of expression is provided by the 1948 Universal Declaration of Human Rights (UDHR),[30] the 1966 International Covenant on Civil and Political Rights (ICCPR),[31] the 1950 European Convention for the

30. Universal Declaration of Human Rights, G.A. Res. 217 (III), U.N. Doc. A/810, at 71 (1948), Art. 19: "Everyone has the right to freedom of opinion and expression; this right includes freedom to hold opinions without interference and to seek, receive and impart information and ideas through any media and regardless of frontiers."

31. International Covenant on Civil and Political Rights, opened for signature Dec. 19, 1966, 999 U.N.T.S. 171 (entered into force Mar. 23, 1976), art. 19 § 2: "Everyone shall have the right to freedom of expression; this right shall include freedom to seek, receive and impart information and ideas of all kinds, regardless of frontiers, either orally, in writing or in print, in the form of art, or through any other media of his choice."

Protection of Human Rights and Fundamental Freedoms (ECHR),[32] the 1969 American Convention on Human Rights (ACHR),[33] the 1981 Banjul Charter of Human and Peoples' Rights (ACHP),[34] and the 1966 International Convention on the Elimination of All Forms of Racial Discrimination (CERD).[35]

Freedom of expression is a pillar of democratic societies, based on pluralism of ideas and thoughts. Even the ideas and thoughts that offend, shock, or disturb the State or part of the population are deemed to have the full protection of the freedom of speech. As the European Court of Human Rights stated in the 1976 landmark case *Handyside*:

> The Court's supervisory functions oblige it to pay the utmost attention to the principles characterising a "democratic society." Freedom of expression constitutes one of the essential foundations of such a society, one of the basic conditions for its progress and for the development of every man. Subject to paragraph 2 of Article 10 . . ., it is applicable not only to "information" or "ideas" that are favourably received or regarded as inoffensive or as a matter of indifference, but also to those that offend, shock or disturb the State or any sector of the population. Such are the demands of that pluralism, tolerance and broadmindedness without which there is no "democratic society." This means, amongst other things,

---

32. European Convention for the Protection of Human Rights and Fundamental Freedoms, opened for signature Nov. 4, 1950, 213 U.N.T.S. 221 (entered into force Sept. 3, 1953), art. 10 § 1: "Everyone has the right to freedom of expression. This right shall include freedom to hold opinions and to receive and impart information and ideas without interference by public authority and regardless of frontiers. This article shall not prevent States from requiring the licensing of broadcasting, television or cinema enterprises."

33. American Convention on Human Rights, opened for signature Nov. 22, 1969, 1144 U.N.T.S. 143 (entered into force July 18, 1978), art. 13 § 1: "Everyone has the right to freedom of thought and expression. This right includes freedom to seek, receive, and impart information and ideas of all kinds, regardless of frontiers, either orally, in writing, in print, in the form of art, or through any other medium of one's choice."

34. Banjul Charter of Human and Peoples' Rights, June 27, 1981, 21 I.L.M. 58 (1982), art. 9 § 2: "Every individual shall have the right to express and disseminate his opinions within the law."

35. International Convention on the Elimination of All Forms of Racial Discrimination, opened for signature Mar. 7, 1966, 660 U.N.T.S. 195 (entered into force Mar. 12, 1969), art. 5 (d) (viii): "In compliance with the fundamental obligations laid down in article 2 of this Convention, States Parties undertake to prohibit and to eliminate racial discrimination in all its forms and to guarantee the right of everyone, without distinction as to race, colour, or national or ethnic origin, to equality before the law, notably in the enjoyment of the following rights: (viii) the right to freedom of opinion and expression."

that every "formality," "condition," "restriction" or "penalty" imposed in this sphere must be proportionate to the legitimate aim pursued.[36]

In international human rights law, freedom of expression is therefore based on the principle expressed by the Handyside paradigm according to which a democracy must not only accept but also protect ideas that are not shared by the majority. Freedom of speech is so fundamental in a democratic society that the States should avoid interference.[37] A vast range of discourses or ideas are protected by the freedom of expression. More than scrutinizing and assessing what is being said, the international bodies tend to analyze the *general aim pursued by the use of freedom of speech* that is defined in a very wide manner.[38] This liberal and pluralist approach is adopted by such other international organs as the Inter-American Court of Human Rights[39] and the United Nations Human Rights Committee.[40]

The freedom of expression is fundamental for democratic societies—there is no doubt on this assertion—and international human rights law confirms it. However, that freedom is not absolute and may be limited by the States under certain conditions. The limitation aims at balancing the freedom of expression and the rights and liberties of others. The limitation rule is expressly provided by Article 10 § 2 of the European Convention,[41]

---

36. Handyside v. UK, no. 5493/72, 1976, §49.

37. This significant role played by the freedom of speech in a democratic society is underlinded by all international organs. For the HRC's position, see for example Mukong v. Cameroun, n°458/1991 (1991), par. 9.7.

38. The European case law dealing with defamation, for example, shows that before deciding whether the domestic condemnation of a journalist for defamation is justified or not, the European Court controls the content of the discourse and the issue it deals with (corruption, justice, public administration, use of public funds, public affairs, health, environmental issues, nuclear policy, historical debate, etc. . .) as well as the person targeted by the discourse (public or private person). See Eur. Court of H. R., judgment of October 8, 2009, Porubova v. Russia; Fedchenko v. Russia and Fedchenko (n°2) v. Russia, no. 33333/04 and 48195/06;, Antica & Company "R" v. Romania, no. 26732/03, 2010. *See also Lehideux and Isorni v. France*, no. 24662/94, 1998; Orban & others v. *France*, no. 20985/05, 2009; Karsai v. Hungry, no. 5380/07, 2009.

39. See for instance Claude Reyes v. Chile, 2006 Inter-Am. Ct. H.R. (ser. c) No. 151 (Sept. 19, 2006).

40. See for an illustration HRC's various decisions concerning the Republic of Korea and Article 19 of the ICCPR: for instance, Kim v. Republic of Korea, n°574/1994, (1999).

41. Article 10 § 2: The exercise of these freedoms, since it carries with it duties and responsibilities, may be subject to such formalities, conditions, restrictions or penalties as are prescribed by law and are necessary in a democratic society, in the interests of national

Article 19 § 3 of the International Covenant on Civil and Political Rights,[42] and Article 13 § 2 of the American Convention on Human Rights.[43]

To be valid, according to the international human rights standards, the restrictions must meet three cumulative criterion: legality,[44] legitimacy,[45] and democratic necessity.[46] When confronted by a restriction to the freedom of expression, the international bodies will apply that three-pronged test.[47] Indeed, to evaluate the compatibility of a limitation to the freedom of the

---

security, territorial integrity or public safety, for the prevention of disorder or crime, for the protection of health or morals, for the protection of the reputation or the rights of others, for preventing the disclosure of information received in confidence, or for maintaining the authority and impartiality of the judiciary.

42. Article 19 § 3: The exercise of the rights provided for in paragraph 2 of this article carries with it special duties and responsibilities. It may therefore be subject to certain restrictions, but these shall only be such as are provided by law and are necessary:
    (a) For respect of the rights or reputations of others;
    (b) For the protection of national security or of public order (ordre public), or of public health or morals.

43. Article 13 § 2: The exercise of the right provided for in the foregoing paragraph shall not be subject to prior censorship but shall be subject to subsequent imposition of liability, which shall be expressly established by law to the extent necessary to ensure:a. respect for the rights or reputations of others; orb. the protection of national security, public order, or public health or morals.

44. Legality requires that the restriction be provided by law. The language may vary from one treaty to another. For instance, the International Covenant on Civil and Political Rights refers to the wording "provided by law," the American Convention requires that the restrictions be "expressly established by law," and the European Convention requires that such restriction be "prescribed by law." Despite these language differences, the idea of all these human rights treaties is similar: a government may not arbitrarily restrict freedom of expression; it may only do so where a law exists allowing it to. The relevant domestic law must be formulated with sufficient precision to enable one to reasonably foresee the consequences that a given action may entail.

45. The legitimacy standard requires that the restriction meet one of the goals of the limitations expressly enumerated in the international human rights treaty. These goals may slightly vary from one instrument to another, but the idea in most of the treaties is to ensure the protection of the interests of national security, territorial integrity, public safety or order, public health or morals, and the protection of the reputation or the rights of others. Some treaties, such as the American Convention on Human Rights or the International Covenant on Civil and Political Rights explicitly allow or oblige restrictions of freedom of expression when such expression consists of advocating national, racial or religious hatred that constitutes incitement to discrimination, hostility, violence, or any similar action against any person or group of persons on any grounds.

46. The proportionality standard entails that the interference must be a suitable and the most lenient means to achieve the goal.

47. Based on these standards, the European Court considers that the limitation must correspond to an "imperative social need." For a description of the European Court's control of a State's limitation to the freedom of speech, see Handyside v. UK, §§48–49.

speech with the international human rights law standards, international bodies take into account the context of the speech and its "weight" in a democracy. Various factors influence the balancing exercise scrutinizing the whole context and depending on various elements such as the speaker, the speech, the target, and the other rights that may be affected by the speech.

As far as the speaker is concerned, the agents of democracy and "watchdogs"—first of all, the journalists, and by extension the editors, writers, artists, historians, scholars, political leaders,[48] and elected representatives of the people[49]—enjoy extensive protection. Therefore, the margin of appreciation of the States to limit their expression is narrower than when limiting the speech of a private person. The journalists and other similar categories of speakers enjoy a greater protection because they contribute to the democratic debates and to the information of the public regarding public matters and concerns.[50] Inevitably, the international bodies assess the method, the context, the content, and the purpose of the expression and of the work of, for instance, the journalist. In one word, "good journalism"—the "serious" kind, based on objective and critical analysis, aiming at informing "in good faith" the general public regarding public matter—enjoys a quasi-absolute protection under international human rights law.[51] On the other

48. Mamère v. France, no. 12697/03, 2006, §20.

49. As stated in Castells v. Spain, no. 11798/85, 1992, at §42: "While freedom of expression is important for everybody, it is especially so for an elected representative of the people. He represents his electorate, draws attention to their preoccupations, and defends their interests. Accordingly, interferences with the freedom of expression of an opposition member of parliament, like the applicant, call for the closest scrutiny on the part of the Court."

50. The Court recalled its position on the matter in the 2009 Aleksandr Krutov v. Russia case. In that case, a journalist had been found liable by the domestic courts for defamation for having written an article describing how the regional prosecutor received "gifts" from the town hall in exchange for support he had provided to some of its members including by shielding them from criminal prosecution. The Court determined that Russia violated Article 10 of the European Convention. Aleksandr Krutov v. Russia, no. 15469/04, 2009.

51. However, even the journalists' protection is not unconditional. They bear duties and responsibilities. The European Court of Human Rights scrutinizes the role played by journalists and evaluates the quality of their work in the context of a democratic society. In the 1994 Jersild v. Denmark case, the Court assessed the journalist's editorial responsibility when editing and broadcasting a television interview featuring a group of racist young people expressing abusive and derogatory remarks about immigrants and ethnic groups. Fundamentally, the Court appraises the quality of the work done in distinguishing, at least implicitly, between informative journalism and sensationalist journalism. In the *Jersild* case, the State argued that the journalist edited the documentary "in a sensationalist rather than informative manner and that its news or information value was minimal" (§ 29).

hand, "bad journalism"—the sensationalist type that does not contribute to the general debate[52] or that aims at using the free speech protection that "when considered as a whole, appeared from an objective point of view to have had as its purpose the propagation of racist views and ideas"[53]—may be limited by the States with a greater margin of appreciation to protecting other rights, such as privacy or the reputation of others.

As far as the person targeted by the speech is concerned, the general principles drawn by the international jurisprudence are that when he or she is a "public" figure, he or she must accept criticisms from journalists or other protected peoples: the consequence is that the State has a narrower margin of appreciation to limit speeches concerning a political leader, for example, than the speeches targeting a private person. The same is true when the person targeted by the discourses is a judge exercising political functions or a civil servant[54] and even more true when the subject of the criticisms is the government itself.[55] However, civil servants acting in an official capacity must be ensured a more extensive protection than politicians, subject to the broader limits of acceptable criticism, and "it cannot be said that civil servants knowingly lay themselves open to close scrutiny of their every word

---

The Court didn't share that point of view. Its assessment was quite extensive and based on the method, the context, the content and the purpose of the contentious show. The main question to solve by the Court was "whether the item in question, when considered as a whole, appeared from an objective point of view to have had as its purpose the propagation of racist views and ideas" (§ 31). Therefore, accordingly the scope of the protection depends of the type of journalism and the type of content. Jersild v. Denmark, no 15890/89, 1994, §§ 29–31.

52. The Court does not credit sensationalist journalism with the same level of protection as it was illustrated in the *Caroline Von Hannover* case. In the latter case, the Court ruled that Germany should have protected a public figure against the publication of photographs related exclusively to a private life, taking into account the fact that the the princess did not exercise any official functions. In its case law, the Court "considers that the decisive factor in balancing the protection of private life against freedom of expression should lie in the contribution that the published photos and articles make to a debate of general interest." Von Hannover v. Germany, no. 59320/00, 2004, § 76.

53. Jersild v. Denmark, § 31.

54. Mamère v. France, §27. *See also*, more recently, Taffin and Contribuables Associés v. France, no. 42396/04, 2010 (condemnation of a person who criticized a civil servant from the tax department; nonviolation of freedom of speech committed by France).

55. *Sürek and Özdemir v. Turkey*, nos. 23927/94, 24277/94, 1999, § 60: "the limits of permissible criticism are wider with regard to the government than in relation to a private citizen or even a politician. In a democratic system the actions or omissions of the government must be subject to the close scrutiny not only of the legislative and judicial authorities but also of public opinion." *See also* Oberschlick v. Austria *(No. 2)*, no. 20834/92, 1997, § 29.

and deed to the extent to which politicians do and should therefore be treated on an equal footing with the latter when it comes to the criticism of their actions." Moreover, "civil servants must enjoy public confidence in conditions free of undue perturbation if they are to be successful in performing their tasks and it may therefore prove necessary to protect them from offensive and abusive verbal attacks when on duty."[56]

As far as the speech is concerned, freedom of speech in a democratic society "covers possible recourse to a degree of exaggeration or even provocation."[57] Any kind of speech or expression is protected under international human rights law, including cartoons[58] and ideas imparted in the form of art.[59] As far as the content of speech is concerned, speech that deals with "public concerns" enjoys a quasi-absolute protection under international human rights law.[60] The European Court decides on a case-by-case basis what "public concern" covers.[61] However, even when the speech pretends to be

---

56. Janowski v. Poland, no. 25716/94, 1999, § 33.

57. As stated in the 1995 Prager & Oberschlick v. Austria judgment dealing with journalists condemned for defamation for having published an article containing criticisms of the judges sitting in the Austrian criminal courts. Prager and Oberschlick v. Austria, no. 15974/90, 1995, § 38. *See also* Kulis & Rózycki v. Poland, no. 27209/03, 2009, § 30.

58. *See* Kulis & Rózycki v. Poland and Alves da Silva v. Portugal, no. 41665/07, 2009, §§ 27–28.

59. Human Rights Committee, Hak-Chul Shin v. Republic of Korea, no. 926/2000, § 7.2, 2004.

60. Regarding political debates, the Court summarized its position in the 1992 Castells v. Spain judgment at § 46: "The limits of permissible criticism are wider with regard to the Government than in relation to a private citizen, or even a politician. In a democratic system the actions or omissions of the Government must be subject to the close scrutiny not only of the legislative and judicial authorities but also of the press and public opinion. Furthermore, the dominant position which the Government occupies makes it necessary for it to display restraint in resorting to criminal proceedings, particularly where other means are available for replying to the unjustified attacks and criticisms of its adversaries or the media. Nevertheless it remains open to the competent State authorities to adopt, in their capacity as guarantors of public order, measures, even of a criminal law nature, intended to react appropriately and without excess to defamatory accusations devoid of foundation or formulated in bad faith."

61. On the contrary, freedom of speech is less protected and must be reconciled with other rights as explained further above, when it does not deal with public concerns or interests, as shown by the *Caroline von Hannover* case at § 63: The Court considers that a fundamental distinction needs to be made between reporting facts—even controversial ones—capable of contributing to a debate in a democratic society relating to politicians in the exercise of their functions, for example, and reporting details of the private life of an individual who, moreover, as in this case, does not exercise official functions." While in the former case, the press exercises its vital role of "watchdog" in a democracy by contributing to "impart[ing] information and ideas on matters of public interest . . ., it does not do so in the latter case."

addressing a "public concern," heinous and violent speech is not protected under international human rights law. Article 20 of the International Covenant on Civil and Political Rights[62] and Article 13 §5 of the American Convention on Human Rights[63] provide that such a discourse should be specifically prohibited. The European Court of Human Rights adopts a similar position, although its recent jurisprudence may soon be the object of serious criticism. In the 2009 Féret v. France judgment, the court found no violation of the freedom of expression for the criminal condemnation of a political leader of an extreme-Right political party–who was member of the Parliament—based on distribution of leaflets presenting immigrant communities "as criminally-minded and keen to exploit the benefits they derived from living in Belgium." For the court, such discourse could be considered an advocation of racial discrimination and therefore was not protected by freedom of expression.[64] Political speech may be considered as the basic pillar of a democratic society promoted by the ideals of the Council of Europe. However, dignity and tolerance are two other fundamental pillars of a democratic and pluralist society, and in these circumstances, the political speech can be limited and restricted.[65] Hate speech and racism are obviously not protected by the European Convention. However, the recent jurisprudence of the court shows that such posture, requested to protect the rights of others and the democracy, may jeopardize free speech, especially political discourses and debates, as well as democratic values.[66] Such danger is clearly exposed in another 2008 case, *Leroy v. France*. A cartoonist was

---

62. This article states that: "1. Any propaganda for war shall be prohibited by law. 2. Any advocacy of national, racial or religious hatred that constitutes incitement to discrimination, hostility or violence shall be prohibited by law."

63. Article 13 § 5: "Any propaganda for war and any advocacy of national, racial, or religious hatred that constitute incitements to lawless violence or to any other similar action against any person or group of persons on any grounds including those of race, color, religion, language, or national origin shall be considered as offenses punishable by law."

64. *See* Féret v. Belgium, no. 15315/07, 2009, §§ 6364.

65. *Id.*, § 64 (to date, the judgment has only been published in French): "Il en résulte qu'en principe on peut juger nécessaire, dans les sociétés démocratiques, de sanctionner voire de prévenir toutes les formes d'expression qui propagent, incitent à, promeuvent ou justifient la haine fondée sur l'intolérance (y compris l'intolérance religieuse), si l'on veille à ce que les « formalités », « conditions », « restrictions » ou « sanctions » imposées soient proportionnées au but légitime poursuivi."

66. The *Féret* judgment was adopted by 4 votes to 3. The three dissending judges feared the consequences of this excessive jurisprudence regarding political discourse over the freedom of expression regime.

criminally charged and convicted for the publication (on September 13, 2001) of a drawing representing the attack on the twin towers of the World Trade Center, with a caption that parodied the advertising slogan of a famous brand: "We have all dreamt of it. . . Hamas did it."[67] The court found no violation of the freedom of expression of the cartoonist taking into account the context of global chaos after the events of 9/11. This ruling shows the danger of the censorship of the expression of ideas and political arguments that may shock or disturb and that are not in conformity with the opinions of the established government. It underlines the challenges of the balancing exercise between freedom of expression and the rights and liberties of others.

It is not surprising in the light of the global regime regarding freedom of expression in international law that the restrictions imposed by the States over denial speech were not deemed a violation of the human rights treaties considered. There is, however, a difference in the posture adopted at the United Nations level and at the Council of Europe level. The Human Rights Committee of the United Nations had to deal with the issue of denial in the 1996 case, *Robert Faurisson v. France*.[68] *In casu*, Robert Faurisson was convicted by a criminal tribunal under the Gayssot Act following the publication of an interview in a newspaper in which he contested the existence of homicidal gas chambers for the extermination of Jews in Nazi concentration camps. Before the Committee, he claimed, *inter alia*, for the protection of his freedom of expression and his academic freedom. After considering the claim admissible, the Committee found no violation of his freedom of expression. The Committee was prudent regarding the Gayssot Act per se. Since the act makes a criminal offence of merely challenging the conclusions and the verdict of the International Military Tribunal at Nuremberg, it may lead, in certain cases, according to the Committee, to decisions or measures incompatible with the International Covenant on Civil and Political Rights.[69]

---

67. Leroy v. France, no. 36109/03, 2008 (in French only—press release available in English).

68. Human Rights Committee, Robert Faurisson v. France, no. 550/1993, 1996.

69. *Id.* at § 9.3. Regarding that issue, Ando Nisuke, member of the Human Rights Committee expressed his skepticism: "As I understand it, the Act criminalises the negation ("contestation" in French), by one of the means enumerated in article 23 of the Law on the Freedom of the Press of 1881, of one or several of the crimes against humanity in the sense of article 6 of the Statute of the International Military Tribunal of Nuremberg (see para. 4.2). In my view the term 'negation' ('contestation'), if loosely interpreted, could comprise various forms of expression of opinions and thus has a possibility of threatening or encroaching the right to freedom of expression, which constitutes an indispensable prerequisite for the proper functioning of a democratic society. In order to eliminate this

The Committee applied the three-pronged test evaluating whether the conditions of the restrictions on the freedom of expression compatible with the International Covenant on Civil and Political Rights were met. The restriction was provided by law: the Gayssot Act. Faurisson was convicted for having violated the rights and reputation of others. The purpose of the restriction was to protect the interests of other persons or to those of the community as a whole. The Committee considered that "[S]ince the statements made by the author, read in their full context, were of a nature as to raise or strengthen anti-semitic feelings, the restriction served the respect of the Jewish community to live free from fear of an atmosphere of anti-semitism."[70] Finally, it considered that the restriction was necessary and noted that the Gayssot Act was intended to serve the struggle against racism and anti-Semitism. The Committee recalled the statement made by a member of the French Government, the then-minister of justice, characterizing the denial of the existence of the Holocaust as the principal vehicle for anti-semitism.[71] The reasoning of the Committee regarding the proportionality test is quite short and does not help to understand the standards that the Committee may apply when appreciating the concrete application of anti-denial laws. Some members of the Committee have expressed their doubts. In their individual opinion, they considered:

> The Gayssot Act is phrased in the widest language and would seem to prohibit publication of *bona fide* research connected with matters decided by the Nuremburg Tribunal. Even if the purpose of this prohibition is to protect the right to be free from incitement to anti-semitism, the restrictions imposed do not meet the proportionality test. They do not link liability to the intent of the author, nor to the tendency of the publication to incite to anti-semitism. Furthermore, the legitimate object of the law could certainly have been achieved by a less drastic provision that would not imply that the State party had attempted to turn historical truths and

possibility it would probably be better to replace the Act with a specific legislation prohibiting well-defined acts of anti-semitism or with a provision of the criminal code protecting the rights or reputations of others in general."

70. *Id.* at § 9.5.

71. *Id.* at § 9.7.

experiences into legislative dogma that may not be challenged, no matter what the object behind that challenge, nor its likely consequences.[72]

For those members, the "good faith" standard is crucial:

> While there is every reason to maintain protection of *bona fide* historical research against restriction, even when it challenges accepted historical truths and by so doing offends people, anti-semitic allegations of the sort made by the author, which violate the rights of others in the way described, do not have the same claim to protection against restriction. The restrictions placed on the author did not curb the core of his right to freedom of expression, nor did they in any way affect his freedom of research; they were intimately linked to the value they were meant to protect—the right to be free from incitement to racism or anti-semitism; protecting that value could not have been achieved in the circumstances by less drastic means.[73]

The European human rights law dealing with the matter dismisses the freedom of expression argument pleaded by deniers as well. However, contrary to the Human Rights Committee, before the European Court, the merits are even not considered by the court since the individual petitions lodged by deniers have been, so far, considered as inadmissible. In the 1996 case, Marais v. France,[74] the European Commission founded the admissibility on the ground of Article 17 of the European Convention that prevents a person from deriving from the Convention a right to engage in activities aimed at the destruction of any of the rights and freedom set forth in the Convention.[75] The article published in that case, pretending to be a scientific

---

72. Individual opinion by Elizabeth Evatt and David Kretzmer, cosigned by Eckart Klein (concurring), § 9.

73. *Id.* at § 10. On the issue of intent, see in this volume the contribution of Thomas Hochmann.

74. Marais v. France, no. 31195/96, Commission decision of June 24, 1996.

75. That does not mean, however, that the authors of hate speech or denials are not protected by the Convention for instance when their reputations are infringed by other speakers. Eur. Court of HR (GC), judgment of October 22, 2007, Lindon, Otchakovsky-Laurens and July v. France [GC], nos. 21279/02, 36448/02, 2007, § 56. Some cases tend nevertheless to indicate that the Court will be more reluctant to limit freedom of speech when the defamed individual is a right-wing extremist. *See* Oberschlick v. Austria *(n°2)*, at § 34; Lopes Gomes da Silva v. Portugal, no. 37698/97, 2000, § 35; Wirtschafts-Trend

demonstration, aimed at denying that gas chambers existed or had been used to commit genocide. The Commission ruled that such speech "runs counter to basic ideas of the Convention, as expressed in its preamble, namely justice and peace." The real goal of the use of freedom of expression revealed in that case is considered by the European Commission as "contrary to the text and spirit of the Convention."[76] In the 1998 Lehideux v. France case, dealing with the conviction for "public defence of war crimes or the crimes of collaboration" based on the publication in a national daily newspaper of an advertisement presenting in a positive light certain acts of Philippe Pétain, the court distinguished between this type of ongoing debate—protected by the Convention—and "the category of clearly established historical facts—such as the Holocaust—whose negation or revision would be removed from the protection of Article 10 by Article 17."[77] The court confirmed that position in the 2003 Garaudy v. France case,[78] considering the application in casu inadmissible under Article 17 of the Convention. Garaudy, a philosopher and writer, was charged and convicted for denying crimes against humanity. The charges and convictions followed the publication of the book entitled The Founding Myths of Israeli Politics in which the applicant questioned various historical events relating to the Second World War, such as the Holocaust. For the Court:

> far from confining himself to political or ideological criticism of Zionism and the State of Israel's actions, or even undertaking an objective study of revisionist theories and merely calling for 'a public and academic debate' on the historical event of the gas chambers, as he alleges, the applicant does actually subscribe to those theories and in fact systematically denies the crimes against humanity perpetrated by the Nazis against the Jewish community.

Zeitschriften-Verlags GmbH v. Austria, no. 58547/00, 2005, § 37. One author characterized this case law as the "horizontal effect" of Article 17. Sébastien Van Drooghenbroeck, *L'article 17 de la Convention européenne des droits de l'homme est-il indispensable ?*, REVUE TRIMESTRIELLE DES DROITS DE L'HOMME 541, 560 (2001).

76. See similar decisions: Remer v. Germany, no. 25096/94, Commission decision September 6, 1995; N.D.P. Bezirkserband München-Oberbayern v. Germany, no. 24398/94, Commission decision November 29, 1995.

77. Lehideux and Isorni v. France, at § 47.

78. Garaudy v. France (dec.).

> There can be no doubt that denying the reality of clearly established historical facts, such as the Holocaust, as the applicant does in his book, does not constitute historical research akin to a quest for the truth. The aim and the result of that approach are completely different, the real purpose being to rehabilitate the National-Socialist regime and, as a consequence, accuse the victims themselves of falsifying history. Denying crimes against humanity is therefore one of the most serious forms of racial defamation of Jews and of incitement to hatred of them. The denial or rewriting of this type of historical fact undermines the values on which the fight against racism and anti-Semitism are based and constitutes a serious threat to public order. Such acts are incompatible with democracy and human rights because they infringe upon the rights of others. Their proponents indisputably have designs that fall into the category of aims prohibited by Article 17 of the Convention.
>
> The Court considers that the main content and general tenor of the applicant's book, and thus its aim, are markedly revisionist and therefore run counter to the fundamental values of the Convention, as expressed in its Preamble, namely justice and peace. It considers that the applicant attempts to deflect Article 10 of the Convention from its real purpose by using his right to freedom of expression for ends which are contrary to the text and spirit of the Convention. Such ends, if admitted, would contribute to the destruction of the rights and freedoms guaranteed by the Convention.

The posture of international human rights law regarding denials turns down the free speech protection to deniers. While the Committee considers that the deniers' petition may be considered admissible, the European Court judges that such claims are in contradiction with human rights standards. The European position corresponds to a clear political goal of the Council of Europe that intends to combat the resurgence of the Nazi ideology and thus refuses to give any room to deniers that may contribute to such resurgence.[79]

---

79. Parliamentary Assembly, Council of Europe, Resolution 1495(2006), April 12, 2006, Combatting the resurgence of the Nazi Ideology, § 8: "Modern Europe has been conceived on the basis of a total rejection of the Nazi ideas and principles, to ensure that such horrendous crimes as those committed by the Nazi regime in the name of 'racial superiority' will never be repeated. The Council of Europe, as the oldest European political organisation aimed at protecting and furthering democracy, human rights and the rule of law, has a special responsibility in preventing the resurgence of the Nazi ideology."

3. Denial as a Crime

Among the means and tools used by States to conciliate freedoms, the key question that arises is whether it implies the use of criminal law to regulate the exercise of the freedom of expression. The law offers various avenues, including torts litigation and criminal prosecution, which can be used against the deniers in order to protect the reputation, honor, or memory of the victims. Education may be the best tool to beat racism, racial discrimination, xenophobia, and related intolerance. However, criminal law often remains the classic mode of regulation used to ease relations between individuals in pluralist and so-called multicultural societies. Criminal law as an expression of the State's constraint power on citizens is equipped with a "*capital symbolique et d'une charge émotive énormes*"[80]: "*sa grande visibilité, l'immédiateté de ses effets, la grossièreté de ses catégories manichéennes qui aplatissent toutes les complexités et les remplacent par un simple code binaire « innocent-coupable », lui garantissent une carrière florissante*,"[81] according to a philosopher who stresses that Western societies are today experiencing an inflation of criminal law. According to him, "*cette inflation est stimulée par le recours irréfléchi à une philosophie pénale solidariste. . . selon laquelle un procès pénal sert à ressouder la communauté autour de ses principes originaires si bien qu'une seule et unique interprétation du passé a droit de cité*."[82]

The relationship between criminal law and human rights is quite complex.[83] Human rights treaties not only oblige States to refrain from violating human rights but also to protect them.[84] Following the positive obligations doctrine, the case law of the European and Inter-American Courts and the Human Rights Committee of the United Nations underlines the significant role played by State organs to ensure the respect of human rights by individuals and private persons. To ensure and protect rights and liberties,

80. Ioannis Papadopoulos, "Pénalisation du discours de haine et premier amendement," www.ihej.org (2003).

81. *Id.*

82. *Id.*

83. Stefan Trechsel, *Comparative Observations on Human Rights and Criminal Law,* 2000 St. Louis-Warsaw Transatlantic L.J. 1 (2000).

84. The Human Rights Committee has admitted the same definition and interpretation of a general obligation of protection relying on States. For its scope and content, *see* its General Comment No. 31, *Nature of the General Legal Obligation Imposed on States Parties to the Covenant:. 26/05/2004. CCPR/C/21/Rev.1/Add.13.*

States may have to use criminalization.[85] In its case law concerning Article 3 of the Convention (inhuman or degrading treatments), the Court has stressed the "element of humiliation" inherent in any criminal sentence.[86] Some scholars currently criticize the "abuse" of proceduralization and the danger raised by the intensive referral to the criminal law. Accordingly, intensive criminal prosecution can violate human rights, namely arbitrary detention, unfair trial, illegal deprivation of liberty, ill treatment in prison or more broadly during the deprivation of liberty, and in the worst situations, imposition of capital punishment. In cases of freedom of speech, the European Court often points out that the use of criminal sanction toward journalists, for instance, keeps them from enjoying their liberty freely. The consequences of the use of criminal prosecution are deterrent. But in the relevant international case law, the use of criminal law is perceived as a tool for a better implementation of human rights, including in private relations. However, while the criminal procedure and a fair and effective punishment of individuals responsible for grave violations of human rights may be considered as one of the best ways to improve respect for human rights and freedoms, criminalization can infringe upon human rights as well. Penal law is ambivalent since it is both a tool to protect and a means to violate individuals' rights.[87]

Regarding the criminalization of certain speech, the international jurisdictions control, with the utmost scrutiny, penal condemnations of journalists, for instance, who allegedly have misused their freedom of speech. This approach, systematically reiterated by the Strasbourg Tribunal, is well described in the 1999 *Surek & Ozdemir v. Turkey* judgment:

> . . . The dominant position which the government occupies makes it necessary for it to display restraint in resorting to criminal proceedings,

---

85. Synthesis work of the internal legislations of the European Commission against Racism and Intolerance (ECRI—body of the Council of Europe) shows that in the European legal systems, a large majority of the States of the Council of Europe use criminal law to fight this kind of speech.

86. *See* Tyrer v. the United Kingdom, no. 5856/72, 1978, § 30; *Ülke v. Turkey*, no. 39437/98, 2006, § 59. *See also* Ivo Appel, VERFASSUNG UND STRAFE 283 (Berlin: Duncker & Humblot, 1998).

87. To illustrate the debate concerning the use of criminal law in the field of the freedom of speech, the dissent opinion of three European Judges under the Féret v. Belgium case (only in French), pointed out the danger of the criminalization of political discourse. For the minority, the use of criminal law in this field is contrary to the freedom of expression, even if it aims at protecting the "spirit" of the European Convention. See also Lindon v. France (dissenting opinion by Tulkens and others), § 7.

> particularly where other means are available for replying to the unjustified attacks and criticisms of its adversaries. Nevertheless, it certainly remains open to the competent State authorities to adopt, in their capacity as guarantors of public order, measures, even of a criminal-law nature, intended to react appropriately and without excess to such remarks . . .[88]

In international human rights law, criminal law may be used to limit specific discourses. Explicit obligations to criminalize hate speech can be found in various international texts. The starting point is, without doubt, the text of the Charter of the United Nations of 1945, to which the Preamble proclaims the faith of the people of the United Nations "in fundamental human rights, in the dignity and worth of the human person, in the equal rights of men and women," and the first article states, among the goals of this new organization that aims at breaking away from the model of the League of Nations, "[t]o achieve international co-operation in solving international problems of an economic, social, cultural, or humanitarian character, and in promoting and encouraging respect for human rights and for fundamental freedoms for all without distinction as to race, sex, language, or religion." This postwar ideal was translated, a few years later, in the first article of the Universal Declaration of Human Rights of December 10, 1948, according to which "all human beings are born free and equal in dignity and rights. They are endowed with reason and conscience and should act towards one another in a spirit of brotherhood." Article 2 of the Universal Declaration reaffirms the principle of nondiscrimination as a corollary of the principle of equality which had just been announced. In a Recommendation adopted in June 2007, the parliamentary Assembly of the Council of Europe reaffirmed "that the speech of hatred towards people, for religious or different reasons, must be set as a penal offence by the law. . .. Speech of hatred, in this way, includes remarks necessarily directed against a person or a particular group of people. The national legislations must be set up as a penal offense of the declarations that call for hatred, discrimination, or violence against a person or a group of people with as a reason their religion.[89]

---

88. Sürek & Özdemir v. Turkey, at § 60; Incal v. Turkey, no. 22678/93, 1998, § 54. Before the Human Rights Committee, see for instance *Coleman v. Australia*, no. 1157/2003, § 7.3, 2006.

89. This resolution refers to the international obligation to incriminate the speech of hatred and especially, when this hatred originates from a racial or religious reason. States and

Article 4 of the 1965 UN Convention on Racial Discrimination[90] provides an explicit obligation to incriminate the heinous remarks, since the States:

> a. Shall declare an offence punishable by law all dissemination of ideas based on racial superiority or hatred, incitement to racial discrimination, as well as all acts of violence or incitement to such acts against any race or group of persons of another colour or ethnic origin, and also the provision of any assistance to racist activities, including the financing thereof;
> b. Shall declare illegal and prohibit organizations, and also organized and all other propaganda activities, which promote and incite racial discrimination, and shall recognize participation in such organizations or activities as an offence punishable by law; . . . .

The European Court of Human Rights, in various judgments, recently referred to the 1965 Convention to recall to the responding States their obligation to fight against racial discrimination in general, and hate speech in particular, even within interindividuals' relationships. In the *Balsyté-Lideikiene v. Lithuania* decision concerning the prohibition and confiscation of a calendar containing racist and discriminatory elements, the court, relying on International Law and especially Article 20, §2 of the ICCPR, the CERD, and the European Framework Convention on national minorities (1995), recalls the international obligation to take measures necessary to protect peoples against discriminatory behaviors and the necessity to *forbid hatred speeches.*[91] As mentioned above, the 1966 International Covenant on Civil and Political Rights required that States prohibit by law calls "to national, racial or religious hatred which constitutes an incentive to discrimination, hostility or violence" (Article 20). It is up to the States to use criminal law to ensure the effectiveness of such a prohibition. The 1969 American Convention of Human Rights required the States to consider as offenses punishable by

---

the international organizations concentrated on this form of hatred and for the time being forsakes the speech of hatred which would be motivated by the gender of the person or their sexual preferences, even if in internal law, the homophobic arguments are sometimes set up as a penal offence. The international obligation to incriminate the speech of racial or religious hatred is manifest; it is more difficult to state the same for the other motives of hatred.

90. One hundred seventy-three States have ratified that Convention.

91. Balsyté-Lideikiene v. Lithuania, no. 72596/01, 2008, § 78. In other judgments as the Féret v. Belgium case, at §§ 72–73, the Strasburg Court does not cite expressly the CERD but other international or domestic sources.

law any "advocacy of national, racial, or religious hatred that" constitutes incitement "to lawless violence or to any other similar action against any person or group of persons on any grounds including those of race, color, religion, language, or national origin" (Article 13, §5).

The rejection of hate speech is so radical in international law that it constitutes an element of the genocide as understood by the Convention of 1948 mentioned above. In this case, and taking into account the development, also since 1945, of international criminal law, this means that the obligation to incriminate and repress does not have only an internal dimension but acquires an international dimension. In Article 4 of the Statute of the International Criminal Tribunal for the Former-Yugoslavia (ICTY) and in Article 2 of the Statute of the International Criminal Tribunal for Rwanda (ICTR) can be found this constitutive component of genocide ("the direct and public incentive to commit genocide") and recently, the ICTR applied it in a judgment of December 3, 2003, in a case known as "*business of the media*" in which the international criminal judge analyzed "the genocide-rhetoric" in the written press as well as through the radio and television, such as the famous radio broadcasts of the Thousand-Hills.[92] The speech of hatred in its absolute form - in which its end is to perpetrate a genocide—is therefore not only an internal infringement but becomes a crime of repressed international law in certain circumstances by international jurisdictions. However, in the definition of genocide in Article 6 of the Statute of the International Criminal Court (ICC), this element is abandoned, which may be regrettable taking into account the dramatic consequences that speeches of hatred have had and continue to have in Rwanda but also today in the Democratic Republic of Congo or in Sudan.

If international law unquestionably requires that States repress the heinous behaviors *lato sensu*, it is more difficult to find an obligation to incriminate the negation of crimes against humanity or genocide. Of course, denials may be assimilated to hate speech.[93] However, specific obligations to criminalize denials are not so explicit in international law. For instance, a draft resolution adopted by States within the General Assembly in January 2007 concerning the "Denial of the Holocaust," only requires "all the Member

---

92. ICTR, judgment December 3, 2003, *Proc. c. Nahimana, Barayagwiza, Ngeze*, 99-52-T (see H. Ascensio and R. Maison, *L'activité des juridictions pénales internationales* (2003–2004), AFDI 2004, p. 462). See also in this volume the contribution of Martin Imbleau.

93. See in this volume the contribution of Robert Kahn.

States to reject without any reserve any denial of the Holocaust as a historical event, may this denial be total or partial, or any activity undertaken in this direction."

While the international human rights bodies seem to be extremely prudent when they deal with criminal law used to prohibit denials and other discourses, some recent international norms explicitely refer to such an obligation. Article 6 of the Additional Protocol to the Convention on Cybercrime, related to the incrimination of acts of a racist and xenophobic nature committed by the means of computer systems requires States to incriminate denials committed by a computing system:

> 1. Each Party shall adopt such legislative measures as may be necessary to establish the following conduct as criminal offences under its domestic law, when committed intentionally and without right: distributing or otherwise making available, through a computer system to the public, material which denies, grossly minimises, approves or justifies acts constituting genocide or crimes against humanity, as defined by international law and recognised as such by final and binding decisions of the International Military Tribunal, established by the London Agreement of 8 August 1945, or of any other international court established by relevant international instruments and whose jurisdiction is recognised by that Party.
> 2. A Party may either:
>   a. require that the denial or the gross minimisation referred to in paragraph 1 of this article is committed with the intent to incite hatred, discrimination or violence against any individual or group of individuals, based on race, colour, descent or national or ethnic origin, as well as religion if used as a pretext for any of these factors, or otherwise
>   b. reserve the right not to apply, in whole or in part, paragraph 1 of this article."

Thus far, it has had relatively little success since it came into effect in 2006. Only 27 States out of the 47 Members of the Council of Europe ratified it and some States, such as Denmark, Lithuania, and Ukraine, have put forth declarations at the time of this ratification, the first abstaining from incriminating genocide denial and the latter two adding constitutive components to the definition of infringement. Lithuania and Ukraine require, for instance, that the negation of crimes against humanity and the genocides be committed with the intention of hatred and discrimination, which shows that to deny such acts is not easily detachable from racist and other intentions of the author.[94] As shown by Laurent Pech in his chapter, the 2008 EU Framework Decision on combating certain forms and expressions of racism and xenophobia by means of criminal law may radically alter the legal landscape in Europe. This Framework Decision explicitly provides for an international obligation among all European States to criminalize "aggravated" denials.[95] The Framework Decision assimilates, or at least groups, hate speech and denials in a formal text confirming that whether the two must be distinguished, they should both be criminalized. Should one feel pleased or uncomfortable with this development? This is a question worth asking if one leaves aside the strict legal treatment of the matter.

4. Prohibiting Denials: Political and Moral Issues

Why would one legally forbid the denial of a crime against humanity? Many pragmatic, moral, and legal-political arguments have been put forward for or against such statutes. Some of them overlap with classical arguments about hate speech regulation, and most of them are analyzed in depth in this volume. An all-comprehensive assessment of these arguments would be out of the scope of this introduction, but some of them deserve to be mentioned here.

A major argument in support of prohibition is the harm that genocide denial is said to inflict to victims and their descendants. Some legal systems

94. See in this volume the contribution of Laurent Pech.

95. Article 1 of the Framework Decision: 1. Each Member State shall take the measures necessary to ensure that the following intentional conduct is punishable:
   (a) publicly inciting to violence or hatred directed against a group of persons or a member of such a group defined by reference to race, colour, religion, descent or national or ethnic origin;
   (b) the commission of an act referred to in point (a) by public dissemination or distribution of tracts, pictures or other material;
   (c) publicly condoning, denying or grossly trivialising crimes of genocide, crimes against humanity and war crimes as defined in Articles 6, 7 and 8 of the Statute of the International Criminal Court, directed against a group of persons or a member of such a group defined by reference to race, colour, religion, descent or national or ethnic origin when the conduct is carried out in a manner likely to incite to violence or hatred against such a group or a member of such a group;
   (d) publicly condoning, denying or grossly trivialising the crimes defined in Article 6 of the Charter of the International Military Tribunal appended to the London Agreement of 8 August 1945, directed against a group of persons or a member of such a group defined by reference to race, colour, religion, descent or national or ethnic origin when the conduct is carried out in a manner likely to incite to violence or hatred against such a group or a member of such a group.

recognize an insult to the memory of deceased persons. Thus, German jurisdictions ruled that the specific circumstances of an individual's death are part of his dignity,[96] which is protected post-mortem in German law.[97] The German Federal Court of Justice has ruled that the dignity of an individual murdered by the State because of his or her origin ("race") is harmed when this crime is denied.[98] No jurisdiction in the United States recognizes tort liability for defamation of the dead,[99] whereas France forbids such expression only when it targets the heirs.[100]

But, of course, denial can also be seen as harming living persons, namely, survivors of a crime against humanity; descendants of victims; and more broadly, members of a group targeted as such by the commission of a crime against humanity. It is unquestionable that some members of such groups feel hurt by denial, as it seems likely that not every person considering himself Jewish or Armenian feels injured by such speech. Some constitutional judges may find that this harm justifies the prohibition of denial; others may find that it allows for punishing denial as an insult. The reality of harm is not subject to any empirical evidence and is much more a judicial ascription. We quoted earlier the German case law describing denial as inflicting harm upon Jews because the Holocaust was part of their "self-perception." The Federal Court of Australia adopted the same reasoning in its ruling about the claims that there is serious doubt that the Holocaust occurred, and that it is unlikely that there were homicidal gas chambers in Auschwitz. According to the judge, each of these imputations:

> challenges and denigrates a central aspect of the shared perception of Australian Jewry of its own modern history and the circumstances in which many of its members came to make their lives in Australia rather than in Europe. To the extent that the material conveys these

---

96. BGHSt 40, 97 (March 15, 1994), 105.

97. BVerfGE 30, 173 *Mephisto* (February 24, 1971), 194.

98. BGHSt 40, 97, 105–06.

99. *See* Lisa Brown, *Dead but Not Forgotten: Proposals for Imposing Liability for Defamation of the Dead,* 67 TEX. L. REV. 1525 (1989); and *Restatement (Second) of Torts,* § 560. Many States do have a criminal statute targeting defamation of the dead, but these statutes seem to have fallen into "desuetude." *See* Raymon Iryami, *Give the Dead Their Day in Court: Implying a Private Cause of Action for Defamation of the Dead from Criminal Libel Statutes,* 9 FORDHAM INTELL. PROP. MEDIA & ENT. L.J. 1083, 1085 (1999).

100. Section 34 of the 1881 statute on the freedom of the press.

> imputations it is, in my view, more probable than not that it would engender feelings of hurt and pain in the living by reason of its challenge to deep seated belief as to the circumstances surrounding the deaths, or the displacement, of their parents or grandparents. For the same reason, I am satisfied that it is more probable than not that the material would engender in Jewish Australians a sense of being treated contemptuously, disrespectfully and offensively.[101]

Another argument in support of the prohibition of genocide denial, closely related to the one of harm, is the idea that denial is a kind of hidden hate speech. According to this idea, a speaker would choose "bare denial" rather than explicit racist speech as a way to avoid a legal punishment. Prohibition of denial would then be a response to this circumvention of the law. This argument has its counterweight: some opponents of denial's prohibition argue that deniers were punished in the absence of specific statutes, hence the pointlessness of such statutes.[102] This claim is partially true: for sure, some deniers were punished on bases other than specific prohibition. Maybe it is also true that deniers will not be able to keep hiding eternally what they have in mind, namely the hate of a group. For practical purposes, it seems that one denying the occurrence of the Holocaust will always end in blaming "the Jews" for having invented or protected this "myth."[103]

But some would argue—and it is another argument raised in favor of denial's prohibition—that the rationale behind a conviction has a strong symbolic significance. Convicting someone for some kind of hate speech (advocacy of hatred, group libel, etc.) is not like punishing him for denial of a crime against humanity. As far as we know, nobody argues that the refusal to specifically prohibit genocide denial would be perceived as its "symbolic endorsement."[104] This argument is not very persuasive and has been rebutted quite effectively by Professor Robert Post: "Just as a library could not function

---

101. Jones v. Toben [2002] FCA 1150 (September 17, 2002), par. 93.

102. *See*, for instance, Madeleine Rebérioux, *Le genocide, le juge et l'historien*, L'HISTOIRE, no. 138, November 1990, 92.

103. *See* Thomas Wandres (above n. 10), 265. See also the selection of Holocaust denying quotations in the contribution of Kenneth Lasson in this volume. For the hypothesis of a nonhateful denial, see the contribution of Thomas Hochmann.

104. The "symbolic endorsement" is part of the argumentation of the "critical race studies" in favor of the regulation of hate speech. See, for instance, Mari J. Matsuda, *Public Response to Racist Speech: Considering the Victim's Story*, 87 MICH. L. REV. 2320, 2338 (1989).

if it were understood as endorsing the views of the authors whose books it collects and displays, so also in a democracy the government could not serve the value of autonomy if it were understood as endorsing the ideas expressed by private persons in public discourse."[105] The argument is more persuasive when it is lessened and presented in another way, namely, that the prohibition of genocide denial sends the symbolic message that a State repudiates this expression.[106]

This, in turn, gives place to the claim that a democracy should not forbid an expression merely because it disapproves of it. Freedom of speech—Europeans argue quoting what has become the European Court of Human Rights' shibboleth—does not protect only inoffensive ideas, it also protects those ideas "that offend, shock or disturb the State or any sector of the population."[107] This formula has been cited so widely that the claim can be made that within the discussion about freedom of expression, the protection of the words that "offend, shock or disturb" is the European equivalent to the American notion of falsely shouting fire in a theatre. This, however, does not make it a strong argument. It is obvious that freedom of speech protects the expression of ideas that "disturb." Actually, the case of a government aiming at forbidding an expression merely because it finds it "shocking" is at best very seldom. "Free speech advocates often claim that governments and others seek to restrict speech with which they 'disagree,' but that is almost certainly false," writes Professor Schauer.[108] Those who wish to restrict speech want much more to avoid some of the consequences they think it would provoke. It is therefore on the question of harm that the debate over the prohibition of denial is the most relevant.

Besides the harm directly inflicted on some individuals and the harm related to hate speech, another consequence of genocide denial has been identified in support of its criminal prohibition. There are strong similarities between the perpetration of a crime against humanity and the denial of its occurrence.[109] Perpetrators of genocide often hide their crime while

---

105. Robert Post, *Racist Speech, Democracy and the First Amendment*, 32 WM & MARY L. REV. 267, 292 (1991).

106. See Robert Kahn's contribution in this volume.

107. Handyside v. UK, at § 49.

108. Fred Schauer, *Is It Better to Be Safe than Sorry? Free Speech and the Precautionary Principle*, 36 PEPPERDINE L. REV. 301, 301, n. 1 (2009).

109. See in this volume the contributions of Lawrence Douglas and David Fraser.

committing it. Primo Levi's account of Wiesenthal explaining how an SS guard told the inmates that nobody would ever believe them, because "we will destroy the evidence together with you" is one of the most cited texts in the literature about denial, memory, and the historiography of the Holocaust.[110]

Another widely quoted sentence is that "those who cannot remember the past are condemned to repeat it."[111] Denial, it is argued, whitewashes the political regime or the ideology responsible for a crime against humanity and therefore strives for its revival. This rationale is especially obvious in the case of Austria, which in 1992 inserted a disposition targeting the denial of Nazi crimes within its Prohibition Act (*Verbotsgesetz*), adopted in 1945, a statute with constitutional rank that forbids the NSDAP and prohibits any act complying with National Socialist aims. The Austrian example is a clear illustration of denial's prohibition as a feature of "militant democracy," this "political and legal structure aimed at preserving democracy against those who want to overturn it from within."[112] Of course, one can argue about the claim that genocide denial increases the likelihood of further genocide. But once again, at least in Europe, the empirical plausibility of the occurrence of harmful consequences caused by speech need not be certain to justify regulation.

One question arises: is this argument in support of denial's prohibition extensible in Europe to crimes against humanity other than the Holocaust? The European Commission of Human Rights ruled in a case involving the Austrian Prohibition Act that treating National Socialist activities differently "has an objective and reasonable justification in the historical experience of Austria during the National Socialist era, and the danger which activities based on National Socialist thinking may constitute for the Austrian society."[113] In a 2003 case involving the prohibition of an Islamic political party in Turkey, the European Court of Human Rights ruled that "each

---

110. PRIMO LEVI, THE DROWNED AND THE SAVED (Raymond Rosenthal trans., New York: Summit Books, 1988), 11–12.

111. ·For more on this post-Holocaust aphorism, *see infra* Thomas Hochmann's contribution.

112. Otto Pfersmann, *Shaping Militant Democracy: Legal Limits to Democratic Stability, in* MILITANT DEMOCRACY (Andras Sajo ed., Utrecht: Eleven International Publishing, 2004), 47. *See also* Karl Loewenstein, *Militant democracy and fundamental rights*, AM. POL. SCI. REV., June 1937, 417–32, and August 1937, 638–58; and Laurent Pech's contribution in this volume.

113. B.H., M.W., H.P. et G.K. v. Austria, no. 1277/87, Commission decision of October 12, 1989.

Contracting State may oppose such political movements in light of its historical experience."[114] A number of authors in this volume and elsewhere claim that they are opposed to the criminalization of Holocaust denial in their respective countries but understand why such a statute was adopted in Austria or Germany. One should emphasize that the German Constitutional Court ruled only very recently with whole clarity that while the criminalization of the glorification of Nazi crimes is not neutral toward opinions as the Constitution requires, it is nevertheless justified by Germany's dark past.[115]

One cannot seriously maintain that the Armenian genocide, for instance, is part of the French "historical experience." Some argue therefore that the French statute recognizing the Armenian genocide is "extra-territorial," and that the criminalization of its denial in France would also be.[116] According to others, the presence of a large population of people with Armenian roots in France is enough to establish a link between "past hate" and the prohibition of denial.[117]

The extension of the prohibition of denial of crimes against humanity in every European Member State raises a similar issue. Indeed, some former Communist countries criminalize the denial of Communist crimes and the display of Communist emblems.[118] As Germany intended to extend to the whole of Europe the prohibition of Nazi signs, these countries insisted that the criminalization of Communist signs should also be implemented in every Member State. This case led to a status quo, and the project was abandoned in 2005.[119] But national history is not the only difference among European Member States. Throughout Europe, there are also various national traditions concerning the freedom of expression, and some countries such as the United Kingdom, Italy, and especially Hungary,[120] are more reluctant toward speech regulation than, for instance, Austria, France, and Germany. Should the European Union press the former countries to criminalize

---

114. Refah Partisi (The Welfare Party) and others v. Turkey, nos. 41340/98, 41342/98 41343/98, 41344/98, 2003, § 124.

115. BVerfG (2009), *Wunsiedel*, 1 BvR 2150/08, par. 64–68.

116. See in this volume David Fraser's contribution.

117. See in this volume Robert Kahn's contribution.

118. See in this volume Martin Imbleau's contribution.

119. See Sebastian Weber, *Strafbarkeit der Holocaustleugnung in der Europäischen Union,* Zeitschrift für Rechtspolitik, 2008 (1), 21.

120. However, in February 2010, the Hungarian Parliament passed a bill that prohibits Holocaust denial.

genocide denial?[121] Here, one must recall that the Framework Decision only requires that the Member States punish aggravated denial, which is an explicit kind of hate speech. But what if something as broad and vague as "bare denial of crimes of genocide, crimes against humanity, and war crimes" was to be criminalized across Europe in the future?

This last concern comes close to "a slippery slope" reasoning, a widespread argument against statutes forbidding Holocaust denial. However, one should not forget that this argument is but an empty shell if it does not draw upon some empirical circumstances.[122] Is the Framework Decision a start down the road toward a European requirement of criminalizing "bare" denial of every crime against humanity and war crime? If one answers this question affirmatively, there is reason for concern. Nevertheless, until now, the "slippery slope" argument has been used mostly retroactively, especially in France to criticize the Gayssot Act penalizing Holocaust denial. Many historians and others have blamed this statute for opening a "Pandora's Box" and leasing to other "memory laws." Nevertheless, this interesting debate was weakened by the widespread confusing failure to differentiate between a norm that forbids denying a crime and a norm that merely recognizes a crime without associating any legal consequences to its denial.[123] No earlier than in 2006, sixteen years after the adoption of the Gayssot Act, did the French National Assembly vote a statute criminalizing the denial of the Armenian genocide. One can assume that without the strong mobilization of numerous historians, this statute would have been adopted by the Senate—France's parliamentary high chamber—rendering the prohibition of denial of the Armenian genocide effective. Whether the sixteen-year period works in favor of or to the detriment of the "Pandora's Box" argument against the Gayssot Act is open to discussion.

The argument that the Gayssot Act opened "Pandora's Box" seems stronger if it is perceived as an argument of "added authority,"[124] namely, the claim that with this statute Parliament began to have a say on history. To put it in a somewhat caricatured way: "I don't want the government to tell me that it occurred because I don't want any government ever to tell me that it

---

121. See in this volume the contribution of Laurent Pech.

122. Fred Schauer, *Slippery Slopes*, 99 HARV. L. REV. 361, 381 (1985).

123. See in this volume the contributions of David Fraser and Emmanuela Fronza.

124. *See* Fred Schauer, *supra* note 122, at 367–68.

didn't occur."[125] The argument claims that the Gayssot Act increases the likelihood of Parliament dealing in other instances with history, and that such a sphere of jurisdiction is unwelcome no matter whether Parliament criminalizes denial or merely "recognizes" a historical fact.[126] Parliament, it is argued, should not enact "official truths." The fact that this claim was used almost exclusively about statutes dealing with the past is quite surprising. After all, it is quite a common thing that a legal norm concerns something that could be characterized as an "official truth." A famous lawmaker even once considered it to be a "self-evident truth" that "all men are created equal."[127] In many countries, statutes forbid the advocacy of the "inequality between human races." One cannot help but observe that no geneticist ever wrote impassioned op-eds or circulated outraged petitions denouncing this "parliamentary imposition of truth." History seems to be a more sensitive domain.

The hostility toward the relationship between Clio and Themis actually has a long history in France. Until 2005 and the uproar—many months after its unnoticed adoption—against a statute asking textbooks to "acknowledge the positive role of the French" colonialism,[128] the criticisms against the meddling of law in history's affairs did not aim at the legislature but at the judge. The judge should not tell the historian how to do his job, it was argued. A courtroom is not the place to talk about history, some added. The criminalization of genocide denial avoids precisely such discussion, and some commentators welcomed these statutes as a way to prevent deniers from using their trials as a forum for their thesis.[129]

But one could also argue that the prosecution and trial of deniers give them a publicity that they would not enjoy were they free to spread their inanities. Another pragmatic argument is that the prohibition of denial "chills" the historical research about the crime against humanity whose denial is punished. It seems neither that this has been the case with the statutes against Holocaust denial nor that it will be with the European

---

125. Alan Dershowitz, *Debate: Freedom of Speech and Holocaust Denial,* 8 CARDOZO L. REV. 559 (1987).

126. See in this volume Emmanuela Fronza's contribution.

127. Declaration of Independence [¶ 2] (1776).

128. Section 4 of the "loi n° 2005-158 du 23 février 2005 portant reconnaissance de la Nation et contribution nationale en faveur des Français rapatriés."

129. See in this volume the contributions of Lawrence Douglas and Martin Imbleau.

prohibition of aggravated denial. Indeed, the inaccurate description of these norms, which exaggerates their scope, creates a much more chilling effect. May the present volume contribute to reduce it. The first part of this book focuses on the relationship between genocide perpetration and genocide denial. Part II concerns the justification of denial prohibition and aims at understanding such limitation of free speech. Part III is dedicated to more purely legal questions.

Genocide Denials and the Law is not a plea in favor of or against the legal prohibition of genocide denial. Admittedly, this introduction expresses the view that the prohibition of some denials of crimes against humanity is in accordance with international law and is constitutional in most of the legal systems studied in the book. But the constitutionality of a regulation does not automatically mean that it is a wise policy. While some of the contributions that compose this book present strong arguments supporting or opposing such a limit to the freedom of expression, the main purpose of the book is to offer a deep analysis of the legal implications of genocide denials and of the prohibition of this kind of speech. When concluding the book, readers may decide for themselves.

PART ONE

From Genocide to Denial

ONE

Law's Holocaust Denial

State, Memory, Legality

–David Fraser

1. Introduction: Law's Holocaust/Law's Amnesia

I begin this chapter not with the law of lawyers and judges, but with the laws of another genre. Recent revelations from within the world of literature about the Shoah establish the fundamental deontological nature of the questions that inform, albeit far too often, by their forgetting, discussions, and treatments of denial(s) and the law. Literature broadly construed plays a significant role in the construction of a social memory of the Shoah.[1] The broader, more flexible epistemological limits that are imposed on the genre and on its relationship to history and truth mean that what is "unacceptable" in literature comes closer to ultimate social limits than that which is "unacceptable" within the stricter professional discourses of law or history, the two genres most commonly linked in debates about denial(s). But the existence of broader and more flexible considerations in relation to literary accounts of the Shoah, including victim memoirs, does not remove the idea of a limit. Recent cases highlight this overarching deontological hermeneutic frame that reinforces the links between and among law, history, and literature when dealing with the truth of the Shoah.

Herman Rosenblat's touching account of the young girl who saved him by passing apples over the fence of the concentration camp where he was imprisoned and of how, as adults, they met by chance in the United States, fell in love, and married was revealed to have been made up by the author to add dramatic effect to his memoirs.[2] Binjamin Wilkomirski played out his role as a Holocaust survivor. He persisted in his claim and in his self-representations as a child survivor of the Shoah, even when confronted with

1. Paul Ricoeur, *Devant l'Inacceptable: le Juge, L'Historien, L'Écrivain*, 67 PHILOSOPHIE 3, 3–18 (2000).

2. Motoko Rich & Joseph Berger, *False Memoir of Holocaust is Canceled*, N.Y.TIMES, Dec. 28, 2008, *available at* http://www.nytimes.com/2008/12/29/books/29hoax.html.

irrefutable factual evidence to the contrary.[3] Belgian author Misha Defonseca's autobiographical account of her escape from the Nazis and survival among wild wolves was revealed to have been a work of fiction.[4] While Rosenblat seems simply to have embellished and romanticized the account of his life as a victim of Nazi persecution, Wilkomirski and Defonseca falsified their status as Holocaust survivors. The reactions to these two cases indicate that the social political reception of revelations of historical and autobiographical fraud evidences the same deontological frame as that which is found in debates about law and history in relation to the denial(s) issue. Wilkomirski's and Defonseca's crime—or, more accurately, their sin—was not to have written fictionalized accounts of the Holocaust. Their error was to have staked a truth claim about their autobiographical status as survivors of the Holocaust. While other recent examples of authors who have offered fictionalized accounts of their lives, only to have these tales revealed not as fact but as fiction abound, the reaction, particularly to the Defonseca account, has carried much higher morally resonant tones of disapproval. The deontological issue is not about having lied at all or to have lied about one's personal experience. The fault is that the authors lied about the Shoah. The judgment that has been imposed on their work by critics, journalists, and the public alike is the same as that which has been imposed on Irving, Faurisson et al., by law and by history. The three genres, for all their methodological and epistemological differences, share, or ought to share, a moral vision of the Shoah. It is at this level that the debate about denial and law should or must occur. Instead, we more often find ourselves mired with assertions that law and history are incommensurable discursive practices that can never be reconciled.

The matrix of issues surrounding debates about denial(s) and the law poses fundamental questions about the nature of law itself and its appropriate function in modern democracies. The political and social phenomena of those who would deny the facticity of various crimes against humanity, genocides, and the Shoah question the taxonomical structures and epistemological bases not

---

3. *See* BINJAMIN WILKOMIRSKI, FRAGMENTS: FROM A CHILDHOOD, 1939–48 (1996); STEFAN MAECHLER, THE WILKOMIRSKI AFFAIR: A STUDY IN BIOGRAPHICAL TRUTH (2001); BLAKE ESKIN, A LIFE IN PIECES: THE MAKING AND UNMAKING OF BINJAMIN WILKOMIRSKI (2002).

4. *See* MISHA DEFONSECA, SURVIVRE AVEC LES LOUPS (1999); Marc Metdepenningen, *Les aveux de Misha Fonseca*. LE SOIR, Feb. 28, 2008; *see* Olivier Mouton et al.; *Misha Defonseca a vécu en trompe l'oeil*, LE SOIR, Feb. 29, 2008; *see* Lawrence Van Gelder, *Holocaust Memoir Turns Out to be Fiction*, N.Y. TIMES, Mar. 3, 2008, *available at* http://www.nytimes.com/2008/03/03/books/03arts-HOLOCAUSTMEM_BRF.html.

just of law but of history and memory. Denial, as the essays in this book demonstrate, raises difficult, if not intractable, questions about the role to be played by legal prescription in relation to historical "fact." At this juncture, it is perhaps desirable to trace in broad terms the social, political, historical, and legal parameters of the debates, with a specific focus on the place of the catastrophe of the killing of six million Jews in the Shoah. I wish to underline an important instance of law's forgetting of itself and its role—not just in the institutional precursors of the Shoah—but in the post-Holocaust, post-Nuremberg construction of militant democracy and its institutional defenses against the rise of fascism, and more particularly, the use of Holocaust denial as an ideological and political tool in a resurgent fascism.

Ricoeur identifies the three principal genres that have been deployed in our collective search for a narrative "truth" about the Holocaust, or, as he puts it, as a judgment about the Shoah.[5] The three forms of judgment that fix collective, social, and political meaning under the broad rubric of memory are the judicial, the historical, and the literary. The constituent elements of moral, legal, and historical characterization and decision making all come together at the point where a judgment is, however tentatively, fixed on facts in order to give them meaning and character according to the rules of the particular enterprise. Important questions about socially constructed knowledge and memory of the Shoah have presented themselves to expert practitioners: judges, lawyers, historians, and authors. Nonexpert interpreters—the body politic—confront the phenomenon of denial and confront those who are in the business of "denying the Holocaust,"[6] or "telling lies about Hitler."[7]

For Ricoeur, each genre—law, history, literature—suffers from its own inherent limits when confronted with the enormity of the "Final Solution of the Jewish Question." For history, the internal rules of epistemology and deontology of the profession are put to the test when dealing with the Shoah on its own terms. How does one go about determining, according to the rules and practices of the historical profession, exactly what happened: to whom, when, where, and why? The very enormity of the Shoah means that not every question can be answered with absolute precision. It is impossible to identify each victim and the place and time of her death, for example. The discipline of historical inquiry

---

5. Ricoeur, *supra* note 1.

6. DEBORAH LIPSTADT, DENYING THE HOLOCAUST: THE GROWING ASSAULT ON TRUTH AND MEMORY (1993).

7. RICHARD J. EVANS, TELLING LIES ABOUT HITLER: THE HOLOCAUST, HISTORY AND THE DAVID IRVING TRIAL (2001).

must also be wary of the demands for a moral or ethical condemnation that are almost inherent in any study of the extremes of human violence.[8] Historians must study the Shoah as dispassionately as possible, while at the same time rendering judgment as the results of their research emerge.

A narrative of the Shoah will confront the same issues while having to cope with the "unwriting" of history that is inherent in the literary genre. In other words, by emphasizing the rhetorical elements of history, literature, by its very presence, undermines history's claim to epistemological status. But a literary rendering—a category in which Ricoeur includes witness testimony—must also confront the basic question of its "reception."[9] For Ricoeur, the intersection at this level of reception, the level of judgment, confronts the citizen historian and the citizen writer, each of whom plays a role in the construction of an ethically informed collective memory. At this moment of engagement with memory, history, and forgetting, Ricoeur argues that all who encounter these texts answer the question of judgment: the question as to whether and how a particular text can, as it must, be subjected to a criterion of acceptability.[10] The question to be asked, in order for judgment to be made, is always whether the text and its narration are likely to assist in the working through of the trauma at the core of collective understanding and memory.

To this hermeneutic circle must be added the citizen judge, lawyer, and juror in legal proceedings relating to mass atrocity (and denials), in general, and the Shoah, in particular.[11] In such circumstances, the law confronts the history of the Shoah in accordance with its own particular rules, practices, and objectives. In a war crimes trial, for example, the principal aim must always be the finding of guilt or innocence of the accused, to be determined based on admissible evidence, the analysis and judgment of witness credibility, and rules relating to the burden of proof. History, by way of original documents and/or expert evidence will play a part, but that role will always be circumscribed by the overarching rules of the criminal trial. The object is not truth in some pure epistemological rendering but a limited truth of the accused's guilt or innocence.

---

8. Ricoeur, *supra* note 1, at 7.

9. *Id.* at 16. *See also* Danièle Voldman, *Le Témoinage et l'Écriture de l'Histoire, in* PASSEPORTS POUR LE VRAI/LE FAUX 147–62 (Françoise Reumaux ed., 2005).

10. Ricoeur, *supra* note 1, at 17. *See generally* PAUL RICOEUR, MEMORY, HISTORY, FORGETTING, (Kathleen Blamey & David Pellauer trans., 2004).

11. Patricia Wald, *Foreword: War Tales and War Trials*, 106 MICH. L. REV. 901, 901–22 (2008).

For some, this situates law as a necessarily marginal phenomenon in relation to the construction of historical truth. Law in such circumstances is not concerned with the "fact" that 800 Jews were killed beside a pit in a Ukrainian forest in the summer of 1942 but with whether the accused can be placed at the pit, actively participating in the killings. If the accused can be shown to have participated in shooting 20 of the 800, for law, that will be sufficient. The law's "truth" is at once more precise and less accurate. The liability of one individual is established, but the broader truth of the mass killing is elided in a way that historians would find unacceptable.[12]

This apparent conflict between truth and law is at the heart of concerns over legal regulation of denial of the Holocaust. Legal truth does not coincide with the broader and more profound issues studied by historians. This conflict between and among law, history, truth, and memory appears concretely for opponents of criminalization of denial in those cases where the state seeks to impose criminal liability on an individual who has denied the existence, for example, of gas chambers for killing Jews at Auschwitz. But at an important level, such objections misunderstand or underestimate the functions of a criminal trial. It is doubtless the case that the primary aim of a criminal trial is always the establishment of the guilt or innocence of the accused. Nor is there any question that such a determination is informed and constrained by the internal rules of procedure and evidence imposed by law itself. But law has other more broadly defined social and political functions, including the ideological, political, and pedagogical.

The fundamental issue that arises is not that of the failings or weakness of law as a genre. It is a debate over "truth." What is at stake in all discussions of denial(s) and the law is a fundamental argument over and between epistemology and deontology, an argument where proponents of competing visions exploit the strengths and weakness of each genre. There can be little doubt that in a trial, history and historians can be, and are, examined and undermined using the skills and tools of cross-examination and the admissibility of evidence. But the existence of various rules of genre does not, by definition, disable law in relation to denial.

Deniers also seek to employ the rules of historical and academic discourse to assert that they are simply engaged in a practice of history: of revising and contesting accepted truth in a way consistent with best practice among

---

12. Donald Bloxham, Genocide on Trial: War Crimes Trials and the Formation of Holocaust History and Memory (2001).

professional historians. Deniers challenge history's very capacity for judgment, asserting that different interpretations are always available with which to confront what constitutes, momentarily, the historical record. In such instances, the legal forum can become, ironically, the venue in which this dispute is resolved. The David Irving defamation case against Deborah Lipstadt is perhaps the most well-known such instance. A similar scenario unfolded, and a similar result obtained in France more recently when Robert Faurisson brought a defamation action against former French Justice Minister Robert Badinter in relation to a statement made by Badinter during a television interview where he accused Faurisson of manufacturing history.[13] In such defamation cases, where "truth is a defense," law and history come together in a way that is much less problematic in the eyes of those who discuss the difficult connections between and among, law, history, and truth, than in criminal prosecutions against deniers.[14] In his review of the recent legal history of European instances in which historians had been sued for defamation, Antoon de Baets is even reluctant to include deniers among the ranks of historians as parties to such disputes. He writes:

> A special type of complainant is the Holocaust denier represented by three cases in the table. This is perhaps telling in light of the gradual growth in the 1990s of this extremist (but extremely diversified) minority trying to rewrite history in an immoral way.[15]

What is intriguing about these instances in which a private law mechanism has been used to determine a historical truth and a truth about history and historiographical method is not to be found at the level of any important distinction that one might choose to assert between private and public law; between the goals, objectives, and internal rules of tort/delict or criminal proceedings, although no doubt these are issues that should be explored and analyzed. The most important element is to be found in the semiotics deployed by historians themselves. Badinter accused Faurisson of being a manufacturer, a counterfeiter or falsifier of history (*un faussaire*). De Baets writes

---

13. BERNARD JOUANNEAU, LA JUSTICE ET L'HISTOIRE FACE AU NÉGATIONNISME: AU COEUR D'UN PROCÈS (2008).

14. Lawrence McNamara, *History, Memory and Judgment: Holocaust Denial, The History Wars and Law's Problems with the Past*, 26 SYDNEY L. REV. 343, 343–94 (2004).

15. Antoon de Baets, *Defamation Cases against Historians*, 41 HIST. & THEORY 346, 352 (2002).

unselfconsciously of an "immoral" rewriting of history. What emerges from this discourse is a clear vision of deontological judgment about truth and history within both legal and historical discourse. A judgment about Holocaust denial has been made and reinforced within a legal frame that confirms the accepted truth of history.

Nonetheless, the incommensurable discourse argument is one that continues to hold sway. Noted French historian Henry Rousso has been vociferous in his defense of this position in the context of Holocaust trials, and he has been joined by many other prominent scholars, both in law and in history.[16] Donald Bloxham is also forceful in his claims that legal proceedings, especially prosecutions of Holocaust perpetrators, are ill suited as *loci* of historical inquiry. The ultimate objectives of historical inquiry and the limited aims of criminal trials make the two incompatible. At the same time, however, Bloxham does not dismiss another form of legal process as a possible preferable way of joining the two distinct disciplines. He finishes his account of the legal-historical or historical-legal failings of Holocaust perpetrator trials by commenting that "Conversely, the actions of the South African Truth and Reconciliation Committee, albeit it in a different historical context, have suggested that it is possible to combine democratic development with some consciousness of the crimes of apartheid but with less 'justice' in the commonly held sense of the term."[17]

It is not possible here to offer an extended critique or analysis either of the South African Truth and Reconciliation experience or of Bloxham's analysis of law and history. It is important to note that Bloxham, while rejecting the examples of war crimes trials, shares a general notion that both history and "law" are engaged in such circumstances in a broader project of democratic development, and that public consciousness about the historical past and the construction of collective memories about it are essential elements in this developmental process. Bloxham then commits three intersecting epistemological errors: First, he writes of the "crimes of apartheid"; apartheid South Africa has raised and continues to raise precisely the same questions about the content and meaning of "the rule of law" as did

---

16. Henry Rousso, The Haunting Past: History, Memory, and Justice in Contemporary France (2002); Le Génocide des Juifs entre procès et histoire, 1943–2000 (Florent Brayard ed., 2000); Jean-Noël Jeanneney, Le Passé dans le prétoire (1998).

17. Bloxham, *supra* note 12, at 228. *See also* Marouf A. Hasian, Jr., Rhetorical Vectors of Memory in National and International Holocaust Trials (2006).

Nazi Germany.[18] To speak of the "crimes" of apartheid is to elide vital historical and jurisprudential issues that go the heart of the question of the legal/historical/moral matrix. Second, Bloxham seemingly asserts that general understandings of "justice" require either a full-fledged trial process or are the equivalent of "vengeance," "punishment," or "retribution." There are serious historical questions that remain unanswered, just as there are questions of jurisprudential significance that are equally passed over. The Truth and Reconciliation process offered amnesty/immunity to all those who were forthcoming about their actions during apartheid. This has two important consequences for law and for history. The "history" of apartheid and the "crimes" committed thereunder is fashioned only by those who sought amnesty and is expressed in the terms of their confessions and confirming victim narratives. This is not an objective historical analysis but the start of a process of compiling evidence and sources for further historical inquiry.

Third, the narrative constructed by victim and perpetrator in the processes of the Truth and Reconciliation Commission is, not surprisingly, a narrative of truth and reconciliation. The genre and the hermeneutic framework imposed by the apparatus, by the "mode of instruction," as Bloxham puts it,[19] determine the nature, type, and content of "history" that is allocuted. There is no evidence from those who do not regret their acts, yet they remain an essential part, not just of the "crimes of apartheid" but important evidence about perpetrator motivation and about the mechanics of the policies of state racism. In other words, there is simply no basis at this point that might allow anyone to determine whether Bloxham's preference for "truth and reconciliation" is justified. That decision is one that must be founded in judgment, not just about truth and reconciliation versus criminal trials but about law versus history and about law and history as discourses and sources of knowledge that may, at certain junctures, become commensurable. The question, demonstrated ironically by Bloxham's intervention, is as always the question of judgment, particularly Which law? Which history? The debate must always be about the ethical groundings of our democratic structures and about the deontological content of our legal normativity, about the morality of historical inquiry and discourse. There is no neutral position

---

18. David Dyzenhaus, Judging the Judges, Judging Ourselves: Truth, Reconciliation and the Apartheid Legal Order (1998); David Fraser, Law After Auschwitz: Towards a Jurisprudence of the Holocaust (2005).

19. Bloxham, *supra* note 12, at 228.

when faced with the pernicious and immoral discourse of denial(s) there is always—as Ricoeur argues—only judgment.

Law's didactic function is specifically and starkly raised in cases in which denial is the object of a juridical proceeding. Lawrence Douglas elucidates the question as to whether law succeeds in such instances in fulfilling the goals beyond a determination of innocence or guilt—or between good and bad history—or between real history and immoral denial disguised as history, between authentic inquiry and counterfeit dissemblance.[20] The series of interrogations that must inform any inquiry into denials and the law, about history and law and their possible intersections and divergence, must necessarily begin with law's own history, with what I argue is law's denial of itself and its problematic disciplinary historical past. In the next section, I turn to face law's troubled past—a past that is always present—because when it comes to denial(s) and the law, we still live "under the shadow of Weimar."[21]

2. Blind in the Left Eye: Weimar, Law's Republic and Denial

The history of Weimar Germany, is oft-told and well known. The republic failed in large part because its legal system was infected both by a narrow legal positivism that ignored the normative requirements of democratic legality and by practitioners who were predominantly, if not overwhelmingly, conservative in ideology, approach, and sympathy. When the time came for a Nazi *Weltanschauung*, the legal profession and the judiciary proved all too ready to adopt the new worldview.[22] This legal historical narrative is a retrospective and almost oedipal reconstruction. As West Germany attempted to reconstruct itself after the end of World War Two—in accordance with the dominant discourses imposed by the International Military Tribunal proceedings—the twelve years of the Hitler Reich were constructed as a period of state criminality. The Nazi state was one that destroyed the preexisting rule of law. It became a criminal state in which the form of law persisted, but the core

20. Lawrence Douglas, The Memory of Judgment; Making Law and History in the Trials of the Holocaust (2001).

21. Under the Shadow of Weimar: Democracy, Law, and Racial Incitement in Six Countries (Louis Greenspan & Cyril Levitt eds., 1993).

22. Ingo Müller, Hitler's Justice (1991).

essence of law was destroyed. The Federal Republic gave rise to the return of law to Germany.[23]

I shall not detail the complex jurisprudential debates as to whether Nazi legality is more accurately described by the formula, *Recht im Unrecht* or by *Unrecht im Recht*, or in Anglo-American terms, where and how Nazi law might be classified in terms of legal positivism and natural law theories.[24] What is important for law's (self-) denial is not the treatment of Nazi law as nonlaw, *Unrecht*, but rather the necessary forgetting of Weimar law within this discourse.

Weimar law has become—in dominant accounts of law's Nazi history—a phenomenon best forgotten or quickly glanced over. Like Weimar itself, it is a sometimes glorious experiment that failed when faced with the Nazi menace. This recounting places law's failures largely in the hands of legal actors, judges, prosecutors, lawyers, and ministry officials who either lacked the moral fiber and courage to stand up to the Nazi onslaught or else were already predisposed to the Nazi worldview. Another story about Weimar can be and has been told, but it is too easily forgotten. This story is one of law and politics; of law and history; and ultimately, in relation to denial(s) and the law, a narrative that could be used to recover law's traumatic memory.

The traditional narrative about Weimar law as failure is about a legal system that was—in the memorable phrase—"blind in the right eye." It was a legal system in which an unwarranted and systematic bias toward the forces of political and social conservatism was inherent and ultimately crippling to the rule of law.[25] It is no small irony that a frame for modern and current European constitutional arrangements and more specific legislative provisions relating to the phenomenon of denial is provided quite explicitly by the dominating historico-legal narrative of Weimar. Within this frame, Weimar

---

23. On the intimate connection with a judicial recognition of the Shoah, *see* Norbert Frei, *Le retour du droit en Allemagne: La justice et l'histoire contemporaine après l'Holocauste- un bilan provisoire*, *in* Brayard, *supra* note 16, at 57–78. *See also* NORBERT FREI, ADENAUER'S GERMANY AND THE NAZI PAST: THE POLITICS OF AMNESTY AND INTEGRATION (2002).

24. *See* H.L.A. Hart, *Positivism and the Separation of Law and Morals*, 71 HARV. L. REV. 593 (1958) and Lon Fuller, *Positivism and Fidelity to Law: A Reply to Professor Hart*, 71 HARV. L. REV. 630 (1958) for the best-known Anglo-American debate. *See also* S. L. Paulson, *Lon L. Fuller, Gustav Radbruch, and the "Positivist" Theses*, 13 L. & PHIL. 313 (1994); Frank Haldemann, *Gustav Radbruch vs. Hans Kelsen: A Debate on Nazi Law*, 18 RATIO JURIS 162 (2005).

25. Moshe Zimmermann, *Blind in the Right Eye: Weimar as a Test Case*, 32 ISR. L. REV. 395 (1998). For a critique of modern German legal practice in relation to its failure to police Holocaust denial from the same perspective, *see* Geoffrey J. Giles, *Blind in the Right Eye: German Justice and Holocaust Denial*, *in* LESSONS AND LEGACIES, VOLUME III, MEMORY, MEMORIALIZATION, AND DENIAL 248 (Peter Hayes ed., 1999).

is still made culpable because it is seen and portrayed always in terms of failure, as part of our own explicitly constructed retrospective jurisprudence of Auschwitz, as the precursor to Nazi law and the Holocaust. Weimar is the negative: the example of a democracy that could not save itself. Its law was too weak to prevent the republic from committing a form of self-immolation under the concerted pressures of Nazism.[26] The failures of Weimar legality led directly to the Nazi takeover of the state apparatus, to the twelve-year rule of *Unrecht,* and to the Shoah. Europe's constitutionalized normative framework for self-preservation—militant democracy—is quite specifically informed by this juridico-historical rendering of Weimar law as failed law. In a general comparative constitutional law context, this legal history is particularly significant. In the more precise domain of comparative constitutional regimes and their views of accepted and acceptable limits on individual freedom, especially in so far as denial is concerned, on "speech," this remembrance of Weimar as constitutional failure has a particularly strong resonance within the European context.[27] Wojiech Sadurski, a skeptic about restrictions on speech, explains:

> In the European context, the call for so-called militant democracy has often been accompanied by an invocation of the most traumatic European experience of weak democracy unable to cope with antidemocratic enemies within—that of the fall of the Weimar Republic, and the emergence of an undemocratic system through the exploitation of democratic freedoms by parties and politicians committed to destroying democracy itself.[28]

The failure of law and democracy is presented in this particular narrative of legal history, collective memory, and politics within Europe as the lesson that must be drawn from the Weimar experience. Those who deny the Holocaust do so not because they are objective historians who dispute the

---

26. For a more sophisticated, nuanced, and convincing study of the way in which a democratic polity and its concomitant rule of law mechanisms can destroy themselves, *see* Vivian G. Curran's account of Vichy, *The Legalization of Racism in a Constitutional State: Democracy's Suicide in Vichy France*, 50 HASTINGS L. J. 1 (1998).

27. *See* RONALD J. KROTOSZYNSKI, THE FIRST AMENDMENT IN CROSS-CULTURAL PERSPECTIVE: A COMPARATIVE LEGAL ANALYSIS OF FREEDOM OF SPEECH (2006). More specifically in relation to denial, *see* Joachim J. Savelsberg & Ryan D. King, *Institutionalizing Collective Memories of Hate: Law and Law Enforcement in Germany and the United States*, 111 AM. J. SOC'Y 579 (2005).

28. Wojciech Sadurski, *European Constitutional Identity?* 15–16 (Sydney L. Sch. Legal Studies Research Paper, Paper No. 06/37, 2007).

facticity of the death chambers of Auschwitz but because they have a particular political agenda that is deeply invested in the legacy of Nazism and in anti-Semitism.[29] Their existence, their political agenda, and their speech are in an open confrontation not just with history and memory but with the constitution of a democratic European body politic. History, specifically the legal history of Weimar, teaches that such speech cannot be allowed to flourish. The simple and simplifying historical narration of the complexities of the rule of law under Weimar leaves much unsaid or underemphasized. A fuller account of law in Weimar can go some way to properly situating and figuring law in the complex matrix of the role of legality and the state in more recent debates about the regulation of denial(s).

In Weimar Germany, Jews attempted to combat anti-Semitic hatred by legal means, invoking the protections of the criminal law, the civil law of defamation, and other legal processes and normative principles. Those who have taken the time to study Jewish self-defense through law in the Weimar era have uncovered a rich history of democratic self-empowerment through law by an endangered minority group and a rich history of law that dismantles many of the dominant understandings of the situation of law under the Weimar Republic. Donald Niewyk concludes that despite the presence of a conservative judiciary, Jewish attempts to seek redress before Weimar courts against racist provocation, defamation, boycotts, and other forms of harassment "produced a creditable record of success."[30] He offers significant proof to back up a wider claim that Weimar law can offer important lessons not just for law's own history in the shadows of Auschwitz and the Shoah but for our current debates about the appropriateness of using law as a tool in the struggle against those who would deny the Shoah and other mass crimes.[31]

Niewyk's study examines how civil rights organizations adopted a self-conscious strategy of using legal action to achieve their aims. Niewyk argues that these groups had available to them a number of substantive legal tools: criminal libel; disturbing the peace; gross misconduct; incitement; insulting the Jewish religion; and common law offenses relating to violence, intimidation, and blackmail. Only 10 percent of prosecutions

---

29. Michael Sherman & Alex Grobman, Denying History: Who Says the Holocaust Never Happened and Why Do They Say It? (2002).

30. Donald L. Niewyk, The Jews in Weimar Germany 88 (2001).

31. Donald L. Niewyk, *Jews and the Courts in Weimar Germany*, 37 Jew. Soc. Stud. 99 (1975).

of anti-Semites resulted in acquittals. A 10 percent acquittal rate is hardly evidence of a judicial system corrupt from head to toe and dominated by proto-Nazi judges and prosecutors. The study also reveals that a significant number of the failures—i.e., acquittals—were due to factors that would inform any prosecution, most commonly, a lack of evidence, combined with an overly optimistic decision to prosecute.[32] In addition, some acquittals were the result not of judicial conservatism and/or bias but of traditional legal arguments based in the taxonomy of the essential elements of the offense. Defendants charged with insulting the Jewish faith could raise the successful defense that their insult was in fact targeted at Jews as a "race" and not at Judaism as a religion. In the absence of a particular prohibition against racial vilification, the charge would fail. While it might be argued that cases of this type highlight a lacuna in Weimar law, in the 1920s, the idea of a crime of racial vilification was unheard of. Moreover, historically, the distinction between classifying Jews as a race rather than focusing on Judaism as a religious faith had a resonance and geographical application well beyond the borders of Germany and a temporal application outside the period of the Weimar Republic. The race/religion taxonomy was part of European liberal legal discourse, even in the Hitler era. The failure of Weimar law in this regard cannot be seen to be anything other than the failure of European law more generally.

Niewyk argues that in relation to a perceived leniency in sentencing right-wing offenders, many instances—which have been invoked by the proponents of the "blind in the right eye" thesis—can be explained by the application of normal legal standards within a recognizable criminal justice discourse. Light sentences were imposed when impecunious defendants could not afford to pay the normal fine; some cases were relatively trivial and deserving of symbolic condemnation but not harsher treatment; many Weimar judges were sensitive to the martyrdom argument and therefore reluctant to create political heroes by imposing harsh punishment on convicted offenders; Weimar judges were also sensitive to general concerns within democracy that restrictions on free speech should not be imposed too lightly.[33] Niewyk attributes unjustifiable conservative prejudice—"blindness in the right eye"—to a mere twenty-one cases between 1919 and 1933, 7 percent of the total.[34]

---

32. *Id.* at 101–02.

33. *Id.* at 103–05.

34. *Id.* at 106.

Udo Beer's later work confirms and further expands upon Niewyk's findings and analysis.[35] Beer highlights the way in which the absence of an effective hate speech standard prevented successful legal action against many vehement anti-Semites. While defamation against identified individual Jews was almost always successfully litigated, Weimar law was inadequate when the issue was the defamation of Jews as a whole, i.e., group libel. Some early success was achieved in cases where the targeted group could be more narrowly defined, such as the Jews in a particular locality, but group libel per se was not actionable in the normative structure of Weimar law. Beer notes: "Yet, in spite of many successes, it was clear that there were some norms of the existing criminal law that failed to accord adequate protection to Jews. Defamation of individuals, apart from a very few exceptions, was always punished. Collective insults were a different matter."[36]

Despite this, Beer documents several instances where collective libels were successfully prosecuted under a variety of extant legal norms.[37] Insults against the Jewish religion were protected under general provisions; and again, they were successfully prosecuted.[38] Jewish economic interests were consistently granted the protection of the law under anti-boycott provisions of Weimar legislation.[39] Niewyk summarizes the situation in regards to the use of law as a self-defense mechanism for Jews in Weimar with a conclusion that refutes the "blind in the right eye" narrative.

> But there can be no question that judicial sternness in prosecuting Jew-haters was much more common and significant and that unexceptionally apposite judgments were typical in an overwhelming majority of the remaining cases. Nor has a single case of an unjust verdict being imposed on a Jewish defendant come to light.[40]

---

35. Udo Beer, *The Protection of Jewish Civil Rights in the Weimar Republic: Jewish Self-Defence through Legal Action*, 33 Leo Baeck Inst. Y.B. 149 (1988). *See also* Dirk Walter, Antisemitische Kriminalität und Gewalt: Judenfeindschaft in der Weimarer Republik (1999).

36. Beer, *supra* note 35, at 161 (footnote omitted).

37. *Id.* at 161–62.

38. *Id.* at 162–67.

39. *Id.* at 176–78.

40. Niewyk, *Jews and the Courts in Weimar Germany*, *supra* note 31, at 112.

Beer echoes this conclusion:

> In the light of the relevant facts, then, it is plain that at least in the field of legal defence the Jews were far more widely recognized as equal citizens with equal rights than has so far been accepted. Indeed, during the life of the Weimar Republic the collective and individual rights of the Jews were effectively protected and enforced by the State and the Jewish-organisations.[41]

Both Niewyk and Beer highlight three intersecting and vital points for our understanding of the legal history of Weimar. It is clear that Jews did have access to both specific and general legal norms to protect their interests—i.e., legal rules aimed at protecting religious practice and belief and rules of general application. While there is some evidence of a conservative bias—the blindness in the right eye of traditional accounts—a careful study of the cases reveals that Jews succeeded in invoking rule of law norms in their defense against Nazi and other forms of right-wing anti-Semitism.

Many of the tools deployed against anti-Semites fell under the general rubric of a legal normativity meant to protect the republic generally. Both Niewyk and Beer highlight the presence of non-Jewish groups in the struggle against right-wing anti-Semitism. Of greater significance for current debates is the fact that those involved shared the understanding—as opponents of anti-Semitism—that the struggle to protect the Jews fell more importantly under the rubric of the defense of republican government. The Weimar Republic was, in other words, a militant democracy, protected—in theory at least—by a series of legal provisions meant to ensure both the survival of the republican form of government and the protection of constituent elements of the body politic, including those most vulnerable to attacks from the Nazis.

The failures attributed to Weimar legality and the defense of its Jewish citizens by both Niewyk and Beer are political rather than legal. While the introduction of a better and clearer set of provisions relating to group libel and a judiciary that might have been more aware of the dangers of certain types of speech may have made some difference, these analyses of Weimar legality point to other factors. The internal failure of German Jews to find a single, unified voice and a collective administrative, political, organizational

---

41. Beer, *supra* note 35, at 176.

structure exacerbated the weakness in the group defamation laws and, more importantly, dispersed political power in an ultimately dangerous way. The failures of Weimar democracy to unite republican adherents against a common enemy in the Nazis—not the bias of Weimar judges or the inadequacies of Weimar law—ultimately led to democracy's downfall. As Beer puts it, "Yet, in the long run the processes of civil law cannot operate successfully unless the poison is taken out of political life, and that did not happen."[42]

The failure of Weimar was not a failure of legality or the result of law's institutional bias toward conservative political positions. It was a failure of politics, both formal and institutional; and more crucially, it was the result of an essential social weakness within the body politic. "Yet, when all is said and done, the fact remains that emotionally motivated mass movements cannot be stemmed by courts of law."[43]

The real lesson to be learned from the experience of Jews under Weimar and their invocation of legal normativity is a lesson that the Jews themselves understood at the time; law was, and is, only a tool that is as strong and weak as the political system of which it is a part. The history of Weimar and its collapse is to be found in a point that we forget—at our peril—and that must inform all current and future debates about the possible utility of denial laws. The empirical evidence demonstrates that while law worked for Weimar's Jews, politics failed them.

This is clearest in the ways in which manifestations of organized anti-Jewish violence were policed. Ironically perhaps, Jewish interests were directly and concretely protected under a series of emergency decrees issued by the president, pursuant to the provisions of the Constitution granting special powers to the police to prevent public disturbances. Anti-Jewish violence was curbed under these measures; anti-Semites were arrested and imprisoned.[44] These emergency decrees which protected Jews and Jewish property were promulgated under the same constitutional provisions which would be used by Hitler to institute a lawful state of emergency from which Germany would only emerge in 1945. What failed was not "law" since the actual normative content of the enabling provisions never changed;

42. *Id.* at 169.

43. *Id.* at 175.

44. *Id.* at 168.

technically, the Weimar Constitution remained in force. What failed was society and the citizens who made up the body politic.

I am not suggesting that law did not play a key role in the unfolding of the Shoah. The continuities between Weimar and Nazi law are incontestable, but this is a debate about law's institutional structures and about the legitimating effect of legality and legal normativity. Such an analysis misses the central point. A focus on the institutional is central to debates about denial(s) and the law since the debate takes place in a current and historical context, which is itself institutionalized. Concerns relate more directly to arguments about competing institutional competences within modern democratic states-courts versus legislatures; the body politic as manifested in the marketplace of ideas or a republican body politic in which the flow of speech can and should be regulated by means other than free competition; law and history as competing institutionalized discourses of truth, etc. The important issue however, always remains that of judgment. We need to judge the substantive worth of the institutional arrangements themselves as tools for the appropriate communication of our collective ideals and identities. The real question becomes how an embodied discourse like "law" can and does deal with the basic epistemological and deontological issues of historical truth in the context of denial(s) as social and political reality.

3. Holocaust and Legal History

Just a few years after Weimar Jews could and did successfully invoke the protections of republican legality, the National Socialist regime made effective use of law in its programmatic identification, exclusion, and killing of Jews. At the end of World War II, combined Allied programs dealt with Nazi anti-Semitic legality by declaring the twelve-year Nazi Reich a period of non-law, creating a jurisprudential amnesia about "Nazi law" as *Unrecht*. At the same time, the records uncovered during the pursuit of Nazi war criminals have become invaluable sources for historical inquiry into the Shoah. From the beginning of the period of post-Nazi law at Nuremberg, there has been a close relationship between legal process and the construction of historical knowledge about the Holocaust.

Whatever criticisms may be made of the Nuremberg processes—either in relation to its flaws and failures as a formal legal instance aimed at the reinstitution of the rule of law or in so far as its failures in dealing with and comprehending the true nature of the Holocaust—there can be little doubt that as a source of primary archival material relating to the processes of the Final Solution, the trials at Nuremberg, and the masses of evidence seized by the Allies and introduced at Nuremberg, have played a primary role in the earliest stages of academic historical study of Nazism. One can temporarily put to one side debates about the appropriateness of the mechanism of the trial as a pedagogic tool, as a history lesson, and instead, focus on the role played by legal processes in the production of primary material about the Holocaust, its victims, and its perpetrators, to be studied by historians. From this empirical perspective, law and history are not deployed as incommensurable discourses suffering from conflicts imposed by the two disciplines' differing methodologies and objectives. Instead, law and history develop a kind of synergistic relationship in which each can and does pursue its own disciplinary agenda. The pursuit of war criminals and the pursuit of knowledge about the Shoah are no longer contentious and mutually exclusive goals.

Trials themselves have become a subspecialty of historical inquiry; the examination undertaken by historians is not a study of the Holocaust based in primary sources and archival research for Nazi documents but instead, Holocaust history is treated as a part of legal history, or the history of legal phenomena. The emergence of a new subgenre of historical inquiry into war crimes trials would not be possible without law's direct concern with historical phenomena relating to war crimes and crimes against humanity.[45] Historical inquiry is intimately related to and informed by the taxonomical structure of law itself; war crimes, crimes against humanity and genocide are, first and foremost, legal categories. Temporally and taxonomically, law precedes and determines history in relation to the Shoah.

Objections to denial laws are often framed not just in terms of general concerns over free speech but by a subcategory of, more specifically, historical concerns about legislating and legalizing a particular version of history.[46] Before turning to the general question, one specific and directly related issue of the law/history nexus in relation to denial must be highlighted.

Perhaps the most well-known Holocaust denial legislation is the French prohibition, known as the *loi Gayssot*. At this stage of the discussion, it is

---

45. Atrocities on Trial: Historical Perspectives on the Politics of Prosecuting War Crimes (Patricia Heberer & Jürgen Matthäus eds., 2008).

46. Eric Stein, *History Against Free Speech: The New German Law Against the "Auschwitz—and Other "Lies,"* 85 Mich. L. Rev. 277 (1986–1987); Eric Stein, *Correspondence on the "Auschwitz Lie,"* 87 Mich. L. Rev. 1026 (1988–1989).

important to note that the *loi Gayssot* only targets denial of the Holocaust. It does so specifically with reference to law. The French legislation incorporates law as the starting point for a legal prohibition on the discourse of history, under the guise of Holocaust denial. Thus the statute criminalizes

> anyone who questions. . . the existence of crimes against humanity as defined by Article 6 of the Statute on the International Military Tribunal annexed to the London Agreement of August 8 1945, committed either by members of a criminal organization determined pursuant to Article 9 of the Statute or by a person found guilty of such crimes by a French or international court.[47]

The French statute makes it an offense not to "deny the Holocaust" but instead to "question the existence of crimes against humanity." Those crimes against humanity are then specifically defined as acts set out in the historical legal document, the IMT statute.

In fact, in law and in history, then, the *loi Gayssot* does not specifically mention the Holocaust, the Shoah, or Jews. The only further requirement is that individuals (or groups) have been found responsible by an international or French court.

The law is notable for legal self-referentiality. The statute defines the Holocaust in terms of crimes against humanity judged by the courts at Nuremberg and afterward. It defines the offense solely in relation to this legal frame. Holocaust denial is denial of the law. The history that is rendered official is not legislative; it is a judicial version of history. Supporters have insisted on its unique juridical progenitor and the judicial form as its true source of legitimacy:

> The real foundation of Article 24 *bis* is not to be found, to invoke Kantian terminology, in the affirmation of an apodictic truth which removes all critical dissenting thought, but instead it is based essentially in the need to ensure respect for both the principles set out in the London Inter-Allied Agreement of 8 August 1945 and for the subsequent judgment of the International Military Tribunal at Nuremberg. It is necessary to add that beside this respect for *stare decisis*, a legitimate concern for the legal

---

47. Loi du 29 Juillet sur la Liberte de la Press [Law of July 29, 1881 on the Freedom of the Press] art. 24 (all translations by the author).

> system, we can place the respect which is due to our highest values, on the moral plane, for the memory of the victims of Nazi barbarism, the suffering endured by those who survived, and the pain of the relatives and friends of those who could not escape. The legitimacy and the utility of the legal regime established on 13 July 1990 therefore seem to me, on both the moral and legal plane, difficult to challenge, even if the debate on this issue is far from over.[48]

These comments underline the idea that denial is intimately centered not in history but in law, both as the source of the "facts" to be protected and in the legitimating instance in which truth and memory are to be located. Law can legitimately concern itself with the protection and recognition of legal precedent. Holocaust denial legislation in France can thus be properly grasped within an almost entirely juridical frame. Law is protecting its own legitimacy by rejecting discourse that calls into question the internally established truths of legal history at Nuremberg. This is not about the unilateral imposition of an "official history" but about the legitimate regulation of attacks against an essential legitimating function of law. The recognition of law's internal legitimacy is also consistent with a deontology of history and memory. The Shoah, its place in public memory, and the ideal of an ethical duty to the memory of the victims sit comfortably beside law's internal self-protection and self-legitimation. The hermeneutic deployed is one of judgment, in which law and the state can appropriate both internal legal legitimacy and deontological status. The unanswered question remains: how can this juridical self-legitimation of Nuremberg and the Shoah be reconciled, historically and jurisprudentially, with a legal history of the Holocaust or more precisely, with a history of the Shoah as a juridical event itself?

4. Memory Laws and Law's Memory

So-called memory laws, of which (anti-)denial laws are an important subset, are on the political and juridical agendas of many different jurisdictions. In April 2007, the Council of the European Union agreed a "Framework

---

48. Jean-Louis Nadal, *Discours d'acceuil, in* LA LUTTE CONTRE LE NÉGATIONNISME 10–13, 12–13 (2003).

Decision on Racism and Xenophobia." Part of the decision requires Member States to prohibit all intentional conduct, "[p]ublicly condoning, denying or grossly trivializing . . . crimes of genocide, crimes against humanity and war crimes."[49]

The Framework Decision refers specifically to the definition of each offense found in Articles 6, 7, and 8 of the Statute of the International Criminal Court. Like the *loi Gayssot*, the European Framework offers a self-referencing juridical framework for denial laws. What is denied is not "history" but rather "law"—i.e., the operative legal definitions of international criminal offenses. But the reference to legal normativity does avoid the potential conflict between the genres of history and law as it presents itself in relation to the legitimacy and/or desirability of memory laws, generally, or denial laws, more specifically. An unresolved problem for both law and history first goes to the temporal aspect of the offense of denial. The denial of genocide, to take the most obvious and problematic example, is dependent upon the definition of the offense. What is denied by the accused must be "genocide." According to the European Framework, what is denied must be genocide as defined by the Rome Statute. Substantive offenses under the Rome Statute are prospective only. There is no retrospective criminal liability.

The real problem operates at the intersection of law and history: at the jurisprudential, deontological, and epistemological bases for the justification of denial laws. In domestic implementation, would such a statute apply to acts or speech in relation to historical events that predate it? Would they apply to historical facts that predate the very concept of "genocide"? Can one deny genocide in relation to historical events that occurred before the jurisprudential idea and the "crime" of "genocide" existed in the legal lexicon? Where, if at all, is the balance to be struck between and among historical analyses, legal prohibition, and the retrospective application not of law directly but of a legal concept? Is "genocide" deontologically retroactive? The debate circulates not around the status and acceptability of law's immersion in history but in history's inaccurate appropriation of law, an appropriation that law would recolonize in denial legislation.

The best example of this phenomenon relates to events in Turkey in the first twenty years of the twentieth century—the massacre of the Armenians by Turkish forces and their Kurdish allies. Debate, fueled by current domestic and international politics and by the politics of history, memory, and

49. Council of the European Union, April 19, 2007.

identity—both inside and outside of Turkey—continues to rage around the exact nature of these acts of mass killing, expulsion, starvation etc.: their origins, their intentionality. Absent historical, ethical or jurisprudential refinement—was it "genocide"?[50]

The denial of the Armenian "genocide" is government policy in Turkey and part of the essential duties of its diplomatic missions. Denial occurs in a network of organized political attempts to rewrite or unwrite history across international borders. It is not my intention to offer a detailed analysis of the Turkish/Armenian case. I bracket a brief introduction of a taxonomical difficulty that informs much of the discussion. I use it as a cursory case study for the wider issue of denial/memory laws and the uncomfortable, deontologically, and epistemologically troubling, if often ignored, appropriation of law by history. The conjoined issues of the legislative recognition of the historical facticity of these events and the criminalization of denial raise a particular semiotic, historical, legal, and ideological question. French legislative action in relation to history and more specifically, the history of genocide, again is deployed here as a case study used to illustrate the general issues of denial/law and memory/history/law. The French case raises this significant and signifying question of the temporality of "genocide" as a legal category and the ways in which this temporality is ignored in historical discourse about denials.

The taxonomical issue relates to the nature, content, and legal definition of the term "genocide." The term "genocide," whatever its current legal and political meaning, is commonly attributed to Raphael Lemkin in his 1944 book, *Axis Rule in Occupied Europe: Laws of OccupationAnalysis of Government—Proposals for Redress.* One concern in all debates about law, history, and memory is that there is a temporal displacement at work. The qualification of the events in what is now Turkey in the early twentieth century as "genocide," is one that can only ever occur ex post facto. At the time of the events themselves, no such concept existed. This does not in an absolute sense entail the rejection of the label. What is does require, as a deontological concern for all involved in these debates—lawyers, judges, historians, politicians, citizens—is a careful acknowledgment of the historical specificity of the term as such and of the inherent dangers of applying new categories to old events. Some concepts may be historically or culturally

---

50. REMEMBRANCE AND GENOCIDE: THE CASE OF THE ARMENIAN GENOCIDE (Richard G. Hovannisian ed., 1999); YVES TERNON, DU NÉGATIONNISME: MÉMOIRE ET TABOU (1999).

specific. Ideas or interpretations that have emerged ex post may also carry with them the specificities of their origins, making such applications inappropriate. Most importantly, the use of a new label or taxonomy by current-day scholars may mean that subtle complexities of the historical record and circumstances that existed at the time of the events under examination will be glossed over or forgotten. The mass killing of Armenians was not *stricto sensu* genocide at the time the massacres occurred, simply because the word itself, as a legal, historical, and political signifier, did not exist. If historians writing about and characterizing these events choose, in exercising their professional judgment, to characterize Turkish actions as "genocide," they do so either within the sense and meaning of the concept as understood and deployed by historians today or by distorting the historical legal record. This does not mean that there is a rule forbidding the use of the taxonomy "genocide" to describe actions against the Armenians. It does mean, however, that great care must be used to explicate the way in which the term is used. "Genocide" in particular contexts has a specific meaning and carries with it political, legal, and ideological messages that are never, in the inevitable interpretive space between signifier and signified, simple recitations of historical "fact." Armenians were killed. To label those killings "massacres," for example, would require specific and detailed reference to historical facts about the nature and manner of killing, some of which may be in dispute, since "massacre," in order to be an accurate representation of historical fact, must include something more than "mere" killing. There are things that have happened, and then there are choices about the language we choose to represent what has happened. To attach the signifier "genocide" to the killings without careful contextualization and historical self-examination in the circumstances of political, historical, cultural, and legal debates about Armenian-Turkish relations is to do something more than to merely describe what happened. Indeed, I would argue that the deployment of this term always does more than describe events; it almost inevitably ascribes motive. It is, in effect, to pass judgment on what happened. This is, of course, precisely what lawyers and historians do within the confines of their own professional discourses and practices. But both disciplines demand care in the deployment of judgment. The term "genocide" carries with it a semiotic baggage situated in the political and juridical gap between signifier and signified. Indeed, the English language is thought by many to be insufficient to properly describe and characterize those who commit "genocide." "Killer" and "murderer" do not suffice. We have adopted the French "*genocidaire*" precisely because genocide is not a simple fact. In a reversal of the usual accusations by historians that law, lawyers, and legal rules of interpretation and application distort history and historical practice, historians who use the term "genocide" in such contexts potentially distort legal meaning and the history of legal taxonomy.

The second issue that should inform all of the debates about "memorial laws" (*lois mémorielles*) is the existence of competing definitions of the word "genocide." If the term did not exist in 1915 as Turks and their Kurdish auxiliaries exterminated Armenian men, women, and children, its existence today is subject to historical and contextual refinement and legal debate. For example, the 1948 United Nations Convention on the Prevention and Punishment of the Crime of Genocide (to which Turkey adhered in 1950), differs from Lemkin's published work, which, in turn, underwent significant evolution as his study progressed. International criminal law has also adopted and adapted corollary concepts of "war crimes" and "crimes against humanity" that figure in many current and proposed denial laws. Those concepts have evolved from their original formulation. Their content is subject to further revision by international and national criminal and other tribunals. "Genocide" is deployed as a particularly strong signifier, which is then attacked as inaccurate by political opponents. Politics become paralyzed by legal semiotic wrangling while thousands die.

Absent political and humanitarian exigency, the taxonomical debate must still have currency. As a matter of historical analysis and putting aside the temporal issues, which definition of "genocide" should we invoke to understand and categorize the events in Anatolia from 1915? Some actions will be included or excluded, at least by law if not by history, depending upon the text one chooses as a guide or taxonomical indicator. Of course, this does not mean that an act that falls outside a particular legal definition of "genocide" did not happen, or that it was not heinous, or that it was lawful. Other common law *(droit commun)* crimes and international criminal offenses (crimes against humanity) can also be invoked to cover most such instances, with at least some more solid historical assertion that the offense actually existed contemporaneously with the facts.[51] What it does mean is that one must be extremely careful as a lawyer, as a historian, and as a legal historian, to establish *a priori* one's methodological, taxonomical, and deontological

---

51. David Scheffer has recently and somewhat controversially suggested the new taxonomy of "atrocity crimes." *See* David Scheffer, *Genocide and Atrocity Crimes*, 1 GENOCIDE STUD. & PREVENTION 229 (2006).

framework when addressing such issues in any particular detail.[52] It is no small irony that members of the same profession, who assail lawyers for their disciplinary insensitivity when dealing with "history" themselves, all too often engage in acts of linguistic and disciplinary imperialism.

Historical inquiry demands almost as condition for its existence, uncertainty, doubt, and a recognition of the unanswered. In cases of genocide and other mass crimes, the possibility/reality of the unanswered and the unknowable also raises fundamental deontological issues. On the other hand, criminal law demands certainty and clarity. When historians seek to analyze, critique, or understand events of the past using modern legal concepts such as "genocide," a potential conflict between the professional practices and discourses of the historian and the lawyer arises. When legislatures intervene to legalize history, the potential conflicts are exacerbated. Many conflicts might and do arise in any attempt to legislate "memory" and/or "history." I turn to concrete examples of the debates that have emerged in France in recent years in order to highlight not just the conflicts but to outline possible ways of conceptualizing the issues that might lessen, if not eliminate, the apparent discord between disciplines and institutional practices of law and of history.

5. Memory/Law-Memory Laws

Heated debate has occurred in France in the past several years on the subject of so-called *lois mémorielles*—memorial laws, or more accurately perhaps, memory laws. Many leading historians and lawyers in France have expressed their anger at what they perceive to be increasingly pernicious legislative intervention into the domain of "history." In addition to intriguing issues about different understandings of the nature and function of the legislative and judicial branches of government in French republican democracy, these interventions by leading French intellectuals proceed from a set of mutual misunderstandings about the intersecting taxonomies and signifiers involved.

It is important to distinguish between and among public acts of memory and remembrance which are, by common agreement, acceptably within the realm of the "political." No one (with the exception perhaps of politicians on

52. Christian Joerges, *Working Through "Bitter Experiences" Towards Constitutionalisation: A Critique of the Disregard for History in European Constitutional Theory* (Eur. Univ. Inst. Working Paper No. 2005/14, 2006).

the Far Right) suggests for example, that Jacques Chirac's public recognition of the role of the French state under Vichy in the Shoah was an inappropriate interference in the domain of "history." In that case, politics and political discourse finally caught up with the facts of Vichy's role in the persecution, deportation, and death of the Jews of France as established by years of historical inquiry and by the judgment of numerous criminal courts. Chirac's statement embodied the politics and practices of apology, expiation, recognition, pardon, and perhaps eventually, amnesty/amnesia and reconciliation that were deployed to deep and lasting sociopolitical effect.

Similarly and more generally, no one in France, or in other countries where similar debates have occurred, suggests that the use of public space and state finances to create and maintain thousands of *lieux de mémoire* to honor the fallen from any number of wars, for example, is in any way improper. The presence of war memorials in every small town and village or the plaques placed on innumerable buildings in Paris and Lyon, marking the spot where various Resistance fighters died in the liberation of the city, do not in anyone's mind constitute inappropriate interference by politics or the political branch into "history."

When debates about such unjustified incursions do occur, they are situated not in the higher realms of fundamental epistemological or ontological categories of "the political" or "the historical" but purely in the domain of the political *tout court*. When nuns seek to establish a convent at Auschwitz or homosexual men or Roma demand recognition for their suffering under the Nazis—in France and Germany in particular—these debates are about "proper" memory, or priority in memory, or about using one memory to obliterate or forget another. They are pleas for a particular reading of historical events, pleas that must be judged according to criteria drawn from the political, legal, historical, and ethical realms. Everyone politicizes history because history in its public manifestations must always be political.[53]

The debates in France about the *lois mémorielles* fall partly into most of these subcategories of concern over the proper political ordering of history and memory. But the debate also falls outside these limits and enters into a juridico-epistemological deployment of other issues. More particularly, the controversies occur around apparently first-order concerns about the proper understanding of history, the academic discipline, the "*science*" of "history,"

53. Jean-Michel Chaumont, La concurrence des victimes: Génocide, identité, reconnaissance (2002).

on the one hand, and another perhaps competing understanding of "law" and its proper role. We return in such cases to claim and counterclaim about disciplinary purity and the incommensurability of competing professional discourses. At another level, because in France, we are dealing with legislative measures, which sometimes carry a penal sanction, we are also faced with understandings of and concerns surrounding the basis of republican legality. In addition, there is a barely articulated but powerful subtext about nation, citizenship, identity, and the "other" that is also always at play.

Only one minor taxonomical issue at the level of technical legal art/science needs to be signaled here; there is a clear distinction, both epistemologically and politically—and clearly as a matter of law—between the two types of *lois mémorielles,* which have been at play in the recent French debates. The first type is the simple declarative statute under which the republic recognizes a particular historical set of events as "genocide"—notwithstanding historico-temporal concerns about the ex post facto use of the term. This kind of legislative intervention into history and/or memory can be placed in a category that resembles legislative acts authorizing the appropriation of a place in a park and the dedication of some public funds for the erection of a monument. In each such instance, the legislative branch makes a political decision to recognize and memorialize a particular event in history. In so doing, it "officializes" that event and marks it in a particular way as a historical truth, recognized and honored as such by the state and thence, by the nation. But legally, such a memorialization, even in a statutory form, has no further direct legal effect.

The second type of legislative intervention is the one that has caused most, but not all, of the public furor in France in recent years. In this situation, the state not only recognizes a particular set of historical events and facts as "true" and worthy of national honor, remembrance, memorialization, and respect, it attaches a penal sanction to the denial of these facts. This is the nature of Holocaust denial legislation in many jurisdictions and of the most recent bill passed in the Assembly in Paris on the Armenian genocide. It is this move to sanction "truth" by criminalizing "lies" that has caused the ire of leading French historians and jurists and has quite natural echoes in other jurisdictions.

5.1 The loi Gayssot

The progenitor of all subsequent memory laws in France and the most problematic of them all from a number of perspectives (few of which I share) is the *loi Gayssot,* which criminalized Holocaust denial (*négationnisme*).[54] This statutory intervention into the fields of law and history came about in a particular set of historical, political, and legal circumstances. It coincided temporally and politically with the prosecution of the wartime collaborationist killer Paul Touvier and the surrounding controversies about state and church collaboration in keeping Touvier out of the hands of the French police and courts for forty years. It also came into being at the time of one of the frequent resurgences of high-profile public examples of Holocaust denial in France. The *loi Gayssot* is, for all its ambiguity and infelicity—for its grant of primacy to law over history and to deontology over immoral claims to epistemological status—aimed solely and uniquely at what we now call the Holocaust or the Shoah. It does not refer to the crime of genocide in general or to any other crimes against humanity beyond those embodied at Nuremberg. It is limited geographically, temporally and in its subject matter; it is Shoah-specific. This limited nature of the *loi Gayssot* has a particular role to play in subsequent French legislative and judicial interventions in the domains of law, memory, and justice.

5.2 Lois Mémorielles

I shall deal briefly with well-known recent cases of memory laws in France. These laws always occur in particular political and historical contexts. The application of general "principles" can often lead to the depoliticization and indeed the dehistoricization of the debate. The battles that led to the legislation were long and difficult and, above all, they were "political." This again is a central point about the nature of these so-called memory laws. A useful working hypothesis in situating and understanding these memory laws is that all debates about the social place of memory and memorialization of specific events or phenomena about "history" and/or "memory," in other words, can best be grasped by placing "memory" and memorialization by legislative means clearly within the realm of the political and, more broadly, the social. This does not mean that "higher" concerns of justice, truth, reconciliation, working through and/or coming to terms with the past, etc., are not present as intended or unintended consequences. Nor does it mean that claims to a particular historical and legal status of events involving them or

54. Loi no 90-615 du 13 juillet 1990 JORF, 14 July 1990 [Law No. 90–615 of July 13, 1990, J.O., July 14, 1990]. VALÉRIE IGOUNET, HISTOIRE DU NÉGATIONNISME EN FRANCE 397–456 (2000).

their ancestors are made in bad faith. It simply positions many of these issues more realistically on contested political terrain and in their rhetorical practices. Each of the French *lois mémorielles* demonstrates that political success is largely determined by the ability of the various actors to translate their demands from the terrain of the politically contingent into some kind of ineffable moral discursive location.

If we proceed within an analytical and hermeneutic frame that gives precedence to the political, a more nuanced analysis of the place, role, and nature of the memory laws in French culture and society and of denial laws, more generally, is possible. Part of this clarity might come at the expense of placing, albeit tentatively—for limited analytical purposes—"history" outside of politics. This minor and contingent methodological cost may be worth paying. When French historians and lawyers proclaim that history is in danger of being "legislated," frozen by fiat, they are invoking this same taxonomical structure, i.e., that history must not be "politicized." Such claims about the apolitical nature of history are themselves arguably political and ideological assertions about history and historical inquiry. They also run the opposite risk of conflating "memory" and "history," particularly when they argue that simple declarative statutes of recognition are violative of the free scientific spirit of inquiry, which informs history in the republican tradition. Again, Chirac's apology for Vichy, public monuments to the fallen war dead of the Franco-Prussian War, or the First and Second World Wars, memorialization in public space of *Résistance* fighters, even the celebration of July 14th, all involve the legislation of history and of memory, and all occur without any credible assertion that such events violate the sacred nature of "history."

After years of political agitation, especially from community groups among the population from the French Antilles and to a lesser extent, Réunion, the French legislature passed the "Law recognizing the slave trade and slavery as a crime against humanity," popularly referred to as the *loi Taubira*.[55] Article 1 of the law embodied the recognition and classification of slavery and the slave trade in the former French colonies of the Caribbean and the Indian Ocean, as well as in France itself, as a crime against humanity. Intriguingly, from the perspective of legal taxonomy, if not from one informed by legal historical accuracy, this provision of a memory law did not classify slavery as genocide but opted for the broader category of crime against

55. Loi no 2001-434 du 21 mai 2001, JORF, no 119, 23 May 2001[Law No. 2001-434 of May 21, 2001, J.O. No. 119, May 23, 2001], p. 8175.

humanity. Slavery is itself also defined in the *Code Pénal* Chapter 11 as "another crime against humanity." Specific reference is made in Article 212-1, which states:

> Deportation, reduction to slavery or the massive and systematic practice of summary executions, of abduction of persons followed by their disappearance, of torture or inhuman acts, inspired by political, philosophical, racial or religious motives, and organised in pursuit of a concerted plan against a group of a civil population are punished by criminal imprisonment for life.

Article 2 of the *Loi Taubira*, which in particular raised the ire of the French historical profession, set forth the proposition that all educational and research programs in history and the social sciences give the question of slavery the place it deserves and encourages the opening of archival sources to researchers. Article 4 establishes mechanisms for the public commemoration of the sufferings inflicted by the slave trade and slavery.

Putting aside the temporal issue, there seems to be no grounds for disagreement or controversy since slavery itself is one of the enumerated crimes against humanity found in the *Code Pénal* Article 212-1, a provision which predates the slavery memory law of 2001. Moreover, it is important to note that the slavery memory law carries with it no direct penal sanctions. Denial or questioning the "fact" of slavery as a crime against humanity is not prohibited. The *loi Taubira* is a memory law in the strictest sense, recognizing and categorizing the horrors of part of France's historical legacy, memorializing and "repenting" publicly for the faults and harms committed. It does not criminalize the denial of the slave trade as a crime against humanity nor does it inflict sanctions on those who might, for example, diminish the suffering of the victims of slavery. In short, it offers an "officialized" French history but does not punish or prohibit.

Some French historians nonetheless objected as a matter of principle to the legislation of history and more vociferously, perhaps, to the potential danger as they saw it to the freedom of "scientific" research and pedagogy. But at some practical, realistic, political level, these objections and fears appear to have been misplaced. There is no evidence in the years since the passage of the law that any such interference has in fact occurred. Moreover, historians, especially French historians who wish to invoke republican tradition, are on very shaky ground indeed if they wish to object to the government or, more accurately, the state having a role to play in education.

The entire controversy over *laïcité* in France was sparked by the *affaire des foulards*, concerning the wearing of "religious" garb by Muslim schoolgirls.[56] The idea and ideal of the public school as a republican space and as a place where children are educated in and inculcated with republican values is central to French political practice and ideological national self-understanding. For the government to insist that slavery is a crime against humanity and contrary to basic republican, and therefore French norms of *libérté, égalité, et fraternité* should strike one both as perfectly natural and as falling clearly within accepted understandings of the proper and necessary role of the French state.

Yet, it was in large part a juristic event grounded in the context of the *loi Taubira* that has given rise to the current rupture between the historical profession and the French state. Noted historian Olivier Pétré-Grenouilleau, author of the leading French study on the slave trade, was sued following statements that he made about the correct characterization of slavery, according to his reading of the historical evidence.[57] He argued that while he had no quarrel with the characterization of slavery as a crime against humanity, the historical evidence did not justify placing the slave trade under the more specific category—"genocide." His position was that slave traders operated on the basis of commercial self-interest, and genocide requires an intention to destroy an identified group. In such a case, it would have been against their own profit motive for slave traders to wish to destroy the group. Therefore, he argued, based on the historical evidence of the capitalist logic that informed the slave trade, the slave trade did not meet the legal definition of genocide.

This is a case in which a leading academic historian, responding to the specific legislative provisions of the *loi Taubira* and comparing and applying historical data and evidence, reached a "scientific" conclusion in his field of expertise. Pétré-Grenouilleau's position does not itself contradict the legislative position of the French Parliament, which classified the slave trade and slavery in the *loi Taubira* itself not as genocide but as a crime against humanity.[58]

This did nothing to assuage the anger of some community groups who brought a legal action against the historian, apparently based in the provisions

---

56. John R. Bowen, Why the French Don't Like Headscarves (2007); Dominic McGoldrick, Human Rights and Religion: The Islamic Headscarf Debate in Europe (2006).

57. Olivier Pétré-Grenouilleau, Les Traites négrières. Essai d'histoire globale (2004).

58. On November 30, 2005, the complaint against the historian failed. *See* Jean-Yves Camus, *The Commemoration of Slavery in France and the Emergence of Black Political Consciousness*, 11 Eur. Legacy 647 (2006).

of the two statutes then in existence as memory laws: the *loi Gayssot* and the *loi Taubira*. In effect, the case on these foundations was doomed to fail; French jurisprudence clearly establishes that the *loi Gayssot* is limited to events as prescribed in its text—i.e., the Shoah—and cannot be applied to other historical circumstances. Nothing in the *loi Gayssot* makes refusing to classify the slave trade as genocide actionable. As for the *loi Taubira*, the statute is one in the form of a law of recognition only, without a concomitant criminalization provision.

For many historians, the *loi Taubira* and the political and legal agitation by the community groups behind its passage and "enforcement" came to symbolize and embody an attack on their professional jurisdiction, their competency, and their ability to carry out their tasks as independent "scientists" and researchers. The so-called memory laws allowed politically active and powerful "community" (*communautaire*) groups to cow parliamentarians into legislating beyond their proper knowledge and competence. More perniciously, the groups then used their legislative victory in order to rely on such memory laws to pursue political agendas through means of legal actions against reputable historians. For leading French historian René Rémond, this was nothing less than the natural consequence of legislative interference in history.[59] Rémond, along with a number of historians—both French and foreign—signed a petition in December 2005 condemning all memory laws and calling upon Parliament to abolish all offending provisions, including the *loi Gayssot*, the *loi Taubira*, and the law on the *pieds noirs* and *harkis*. The petition asserted that history was not a religion, not about morality, not a slave to current events, not the same as memory, and not a legal question.[60] The signatories demanded that history be left out of all these irrelevant considerations and that they be left alone to get about the business of "real" historical research without government fiat.

Yet the historians themselves were compelled to recognize that they ran the risk of overstepping the mark on several points. Their press release had to recognize—and Rémond repeatedly reasserted the point—that as historians attacking the very concept of memory laws they were not staking an elitist and therefore potentially anti-democratic and anti-republican,

59. René Rémond, Quand L'État Se Mêle à L'Histoire 39 (2006).

60. *Liberté pour l'histoire!*, Libération, Dec. 13, 2005, *available at* http://www.liberation.fr/tribune/0101551004-liberte-pour-l-histoire.

claim to professional monopoly status in so far as "history" was concerned. History in the Republic belongs to every citizen. Memory laws—so the historians' argument goes—in effect, misappropriate history and remove it from the democratic citizenry of the Republic. The signatories merely wanted freedom for "history" and had never claimed freedom for "historians." This might appear to be an example of self-indulgent sophistry when referring to a petition signed by none other than 600 professional historians proclaiming the right to free scientific research. Nonetheless, the historians insisted that their goal was to preserve history from politics.

They also tried to strike a balance between the appropriate function for legislative intervention and those domains: in this case, all memory laws where the parliament had overstepped its own competence and proper jurisdiction in a republican democracy. In the press release, the group underlined that it wished to:

> Recall that if it is traditionally the role of Parliament or the government to decide about commemorations, celebrations or indemnities, it is not within the competence of Parliament to pass laws which aim to declare a kind of official historical truth and to establish thereby, through the court system, control over the writing or even the teaching, of history at every level.[61]

The rhetoric of the historians, which attempts to draw lines of distinction, is inaccurate and misplaced. Not all of the laws in question, in fact, sanctioned a declaration of historical truth with a penalty. The judicial apparatus was uninvolved in all but the *loi Gayssot.* It is difficult to see how a simple parliamentary declaration classifying slavery as a crime against humanity, after that same parliament had passed a general provision of the *Code Pénal,* including slavery in a list of crimes against humanity is, first of all, inappropriate as an exercise of the legislative function. Secondly, it is difficult if not impossible to glean from the petition itself exactly where the "scientific" taxonomical line between a commemoration of slavery or a law granting compensation to the descendants of slaves, each of which is apparently, and without question, acceptably within the jurisdictional limits of a legislative body, and the establishment of a "historical truth" by legislation, might lie.

---

61. *Id.*

One more easily understands why and how historians might object to memory laws that would criminalize real historical research and the dissemination of theories, interpretations, and understandings of historical events based on that research. But this is not the position in French law under any of the memory law provisions. The *loi Gayssot* has never been used to prosecute or intimidate any serious French or other historical inquiry into the Holocaust. Nor has this ever happened in any other jurisdiction in which similar laws exist. Holocaust denial laws, a particular type of memory law, have been used to pursue and penalize deniers; this has been met with mixed success. These deniers are anti-Semites and/or neo-Nazis who couch their statements and writings in the guise of serious academic inquiry and debate but who pursue a self-evident political and ideological agenda to sanitize Nazism and to attack Jews. The fact that these laws exist in modern European liberal democracies indicates that they have received, formally at least, a serious public vetting and have been subject to debate, objection, and scrutiny. Denial laws do not simply emerge out of thin air. Nor do they come into being without careful thought, consideration, and debate about the dangers inherent in officializing history and/or limiting freedom of speech.

Such laws are doubtless political. This has many consequences, not the least of which is that their abuse in a real democracy is controlled and limited by their very political nature and context. They are also political in the sense that they give voice to and embody both a broadly held belief in the essential importance of preserving the history and the memory of the Holocaust within Europe's borders, and in the state's valid and necessary role in the protection of vulnerable minorities within the republican polity. The American position, which prioritizes free speech in such instances, takes a different view, a view that is not without its consequences: In relation to hate speech, generally, Jeremy Waldron has recently written of the reality of the First Amendment worldview:

> The question is about the direct targets of the abuse. Can their lives be led, can their children be brought up, can their hopes be maintained and their worst fears dispelled, in a social environment polluted by these materials. Those are the concerns that need to be answered when we defend the use of the First Amendment to strike down laws prohibiting the publication of racial hatred.[62]

---

62. Jeremy Waldron, *Free Speech & the Menace of Hysteria*, 55 N.Y. REV. BOOKS 40, 44 (May 29, 2008).

The debate, as Waldron's comments indicate, is not simply legal, nor in any context is it simply about "history." It is at once about a politically engaged debate on issues of definitional import to the republic and to the ethical content of memory in the republican body politic. On the facts and in the context of French law, the case allegedly brought under the *loi Taubira* failed precisely because of the limited nature of the *loi Gayssot* and the fact that the slavery memory law does not itself contain any provision extending beyond simple "recognition." The historians' petition is based on fears that are ill founded and that have no basis in political or legal reality in the modern-day French republic. They create a straw-man argument that simply ignores both the concrete facts and the cultural and political contexts in which these laws really operate. If memory laws are political, they are so in a limited context and in relation to other contextual elements, not the least of which are the legal and deontological limits placed on them. It is not overly naïve to state that no French government, magistrate, or police force will pursue historians doing history, with or without memory laws. These *lois mémorielles*, even in their most severe manifestation, like the *loi Gayssot*, are political in that they have a particular political target: *négationnisme*. Holocaust denial laws do not threaten historical inquiry because no historian, professional, or amateur challenges the historical reality of the Shoah.

In addition to a misapprehension or an ill-defined understanding of the limits on the legislative branch, the historians also fail to grasp the proper role of courts and legal proceedings in a republican democracy. Courts do adjudicate facts, whether they are concrete issues relating to an automobile accident or a murder or bank robbery or—as evidenced in the *Barbie*, *Touvier* and *Papon* cases—to facts surrounding the Shoah and the occupation in so far as they are relevant to a particular criminal offense.[63] Historian Henry Rousso's position in relation to the law/history divide becomes strikingly bizarre, if not obtuse. Called as an expert witness in the *Papon* case, Rousso refused, largely on the grounds that history and historians could play no useful role in the prosecution. The facts were by then sufficiently well known, especially after the *Barbie* and *Touvier* cases. His testimony could add nothing.[64] Despite his repeated assertions that history and law were incommensurable and that the confusion between history and memory has had a deleterious and politicizing effect on real historical inquiry, Rousso agreed to

---

63. Béatrice Fleury & Jacques Walter, *Médias, Témoin-Expert et Contre-Expertise Historiographique*, 88 VINGTIÈME SIÈCLE 63 (2005).

64. Rousso, *supra* note 16, at 85–86.

appear as an expert witness for the defense in Robert Faurisson's libel suit against Robert Badinter. In doing so, he positioned himself purely and simply as a defender of history. Rousso asserts:

> I do not consider that this trial has as a goal the judgment of History, we are here to judge the words of a certain number of individuals. This is a contemporary case which calls into question the rights and duties of everyone who claims to write History, the rights and duties of anyone who claims to exercise the profession of an historian. And, in this case, I think that the terms used to qualify the work of Mr. Faurisson over the past twenty-five years, i.e. as that of a falsifier or faker, seem to me, as they did twenty-five years ago, to be the only possible way of categorizing them.[65]

Even for Rousso, a vehement critic of the misuse of history in a legal context, Holocaust denial is another kettle of fish—it is the opposite of history: it falsifies and manufactures a fake and counterfeit version that is then passed off as history.

French courts have shown themselves ready and able to adjudicate in such matters concerning memory laws and their corollaries in private law actions in delict, within a self-defined professional understanding of the judicial function, just as Rousso is able to distinguish within a legal and historical professional context between real and fake history. One irony, probably unintended, of the historians' petition against all memory laws, is that they are unconcerned about making categorical statements about institutional competence in so far as that relates to the parliament and the judiciary, while at the same time rejecting any legislative attempt to circumscribe their own jurisdiction. Again, in the midst of a political debate about the nature and content of law, they rhetorically situate themselves outside the political realm. In so doing, they replicate and mirror in important ways that the position adopted by the proponents of the very legislation they seek to overturn.

At some level at least, the call for the abolition of all *lois mémorielles* might strike the observer as over-kill or at least, as being poorly articulated in terms of its limiting and self-defining premises. There is confusion about the content, form, and function of the different laws attacked by the historians and about important issues concerning the role of republican institutions.

---

65. Jouanneau, *supra* note 13, at 125.

It would seem more logical and coherent—though still unacceptable in my view—to object to provisions that penalize speech and inquiry or which overreach in terms of pedagogical needs and jurisdictional competence based on some shared political understanding of the importance of free speech in a democratic society.[66]

The recognition of the Armenian genocide in French law places the law/history/nexus contextually in relation to the more general debates about "*lois mémorielles*" in France, which might then lead back to a way of more fruitfully situating law and denial(s) in their proper social setting.

5.3 The Armenian (Genocide) in French Law

Whatever one's view of the French memory laws outlined above, they do share one very specific and important characteristic: they are "French" *lois mémorielles*. The *loi Gayssot* deals specifically with the phenomenon of Holocaust denial (*négationnisme*) in that country. While its definitional elements point to international criteria (the IMT), it deals, especially in light of the historical origins of its passage, with the Shoah in France and the complex cultural, political, and social circumstances surrounding, on the one hand, the killing of French Jews and, on the other, the rise of Holocaust Denial as a French political phenomenon.[67] Similarly, the *loi Taubira* and the provisions relating to *pieds noirs* and *harki* history can be placed easily as a matter of taxonomy within a set of debates about "French" history and the current competing political and social understandings of its colonial past and heritage. These laws also fit into deeper issues of the nature of French citizenship, identity, and belonging in light of the presence of this colonial heritage on French national soil in the form of immigrants from the areas affected by the French imperial adventure; they are all laws about French memory. If *lois mémorielles* are an available and acceptable form of national memory building and recognition, they can each be fitted into some understanding of "Frenchness."

66. This seems to be at least a more productive, if doomed, line of jurisprudential debate and inquiry. *See* Laurent Pech, *Genocide-denial laws: A misguided attempt to criminalize history* (NUI, Galway, Faculty of Law Conference Papers, 7 Law CPS 2006). *See also* "Appel de 56 juristes à l'abrogation des 'lois mémorielles,'" LDH TOULON, Nov. 29, 2006, *available at* http://www.ldhtoulon.net/spip.php?article1683.

67. JOAN B. WOLF, HARNESSING THE HOLOCAUST: THE POLITICS OF MEMORY IN FRANCE (2004).

Any legislative recognition of the Armenian genocide, on the other hand, fits less easily into a common understanding of French citizenship, history, and culture. The presence of a significant Armenian population on French soil—vitally important to the politics of Armenian genocide memory laws in the country—does not, per se, create any condition for a justification—in an epistemological or even a deontological sense—for a national law recognizing the Armenian genocide in 1915 and qualifying it as such. There are many immigrant groups present in France and historical events of cultural and national significance to them—outside of those with a direct French colonial past—have not been recognized and memorialized.

The Armenian genocide did not occur in France nor did it really affect French citizens in any way. French memory laws relating to the Armenian genocide must be based on another connection with France. It is the non-Frenchness of the Armenian genocide that makes French legislative and legal recognition of the events so intriguing in the context of a general debate and discussion and argument about *lois mémorielles* and about their place in the debate about Europe's dark legacy and its laws' (and history's) attempt to come to terms with it. This also raises important and increasingly significant issues of postnational identity and in the legal/historical domain, questions about understandings of universal jurisdiction and the appropriate situation of "crimes against humanity" within the legal systems of nation states. If one can argue that the Shoah, slavery, and colonialism are historical events which must be understood and engraved in French national memory by means of legislation—because they are essential to a proper understanding of the modern day *Vième République*—how can similar legislative and judicial intervention be justified in relation to events that occurred in what is now Turkey, in the early part of the twentieth century? One might begin to categorize the question of the Armenian genocide as a French issue by placing it in some context of the responsibility, historical or otherwise, of France as a Great Power whose inaction aided and abetted the genocide in the first place and whose complicity with the Ataturk and subsequent Turkish regimes allowed the amnesia and amnesty of the Armenian genocide to install themselves across Europe.[68] Into this mix, one would need to add the important factor that the Armenians were Orthodox Christians and that the

---

68. Mark Levene, *Creating a Modern "Zone of Genocide:" The Impact of Nation- and State-Formation on Eastern Anatolia, 1878–1923*, 12 HOLOCAUST & GENOCIDE STUD. 393 (1998); DONALD BLOXHAM, THE GREAT GAME OF GENOCIDE: IMPERIALISM, NATIONALISM, AND THE DESTRUCTION OF THE OTTOMAN ARMENIANS (2005).

genocide was perpetrated by Muslim Turks and Kurds; both the historical and current understandings of the "Muslim Other" and of a Christian Europe must necessarily be understood as informing—if not determining—factors in the politics of the Armenian genocide outside Turkey.

Even before the 1915 genocide, French politicians positioned themselves as the protectors and advocates of the Armenian population of Turkey. In 1896, following the massacres of that era, the French Socialist Deputy Jean Jaurès invoked the "European conscience" as a basis for the defense of the Armenians.[69] Jaurès also situated a theme still applicable today in discussions seeking to justify French legal recognition of the Armenian genocide, one which places France as the country that is the birthplace of human rights (*les droits de l'homme*). As such, a special burden is placed on the French nation to protect these universal truths and advocate for the freedom of all oppressed peoples. Part of the French civilizing mission (*la mission civilisatrice*) is to defend human rights and to protest their violation everywhere they might occur. On this vision of "Frenchness," therefore, one might argue that all genocides—of which the Armenian case is the first example of the twentieth century—have a special significance for France. Their recognition by way of *lois mémorielles* would therefore be intimately associated with a concrete and ideological vision of France as the home of *les droits de l'homme*. A similar argument grounded in a vision of "Europe" as a polity that has successfully emerged from its dark shadows and has a special sense of duty in relation to genocide and crimes against humanity could also be invoked as a political and deontological justification for the general denial provisions envisioned in the Framework Decision of April 19, 2007.

Of course, one obvious question (beyond the one that might ask about where France has been in relation to other violations of human rights both domestically and internationally) is—if the protection and enshrining of human rights are essential and core republican values—why haven't the French adopted the broader European and Swiss approach and enacted, for example, a general statute criminalizing all denials of all genocides and all crimes against humanity? The provisions of the *Code Pénal* have potential universal application. On the other hand, the *loi Gayssot* is specific to the Shoah. Something else, some other factor or factors, beyond French culpability as a Great Power or its special responsibility as the cradle of human

---

69. Jean Jaures, Speech to the National Assembly (Nov. 3, 1896) *in* IL FAUT SAVUER LES ARMENIENS 18 (Paris: Mille-et- Une- Nuits, 2005) 18.

rights, must be at play in the creation of a memory law in relation to the Armenian genocide.

The political and legislative struggle for such a *loi mémorielle* was long and difficult. It was possible, in light of recent political practice, to argue that the commemoration of the Armenian genocide at the Arc de Triomphe every April 24th, in the presence of high-ranking representatives of the republic, already constituted a de facto recognition of the events of 1915. On this view, the statute merely formalized this state of affairs, transforming de facto recognition into de jure memorialization within the competence of the French legislature.

But the struggle to achieve this taxonomical transformation was a long one. While the Report to the National Assembly on the proposed Armenian memory law was issued in May 1998, the bill was not passed into law until January 2001.[70] Eventually, the French Parliament overcame presidential reluctance, based largely in the geopolitics of Turkey's position as a potential member of the EU and did legislatively enshrine and recognize the historical factuality of the Armenian genocide. The 2001 *loi mémorielle* was simple and to the point; traditional and legally unproblematic, it fit perfectly into the first type of memory law, one which offers a legislative recognition of an historical event suitable for memorialization. It contains only one article, which reads: "France publicly recognizes the Armenian genocide of 1915."[71]

The question as to why the French Republic should and did recognize this particular "foreign" genocide as opposed to all others remains. Clearly the presence of the strong, politically astute Armenian population in France played a key role. But other factors were equally at work. The law was constructed as one that served a number of mutually reinforcing goals, all of which were, by definition, important to France. Thus, the Report of the Foreign Affairs Committee characterized the bill as intended both to break the cycle of forgetting, which had heretofore defined the Armenian genocide and to encourage Turkey to officially recognize the genocide. Such recognition would then serve to allow that country to fulfill its proper role on the border of Europe and Asia, in the Caucuses, and to strengthen its ties with the European Union.[72] The memory of the Armenian genocide, as legislated

70. Assemblée Nationale, Rapport, René Rouquet, Député, 26 May 1998; Loi no 2001-70 du 29 janvier 2001, JORF, 30 January 2001 [Law No. 2001-70 of January 29, 2001, J.O., January 30, 2001].

71. Loi no 2001-70 du 29 janvier 2001, JORF, 30 January 2001 [Law No. 2001-70 of January 29, 2001, J.O., January 30, 2001].

72. *Id.* at 4.

in France, was meant on this understanding of parliamentary motive, to promote a reimagining of Turkey's self-understanding, and to help kick-start its own processes of coming to terms with its past. The dark legacy of Turkey became at some level, however attenuated, the dark legacy of France and of Europe. More precisely perhaps, the French Parliament recognized this process of coming to terms with the historical past through rule of law mechanisms as a necessary prerequisite to being "European." Of course, one might ask therefore why no such demands—beyond generalized requirements for constitutional and good governance reforms—had been imposed at French insistence in a significant way on any other EU aspirant country.

In addition to allowing Turkey to flourish as a democratic state in Europe, the report listed several justifications for the memory law. The law concretized France's commitment to human rights and universal values, as the home of *les droits de l'homme.* The law would also reaffirm the basic principle of French law that there was no statute of limitations on crimes against humanity. By recognizing the present-day importance of a genocide committed over eighty years ago, the French Parliament was inscribing genocide as part of the dark legacy of humanity that can and must never be forgotten. The other justifications laid out in the report are more directly related to French political reality. The law would honor commitments to the Armenian community in France and would serve as a salve for the wounds to their collective and individual psychological well-being caused by the lack of recognition of the genocide. Finally, and this brings us back to a central juridical understanding of memory laws, the law would serve to combat denial and to educate future generations.[73] These themes would all be repeated in debates in the Assembly and the Senate as the bill made its way slowly through the legislative process.

It is perhaps difficult to see why this law—with its one Article recognizing events in 1915 as genocide—would cause concern among historians in France. Even so, the law fits in the list of *lois mémorielles* enumerated in the petition "Liberty for History." In reality, such a simple declaration—an official recognition of the genocidal character of the Armenian matter—in no way affects or impacts the rights and freedoms of historians. There is no pedagogical imperative to teach the Armenian genocide in a compulsory curriculum. It is clearly within the role of parliamentarians to identify and pass legislation concerning social phenomena that they find to be causing harm to the nation. If Parliament identifies denial of the Armenian genocide

73. *Id.* at 22.

as a *malum in se* after political debate and public discourse on the matter, there can be little doubt as a constitutional and political issue that it is acting within its rights and duties to decide the appropriate measures to be taken. In this case, the French-elected officials decided to proceed to combat denial and to introduce a form of social pedagogy not by introducing measures similar to the *loi Gayssot*—imposing criminal sanctions on denial of the Armenian genocide. The parliament offered a declarative statement.

In addition to the aforementioned statutes, the proceedings under the *loi Taubira* and the backlash from declarations about the overwhelmingly positive character of French colonialism, the National Assembly in 2006 approved an amendment to the 2001 statute that imposed criminal sanction relating to denial of the Armenian genocide. This was done by incorporating part of the *loi Gayssot* as Article 2 of the 2001 law.

> The punishment set out in Article 24 *bis* of the law of July 29, 1881, on the freedom of the press will be applied to anyone who contests, by any of the means set out in Article 23 of the same law, the existence of the Armenian genocide of 1915.[74]

The 2001 statute recognizing the Armenian genocide, in addition to falling into the "declarative" category, does raise a fundamental question of "extraterritoriality," not in the strict legal sense but in the "memorial" context. Despite claims about the universality of genocide as a matter of concern and notwithstanding the rhetorical invocation of the status of France as the home of the "Rights of Man," the 2001 statute is unique in that it relates to specific events in which the French had no direct stake. However persuasive or unpersuasive one finds the justifications for passing such a law in France, it does raise a vital question of and for French memory.

Among the concerns raised by those historians and jurists who now seek the abrogation of all *lois mémorielles*—whatever their nature—is the question of "communalism." By this, they mean that various racial and ethnic groups have turned to the state and the law and insisted on the recognition of their particular claims; these groups insist that their particular national and/or ethnic histories are also of universal significance within the French polity. For many French intellectuals, this is dishonest and dangerous to the

---

74. Assemblée Nationale, Proposition de Loi, no 3030 (rectifiée), *complétant la loi no 2001-70 du 29 janvier 2001 relative à la reconnaissance du génocide arménien*, Assemblée Nationale, Rapport, M. Christophe Masse, 15 May 2006; Assemblée Nationale, Compte-rendu intégral, 12 Octobre 2006.

republic. When such self-identifying groups argue for general recognition of their communal interests, the Parliament (and the courts, depending on the circumstances), become political tools in the service—not of the nation or the republic—but of identity politics. This French phenomenon of "communalism," so opponents of memory laws claim, betrays the ideals of French citizenship and the nation as universal and republican. Opponents of these laws deem them to be concrete manifestations of the breakdown of the republic and universalist ideals in favor of a disastrous "Anglo-Saxon" version of multiculturalism. This, they argue, can be achieved by the rhetorical strategy of transforming the local and the contingently political into the universal and deontological. The debate about memory laws moves beyond ideas of the proper role of parliaments and historians—of the nature and practice of historical inquiry—to encompass more fundamental questions of republican citizenship. *Lois mémorielles* must be situated and understood in the context of a malaise within French society about the very meaning of citizenship and Frenchness. Riots in the *banlieues*, striking students, racist police and discrimination in employment, and proclamations about France as a nation not of ethnic groups but of citizens, all circulate as the undercurrent of political discourse in France. This political discourse undergirds and informs both historical and legal practice. When a bill attempts to criminalize denial of events in Turkey in 1915, the politics of ethnic lobbying come to the surface and ignite concerns about the state and fate of the republic.

Historians and jurists who now seek the abrogation of all memory laws have, on their side and to their credit, the benefit of "universalism." They do not seek to distinguish between "good" and "bad" memory laws or between simple declarative memory laws and those that carry additional elements such as penalization or pedagogical imperatives. They want all such laws, whatever their individual characteristics, eliminated. This allows them to avoid what has always been a problematic and highly emotive subtext in the context of French *lois mémorielles.*

This issue that goes to the heart of much of the debate is that of the specificity and uniqueness of the Shoah. Because of basic issues about the constitutive role of Vichy's involvement in the legalized killing of French Jews, the question of the Shoah has always had a special place, albeit one that was historically underarticulated. In the eyes of many, the *loi Gayssot* was, and is, justified because it deals with the "modern" European phenomenon of mass killing in Europe. It directly concerns the French state's recognition of the harm caused to French society as a whole by anti-Semitism and denial as a manifestation of that harm. It is a legalized form of France coming to terms not just with its dark legacy but with the dark shadow cast on present-day France by the *malum in se* of *négationnisme*. The Shoah is not about colonialism and the tragedies and horrors of slavery as "historical" memory and reality; the Shoah is Europe's and France's immediate dark past and ominous present. The real debate, which has occurred only at the margins, is not about the question of *lois mémorielles* in general but about the 2006 bill and its taxonomy.

By incorporating the same language as the *loi Gayssot*, the 2006 bill can be seen as an attempt to legislate an equivalency between the Armenian genocide and the Holocaust.[75] This is for some a politically sanctioned Holocaust denial because it tends to relativize the Shoah. Complex debates about contextualization versus relativization—about comparison versus equivalency—become lost in the emotional and psychological as well as the political investment of all parties in the recognition and memorialization of "their" genocide. In fact, "communalism"—which informs the political debate around these memorial/memory laws in France—relates back to the issue of "Frenchness."

The Shoah and therefore the *loi Gayssot* as its memory law, directly implicate the French state and the French nation. The Armenian genocide, despite arguments about Great Power complicity, Christian solidarity, and human rights universalism is a distinctly "foreign" event. The issues are complex and intertwined. Not only is the plan to exterminate the Jewish population of Europe different in nature, type, and extent from the Armenian genocide, but it is part of the dark legacy of "Europe" and France. This means that it deserves special recognition and remembrance. The Armenian genocide does not share this fundamental and distinguishing characteristic. This specificity in relation to the Shoah and to the *loi Gayssot* manifests itself even among those who have decided to opt for a position of total opposition to memory laws. The late René Rémond, then the leading spokesperson for the movement "Liberty for History," expressed his ambivalence as follows: "by constantly increasing examples of genocide, we run the risk of eliminating the exceptional nature of the Shoah. This plays indirectly into the hands of the Deniers by diluting the specificity of Nazi criminality in a multiplicity of massacres."[76]

Rémond recognized that the particular rise of anti-Semitism in France and the danger posed by deniers in that country raise special national and political concerns. As a result, he struck an ambivalent pose by insisting that the abolition of all memory laws is the only way to preserve the liberty of

---

75. Vahakn N. Dadrian, The History of the Armenian Genocide (2007). *See also* Neela Banerjee, *Armenian Issue Presents a Dilemma for U.S. Jews*, N.Y. Times, Oct. 19, 2007, *available at* http://www.nytimes.com/2007/10/19/us/19genocide.html.

76. Rémond, *supra* note 59, at 31.

history, while conceding that the decision on the *loi Gayssot* is a difficult one. The solution must be left to the judgment of politicians.[77]

Memory laws are distinctly political phenomena born of specific historical, social, political, and legal contexts. They are not—except perhaps by virtue of a political and ideological choice—members of the same genre. The taxonomical game in relation to these *lois mémorielles* is hidden in the general statements of principle emanating from their proponents and their opponents. Every choice in relation to basic questions about "human rights," "crimes against humanity," "genocide," and the fixing of historical and political truth in memorial laws, is an ethical one. The real debate again is at the deontological level rather than at the more prosaic level of disciplinary discursive boundaries. The response to the question posed by the *loi Gayssot* and by the 2006 amendment to the 2001 law on the Armenian genocide must be contextualized and differentiated according to the circumstances. All choices carry with them a risk, and it is this risk that the historians' and jurists' petitions attempt to eliminate from politics (and from law). It is also the risk they wish to eliminate by rejecting a choice between crimes against humanity, genocides, and national and collective memory and by refusing in principle any distinction between and among the various memory laws—- and indeed between and among different historical phenomena.

But even this tactic, legislative abrogation of all memory laws, would not in and of itself succeed in removing the issues and controversies about the Armenian genocide—including continuing Turkish denial—from the political realm. It might assuage the feelings of historians who feel themselves under assault from short-sighted legislators who act out of momentary political expediency. Nonetheless, the question of the Armenian genocide will remain on the political and cultural agenda as long as the question of Turkey and Europe remain on the national and international agendas. Moreover, the question of denial of the Armenian genocide will not be removed from the judicial arena even if René Rémond and his colleagues were to win the day.

6. Conclusion

Adolf Hitler famously asked, "Who, after all, speaks today of the annihilation of the Armenians?" The answer at this moment, somewhat bizarrely

77. *Id.* at 42–55.

perhaps, would be "the French" but again, in an attenuated manner. The 2001 general recognition statute remains on the books, but the criminalizing amendment of 2006 will advance no further.

French claims of deep attachment—at the cultural and ideological, if not the governmental, level—to its heritage as the home of *les droits de l'homme,* are despite everything, credible. In fact, the deep resonance of the Shoah in French life and collective commemoration and memory—from the *loi Gayssot* to Chirac's apology for the role of Vichy and therefore of the French state in the Holocaust—can only be grasped if one recognizes the deep cultural dissonance caused by the concomitant historical realities of the persecution, deportation, and killing of French Jews with the active assistance of the French state and French ideals of universalism and human rights. But still this does not completely explain why the French have opted for a memory law for the Armenian genocide and not for any other "non-French" genocide.

We ignore at our peril the political stakes of the recognition of history by way of a *loi mémorielle* and of the criminalization of hate speech in the guise of "history" by means of denial laws. In all these political and legal debates, we must not forget the ethical duty to ensure that in Europe, "we" do not forget our own dark past. As lawyers and historians, we have a specific duty to guard against their misuse as well as a deontological imperative to resist the pull of internal disciplinary amnesia.

The entire tradition of the lay republic (*laïcité*) is threatened both by conceptions of Europe as "Christian" and by any notion of a "Muslim" Europe. The recognition of the Armenian genocide, of Turkey's collective and historical guilt, serves to reinforce the importance and centrality of a European government and citizenry that is constitutively secular.

This is the true dark legacy—the ethical challenge of law and memory in Europe and of our attempts to bring light into the historical obscurity in which that legacy has lived and is alive. Evil brought into the light is still evil.

TWO

From Trying the Perpetrator to Trying the Denier and Back Again

Some Reflections

–Lawrence Douglas

1. The Logic of the Law: Denier as Perpetrator

The idea that perpetrators of the gravest human rights abuses should have to answer for their conduct in courts of criminal law hardly constitutes a subject of controversy. Jurists might argue about form, venue, and procedure; they might disagree about whether, for example, domestic institutions are to be preferred over international tribunals; about whether it is proper to impose capital punishment upon those who grossly violate international humanitarian law; about whether continental or Anglo-American norms of procedure better develop the aims of complicated war crimes trials; about whether it is efficacious or fair to try individuals for crimes committed more than half a century ago; and about whether principles of universal jurisdiction further or frustrate the cause of justice. Jurists might even squabble about the wisdom of trying perpetrators in light of specific conditions "on the ground"—whether, for example, the interests of transitional democracy or negotiated settlement might counsel in favor of reliance on a South African-style "Truth and Reconciliation Commission."

But the deeper logic and normative appeal of trying perpetrators of atrocity is generally accepted as self-evident. At its most basic, the perpetrator trial is seen as a fundamental core requirement of any meaningful system of justice. It gives powerful expression to the idea that impunity is a wrong—both in itself as a violation of the basic moral norm that no one should benefit from his or her wrongdoing and instrumentally, inasmuch as unpunished crimes serve to destabilize the ever-precarious balance of domestic and international power.[1] This latter idea often finds expression in the claim that criminal trials—by serving as acts of impersonal

1. WILLIAM SCHABAS, GENOCIDE IN INTERNATIONAL LAW: THE CRIME OF CRIMES (2d ed. 2009) and GERHARD WERLE, PRINCIPLES OF INTERNATIONAL CRIMINAL LAW (2d ed. 2009).

state or internationally sanctioned retribution—serve to break the cycles of revenge that often erupt in spasms of mass atrocity. In addition, the criminal trial serves as a means of honoring the experience of victims. It provides victims with a venue for expressing their pain and confers public recognition upon the suppressed history of their victimization and, in so doing, helps transform narratives of woe into legally probative testimony. This idea, in turn, is closely related to the pedagogic aim of the trial, which as I've argued elsewhere,[2] invariably plays a major role in the staging of perpetrator trials. Add to this the goal of deterrence, and we have a sense of the range of arguments that support the impulse to try perpetrators of atrocity.

That the coercive arm of the law should be used to punish those who *deny* the acts of perpetrators is a far more problematic claim. What, after all, is the crime in denial? Murder is a horrific crime, but few would think it proper to criminalize the act of denying that a murder took place or that a specific perpetrator was the murderer. A law, for example, that punished a denial that Lee Harvey Oswald assassinated John Kennedy would seem bizarre, but not because of lingering doubts among conspiracy theorists about Oswald's complicity in the slaying. There is no equivalent doubt surrounding the assassination of Abraham Lincoln; yet a law that criminalized denying the killing of America's sixteenth president or the identity of his assailant would strike us as no less bizarre. Speaking more generally, the act of criminalizing the denial of *any* historical statement sounds odd; in part, this might betray our queasiness about permitting the state to punish statements about which reasonable people might express reasonable doubt. A consensus might exist among historians that the humiliations associated with the terms of the Versailles Treaty helped pave the way to the rise of Nazism in Germany, but are we really so confident in our beliefs that we would ever consider slapping a criminal sanction upon those who argue otherwise? And yet, as in the Lincoln example, our discomfort with using the criminal law to punish the denial of a historical fact cannot fully be explained in terms of our doubt concerning the state's capacity to distinguish adequately between statements of historical fact and less stable interpretations or judgments. That the earth is spherical is not a matter open to contestation, and yet a law that

---

2. Lawrence Douglas, The Memory of Judgment: Making Law and History in the Trials of the Holocaust (2001).

made actionable the writings or utterances of flat-earthers would seem grossly inappropriate. Why?

The answer, I think, has little to do with standard Millsian arguments about the valuable role that false statements play in the exposition of truth. It has more, I think, to do with a belief in norms of human autonomy. A respect of human personality and individuality tells us that there is something wrong and even ugly when the state mobilizes its coercive force against an individual to punish the content of his utterances or statements—however false, silly, or eccentric they might be. We might consider it entirely proper for the state to engage in public pedagogy or some other form of instruction intended to correct false statements of fact. We might even approve of the use of the criminal law if a nexus can be demonstrated between the false statement and some other harm—say, to public health arising from false claims made about a prescription drug. But provided that no other demonstrable harm is associated with false beliefs or statements, the state's reliance on the criminal law as a means of correction appears more objectionable than the falsehoods the state seeks to silence. Thus, as opposed to criminalizing acts of atrocity, the criminalization of the denial of atrocity requires some special justification.

In the specific case of Holocaust denial, many purport to find that special justification in the link between denial and incitement to acts of racial hatred. Holocaust denial, it is argued, constitutes a special instance for the application of state force because it constitutes a particularly virulent form of hate speech. Certain European legal codes either specifically classify or treat Holocaust denial as a form of incitement to crimes of hate (Germany provides an example of the former; the Netherlands, the latter).[3]

In Anglo-American circles, incitement has a long history as a common law crime, understood as a form of encouraging, persuading, or instigating someone to commit a crime. But the logic behind likening negationism to incitement is far from clear. The implicit claim, that denying the Holocaust can incite outbreaks of anti-Semitic violence, seems vaguely incoherent. To make the claim work, we must imagine that neo-Nazis will be so enraged to learn that Jews were never the victims of genocide that they will race out to commit acts of anti-Semitic violence.

3. *See, e.g.,* Volksverhetzung [Agitation or Incitement], StGB, § 130; *see also* Section 137d of the Dutch Penal Code.

Even if we acknowledge that many forms of Holocaust negationism hatefully dismiss the Holocaust as a phantasm of the Zionist imagination designed to extort money from the hapless German state, it's not clear how such statements work to incite. Here, we must imagine that neo-Nazis will be so enraged to learn that they've been duped by Jews that they will now target Jews for acts of retaliatory mass violence. That the logic doesn't parse doesn't, of course, mean that it is not compelling; it might well be that the law's own paralogical processes accurately track the dim pathways of the neo-Nazi mind. But it does suggest the difficulty of conceptualizing and defending Holocaust denial as a classic form of incitement.

The phenomenon of denial might be better understood as inciting the class of *victims* and their relatives to acts of retaliatory violence. Enraged by the denial of the horror that they or their loved ones endured and dismayed by the absence of a state response, victims might be prompted to take matters into their own hands. In this understanding, the state must punish deniers in order to safeguard them from being physically threatened by the targets of their lies.

Clearly, this logic fails to convince. Nor do arguments that appeal to other forms of legal harm. Elie Wiesel has likened Holocaust denial to defamation, a false and noxious claim designed to insult and hurt. Until 1994, the German criminal code treated Holocaust denial as a form of criminal insult (*Beleidigung*).[4] Certainly to those who lost relatives and loved ones in the Holocaust and to those who survived Nazi genocide, the arguments of deniers must cause acute pain and disgust. Even here, however, it is difficult to sweep this pain and disgust under conventional legal categories such as group defamation, which is better applied to cases in which false, hateful, and *derogatory* statements are made about a class of persons.

Holocaust denial may be false and hateful, but it is not invariably derogatory; it need not do damage to the groups' reputation. In its simpler and therefore more insidious form, Holocaust denial often eschews explicitly blaming Jews for the myth of their own victimization and limits itself to challenging the facticity of the genocide. This form of denial typically dresses itself up in the garb of pseudo-scholarship and comes adorned with myriad footnotes and copious sources.

---

4. *See* Eric Stein, *History Against Free Speech: The New German Law Against the "Auschwitz"—And Other—"Lies,"* 85 U. MICH. L. REV. 277 (1986).

For years, I have been the unwitting recipient of a steady stream of such denial material. Today's mailing, from somewhere in Pennsylvania, includes reprints of a speech delivered by Reinhardt Heydrich, dated February 4, 1942; a report by Eugene Kulischer submitted to the American Jewish Committee in 1943; and an excerpt from the diaries of Josef Goebbels—all to the end of challenging Peter Longerich's use of documents in his recently published biography of Heinrich Himmler.[5] Anyone reading through this material without knowing the codes and strategies of deniers might mistake it for a debate between rival academics. Conspicuously absent from this material is any explicitly anti-Semitic rants or allegations; the tone is sober and seemingly respectful of Longerich's work. Such material thus presents particular dilemmas. At the very least, it would be a stretch to argue that this variety of denial constitutes group defamation. After all, it is one thing to hatefully decry an entire race as genetically inferior or morally depraved, another simply to deny its status as a victim class.

Perhaps, then, Holocaust denial can be better understood as the kind of wrong conceptualized in American tort law as the "intentional infliction of emotional distress." This specialized cause of action was used by lawyers for Mel Mermelstein, a survivor of Auschwitz, in his well-publicized suit against the Institute for Historical Review, the negationist "think tank."[6] Several countries that lack statutes specifically criminalizing Holocaust denial—and these include Canada and Australia—treat Holocaust denial as this kind of wrong, albeit not as a tort, but under the rubric of the criminal law. The Australian Racial Discrimination Act, for example, prohibits public acts that are "reasonably likely, in all circumstances, to offend, insult, humiliate, or intimidate another person or group of people."[7]

Even this approach, however, is not without its problems. By turning Holocaust denial into a form of collective insult, Australian law brackets the question about lying about history, as the truthfulness of the insult provides no defense to the charge of insult. (It would be no defense to the charge of having ridiculed a classmate as fat to argue that the classmate is, in fact, clinically obese.) As a consequence, Australian courts, in their encounters

---

5. *See* PETER LONGERICH, HEINRICH HIMMLER: EINE BIOGRAPHIE (2008).

6. *See* Judgment of Superior Court of California, Los Angeles county, in Mermelstein vs. Institute for Historical Review, at http://www.nizkor.org/ftp.cgi/people/m/mermelstein.mel/ftp.py?people/m/mermelstein.mel//mermelstein.order.072285 (last accessed Sept. 14, 2009).

7. Racial Discrimination Act of 1975, s. 18C (1)(a).

with deniers, do not pass judgment on the bald falsification of history and instead focus on the violation of the victims' "deep seated beliefs as to the circumstances surrounding the deaths" of the Jews of Europe.[8] As David Fraser has rightly observed, this "bizarre and unsatisfactory" approach treats Holocaust denial as a "matter of group psychology and theology."[9]

Then, of course, there are those laws that simply criminalize denying the Holocaust outright. As I've noted, thirteen European countries presently treat Holocaust denial as a criminal offense.[10] These statutes share certain similarities. The Belgium criminal code, for example, provides:

> Whoever . . . denies, grossly minimizes, tries to justify or approves of the genocide committed by the German National-Socialist regime during the Second World War will be punished by imprisonment of eight days to one year and a fine of twenty-six to five thousand francs.[11]

The criminal code of Luxembourg likewise holds that it is "forbidden to contest, trivialize, justify, or deny publically the existence of crimes against humanity or war crimes linked to the Holocaust."[12] Similarly, Austrian law holds that a "person shall . . . be liable to penalty. . . . if he denies the National Socialist genocide, or other National Socialist crimes against humanity, or seeks to minimize them in a coarse manner or consents thereto or to justify them."[13]

On one level, these statutes raise a similar evidentiary question, inasmuch as they share the common feature of criminalizing not simply denial outright but also the act of trivializing or minimizing the Holocaust. At what point does trivialization become "gross" and therefore actionable? Such questions might seem crippling to students, and yet courts are called upon to make such thorny interpretive judgments all the time. If there's any reason to believe that such judgments will prove trickier or more problematic in

8. Jones v. Töben (2002) FCA 1150, *quoted in* David Fraser, *On the Internet, Nobody Knows You're A Nazi: Some Comparative Legal Aspects of Holocaust Denial on the WWW*, *in* EXTREME SPEECH AND DEMOCRACY 535 (Ivan Hare & James Weinstein eds., 2009).

9. Fraser, *supra* note 8, at 535.

10. *See* Michael Whine, *Expanding Holocaust Denial and Legislation Against It*, *in* EXTREME SPEECH AND DEMOCRACY (Ivan Hare & James Weinstein eds., 2009) (Spain has repealed its denial law).

11. *Id.* at 544.

12. *Id.* at 545.

13. *Id.* at 544.

dealing with Holocaust deniers, it is only because deniers appear to take particular relish in shaping their arguments to provoke conflict with the law and to expose the gray areas in statutory line drawing.

These statutes share a further common feature, which I find more interesting. They all criminalize both acts of Holocaust denial and Holocaust *justification*. This is hardly surprising—it would be grotesque for the law to prohibit denying the Holocaust but to permit gestures of praise or tribute.

And yet it appears that the two impulses—denial and justification—pull in the opposite direction. Justification arguably seems the more radical act, as it accepts both the facticity and the propriety of genocide. Denial, at least ostensibly, has a peculiarly self-defeating character. The act of denying the Holocaust appears to concede the absolute criminality and indefensibility of mass extermination. It seemingly acknowledges that genocide constitutes an *unimaginable* bad, a crime so extreme and horrific in scope and methods that it could not possibly have occurred. For the denier, the Holocaust has given anti-Semitism a bad name; any effort to revive anti-Semitism and to rehabilitate Nazism must start with erasing the taint of genocide.

This insight, however, fails to attend to a crucial fact that returns us to my point of departure—the affinities between perpetrators and deniers of genocide. Those who question the wisdom or need for criminalizing Holocaust denial often observe that far from clouded in obscurity, the Holocaust is perhaps the most thoroughly researched event in all of human history.

Scholars might continue to advance our knowledge of the Nazi genocide—witness the recent work on the killing fields of the Ukraine.[14] Still, the Holocaust can hardly be said to suffer a want of academic attention or public curiosity. Others who question the wisdom of criminalizing Holocaust denial conjure a criminal code clogged with statutes prohibiting the denial of American slavery or European colonialism or the bombing of the World Trade Center by Al Qaeda.

What both set of arguments overlook, however, is the specific role that denial played in the perpetration of the Holocaust. Recently, historians have written about how much the Germans knew of the Holocaust at the time, challenging the postwar myth of *"Davon haben wir nichts gewusst!"* ("We knew nothing about that!")[15] Nonetheless, it remains accurate to say that the

---

14. *See* Patrick Desbois, The Holocaust by Bullets: A Priest's Journey to Uncover the Truth Behind the Murder of 1.5 Million Jews (2008).

15. *See* Peter Longerich, "Davon haben wir nichts gewusst": Die Deutschen und die Judenverfolgung 1933–1945 (2007).

SS strove not simply to keep genocide a secret but to shroud it in decoys and camouflage.

This fact remains important, as it reminds us that Holocaust denial must be seen *as an invention of the perpetrators* themselves, not of postwar anti-Semites and neo-Nazis. Here we recall the taunt that Primo Levi heard from an officer of the SS: "And even if some proof should remain and some of you survive, people will say that the events you describe are too monstrous to be believed: they will say that they are the exaggerations of Allied propaganda and will believe us, who deny everything, and not you."[16] We recall also Himmler's notorious speech before an audience of generals of the SS, delivered in Poznan in 1943, in which the head of the SS describes the extermination of European Jewry as *"ein niemals genanntes und niemals zu nennendes Ruhmesblatt"* of German history—"an unnamed and never to be named page of glory."[17]

Holocaust denial must, then, be understood not simply as an attempt to paper over atrocity post hoc; rather, it is an act fully consonant with the original methods of the perpetrators. Moreover, the tactics of denial used by the perpetrators were not simply designed to cover their tracks from the Allies or to hide their actions from the German population. Rather, *denial was a means of performing genocide.* From the vans marked with the symbol of the Red Cross that carried Zyklon-B, to the use of code words such as "*Umsiedlung*" ("resettlement") and *"Evakuierung"* ("evacuation"), denial was itself an instrument of extermination. Thus the latter-day act of challenging the existence of "homicidal gas chambers" constitutes something more than a characteristic rhetorical ploy of deniers; it is a gesture that recapitulates the perpetrators' original attempt to decoy gas chambers as innocuous public showers.

Once we appreciate that the methods of deniers represent an extension and reimplementation of strategies and tactics first designed and deployed by the perpetrators, we are better positioned to grasp the logic behind criminalizing denial, at least in countries such as Germany and Austria. As Dieter Grimm has observed, Germany offers a special case for such laws.[18] In Germany, a tolerance of Holocaust denial would powerfully

16. PRIMO LEVI, THE DROWNED AND THE SAVED 11–12 (Raymond Rosenthal trans., 1988).

17. http://www.holocaust-history.org/himmler-poznan/speech-text.shtml (last accessed Sept. 14, 2009).

18. *See* Dieter Grimm, *The Holocaust Denial Decision of the Federal Constitutional Court of Germany*, *in* EXTREME SPEECH AND DEMOCRACY (Ivan Hare & James Weinstein eds., 2009).

suggest the state's acceptance of attempts to whitewash the methods of the perpetrators.

As a crime coordinated and sponsored by the German state, the Holocaust necessarily continues to implicate state interests and concerns in Germany. And inasmuch as denial attempts to conceal the state's *own* history as a perpetrator of atrocity, the state's willingness to tolerate or protect such speech could invariably be understood as a threat emanating from the state to survivors of genocide.

The act of proscribing Holocaust denial in Germany thus represents something more than an attempt to protect the sensibilities of a small minority from hate speech; rather, it aims to protect the very legitimacy of the state. Put another way, the failure to accept the truth of the state's past role as perpetrator of genocide is less an assault upon a minority group than an attack on the foundations of the Federal Republic as a liberal democratic state.

As Grimm notes, "It has become part of the identity of post-war Germany that atrocities like these should never happen again under the responsibility of the German state. The criminalization of . . . Holocaust denial symbolizes this deep conviction and thus is a uniquely German justification."[19] Here we should note that Grimm's defense of the prohibition of Holocaust denial in Germany does not support the extension of such prohibitions to other nations. As Grimm puts it, ". . . this justification would not be available to a prohibition . . . in countries that do not bear the same historical responsibility."[20] Of course, the key term here is "same." While no other nation shares the *same* responsibility as Germany, many European nations, such as Austria and France, remain dodged by a shameful record of complicity in genocide.

The Holocaust continues to vex the memory of many liberal democratic states; paraphrasing Isaiah Berlin, Johannes Houwink ten Cate writes, "in the post-Holocaust era, awareness of the necessity of a moral law is sustained no longer by belief in reason but by the memory of horror."[21] Criminalization of Holocaust denial thus stands as a symbolic declaration, a legal recognition of the ties that bind perpetrator and denier. As a symbolic gesture, it aims to redeem the state's claim as a protector, and not as an annihilator, of human rights.

---

19. *Id.* at 561.

20. *Id.* at 561.

21. Johannes Houwink ten Cate, *On the Outlawing of Holocaust Denial* at 6, CEJI, *available at* http://www.ceji.org/advocacy/On%20the%20Outlawing%20of%20Genocide%20Denial.pdf.

To reconstruct the logic behind the criminalization of Holocaust denial is not, however, to endorse the wisdom of prosecutions based on such statutes. There is some sociological evidence to support the claim that the aggressive prosecution of Holocaust deniers succeeds at deterring, if not other hate crimes, at least the activities of other deniers, at least, temporarily.[22]

Some point to the resounding success of the Irving-Lipstadt trial as proof that the law can successfully lay bare the mendacity and bad faith of deniers' pseudo-scholarship. My goal is not to review the Irving-Lipstadt case, though I believe it is worth noting two points. First, as a civil libel suit brought by Irving, the case was controlled by evidentiary standards considerably less exacting than those that control criminal trials. This permitted a broader range of material and testimony into the courtroom than would have been available in a criminal court. Second, and more crucially, the Irving-Lipstadt trial was, in the words of Christopher Browning, something of a "perfect storm."[23] Many contingencies—the quality of Professor Lipstadt's legal team; the excellence of the presiding judge; and most notably, the plaintiff's decision to present his own case, which he did with a flair for ineptitude that suggested willful self-destructiveness (on one occasion, inadvertently addressing the judge as "Mein Führer")—worked to make that litigation into the kind of success that cannot be easily repeated.[24]

Certainly, it is important to remain mindful of the pitfalls in using the law as a means of responding to Holocaust denial. These include, but are not limited to, the chilling effect that such statutes may exercise upon discourse that deserves free speech protection. In one particularly notorious episode, Bernard Lewis, the prominent Princeton historian, was fined by a French court in a civil proceeding for denying the Armenian genocide.[25] In an article in *Le Monde*, Lewis had characterized the atrocities against the

---

22. *See* Rafael Medoff & Alex Grobman, *Holocaust Denial: A Global Survey—2006*, DAVID S. WYMAN INSTITUTE FOR HOLOCAUST STUDIES, at http://www.wymaninstitute.org/articles/HolocaustDenial2006.pdf.

23. Christopher Browning, *Law, History, and Holocaust Denial in the Courtroom: The* Zündel *and* Irving *Cases*, *in* NAZI CRIMES AND THE LAW 197–215 (Nathan Stolzfus & Henry Friedlander eds., 2008). Browning used the phrase "perfect storm" to describe the Irving case in a presentation of the above cited essay in a conference, *The Holocaust in the Courtroom*, organized by the United States Holocaust Memorial Museum, January 13, 2005, Washington, D.C.

24. D.D. GUTTENPLAN, HOLOCAUST ON TRIAL (2002).

25. *See* CHRISTOPHER CALDWELL, REFLECTIONS ON THE REVOLUTION IN EUROPE 91–92 (2009).

Turkish-Armenian population during the First World War as mass killings but had shied away from calling them genocide, as they lacked, he argued, the central coordination and specific intent required of that crime. In fining Lewis a symbolic amount, the French court concluded, "by concealing elements contrary to his opinion, he [Lewis] neglected his duties of objectivity and prudence." One might disagree with Lewis's assessment of the Armenian catastrophe and yet remain deeply discomfited by a court scolding a prominent historian for violating scholarly norms and lumping his work with the bald lies of negationists. These problems will no doubt loom larger as other groups clamor to use the criminal law as a means to protect their status as victims and to have official recognition conferred upon their history of suffering.[26]

But even bracketing the issue of free speech, we should remain concerned about using the criminal law as a means of safeguarding the facticity of the Holocaust. Cases such as the *Zundel* affair in Canada vividly illustrate the dangers associated with denial trials, dangers altogether distinct from concerns about free speech. As I've argued elsewhere, denial trials create the risk of distorting the very history they mean to protect.[27] By offering a legal stage for the rehashing of denier arguments—that is, a stage with broad media access and one controlled by legally insular roles of procedure and norms of proof—such trials, designed to silence the hateful voice of deniers, only create a new obligation to listen.

Moreover, the criminal law tends to make martyrs out of those subject to its coercion. This problem, I fear, will loom larger in the future as Holocaust denial cases assume a new complexion. Mention Holocaust denial, and one typically imagines an Aryan Nation pseudo-scholar. Recently, however, the rhetoric of Holocaust denial has been powerfully appropriated and deployed by leaders within the Muslim world, most notoriously and openly by Iran's Mahmoud Ahmadinejad.[28] While the phenomenon of "Holocaust inversion"—the attribution of Nazi-like methods and ambitions to the Israeli state—has been a staple of political discourse in the Arab world for decades, the move to more explicit negationism is of more recent vintage. It's just a matter of time before a European court will be confronted with

---

26. *See id.* at 89–99.

27. DOUGLAS, *supra* note 2, at 221–56.

28. *See* Matthias Küntzel, *Unholy Hatreds: Holocaust Denial and Antisemitism in Iran,* Posen Paper in Contemporary Antisemitism No. 8 of The Vidal Sassoon International Center for the Study of Anti-Semitism (SICSA), 2007.

trying a Muslim citizen or resident with Holocaust denial. The changing complexion of the denier promises to change the very meaning of the law's engagement with denial as well as the reception and support for such legal interventions.

2. The Risks of Trial: Perpetrator as Denier

We have already seen how the methods of Holocaust deniers represent a furtherance and extension of the tactics of the perpetrators. As a further matter, we should note how the perpetrator trial can turn into a forum for the arguments and strategies of the denier. This is a phenomenon overlooked in most scholarship on denial, largely because the vast majority of Nazi war criminals never explicitly denied the reality of Nazi genocide. Some, like Goering and Kaltenbrunner, may have denied having known about the unfolding genocide. Others, such as Eichmann and Ohlendorf, might have acknowledged knowing and yet steadfastly denied their personal agency, insisting that they were simply following the orders of superiors. Virtually none, however, denied the genocide itself. Nonetheless, if few perpetrators have engaged in outright denial, several of the most notorious have relied on a defense of trivialization and inversion.

Perhaps the best example of this remains the case of Klaus Barbie, the so-called "Butcher of Lyon," who was tried in France in 1987 for crimes against humanity. Barbie was defended by Jacques Vergès, a charismatic and mercurial figure who had fought with the Algerian resistance, befriended the young Pol Pot, and who used the opportunity of defending Barbie to launch what he called a "defense of rupture." Vergès's goal was to use the trial to reveal the pervasive complicity of ordinary Frenchmen in the crimes attributed to the aging German.

Vergès's revisionism differed from standard Holocaust negationism in one important respect. Rather than deny Nazi crimes, Vergès did just the opposite—he globalized them. In his telling, there was nothing special or unique about Nazi offenses; they were of a kind with the normal excesses of war. Insisting "The word Nazi doesn't exist," Vergès sought to deny not the existence of Nazi crimes but their distinctiveness.[29] Adding a neo-Marxist edge to this critique, Vergès argued that "crimes against humanity" were no

29. Guyora Binder, *Representing Nazism: Advocacy and Identity at the Trial of Klaus Barbie*, 98 YALE L.J. 1321 (1989), 1355.

more than the rhetorical window dressing that Europeans used to describe crimes committed against fellow Europeans, as distinguished from those perpetrated against colonized subalterns. Everyone by this measure could be considered a Nazi: the French in Algeria; the Americans in Vietnam; and, of course, the Israelis in Palestine. Vergès's cocounsel, Nabil Bouaita, railed against the "Nazification of the Jewish-Israeli people" that had led to the "Palestinian genocide"[30] and called the 1982 Israeli invasion of Lebanon a holocaust.

While conceptually distinct from classic Holocaust denialism, Vergès's arguments openly embraced the rhetoric of Holocaust trivialization and inversion. By the end of the trial, Michel Zaoui, an attorney for the Jewish victims, appeared more troubled by the tactics of the defense attorneys than by the crimes attributed to their client. In his summation before the court, Zaoui struggled to give words to his outrage. "Your condemnation of Barbie," he argued to the judges and lay jurors, "will serve as a rampart against such rumors, based on lies and inexactitude . . . we must preserve the memory of what took place for this memory can serve to prevent evil."[31]

Zaoui's plea sounds all the more desperate in light of the fact that the Barbie trial was staged, at least in part, as a means of publically pushing back against what was perceived as a rising tide of Holocaust denial. Elie Wiesel, who testified in court, saw the trial as an answer to deniers—"to stop the killer from killing again." And yet, in Zaoui's final plea, the lies to be rebutted were not those of the Holocaust denier conjured by Wiesel but the very distortions produced by the defense lawyers themselves. The attorney for the Jewish victims found himself pleading for a guilty verdict in order to prevent history from being abused by the trial itself.

The Barbie case was hardly unique in using the trial of a perpetrator as a bulwark against the falsification of the historical record. In a sense, all high-profile war crimes trials mean to accomplish the dual goal of doing justice to the accused and insulating the historical record from crass manipulation. Martha Minow, Harvard Law School's dean, among others, has observed that one of the principal aims of the perpetrator trial is to establish a public record or a baseline account of an episode of atrocity.[32] Such a baseline account cannot supply the kind of nuance, detail, sophistication, and balance that

---

30. *Id.* at 1362.

31. *Id.* at 1363.

32. MARTHA MINOW, BETWEEN VENGEANCE AND FORGIVENESS: FACING HISTORY AFTER GENOCIDE AND MASS VIOLENCE 50 (1998).

might issue from the pen of a professional historian, but it can provide the kind of broad overview that makes history publically available and discredits those who would patently deny the episode of atrocity. The trial of the major war criminals at Nuremberg remains a powerful example of a proceeding staged, at least in part, to lay before the German people irrefutable evidence of Nazi crimes and thus to discredit any claims that Allied allegations were simply the stuff of rumor.

At the present writing, the eighty-nine year-old Ivan Demjanjuk awaits his trial in München as an accessory to the murder of 28,060 Jews. Responding to those who question the wisdom of trying an ailing octogenarian decades after the commission of his crimes, Dieter Graumann, vice president of Germany's Central Council of Jews, recently observed: "Now, at a time when there are so many Holocaust deniers . . . it's all the more important that in such a trial it's made clear once again what happened, what took place."[33]

Graumann's insistence, in turn, echoed the position adopted by the Israeli prosecution at the time of Demjanjuk's first trial, the calamitous "Ivan, the Terrible" proceeding that took place in a Jerusalem court in 1987–1988. At the time, Israeli chief prosecutor Yonah Blatman explicitly defended the trial as a response to "those who wish to rewrite history." In his summation before the court, Blatman again tied the case against Demjanjuk to the fight against Holocaust negationism. "The Holocaust," he declared, "seems to have been forgotten from the collective memory. . . . Moreover, this is fed by a phenomenon that is to be condemned outright, the denial of the Holocaust."[34]

However, as the Barbie trial first revealed, caution must be used in relying on a perpetrator trial to answer negationists. When history enters the courtroom, it does not serve exclusively at the behest of the prosecution. In the "trial of rupture," as pioneered by Vergès, the defense lawyer serves less as a conventional advocate, focusing on the conduct of the accused, and more as a radical historical revisionist. Slobodan Milosevic, who, as we recall, launched a pro se defense in his trial before the International Criminal Tribunal for the Former Yugoslavia, borrowed from and expanded upon the tactics of Vergès. In ceaselessly challenging the legitimacy and neutrality of the Tribunal, Milosevic attempted to turn the prosecution's historical

33. Roland Losch, *Demjanjuk Faces 27,900 Counts in Trial*, THE BOSTON GLOBE, July 14, 2009, at A3, *available at* http://www.boston.com/news/world/europe/articles/2009/07/14/demjanjuk_faces_27900_counts_in_trial/.

34. TOM TEICHOLZ, THE TRIAL OF IVAN THE TERRIBLE: STATE OF ISRAEL VS. JOHN DEMJANJUK 269 (1990).

narrative into a partisan distortion of history. For long stretches of the trial, he struggled, not without success, to deflect attention away from his own alleged crimes and to turn the trial into a contestation over rival understandings of history.[35]

At points, Milosevic's strategy imitated not simply Vergès's, but that of standard negationists. Here we need to bear in mind some of the standard forensic tactics of the Holocaust denier. First, we typically encounter a challenge to the number of victims. The denier will argue that hundreds of thousands may have died but certainly not millions. Second, we find a rejection of the idea of a centralized plan for, and administration of, genocide. Outrages may have occurred, but these were excesses associated with the brutality of armed conflict, not part of any overarching, state-orchestrated campaign of extermination. Third, we encounter an attempt to discredit the accuracy of memory, particular the memories of victims. Victim memory, it is argued, cannot be trusted because it is either born of trauma, and thus subject to unintentional distortion, or biased—that is, the product of intentional falsification.

Although commonly associated with Holocaust negationism, these strategies can be better understood as generic features of the arguments of those who deny *any* episode of mass atrocity—be it the Armenian genocide, the Rape of Nanjing, the Cambodian killing fields, or the ethnic cleansing in the Balkans.

These same arguments found their way into Milosevic's spirited and tendentious defense. Killings may have occurred in Srebrenica, but the prosecutor's numbers were wildly inflated; even if the killings constituted a massacre, certainly there was no centralized policy of ethnic cleansing; those who bore witness to the atrocities were themselves partisans who could not be counted on for accurate statements. These strategies, in turn, were used by Saddam Hussein in his pugnacious courtroom grandstanding in both of his trials before the Special Iraqi Tribunal.

We've observed that one particularly virulent form of Holocaust denial alleges that Jews fabricated the story of the Holocaust in order to extort money from Germany. This form of argument, in which the perpetrator is cast as victim, also describes a generic feature of the arguments of the denier of state-sponsored atrocity. Slobodan Milosevic never tired of presenting

35. Gideon Boas, The Milosevic Trial: Lessons for the Conduct of Complex International Criminal Proceedings (2007).

himself as the victim of Croatian fascism and NATO expansionism. Reviving the ghosts of World War II, Milosevic cast the Serbs, like the Jews, as the victims of Croat and Nazi genocide. In the battle over victimhood, the number of Serb dead became dramatically inflated in the defendant's passionate enumeration.

One might respond to the above observations by pointing out that Barbie and Hussein were both convicted, and Milosevic, had he lived, probably would have been convicted of war crimes and crimes against humanity. But such an observation misses the point. Prosecutorial success—winning a conviction—does not necessarily translate into the success of the proceeding as a bulwark against negationism. Particularly those defendants who are intent on being martyred can use their conviction as further evidence of the partisanship of justice and of the picture of history that the prosecution hopes to establish at trial.

But if prosecutorial success—winning a conviction—does not suffice to guarantee the success of the trial as a bulwark against negationism, it certainly is a necessary condition. This, then, is perhaps the greatest problem with relying on the perpetrator trial as a means of refuting negationism: the measure of the truth of a historical event becomes bound up with the project of proving the legal guilt of a defendant in a court of law. Using legal guilt as a yardstick of historical truth thus runs the risk of calamity in situations in which courts fail to convict.

Needless to say, there are all sorts of reasons why a defendant might be found not guilty at the conclusion of criminal trial or why an original conviction might be overturned on appeal. In a conventional criminal case, the failure to adduce the guilt of the accused does not call into question the claim that a crime was committed in the first place. Yet, in the case of high-profile trials designed to refute the arguments of deniers, the failure to prove the defendant's guilt can be manipulated by negationists to cast doubt on the underlying history itself. Slobodan Milosevic, as we recall, died before the conclusion of his four-year trial, and so it is difficult to predict what the outcome of his case would have been. And yet during the course of the trial, many prosecutors and jurists came to fear that Milosevic would be acquitted of the genocide charges brought against him.

As a crime of specific intent, genocide is extremely difficult to prove, and many within the Office of the Prosecution of the ICTY had strongly resisted indicting Milosevic for this crime, arguing that the trial could be better organized around the more manageable—though also grave—charges of war crimes and crimes against humanity. Carla del Ponte, at the time the ICTY's chief prosecutor, insisted on going forward with the genocide indictment over the vehement objections of Geoffrey Nice, the lead prosecutor who assumed the day-to-day responsibility of presenting the case against Milosevic.[36] Many jurists worried that even if Milosevic had been convicted as a perpetrator of war crimes and crimes against humanity, acquittal on the genocide charge would have been used by Serb nationalists as evidence that such crimes were never committed in the Balkans, at least not by Serbs.

3. Trying the Perpetrator to Answer the Denier

The most spectacular example of the dangers of using a perpetrator trial as a bulwark against negationism remains the Jerusalem trial of Ivan Demjanjuk. To appreciate the court's missteps, we need to remember the profile of the case. Demjanjuk was born in the Ukraine in 1920, and, in the early fifties, immigrated to the United States. He settled in Cleveland, Ohio, where he worked as a machinist in a Ford plant, raised a family, and was known as an affable neighbor—"the kind of guy who would stop to help you fix a flat on the road."[37]

In the late seventies, prosecutors for the United States Immigration and Naturalization Service[38] (INS) first learned of Demjanjuk through an obscure Soviet organization that supplied the INS with a list of possible former Ukrainian Nazi collaborators residing in the United States.[39] This evidence strongly suggested that Demjanjuk had served as a guard at Sobibor, one of the three "pure" extermination facilities, along with Treblinka and Belzec, constructed by the SS in the spring of 1942 in Poland as part of Operation Reinhard—arguably the most murderous single stage in the Holocaust.

The strongest evidence against Demjanjuk was a copy of his photo identification card from his service in the Trawniki training camp—an SS *Ausbildungslager*—a facility used to prepare Ukrainian and ethnic German

36. For del Ponte's take on the contretemps, *see* CARLA DEL PONTE, MADAME PROSECUTOR: CONFRONTATIONS WITH HUMANITY'S WORST CRIMINALS AND THE CULTURE OF IMPUNITY (2009).

37. TEICHOLZ, *supra* note 34, at 49.

38. In 1979, the investigation and prosecution of Nazi war criminals was transferred to the newly established division of the Justice Department, the Office of Special Investigations (OSI).

39. *See* TEICHOLZ, *supra* note 34.

POWs who had volunteered for service as death camp guards.[40] The man pictured in the photo ID was unmistakably a more youthful Ivan Demjanjuk, and the card clearly noted that he had been assigned to Sobibor.

The majority of Sobibor survivors—and these numbered no more than a handful—lived in Israel, so the INS asked a Special Unit of the Israeli Police, which specialized in the Investigation of Nazi Crimes, to assist its investigation of Demjanjuk. Officials in the INS were hopeful that the survivors of Sobibor would be able to offer positive identification of, and supply information about, the former guard.

Yet an odd thing happened at the identification parades conducted by the Israeli police. The Sobibor survivors failed to pick out Demjanjuk's Trawniki picture from a photo spread of suspects. However, a number of Treblinka survivors enlisted to assist the investigation of a completely unrelated case, blanched at the photo of Demjanjuk. This, they declared, was the operator of the Treblinka gas chamber, a guard whose unusual cruelty and viciousness had earned him the sobriquet *Ivan Grozny*, Ivan the Terrible.

At first, the Israeli investigators doubted these identifications. The Trawniki card clearly listed Demjanjuk as having been assigned to Sobibor, not Treblinka. But after ten Treblinka survivors had all identified Demjanjuk as "Ivan the Terrible," Israeli investigators became convinced of the accuracy of these statements. After extensive negotiations with American authorities, the Israelis agreed to request the extradition of the machinist from Cleveland. After his American citizenship was revoked and the extradition petition accepted, Demjanjuk found himself on February 27, 1986, on an El Al 747 bound for Ben Gurion Airport.

Demjanjuk's arrival in Israel created a stir that reminded many of the capture of Adolf Eichmann a quarter-century earlier. "Ivan the Terrible's" trial would be the first of a Nazi perpetrator trial in Israel since Eichmann's. Like Eichmann, Demjanjuk was to be tried not in a conventional courtroom but in a theater-like public space that could accommodate over 300 spectators. In 1961, Israelis had followed the Eichmann trial live on radio, the first trial so broadcast; now they could watch the Demjanjuk trial live on television, the first trial to be televised in Israel's history.

Demjanjuk's trial, as I've noted, was meant in part to discredit Holocaust negationism; here, too, it patterned itself after the Eichmann trial, which also intended to serve as a tool of collective pedagogy. Alarmed by the

40. At trial, the prosecution was able to submit the original Trawniki card.

persistence if not renaissance of anti-Semitism, particularly in Europe, Israeli Prime Minister David Ben-Gurion and Attorney General Gideon Hausner hoped Eichmann's trial would make clear the full horror of Nazi crimes against the Jewish people.[41]

But if the Demjanjuk case was meant to rebut Holocaust denial, it also served as a flashpoint for deniers. Demjanjuk's defense, particularly in the early stages, was closely linked to, and partially subsidized by, Jerome Brentar, a Cleveland travel agent who maintained close ties to denial groups. (Brentar testified as a character witness for the notorious Holocaust negationist Ernst Zundel, at the time of Zundel's first Canadian denial trial.)[42] Moreover, the Demjanjuk family's staggering ignorance about the Holocaust and strange views about Jews—apparently Demjanjuk's wife long labored under the belief that Eichmann was Jewish[43]—provided a model of the mindset receptive to negationist claims.

The Demjanjuk trial patterned itself after the Eichmann trial in another key way. Like its famous predecessor, it strove to tell the story of the Holocaust through the testimony of survivors. It is by now familiar that the Eichmann prosecution rejected the evidentiary strategy used by prosecutors in the trial of the major war criminals before the International Military Tribunal (IMT) at Nuremberg. The IMT prosecutors favored a trial by document, which made for a tight but lethally dull case. Hausner, by contrast, wanted the Eichmann trial to capture the hearts and minds of the public and so chose to structure the state's case around the testimony of survivors, a strategy followed by the Demjanjuk prosecution.

Demjanjuk prosecutor Michael Shaked began his opening argument with the poignant observation, "This may be one of the last trials where it is possible to bring to the stand witnesses who can say 'we were there'. . . . The subject sooner or later will have to step down from the witness stand and become a part of history."[44] Here, perhaps for the last time, the testimony of aging survivors would provide the ultimate bulwark against the spread of negationist lies.

And yet Demjanjuk's trial turned into less a reenactment than a dreadful caricature of its famous predecessor. Part of this had to do with the contrasts

41. *See* Hanna Yablonka, The State of Israel vs. Adolf Eichmann (2004).

42. See testimony of Jerome Brentar, February 15, 1985, in transcript of *Queen v. Zundel* in the District Court of Ontario, 3513–64.

43. Yoram Sheftel, Show Trial: The Conspiracy to Convict John Demjanjuk as "Ivan the Terrible" 102 (Haim Watzman trans., 1994).

44. Teicholz, *supra* note 34, at 103.

between the defendants themselves. It would be no exaggeration to claim that Eichmann helped make his trial a tremendous success. In contrast to the hectoring antics of Slobodan Milosevic and Saddam Hussein, Eichmann was an ideal defendant, snapping to his feet when the judges entered the chamber, answering their questions with precision and deference. Arguably, the very craven obedience to authority that helped turn Eichmann into a perpetrator of genocide served to make him into a model defendant. And with his dour bank teller appearance, humorless demeanor, and formal manners, Eichmann delivered an unforgettable image of what Hannah Arendt called "the banality of evil."

Demjanjuk, by contrast, looked like he had just been plucked from a bar or beer hall. Beefy and boisterous, Demjanjuk enjoyed, during lulls in the trial, entertaining his guards with the bits of mangled Hebrew he had picked up in his jail cell. On the stand, he proved to be a terrible witness on his own behalf—not because he betrayed traces of his alleged former cruelty but because he seemed incapable of telling a coherent story. He claimed never to have set foot in the Trawniki SS facility, never to have worked as a camp guard anywhere, at any time. He insisted that he himself had been a prisoner of war, surviving the latter half of the war in a brutal German POW camp. But when asked to name the camp, he could not, and when pressed to describe his activities as a POW, he openly contradicted himself. When asked to explain why he had had a tattoo removed from his left armpit—members of the SS, including Ukrainian Hiwis (*Hilfswilliger,* or "voluntary assistants"), had had their blood type tattooed in this spot—he stammered an unintelligible reply.

Demjanjuk's story was so implausible, the gaps in his memory so large and unbelievable, his testimony so riddled with contradictions, that the presiding judge felt obliged to explain to him the importance of an alibi in a criminal trial. But if anything, Demjanjuk appeared baffled by the very need to account for his actions. During his cross-examination, he memorably babbled: "Why are you making such a fuss of my matter, like with Eichmann? Eichmann was big, while Ivan is little, and what more it isn't he [Ivan], as there is a mistake in identification."[45]

The tactics and conduct of the defense lawyers also upset the prosecution's decision to use the lived memory of survivors as a means of safeguarding Holocaust history. Demjanjuk's lawyer, Mark O'Connor, an

45. CrimC (Jerusalem) 373/86, Israel v. Ivan (John) Demjanjuk (Apr. 18, 1988) *available at* THE DEMJANJUK TRIAL 381 (1991) [hereafter The Demjanjuk Trial].

American attorney with little trial experience, left the court numb with his rambling, disorganized presentations. His cross-examinations of the survivors from the Treblinka death camp appalled judges and spectators alike. In an effort to undermine the accuracy of the survivors' identifications of his client, O'Connor bombarded them with questions seemingly designed to question their very internment in the death camp. He harassed survivors to offer precise descriptions of the color, height, and intensity of the flames that issued from the death camp's crematoria.[46]

O'Connor's tactics echoed those used by Holocaust denier Ernst Zundel's defense lawyer, Douglas Christie. In Zundel's first Canadian trial, Christie similarly tried to discredit the testimony of survivors, asking, for example, Auschwitz survivor Rudolf Vrba whether he had ever seen an autopsy report indicating gas as the cause of death of those who had perished at Birkenau.[47]

But the trial's most dreadful missteps were committed by the court, a three-judge tribunal presided over by Dov Levin, a sitting member of the Israeli Supreme Court. At the heart of the Demjanjuk trial stood a simple and narrow question: Was Demjanjuk Ivan the Terrible? Whatever indirect ties Demjanjuk's defense team might have had with denial causes, neither the defendant nor his lawyers ever denied that Treblinka had served as an extermination center; they simply denied that the accused had played any roll in the killing process.

In principle, the prosecution could have efficiently presented its case against Demjanjuk without revisiting the larger history of the Final Solution. However, such a narrow presentation would not have served the broad pedagogic aim of the prosecution, and the court openly shared the state's assessment of the importance of the trial as a bulwark against denial and as a means of teaching history. And so, when asked to frame the questions that lay at the heart of the trial, the court did not limit itself to the question of accurate identification but included issues almost metaphysical in their breadth and generality:

> Is it possible that one of the nations of this world, which has produced people of the spirit, and of morality, giants of culture and science, should set before itself, as a target a supreme objective, "to destroy, to kill, and to cause to perish, all Jews, both young and old, little children and women" (like the plot of Haman the Agagite, Esther 3:13)?[48]

---

46. SHEFTEL, *supra* note 43, at 43, 45.

47. See Douglas, *supra* note 2, at 227–31.

48. *The Demjanjuk Trial: District Court*, *supra* note 45, at 11.

"We are charged with the duty to determine," the court continued, "through due process of law, historical truths in regard to the events that befell our world in one of the darkest periods in the history of all nations."[49] Most astonishingly, it described its own judgment as a "monument":

> We shall erect in our judgment, according to the totality of the evidence before us, a monument to their [the victims'] souls, to the holy congregations that were lost and are no more, to those who were annihilated and did not receive the privilege of a Jewish burial because hardly a trace remained of them, to those who were burned on the pyre and whose skeletons became ashes and dust, used to fertilize the fields of Poland, which they made fertile when alive, and on which they found their horrible death.[50]

Convinced of the importance of the trial, the court permitted the prosecution to launch into a sweeping presentation on all aspects of Nazi genocide, rejecting out of hand a motion from the defense to narrow the scope of the testimony of the survivor-witnesses to the question of identification. Survivor-witnesses were given the freedom to tell riveting, though arguably irrelevant, stories of the Holocaust. The court justified this approach as a legal matter with the argument that the truthfulness and accuracy of the survivors' larger narratives provided an index of the reliability of their identifications of Demjanjuk as Ivan the Terrible.

This proved to be a disastrous misstep. In framing its inquiry in these terms, the court briefly entertained "the possibility of treacherous memory"—that the survivors might have sincerely misidentified the defendant as Ivan the Terrible. Yet, here again, the court posed its basic query in terms nothing less legal than theological:

> We must ask: is it at all possible to forget? Can people who were in the vale of slaughter and experienced its horrors, who lived in an atmosphere of oppression, terror, fear, and persecution within the narrow confines of the extermination camp; people who saw, day after day, the killing, the humiliation, the brutality, the abuse by the German oppressors and their Ukrainian vassals in the Treblinka camp, forget all this?[51]

---

49. *Id.* at 2.

50. *Id.* at 39.

51. *Id.* at 10.

The court answered its own rhetorical question with the simple pronouncement: "No, it is not possible to forget the scenes of horror, the atmosphere of terror, all that took place in the extermination camp. It is impossible to forget Ivan the Terrible and his atrocities."[52]

In using the survivors' memories of the Holocaust as proof of the reliability of their identifications of Ivan, the court had boxed itself into the impossible position in which it could not doubt the latter without implicitly calling into question the accuracy of the former. And so the court accepted at face value the tortured testimony of Pinchas Epstein: "I see Ivan every single night . . . I dream about him every night . . . He is etched in me, in my memory, every night. I cannot free myself of this."[53] Worse, the court discounted evidence suggesting that the initial identification parades conducted by the Special Unit of the Israeli Police had fallen far short of satisfying normal police practice, and downplayed the troubling fact that several of the survivors had identified Demjanjuk only *after* learning that he had been picked out by other witnesses.

The court likewise dismissed the relevance of the testimony of defense witness Willem Wagenaar,[54] an experimental psychologist from the University of Leyden and a leading expert on memory problems. Wagenaar testified that persons undergoing trauma often cannot reliably recount their experience. But because Wagenaar's studies focused on isolated moments of trauma—such as a rape or violent mugging—the court reasoned they had no bearing on the Demjanjuk case, which involved a repeating pattern of horror experienced on a daily basis for months on end.[55] But instead of limiting itself to this point, the court tendentiously concluded:

> There is no room whatsoever for comparing the trauma experienced by the survivors of Treblinka with the traumatic experience undergone by a person who was a victim of harsh violence, rape, or similar crimes. . .

---

52. *Id.* at 93.

53. *Id.* at 199.

54. The defense's first choice was Elizabeth Loftus of the University of Washington, perhaps the most renowned expert on memory problems. Loftus, however, decided not to testify apparently out of respect to members of her own family who had survived the Holocaust. *See* Amy Wilson, *War & Remembrance*, ORANGE COUNTY REG., Nov. 3, 2002, *available at* http://williamcalvin.com/2002/OrangeCtyRegister.htm.

55. Wagenaar's critique of this conclusion as well as his attack on the identification parades can be found in WILLEM WAGENAAR, IDENTIFYING IVAN: A CASE STUDY IN LEGAL PSYCHOLOGY (1988).

> The traumatic shock suffered by the victims of Treblinka is a thousand times greater in its intensity and influence.[56]

Finally, the court dismissed the importance of an affidavit of a former Sobibor guard, submitted after the summations of the parties, stating in great detail that he had known Demjanjuk as an "experienced and efficient" guard at that camp and not at Treblinka.[57] In light of the information recorded on the Trawniki card, the court was prepared to believe that Demjanjuk might have served at both Treblinka and Sobibor. However, the court was not prepared to accept the idea that there had been "two *Wachmans* (guards) from Trawniki, one in Treblinka and one in Sobibor, both Ukrainians named Ivan . . . and both with protruding ears, both the same age and becoming bald in the same way." This, the court noted, was simply "far-fetched."

And so Demjanjuk was convicted and sentenced to death. No one had been executed in Israel since Adolf Eichmann in 1962; in fact, the death penalty had long been abolished for all crimes other than those associated with Nazi genocide. In these capital cases, the process of appeal was mandatory and went directly to the Israeli Supreme Court. Usually, the appellate process moved swiftly; as a result of happenstance, Demjanjuk's dragged on for years.

During this time, information emerged from files in the crumbling Soviet empire suggesting precisely what the trial court had dismissed as far-fetched: that, in fact, there had been two Ukrainian Ivans, one at Sobibor and one at Treblinka, who bore a small but not entirely negligible resemblance to one another. According to this material, Ivan the Terrible had been one Ivan Marchenko, a death camp guard who, as the German war effort collapsed, had vanished from Treblinka and had last been seen serving with Yugoslavian partisans in the Balkans.[58] None of this information entirely exculpated Demjanjuk—in fact, it only strengthened the certainty that he had served at Sobibor. But it did cast doubt on whether Israel was about to execute the right man as Ivan the Terrible of Treblinka.

In July 1993, the Israeli Supreme Court voided Demjanjuk's conviction. The court's 400-page decision is an elaborate exercise in legal damage

---

56. The Demjanjuk Trial: District Court, *supra* note 45, at 199.

57. TEICHOLZ, *supra* note 34, at 278.

58. SHEFTEL, *supra* note 43, at 322. Adding to the confusion was the fact that Demjanjuk had originally stated that his mother's maiden name was Marchenko, a common Ukrainian surname.

control. In it, the High Court refused to castigate the trial court for derogating its judicial function or for losing control of the trial, insisting instead that the trial court had merely suffered a legal misfortune. Its verdict had been undermined by facts about which it could not have possibly known at the time. Still, the *tone* of the Supreme Court's decision revealed its dissatisfaction with the trial court.

Compared to the theological excess and poetic anguish of the district court's verdict, the Supreme Court produced an astonishingly dull document. But that was the point. In overturning Demjanjuk's conviction, the Israeli Supreme Court was not about to let the desire to teach Holocaust history upend the rule of law.

In the Demjanjuk trial, the living memory of survivors was meant to serve as the instrument of indictment, as a tool for preparing the gallows, and as a means for vouchsafing history against the hate of deniers. In the end, it only revealed the foibles of traumatic memory—its vulnerability to suggestion and misidentification. In so doing, the trial inadvertently invited negationists to attack the larger truths contained in survivor narratives. This was the sad result of the fatal logic of the trial court, which insisted on linking the accuracy of identifications with the veracity of memories of the camp.

We may rightfully insist that the harrowing descriptions of Treblinka were not impeached by the misidentifications, but it was the court that disastrously maintained that the accuracy of the identifications and the truthfulness of the survivor narratives had to be treated as a whole. This problem was not lost upon the prosecution; it understood all too clearly the calamitous consequence of an acquittal. As the appellate process dragged on, a senior member of the prosecution expressed his concerns to a leading Israeli newspaper: "The most important thing now is at least to prove that Demjanjuk was part of the Nazi extermination machine . . . otherwise . . . we will be making a great contribution to the new world-wide movement of those who deny the Holocaust took place."[59] It as an astonishing statement, insisting that Demjanjuk be condemned—presumably for having served as guard a Sobibor, a crime that the accused had never been charged with or tried for—lest an acquittal send the wrong signals to gleeful deniers.

In this essay, I have tried to make clear that far from a post hoc phenomenon, Holocaust denial represents a continuation and extension of the

59. *Id.* at 342.

methods of the original perpetrators. We have also seen how perpetrators on trial have deployed the arguments and strategies of deniers. Finally, we have observed how the criminal law has tried to silence deniers not only by relying on specialized legal instruments that proscribe Holocaust negationism but also by trying perpetrators of the original atrocities.

The Israeli prosecution of Ivan Demjanjuk presented a cautionary tale. Staged, in part, to establish a bulwark against denial, the Demjanjuk trial remains the most powerful reminder of the perils of relying on the perpetrator trial as a means of answering the denier. Demjanjuk's Munich trial will presumably be the last of the high-profile trials of Nazi-era war criminals. Significantly, it has been staged largely without the testimony of Sobibor survivors, and entirely without survivors able to identify the former guard. We have arrived at the point that Demjanjuk's first trial presaged: where living memory can no longer vouchsafe history.

PART TWO

Balancing Denial Prohibition

THREE

Holocaust Denial and Hate Speech

–Robert A. Kahn

1. The Problem of "Bare" Denial

In a 2007 letter to the german federal minister of justice opposing the proposed European ban on genocide denial, Dr. Agnes Callamard, executive director of Article 19, a civil liberties group, argued that such laws were unnecessary to combat denial and went "beyond the international law standard of incitement to hatred by elevating a historical event to dogma[.]"[1] Almost a decade earlier, the Institute for Jewish Policy Research (JPR) made a similar point in a report opposing a Britain-wide ban on Holocaust denial—hate speech laws (if modified) were enough to address the problem.[2] The report quoted a study by G. Bindman, who after surveying a number of successful prosecutions under the explicit denial laws of France and Germany, concluded that in almost every case, "the evidence would have equally have supported a charge of racial incitement[.]"[3]

What should we make of this claim? Is it merely an argument used by civil libertarians—who, given their druthers, would also oppose hate speech laws—to argue against a new restriction on speech? Or does the argument reflect a sense that laws restricting hate speech have more legitimacy in the liberal democratic societies of Europe and North America than explicit bans on genocide denial? Assuming the latter view is correct, does hate speech theory capture the harm that Holocaust denial poses to society? Or does it draw attention away from the denial of the facts of the Holocaust

---

1. Letter from Dr. Agnès Callamard, executive director of Article 19, to German minister of justice, Re: Proposed EU ban on Genocide trivialization (Feb. 12, 2007).

2. Institute for Jewish Policy Research, *Combating Holocaust Denial through law in the United Kingdom*, JPR Report No. 3,1 (2000), *available at* http://www.jpr.org.uk/Reports/CS_Reports/no_3_2000/index.htm (last accessed Sept. 14, 2009).

3. *See* Geoffrey Bindman, *Outlawing Holocaust Denial*, 147 N.L.J. 466 (1997), *quoted in id.* at 5, n. 20.

(bare denial) to other racist and/or anti-Semitic comments the denier might make at the same time?

Bare denial is the place where the connection between hate speech theory and efforts to regulate Holocaust denial seems to break down. One can make a pretty strong argument that the norm against hate speech applies when a denier blames the Holocaust "hoax" on Jews or Zionists. One can even argue that the norm applies when the denier refers to the Holocaust as a "lie," since this language leads one to ask: who lied? The harder question is whether, returning to the JPR report, the statement "that 500,000 rather than 6 million Jews died in the Holocaust" is "an expression of hatred against Jews."[4]

Note that this question, standing alone, does not tell us whether a state should prosecute deniers either (i) with a generic ban or (ii) on a case-by-case basis under hate speech laws. On the one hand, noted civil libertarian Alan Dershowitz, somebody who has repeatedly stated his opposition to all prosecutions of deniers, has called denial "quintessentially anti-Semitic."[5] On the other hand, hate speech is not the only theory under which one could prosecute denial. For example, a state might prosecute denial as an assault on truth and memory or as a challenge to the democratic order of modern states, especially those with direct experience of Nazi rule.

What the "bare denial" problem does show, however, is an ambiguity in the position of those who distinguish hate speech laws acceptable to libertarians from broad blanket bans on denial. When organizations like Article 19 argue that hate speech laws are "sufficient" to respond to denial, are they arguing that current hate speech laws (and the theory of hate speech that supports them) are sufficient to catch bare denial in their purview? Or are they saying that bare denial, while reprehensible, is nevertheless the type of offensive statement citizens of a modern democratic society must endure?

To explore this issue, I look at the connection between Holocaust denial and hate speech over the thirty years since the emergence of Holocaust denial on the public scene in the mid-1970s. To foreshadow my conclusion, I believe there is a strong case—at least in countries with direct experience with Nazi rule (and possibly those with large populations of survivors)—that even "bare" Holocaust denial constitutes hate speech. Or to put it another

---

4. JPR Report, *supra* note 2, at 3.

5. Dershowitz added that denial could have "no other motive" or "intended effect." *See* Jamie Glazov, *Symposium: Criminalizing Holocaust Denial*, FRONTPAGEMAGAZINE.COM, July 27, 2007 *at* http://97.74.65.51/readArticle.aspx?ARTID=27525 (last accessed Sept. 14, 2009).

way, Alan Dershowitz is at least partially correct when he calls Holocaust denial inherently anti-Semitic.

2. A "Minor Province of Censorship?"

This gets too far ahead. Instead, let's begin with "hate speech." What claim does hate speech place on society? In *A Worthy Tradition: Freedom of Speech in America*, Harry Kalven refers to the "minor jurisdictions of censorship"—areas such as obscenity and libel where (i) "the popular view has been that speech is surely subject to regulation"; and yet (ii) courts, while acknowledging this, seek to render the prohibited domain "as narrowly as possible."[6] While the United States generally takes a more libertarian approach to hate speech than other advanced industrial democracies, the Kalven definition highlights the fluid nature of speech regulation. What one generation—or society—accepts as a domain of regulation might in another time and place stand at the core of protected speech.[7]

This is important because the development of American and European attitudes toward hate speech has evolved over time.[8] Before World War I, while much speech was banned—typically speech offending morals[9] or fomenting class struggle[10]—speech targeting racial, ethnic, and religious minorities was not. The Weimar Republic, however, did ban religious insults.[11]

---

6. Harry J. Kalven, A Worthy Tradition Freedom of Speech in America 23–24 (1988).

7. Think, for example, of blasphemy. Writing in 1974, Kalven viewed it—along with heresy—as part of the consensus on untouchable content. *Id.* at 6–11. In an earlier time, however, it stood at the center of speech controversies. *See* Leonard W. Levy, Blasphemy: Verbal Offense Against the Sacred, from Moses to Salman Rushdie (1993).

8. For a brief overview of the development of hate speech law in the United States, *see* Samuel Walker, Hate Speech: The History of An American Controversy, 9–11 (1994). Walker makes the argument that the extent of hate speech laws depend on the ability of victim groups to create a political coalition favoring such laws. *Id.* at 14. This, in turn, depends on context, which explains why even though the United States as a whole is hostile to hate speech laws, they are a feature of life at many private colleges and universities. *Id.* at 16.

9. *See* Robert Rabban, Free Speech in its Forgotten Years (1997).

10. For an overview, *see* Alex Hall, Scandal, Sensation and Social Democracy: The SPD Press and Willhelmine Germany, 1860–1914 (2008).

11. Cyril Levitt, *Under the Shadow of Weimar: What are the Lessons for the Modern Democracies? in* Under the Shadow of Weimar: Democracy, Law, and Racial Incitement in Six Countries 16, 19 (Cyril Levitt & Louis Greenspan eds., 1993).

Later, during the 1930s, France[12] and several American states passed laws banning hate speech[13]—largely in reaction to the rise of the Nazis to power.[14] These laws reflected a repudiation of Nazi doctrine as well as concerns about potential pro-Axis fifth column movements.

The Nazi defeat in World War II, combined with the horror, shock, and anger that accompanied the liberation of the concentration camps in 1945[15] deepened these concerns. As a result, both the Federal Republic of Germany and Austria enacted a wide range of statutory and constitutional restrictions on Nazi activity.[16] The major growth in hate speech laws, however, did not come until the 1960s after a wave of anti-Semitic incidents across Europe.[17] Laws were passed in a number of countries, including Germany (1960), Canada (1970), and France (1972).

The same period saw a growing international consensus around hate as a permissible reason to restrict speech. Section 20 of the 1966 International Covenant of Civil and Political Rights held that freedom of speech did not extend to comments that advocate racial, national, or religious hatred. Meanwhile, § 4 of the 1970 Covenant of the Eradication of Racial Discrimination imposed a positive duty on states to pass such laws. More recently, the European Courts have used Article 17 of the European Convention for the Protection of Human Rights and Fundamental Freedoms—which withholds rights protections to acts that "aim at the

12. Roger Errera, *French Law and Racial Incitement: On the Necessity and Limits of the Legal Responses*, *in* UNDER THE SHADOW OF WEIMAR: DEMOCRACY, LAW, AND RACIAL INCITEMENT IN SIX COUNTRIES 39 (Cyril Levitt & Louis Greenspan eds., 1993).

13. WALKER, *supra* note 8, at 40–42.

14. Interestingly, during this same period, many American states also passed laws targeting the Ku Klux Klan. *See* DAVID M. CHALMERS, HOODED AMERICANISM: THE HISTORY OF THE KU KLUX KLAN (1968).

15. For a fascinating account of this period that brings alive the way the discovery of Bergen-Belsen and Buchenwald led to widespread feelings of disgust directed at Nazis (and Germans), *see* DAVID STAFFORD, ENDGAME, 1945: THE MISSING FINAL CHAPTER OF WORLD WAR II (2007).

16. The Federal Republic banned the Nazi party, the Swastika, and the first verse of *Deutschland Über Alles*. *See* DONALD KOMMERS, THE CONSTITUTIONAL JURISPRUDENCE OF THE FEDERAL REPUBLIC OF GERMANY (1997). Austria passed the 1945 prohibition law, which, in its initial form barred former Nazis from political life. *See* Michael Whine, *Expanding Holocaust Denial and Legislation Against It*, 20 JEWISH POL. STUDS. REV. 1–2, 4 (2008).

17. The incidents included explicit anti-Semitic acts, such as cemetery desecrations, as well as the revelation that former Nazis occupied high positions in the Federal Republic of Germany. *See* ROBERT A. KAHN, HOLOCAUST DENIAL AND THE LAW: A COMPARATIVE STUDY 66 (2004) [hereinafter, KAHN, HOLOCAUST DENIAL].

destruction of any of the rights or freedoms" set forth elsewhere in the Convention—to uphold state bans of hate speech (and Holocaust denial).[18]

In the United States, events unfolded very differently. Although in the 1940s and '50s, the Supreme Court upheld the right of states to ban "fighting words"[19] and "group libel,"[20] the role that freedom of speech played in the movements for civil rights and against the Vietnam war led to a sea change,[21] one evident by 1978 when a federal court and a large segment of the citizenry (including many Jews) defended the right of neo-Nazis to march through Skokie, Illinois, a town with a large number of Holocaust survivors.[22] During the 1980s and '90s, lower courts rejected hate speech laws passed by municipalities and public universities.[23] American rejection of hate speech laws, however, had one exception—Klan-related activity. During the 1990s, lower courts upheld bans on masked demonstrations in Virginia[24] and Georgia.[25] While the Supreme Court in *R.A.V. v. St. Paul* (1992)[26] threw out a broadly worded ban on cross burning, in *Virginia v. Black* (2003),[27] the court held that states could ban "intimidatory" cross burning.[28]

Overall, however, by the late twentieth century, hate speech was a well-established "province of censorship" in a large part of Continental Europe

---

18. *See, e.g.*, Witzsch v. Germany, No. 7485/03, Feb. 4, 2003, 5–6.

19. Chaplinsky v. New Hampshire, 315 U.S. 568 (1942).

20. Beauharnais v. Illinois, 343 U.S. 250 (1952).

21. *See* WALKER, *supra* note 8, at 104–13. For a great discussion of how speech restrictions hampered the ability of the press to cover the civil rights movement, *see* GENE ROBERTS & HANK KLIBANOFF, THE RACE BEAT: THE PRESS, THE CIVIL RIGHTS STRUGGLE, AND THE AWAKENING OF A NATION (2007).

22. Collin v. Smith, 578 F.2d 1197 (7th Cir. 1978).

23. WALKER, *supra* note 8, at 132–36. Private universities were allowed to keep their hate speech codes because the First Amendment only covers state action. Robert A. Kahn, *Informal Censorship of Holocaust Revisionism in the United States and Germany*, 9 GEO. MASON. U. CIV. RTS. L.J., 125, 137 (1998); for an interesting discussion of the constitutional status of hate speech codes at private colleges and universities, *see* ROBERT M. O'NEIL, FREE SPEECH IN THE COLLEGE COMMUNITY, 218–39 (1997).

24. Commonwealth v. Hernandez, 406 S.E.2d 398 (Va. Ct. App. 1991).

25. State v. Miller, 398 S.E.2d 547 (Ga. 1990).

26. R.A.V. v. City of St. Paul, 505 U.S. 377 (1992).

27. Virginia v. Black, 538 U.S. 343 (2003).

28. Robert A. Kahn, *Cross-Burning, Holocaust Denial, and the Development of Hate Speech Law in the United States and Germany*, 83 UNIV. DET. MERCY L. REV. 163,180 (2006) [hereinafter, Kahn, *Cross-Burning*].

but not in the United States.[29] This situation opened the door to a series of debates over the legitimacy of hate speech laws between civil libertarians (usually, but not always from the United States) and supporters of the laws (often from Canada or Europe). The civil libertarians argued that the hate speech laws would lead to more regulation (Lee Bollinger's "fortress model"),[30] were often used against opponents of racism,[31] and would generate free speech martyrs.[32] In response, supporters argued that the exceptional stability of U.S. political democracy blinded Americans to the threats posed by a Nazi resurgence.[33] Pointing to history as well as the many types of speech the United States does ban (such as individual libel and obscenity), they often accused the Americans of absolutist naïveté, if not outright hypocrisy.[34]

3. Judging Hate by Its Content

Despite differences over whether to ban it, by the 1980s, there was an emerging agreement about what hate speech was. This consensus was expressed in international documents, case law, and academic writings on hate speech.

---

29. The British were a bit more wary of hate speech, as were the Canadians. Both countries had such laws but few prosecutions. One reason for this is procedural. The role played by adversarial attorneys and the jury make hate speech prosecutions more difficult affairs in common law countries. For more, *see* Kahn, Holocaust Denial, *supra* note 17, at Chapters 1 and 2.

30. The basic idea is that if free speech is allowed to weaken on the fringes, the forces of censorship will advance to the citadel of pure political speech. LEE C. BOLLINGER, THE TOLERANT SOCIETY: FREEDOM OF SPEECH AND EXTREMIST SPEECH IN AMERICA 76–101 (1986). Bollinger, however, is a critic of the model and prefers to defend extremist speech on its own terms as a way to create a more tolerant citizenry. *Id.* at 11, 102.

31. *See, e.g.,* Sandra Coliver, *Hate Speech Laws: Do They Work?, in* STRIKING A BALANCE: HATE SPEECH, FREEDOM OF EXPRESSION AND NON-DISCRIMINATION 363, 368–69 (1992).

32. This is the position Alan Dershowitz takes on prosecutions of Holocaust deniers. *See* ALAN DERSHOWITZ, THE VANISHING AMERICAN JEW: IN SEARCH OF JEWISH IDENTITY FOR THE NEXT CENTURY 115 (1996).

33. For a version of this argument raised by two U.S. critical race theorists, *see* RICHARD DELGADO & JEAN STEFANCIC, MUST WE DEFEND NAZIS? HATE SPEECH, PORNOGRAPHY AND THE NEW FIRST AMENDMENT 122–31 (1997).

34. Some of the harshest critiques on this score often came from Canadians who traced U.S. free speech "absolutism" to its revolutionary past and "melting pot" ideology. For more, *see* Robert A. Kahn, *Hate Speech and National Identity, The Case of the United States and Canada*, (Univ. of St. Thomas Legal Studies Research Paper, No. 08-02), *available at* http://ssrn.com/abstract=1104478 [hereinafter, Kahn, *Hate Speech*].

Although there were outliers, the typical hate speech law required a threat or abusive language directed at the target group. For example, the 1986 Public Order Act requires "threatening, abusive or insulting words,"[35] while § 130 of the German Criminal Code until 1994 required "inciting hatred," calling for "violent or arbitrary measures" against the target group, or "insulting" the target group.[36]

The requirement of abusive, insulting, or threatening language narrowed the scope of hate speech laws. This showed how even in Europe and Canada, hate speech was at best a "minor" province of censorship. In fact, the insistence on a threat or insult bore a logical similarity to the strongly libertarian "fighting words" doctrine in the United States, under which speech was restricted only when the speaker used words that "by their very utterance inflict injury or tend to incite an immediate breach of the peace."[37]

The difference between the first generation of hate speech laws and the American approach turned instead on "incitement." While European and Canadian hate speech laws often have an incitement requirement,[38] this did not in practice pose an obstacle to prosecutions. By contrast, the United States generally follows the test laid out in *Brandenburg v. Ohio*,[39] under which the state can only punish that speech which leads to "imminent lawless action."[40] The facts of *Brandenburg* show the test's power. Even though the case involved a Ku Klux Klan "organizer's meeting" at which the speakers uttered racist and anti-Semitic epithets—the bread and butter of most hate speech laws—the Supreme Court held that the speakers had engaged in "mere advocacy."[41]

Like their American counterparts, European and Canadian courts have sought to narrow the scope of their hate speech laws. But instead of relying on the lack of incitement, they ask whether the statements in question

---

35. JPR Report, *supra* note 2, at 8.

36. In 1994, the law was modified to cover Holocaust denial directly. The pre-1994 requirements still apply in other cases.

37. *Chaplinsky*, 315 U.S. at 572.

38. The Public Order Act of 1986 requires that the accused both intends to "stir up" racial hatred, and that, given "all the circumstances," such hatred "is likely to be stirred up[.]" Likewise, German Criminal Code § 130 requires that the statements be made "in a manner capable of disturbing the public peace."

39. Brandenberg v. Ohio, 395 U.S. 444 (1969).

40. *Id.*

41. *Id.* at 445, 449.

were "hateful." This has doctrinal consequences. While Americans, post-*Brandenburg*, debate about the impact of the words on an audience, Europeans debate the meaning of the words themselves. As a result, pro-speech rulings by European courts often take the form of a claim that the speech in question was not harmful.

This tendency goes back a long way. For example, in 1923, the German Supreme Court held that the phrase "Jew Republic" was not an insult against the Weimar Republic as prosecutors alleged but merely a factual claim about the "disproportionate power . . . and influence" many Germans felt Jews wielded in the new republic.[42] While the "Jew Republic" is surely a product of its time—and the result of a judiciary trained to be "blind in the right eye"[43]—the broader trend has been a staple of European jurisprudence.[44]

There is nothing unusual about this kind of doctrinal regime. A focus on content follows logically in a legal system that bans a fair amount of speech. While toleration of all (or almost all) offensive speech provides an easy bright-line rule for court, lawyers, and potential speakers to follow, a regime that punishes speech has to provide convincing public arguments about what is and is not punished. In making these arguments, courts will try to draw clear lines. But the search for dividing lines can protect speech that—seen from a more context-sensitive perspective—is just as worthy of prosecution as speech that the society bans.

4. Is Bare Denial Hateful?

While problems with line drawing can arise in any doctrinal area where speech is routinely proscribed—such as libel and, in the United States, obscenity—the difficulties are particularly acute in the area of Holocaust denial. Traditional hate speech laws require insulting or abusive words—a

42. INGO MÜLLER, HITLER'S JUSTICE: THE COURTS OF THE THIRD REICH 18–19 (Deborah Lucas Schneider trans., 1991).

43. The phrase reflects the understanding that during the Weimar period, the German judiciary was much more lenient with the extreme Right than it was toward the extreme Left. *See* KAHN, HOLOCAUST DENIAL, *supra* note 17, at 65. Nor was the "Jew Republic" case unique. *See* Cyril Levitt, *supra* note 11.

44. For example, in the years after 1945, German courts have expanded the type of offensive speech allowed under the nation's insult laws. For a discussion of this trend in the area of political speech, *see* Winfried Brugger, *Ban on or Protection of Hate Speech? Some Observations Based on German and American Law*, 17 TUL. EUR. & CIV. L. F. 1 (2002).

requirement that appears to exclude bare Holocaust denial. But is bare denial hate speech at all? There are two reasons to think that it is.

First, even bare denial inflicts harm on Holocaust survivors, Jews, and other potential victims. This is a harm that comes from the content of the message rather than how it is expressed. Critical race theorist Mari Matsuda has referred to as the "cold" nature of Holocaust denial tracts, which are—in her words—"cunningly devoid of explicit hate language."[45] Yet, when Matsuda received a flyer in the mail denying the Holocaust, she felt "fear and revulsion," wondered if she had been targeted for giving a recent talk on hate speech regulation, and was relieved when she saw an out-of-state postmark on the letter.[46]

Matsuda felt harmed even though the flyer did not appear to contain any explicit anti-Semitic language. In fact, she did not initially recognize the flyer for what it was.[47] Her experience corresponds to her description of the harms posed by hate speech more generally:

> To be hated, despised, and alone is the ultimate fear of all human beings. However irrational racist speech may be, it hits right at the emotional place where we feel the most pain. The aloneness comes out not only from the hate message itself, but also from the government response of tolerance.[48]

Moreover, most human societies respect the dead. By stripping away this respect from the victims of the Holocaust, denial defames the dead[49] and isolates those connected to the victims (principally Jews and survivors) from the rest of the human race. This view is not that different from Hannah Arendt's definition of genocide as a crime against the "human status" of the victims.[50]

---

45. Mari Matsuda, *Public Response to Racist Speech: Considering the Victim's Story, in* Words That Wound: Critical Race Theory, Assaultive Speech and the First Amendment 41 (Mari Matsuda, Charles R. Lawrence III, Richard Delgado & Kimberle Williams Crenshaw eds., 1993).

46. *Id.*

47. *Id.*

48. *Id.* at 25.

49. Matsuda makes the same point when she quotes Elie Wiesel's statement that Holocaust denial defames the dead. *Id.* at 42.

50. Hannah Arendt, *Eichmann in Jerusalem: A Report on The Banality of Evil* 268 (1963).

Another connection between Holocaust denial and hate speech is genealogical. As noted above, revulsion against Nazi Germany's race policies and crimes sparked the passage of hate speech laws in the years after World War II. While the laws had many goals, one key purpose was to forestall any attempt to politically rehabilitate Hitler and the Nazis. But this is precisely what Holocaust denial does. One can see this connection in the title of Ernst Zundel's pseudonymously written book, *The Hitler We Loved and Why*,[51] as well as in the calls dating back to the 1980s, by then West Germany, for the Canadian government to suppress Zundel's printing press.[52] The harm—here a danger of a neo-Nazi revival—does not depend on whether the speakers used explicitly racist or anti-Semitic language.

5. The Limits of Traditional Hate Speech Laws

The claim that bare Holocaust denial is a form of hate speech, if not easy to make, is at least plausible. The difficulty arises, however, when we turn to law. Ideally, hate speech laws should not only punish the deniers (and prevent future denial); they should also send a "didactic" message to the rest of society that the world repudiates Holocaust denial.[53] However, the prosecutors often faced trouble on both counts.[54] They would struggle—sometimes successfully, sometimes not—to show that the denier in question had, in fact, made an explicitly racist or anti-Semitic statement. However, even when they succeeded

---

51. Zundel published the book under the pseudonym "Christof Freidrich," a combination of his two middle names. *See* STANLEY A. BARRETT, IS GOD A RACIST? THE RIGHT WING IN CANADA 158 (1987).

52. *Id.* Earlier, the Canadian government had tried unsuccessfully to restrict Zundel's mailing privileges. *Id.* at 160–61.

53. *See* LAWRENCE DOUGLAS, THE MEMORY OF JUDGMENT: MAKING LAW AND HISTORY IN THE TRIALS OF THE HOLOCAUST 3 (2001). Douglas has been criticized for suggesting that war crimes trials should have "didactic" objectives. *See* Vivian Grosswald, *Atoms of the Law*, 53 UNIV. TOR. L. J. 305 (2003). But this criticism misses the point. Any high profile trial—and many trials of Holocaust deniers fall into this category—will convey "lessons" to the broader society about law and justice. Given this reality, it is only fair to ask what type of messages a particular trial is sending.

54. They are not always successful. While one can try—as Roger Eatwell has done—to distinguish between racist deniers who make glowing references to Hitler and the Nazi party, from more "moderate" deniers, who try to present their views as "scientific" in nature. However, there is often overlap between the two groups. *See* Roger Eatwell, *The Holocaust Denial: A Study in Propaganda Technique*, *in* NEO-FASCISM IN EUROPE 120 (Luciano Cheles, Ronnie Ferguson & Michalina Vaughan eds., 1991).

in court, the victories came at a high "didactic" cost; instead of focusing on the societal dangers posed by Holocaust denial, the legal debates turned on whether the accused had "crossed the line." To many outsiders, these debates appeared to trivialize the Holocaust—a result that led in the 1990s to new second generation laws that banned Holocaust denial explicitly.

These obstacles were most evident in Germany, where since the late 1970sHolocaust deniers were prosecuted under Criminal Code § 130 (which bans hate speech) and § 185 (which bans insults). In 1979, the German Supreme Court seemed to offer a solution. Interpreting the law against insults, the court held that defendant's claim that only 2 million Jews died in the Holocaust was a "direct attack" on the "self-conception" of Jews living in the Federal Republic.[55] Moreover, Germans had a duty to "guarantee against the repetition" of the Holocaust: only this would allow Jews to feel secure living in the Federal Republic with respect.[56]

If this language was potentially very wide reaching—especially in its suggestion that the descendants of perpetrators have special obligations to respect the memory of past atrocities—the context of the case itself was narrower. For one thing, the defendants did not limit themselves to bare denial. Instead, they referred to the Holocaust as a "lie" and a "Zionist swindle."[57] Also because the complainant was not Jewish—but instead had a Jewish grandfather who perished at Auschwitz—the courts took up whether he had the standing to suc. In answering this question the Supreme Court turned to the Nazi-era race laws.[58] This led to both an outcry and the passage of a 1985 law that removed standing requirements in Holocaust denial cases.[59]

While the 1979 decision said nothing about the hate speech laws, the assumption was that these also covered bare denial. This belief was shattered in 1994 when the Supreme Court held that, for purposes of the hate speech laws, the prosecution would have to show more than bare

55. BGHZ (*Entscheidungen des Bundesgerichtshofes in Zivilsachen*) 75 (1979): 160, 161 (BGH, Sept. 17, 1979)("The Zionist Swindle Case"). For more, see KAHN, HOLOCAUST DENIAL, *supra* note 17, at 18–19.

56. The Zionist Swindle Case, *supra* note 55, at 161.

57. *Id.* The defendants did stop short of explicitly blaming the Jews for the Holocaust, which may be why the court took up the bare denial issue.

58. *Id.*

59. For more, see Eric Stein, *History against Free Speech: The New German Law against the "Auschwitz" and Other—"Lies,"* 85 MICH. L. REV. 277 (1986).

denial.[60] The case, which featured Günter Deckert, leader of the Far Right National Democratic Party (NDP), showed the legal and political limits of the hate speech laws in the fight against Holocaust denial.

The case began in 1991 when Deckert invited Fred Leuchter—an American Holocaust denier famous for claiming on "scientific" grounds that the gas chambers at Auschwitz could not have possibly worked—to give a speech in Wertheim, Germany.[61] This was a time when Germany was facing a wave of antiforeigner violence and right-wing extremism, and there were concerns that the NPD would gain 5 percent of the vote, giving Deckert a place in the Bundestag.[62] After the event, mostly attended by partisans of the extreme Right, Leuchter and Deckert were charged with violating the hate speech laws.

Because Leuchter fled to the United States, the 1992 trial focused on Deckert. A local court in Mannheim found Deckert guilty.[63] He then appealed to the Supreme Court, which, as noted, held that bare denial was not sufficient for a conviction under § 130 and remanded the case for an examination of what Deckert and Leuchter had actually said.[64] A few months later, the Mannheim trial court found Deckert guilty of inciting hatred.[65] They suspended his sentence, however, and in a written opinion praised him for standing up against "Jewish financial pretensions" about the Holocaust.[66] This triggered a widespread scandal that forced the retirement of the judge who wrote the opinion.[67]

The scandal that engulfed the court, however, should not overshadow the first part of the opinion, which struggled to show that Deckert was, in fact, guilty of racial incitement. To justify its ruling, the court went into an extensive analysis of Leuchter's speech, how Deckert translated it, and how both

---

60. NJW (Neue Juristische Wochenschrift) (1994), 1421 (BGH, Mar. 13, 1994) ("The First Deckert Case").

61. *See* Robert A. Kahn, *Who Takes the Blame? Scapegoating Legal Responsibility and the Prosecution of Holocaust Revisionists in the Federal Republic of Germany and Canada*, 16 GLENDALE L. REV. 17, 20-21(1998) [hereinafter, Kahn, *Scapegoating*]. For more about Leuchter, *see* DEBORAH LIPSTADT, DENYING THE HOLOCAUST—THE GROWING ASSAULT ON TRUTH AND MEMORY 162–73, 177–79 (1994).

62. Kahn, *Scapegoating*, *supra* note 60, at 20.

63. *Id.* at 22.

64. The First Deckert Case, *supra* note 60, at 1421.

65. NJW (1994), 2494 ("The Second Deckert Case")

66. *Id.* The court also seemed to suggest that denying the Holocaust was not a crime in Germany. *Id.* For more, *see* KAHN, *supra* note 17, at 70–73.

67. KAHN, HOLOCAUST DENIAL, *supra* note 17, at 73–77.

speakers sought (eventually unsuccessfully) to temper their language to avoid running afoul of Germany's hate speech laws. Taken as a whole, the ruling shows how the requirement of an explicit racial or anti-Semitic slur complicated the prosecution's task and distorted the trial's message.

The court appeared to accept that Deckert, by translating Leuchter's speech, was liable for its contents.[68] Nevertheless, in looking for evidence of hate, it passed over Leuchter's "scientific" denial of Auschwitz.[69] This was less relevant than minor wording changes that Deckert made in translating Leuchter's speech. For example, the Mannheim court found an anti-Semitic intent (and thus evidence of inciting hate) in Deckert's decision to refer to "Silverman" as "Silbermann" and in his decision to shorten the word "Holocaust" to "Holo."[70] On the basis of these wording changes, the court found an intent to treat Jews as "inferior beings."[71]

Meanwhile, the transcript of the event—attached to the judicial opinion as an appendix—shows that Deckert had a very similar reading of the law. He promised to let Leuchter know when he crossed the line into explicit anti-Semitism.[72] For the same reasons, when translating the speech he dropped Leuchter's references to "Jewish persecutors" and "the problem Jewish elements."[73] While Deckert was not consistent—at one moment toward the end of the speech, he called for the Holocaust "lie" to be swept away[74]; his willingness to avoid anti-Semitic language highlights the difficulty of prosecuting Holocaust denial under traditional hate speech laws.

Similar problems arose when deniers were sued for "falsifying history" as occurred in both *R v. Zundel* and the 1979 lawsuit brought by deportees and civil rights groups against Robert Faurisson under the French Civil Code. While both cases show the difficulty of using courts to establish a historical fact, they also share a second common trait relevant here. In each instance, the story of the trial tended to shift from rebutting Holocaust denial as false history to exposing the unsavory political associations of the denier. In the

---

68. *See* Kahn, *Scapegoating, supra* note 61, at 24, n.38.

69. Leuchter's speech included a lengthy discussion of the gas chambers. The Second Deckert Case, *supra* note 65, at 2494.

70. *Id.*

71. *Id.*

72. *Id.*

73. *Id.*

74. *Id.*

1985 Zundel trial, this came from the prosecutor who, on cross-examination, entered evidence of Zundel's love of Hitler.[75] In the Faurisson case, the impetus came from the court of appeals that tried to base its ruling in favor of the civil plaintiffs on Faurisson's sloganeering and disrespect for Holocaust survivors—rather than on his views themselves.[76] In each instance, the specific harm posed by Holocaust denial and the symbolic power of the court to repair it are pushed off center stage.

Once these problems emerged, two outcomes were possible. One possibility was libertarian. If prosecuting Holocaust deniers under hate speech laws sidesteps the real issues, why bring in the law at all? Or, to put it another way: by all means, prosecute a Faurisson or Zundel if they make an explicitly anti-Semitic or racist statement, but do so as hate speech rather than Holocaust denial. This is the implicit position of those who claim that traditional hate speech laws are sufficient to battle Holocaust denial. On this view, Holocaust denial—as the glue that keeps the Radical Right together—remains a fertile ground for other hate speech offenses; but standing alone, it is not hate speech.

The other possibility points in the direction of tougher laws—ones that take the criminality of Holocaust denial as a starting point. This path has been taken by a number of countries, including France, that passed the Gayssot law in 1990 and Germany, which four years later—and largely in response to the *Deckert* case—amended § 130 of the Criminal Code to explicitly outlaw denial or trivialization of the Holocaust. These laws, however, raised a new set of questions: Does a liberal state have the authority to establish an official truth? If the state can ban Holocaust denial, what's next? More generally, is a statute that bans the denial of a historical event still a hate speech law? It is to these questions that we now turn.

6. The Perils of Blanket Denial Laws

Since the passage of the Gayssot Law, thirteen countries[77]—mainly in Europe—have passed laws making it illegal to deny the Holocaust. These laws

---

75. Robert A. Kahn, *Rebuttal or Unmasking: Legal Strategy in* R. v. Zundel, 34 PATTERNS OF PREJUDICE 1, 12 (2000) [hereinafter, Kahn, *Rebuttal*]. This tactic was so successful that at Zundel's 1988 retrial, a new prosecutor presented this evidence in his case in chief. *Id.* at 13.

76. Cour d'appel [CA] [regional court of appeal] Paris, Apr. 26, 1983, 9.

77. As of 2008, the following thirteen European countries ban Holocaust denial: Austria,

ease the burden of the prosecution by making denial itself the offense. So, instead of having to prove that a denier incited hatred (or falsified history), the prosecutor need only show that the accused, in fact, denied the Holocaust.[78] The lighter burden of proof could produce dramatic results. For example, the same Paris court that in 1981 had struggled to find that Robert Faurisson "falsified" history, a decade later easily convicted him under the new law.[79]

The promise of easy prosecutions, however, came at a cost. From its very inception the loi Gayssot law came under criticism. Some of the critics were aligned with the political Right, but others were less expected. For example, Pierre Vidal Naquet, a historian of antiquity and an early critic of Faurisson, came out against the Gayssot law, even though he criticized the pre-Gayssot court rulings against Faurisson for being too mild.[80] Nor was he alone. A number of historians, intellectuals, and opponents of anti-Semitism opposed the Gayssot law—often while supporting hate speech laws.

The main concerns about the Gayssot law fell into two main categories. First, there were those who opposed the law as a state imposition of an official view of history. This perspective was present in the debates over the law's passage where opponents, referring to the then recent breakup of Soviet rule in Eastern Europe, noted with irony how, at a time when liberty was spreading to the East, the National Assembly was considering imposing a Stalinist-style official truth on France.[81]

While the reference to Stalin highlighted the political passions that accompanied the passage of the Gayssot law,[82] other opponents made

---

Belgium, the Czech Republic, France, Germany, Lichtenstein, Lithuania, Luxembourg, Poland, Portugal, Romania, Slovakia, and Switzerland. Israel also bans denial. For an overview, *see* Whine, *supra* note 16, at 3–5. Although Whine includes Spain on his list, this country has repealed its denial law.

78. This was not always easy. In one case under the Gayssot law, the accused argued that there were no "homicidal" gas chambers within the boundaries of 1937 Germany, which made the court uncomfortable about judging history. KAHN, HOLOCAUST DENIAL, *supra* note 17, at 111–13.

79. *Id.* at 108–11.

80. *See* PIERRE VIDAL-NAQUET, ASSASSINS OF MEMORY, ESSAYS ON THE DENIAL OF THE HOLOCAUST (Jeffrey Melhman trans.,1992). Nazi hunter Serge Klarsfeld also came out against the law. *See* KAHN, HOLOCAUST DENIAL, *supra* note 17, at 107.

81. For an overview of the debate, *see* KAHN, HOLOCAUST DENIAL, *supra* note 17, at 105–08.

82. The Left vs. Right tendency was reinforced by the fact that the law's sponsor—Jean Claude Gayssot—was a member of the Communist Party and that the bill was passed largely on a party line vote. *Id.*

the more politically neutral point that the state had no business interfering with history. For example, in 2005, nineteen French historians, including Pierre Nora and Pierre Vidal-Naquet, opposed the Gayssot law on the grounds that history is not a "judicial object," adding that in a "free" society, Parliament, not the judiciary, has the task of "defin[ing] the historical truth."[83]

Second, opponents worried about the expansion of the Gayssot model to other areas of history. These arguments did not always fit into a Left vs. Right paradigm. For example, Pierre Nora, discussing the French denial of the Armenian genocide, said the path represented by the Gayssot law, one "taken with the best intentions" nevertheless "has led more and more groups" to want "their interpretation of history" to be supported by law.[84] Not only that, some of the groups pushing for the new laws live in states that have little apparent connection to the historical events in question. This troubled Timothy Garton Ash, who, speaking of the proposed Armenian genocide law, asked "[w]hat right has . . . France to prescribe by law the correct historical terminology to characterize what another nation did to a third nation ninety years ago."[85] While he could understand why France might want to make it a crime to "deny the complicity of Vichy in the deportation . . . of French Jews," the Armenian genocide law stuck him as little different from Germany making it illegal to deny the Soviet gulag or Turkey making it illegal to deny that France used torture during the Algerian Wars.[86]

There are also concerns about the expansion of the types of historical events protected from denial. While the current laws only cover genocides, the justification for these laws could potentially go much further. For example, the German Federal Constitutional held that there was no expressive

---

83. *France: Call by 19 Historians for Repeal of Several Statutory Clauses,* AGENCE FRANCE PRESSE, Dec. 12, 2005, *available at* http://theholocauststory.blogspot.com/2006/01/agence-france-presse-december-12-2005.html#links.

84. Sabine Seifert, *Should Holocaust Denial Be Banned?,* EURO TOPICS, Apr. 18, 2007, *at* http://www.eurotopics.net/en/archiv/magazin/geschichte-verteilerseite-neu/holocaust_leugnung_2007_04/debatte_holocaustleugnung/(*quoting* Nora).

85. Timothy Garton Ash, *This is the moment for Europe to dismantle taboos, not erect them,* GUARDIAN, Oct. 19, 2006, *available at* http://www.guardian.co.uk/commentisfree/2006/oct/19/comment.franc.

86. *Id.* Garton Ash's argument reflects a broader Euro-skepticism that has also surfaced in the hate speech debate. Writing about European efforts to "harmonize" its hate speech laws, Roger Kimball has warned of a future in which "of you are British and you say something nasty about the French while on vacation in Greece, you might wind up on a Greek jail for two 'or more' years." Glazov, *supra* note 5, at 17.

value in the presentation of "false historical facts,"[87] a far-reaching rationale that potentially targets a wide range of historical facts, including those that do not relate to genocide at all.[88] Another more specific concern involves people like General Lewis McKenzie, who claim that fewer than 8,000 people died at Srebrenica.[89] When asked whether McKenzie would be subject to a European-wide genocide denial law, a German spokesperson said the issue would have to be decided on a case-by-case basis.[90]

In expressing concerns about the potential scope of the blanket denial laws, the critics are following tradition of Harry Kalven—having encountered a new "province" of censorship, they want to make sure that its boundaries are narrowly confined. This, however, is a hard task—at least when the Holocaust denial bans are presented as an end in and of themselves. Under these circumstances, questions abound. Should the blanket bans be limited to Holocaust denial, or should other genocides be included? Does it matter which nation is doing the excluding? How, for that matter, does a legislature decide when a historical event is terrible enough to merit the category of "genocide"?

If one reads the recent debates carefully, however, a powerful answer to these questions begins to emerge. In 2007, Deborah Lipstadt discussed the proposed laws in an online forum with Roger Kimball, Alan Dershowitz, and Jamie Glazov.[91] For most of the debate, Lipstadt agreed with Dershowitz and Kimball that banning Holocaust denial was a bad idea.[92] However, as a "last caveat," she said that she understood "how Germany and Austria would have a different perspective on this issue."[93] These countries were

---

87. NJW (1994), 1781 (case involving a speech by David Irving. Although the Irving case involved the constitutionality of Holocaust denial prosecutions, the case was decided before Germany enacted its blanket ban on denial).

88. For example, the "false historical fact" standard could be used against those who argue that United States President Franklin D. Roosevelt had foreknowledge of the Japanese attack on Pearl Harbor.

89. Bruno Waterfield, *EU plans far-reaching 'genocide denial' law,* TELEGRAPH, Feb. 3, 2007, *available at* http://www.telegraph.co.uk/news/worldnews/1541411/EU-plans-far-reaching-genocide-denial-law.html.

90. *Id.*

91. *See* Glazov, *supra* note 5.

92. *Id.* Glazov took a more nuanced stance. For him, the question "boils down to anthropology." Is Holocaust denial a threat? If the answer to that question is "yes," then there is at least an argument to be made for banning denial. *Id.*

93. *Id.*

where "the Holocaust was nurtured and grew to fruition."[94] As a result, denial has "a different resonance in those countries than it does in other places."[95] She then turned to the United States and explained that because of the history of the Ku Klux Klan, wearing a hood had a different impact in Stone Mountain, Georgia—one of the birthplaces of the Klan—than it would in Seville.[96]

The focus on the national past of the country in question—something also present in Garton Ash's willingness to tolerate French law's banning of the denial of Vichy crimes—suggests a different way to view genocide denial laws, one consistent with Kalven's injunction to censor narrowly. The purpose of genocide denial laws is to not impose an "official history" but to make sure that the historical atrocities perpetuated or supported by the state are remembered. As the German Supreme Court pointed out in the 1979 *Zionist Swindle* case,[97] only in this way can the survivors feel secure as full-fledged members of the post-genocidal society.

This perspective also helps clarify the connection between Holocaust denial and hate speech. Normally, hate speech conveys an element of immediacy. The recipient of the racial, sexist, or anti-Semitic epithet is literally stunned into silence. Holocaust denial does not necessarily do this. As Matsuda points out, at least some deniers are very good at avoiding ethnic and racial slurs. The hateful aspect of Holocaust denial comes from what it says about the past. By denying past acts of hatred and violence targeting the victim group, the denier opens the door to future attacks and isolates the victim from the rest of humanity. When a state that facilitated the prior acts of violence condones denial, it sends the message that the victim group is not worthy of protecting.

7. Bringing "Hate" Back In

On a more practical level, viewing the offense as the denial of "past hate" has three benefits. First, it helps explain how supporters of genocide denial laws

94. *Id.*

95. *Id.*

96. *Id.* I make a similar connection in my 2006 article on cross burning and Holocaust denial. *See* Kahn, *Cross-Burning, supra* note 28.

97. See *supra* text accompanying note 55.

see them. Second, it reflects the way that the European and international courts have viewed the laws when reconciling them to freedom of speech. Finally, it offers a yardstick to distinguish narrowly crafted genocide denial laws from other attempts to regulate history.

7.1 Past Hate as a Rationale for Genocide Denial Laws

One of the most striking things about the Gayssot law debate is how supporters viewed the law as a tool in a larger battle against hate speech and right-wing extremism. In particular, supporters linked the law to Jean Marie Le Pen, whose Far Right National Front Party had been gaining at the polls with anti-immigrant appeals.[98] For example, one socialist deputy argued that "bearers of racist ideology depend on loss of memory . . . to make their ideas prosper anew," while another referred to the "revisionist machine" that, by denying the gas chambers, sought to rehabilitate the extreme Right.[99] Justice Minister Pierre Arpaillange made the point more directly; he stated that denial has a "racist resonance."[100]

The focus on racism also carried over to the legal hopes that supporters had for the new law. Given the outcome of the Faurisson falsification of history case in which the French courts expressed a reluctance to judge Faurisson's "historical" views, one might have expected supporters of the law to discuss how by making Holocaust denial itself the crime, the Gayssot law freed French courts from the burden of judging history. This argument, however, was almost never raised. Instead, supporters pointed out how, under the Gayssot law, it would be possible to prosecute deniers even when there were no explicit racist or anti-Semitic statements.[101]

The antiracist arguments were very powerful, in part, because they were tied into the French experience of collaborating with the Nazis during the Occupation. In this regard, Le Pen was not simply a racist who sought to benefit from Holocaust denial—he was also a symbol of France's failure to

---

98. For a discussion of Le Pen's growing popularity in the late 1980s, *see* KAHN, HOLOCAUST DENIAL, *supra* note 17, at 103–04.

99. *Id.* at 106 (*quoting* Jean-Claude Boulard and François Asensi).

100. *Id.* (*quoting* Arpaillange).

101. *Id.* Asensi noted how it was hard to prosecute Faurisson under France's hate speech laws because he usually avoided making statements that were explicitly anti-Semitic. KAHN, HOLOCAUST DENIAL, *supra* note 17, at 106.

face its past. Using Le Pen's characterization of the Holocaust as "a detail in history," one supporter of the law asked whether "the deportation of infants from Izieu" was also a detail.[102] In response, opponents of the law, such as Marie-France Stirbois—the lone National Front deputy in the National Assembly—touted their Resistance credentials.[103]

As the Gayssot debate became part of a larger debate over French responsibility for the crimes of the Vichy period, Holocaust denial took on a political resonance: one that helps explain why the French passed the Gayssot law in 1990 (after the Barbie trial) rather than after the first round of *Faurisson* litigation ended in 1983. It also helps further Lipstadt's insight that denial laws have a larger role to play in countries that have direct experience with the Holocaust. In fact, the list of European countries that have Holocaust denial laws roughly corresponds to those countries that saw large-scale deportations of Jews under Nazi rule.[104] One can make a similar point about the United States: the states where courts are most likely to uphold antimask laws are those (such as Georgia and Virginia) with a history of Klan activity.[105]

7.2 Past Hate as a Justification for anti-Denial Laws in European Jurisprudence

It is one thing to posit a link between Holocaust denial laws and a country's past experience with the Holocaust but quite another to show that it carries

---

102. *Id.* (*quoting* Jean-Claude Boulard). Le Pen made his "detail in history" comment during a 1987 interview about Holocaust denial. *Id.* at 102. In 1944, Klaus Barbie ordered the deportation of forty-four Jewish children who had been in hiding. The order played a role in his trial, which had just been completed. *See* HENRY ROUSSO, THE VICHY SYNDROME: HISTORY AND MEMORY IN FRANCE SINCE 1944, at 204 (Arthur Goldgammer trans., 1991).

103. Stirbois described the role her father played in the Resistance. KAHN, HOLOCAUST DENIAL, *supra* note 17, at 107.

104. For example, the Netherlands, Belgium, Poland, and Romania have explicit denial laws, while the United Kingdom and Denmark do not. The major exception here was Hungary, before the vote of a statute in February 2010. The previous situation could have been explained by the fact that the deportations occurred in April 1944, after the Nazis staged a coup to remove the Hungarian government, which had, until then, shielded its Jewish population from the worst excesses of the Holocaust. (Italy, where the deportations took place after the fall of Mussolini, may be similar). *See* RANDOLPH L. BRAHAM, THE POLITICS OF GENOCIDE: THE HOLOCAUST IN HUNGARY, 13–14 (1994); SUSAN ZUCCOTTI, THE ITALIANS AND THE HOLOCAUST: PERSECUTION, RESCUE AND SURVIVAL, xxv–xxviii (1987).

105. By contrast, free speech challenges to anti-mask laws were more successful outside the South. *See, e.g.,* American Knights of the Ku Klux Klan v. Goshen, 50 F. Supp. 2d 835 (N.D. Ind. 1999) (invalidating Goshen, Indiana anti-mask law on First Amendment grounds).

doctrinal weight. Yet a careful reading of the Europe-wide case law on Holocaust denial shows courts—in deciding whether a given denial law is "justifiable" in a democratic society—turn to that particular society's historical relationship to the Holocaust.

The "past hate" theory helps clarify the European and international case law on Holocaust denial. Take, for example, *Faurisson v. France*, decided by the UN Human Rights Committee in 1996, which upheld the Gayssot law as it applied to France's 1991 prosecution of Robert Faurisson.[106] In trying to show that the case did not grant states the right to pass blanket denial laws, Dr. Callamard of Article 19 argued that Faurisson's statements at issue were "racist" and, therefore, went beyond "mere denial."[107] She pointed to concurring opinions that talked about Faurisson's use of the words "myth" and "magic" to describe the gas chambers—a usage that could suggest racism (since a "myth" can be the product of lying)—as well as his call to prosecute Jewish historians who reported the findings of the Nuremberg Tribunal.[108]

Dr. Callamard's interpretation of the case, if accurate, would return the courts to the regime of traditional hate speech laws in which prosecutors were forced to pick through statements of deniers to find evidence of explicit hate. The statement at issue in the 1991 trial, however, is far more intelligibly read as "bare denial." Faurisson, who sought to challenge the Gayssot law on its own terms, said that he had "excellent reasons for not believing in the policy of extermination of the Jews" and spoke critically of how "the myth of the gas chambers" had been made "official" by the French government "with the approval of the court historians."[109] To put it another way, Faurisson's directness in his repudiation of the Holocaust made his an easy case under the Gayssot law.[110] Had the case been brought under a traditional hate speech law, the prosecution's task would have been much harder.

---

106. *Faurisson v. France*, Communication No. 550/1993, U.N. Doc. CCPR/C/58/D/550/1993 (Nov. 8, 1996).

107. Callamard Letter, *supra* note 1, at 2, n.5.

108. *Id.* at para. 10 (concurring opinion of Judges Evatt and Kretzmer).

109. KAHN, HOLOCAUST DENIAL, *supra* note 17, at 108. Faurisson made his comments in *Le Choc du Mois*, a right-wing newspaper.

110. Other cases have been more difficult. *See* KAHN, HOLOCAUST DENIAL, *supra* note 17, at 111–15. For example, a French court held that a flyer stating that "Auschwitz, 125,000 deaths" did not, by itself, constitute Holocaust denial. *Id.* at 114. Likewise, Germany's blanket ban on denial did not stop a German administrative law judge from acquitting a denier with strong right-wing associations for using the phrase "Auschwitz Myth" in the context of Steven Spielberg's film *Schindler's List*. *Id.* at 77–82.

Moreover, Dr. Callamard's description of *Faurisson v. France* leaves out the reasoning by which the majority and concurring opinions decided to uphold the Gayssot law. This reasoning focuses directly on the connection between Holocaust denial, French history, and anti-Semitism. For example, the majority opinion concluded that Faurisson's statements—when "read in their *full* context" (emphasis added)—"were of a nature as to raise or strengthen anti-Semitic feelings [.]"[111] In making this connection, the majority did not dissect Faurisson's use of words like "magic" and "myth." Instead, it relied on the statement of the then French minister of justice that "characterized the denial of the existence of the Holocaust as the principal vehicle of anti-Semitism."[112]

While Evatt and Kretzmer's concurring opinion does mention "magic" and "myth," the judges also argued that "in the conditions of present day France," the idea that "Holocaust denial may constitute a form of incitement to anti-Semitism cannot be dismissed."[113] In explaining how they reached this conclusion, the judges added:

> This is a case where, in a particular social and historical context, statements that do not meet the strict legal criteria of incitement can be shown to constitute part of a *pattern* of incitement against a given racial, religious or national group, or where those interested in spreading hostility and hatred adopt sophisticated forms of speech that are not punishable under the law against racial incitement even though there effect may be as pernicious as explicit incitement, if not more so.[114] (emphasis in original)

Most of the other concurring judges made similar statements,[115] while no other judge focused on the potentially anti-Semitic connotations of Faurisson's specific words.[116]

---

111. Faurisson v. France, para. 9.6.

112. *Id.* at para. 9.7.

113. *Id.* at para. 6 (concurring opinion of Judges Evatt and Kretzmer).

114. *Id.* at para. 4.

115. *See, e.g., id.* at para. 9 (concurring opinions of Judge Lallah and Judge Bhagwati).

116. Dr. Callamard also mentions *Lehideux and* Isorni v. France, 55/1997/839/1045 (Sept. 23, 1998) (case in which the Counsel of Europe reversed a conviction under a Nazi apologia law of the authors of a flyer that denied that Marshall Petain, head of the Vichy government, had any complicity in the deportations of French Jews). However, the authors of

The strong connection between denial and anti-Semitism in *Faurisson v. France* also explains the doubts the author of the JPR report had about the validity of a British Holocaust denial law. After stating that restrictions on speech must be "proportionate" to the problem at hand and noting the strong connection between Holocaust denial and anti-Semitism in France, the author concluded that in Britain, a denial law would fail the proportionality test because denial is unlikely "to become a very significant problem" and "is not a major manifestation of antisemitism."[117]

Where, however, denial is a significant problem, courts have been more willing to support blanket denial laws. For example, in *Nachtmann v. Austria*, the European Commission on Human Rights upheld a prosecution brought under Holocaust denial provisions contained in Austria's National Socialism Prohibition Law.[118] In explaining why a ban on denial is consistent with freedom of expression, the court noted that "National Socialism is a totalitarian doctrine incompatible with democracy and human rights[.]"[119] Here, however, the rationale has changed slightly. Owing perhaps to the small Jewish population in Austria, direct incitement of anti-Semitism is less of a direct concern. Instead, concern is that Holocaust denial will harm the state by rehabilitating the Nazi party.

While the reasons are different, the larger structure of the argument parallels *Faurisson v. France*. Under ordinary circumstances, European and international courts will interpret the protections of freedom of speech broadly and reject broad bans of speech—including laws banning the denial of historical facts. When, however, the act of denial in question involves an act of past hate in which members of the society were involved—either as direct perpetuators or as collaborators—the European courts are more likely to give the state in question some leeway.

In this process, we see a curious return of "hate" to Holocaust denial jurisprudence. In the cases brought under the early hate speech laws, prosecutors struggled to prove that denial was a "hateful" act—as opposed to a bizarre, perverse view about history. After a series of difficult prosecutions, opponents of denial enacted laws that sought to remove hate (and history) from

---

the flyer never denied the Holocaust itself: something the court itself found distinguished the case from Holocaust denial. *Id.*, at para. 17.

117. JPR Report, *supra* note 2, at 11.

118. *Nachtmann v. Austria*, Application No. 36773/97 (Sept. 9, 1998).

119. *Id.*

the trials by making denial itself the offense. These laws, however, ran into trouble because of their potential breadth. If the state can ban denial of the Holocaust, what else can it ban? In response, international courts judging these laws have returned to "hate" and upheld anti-denial laws where—in the country in question—there is a link between Holocaust denial and either anti-Semitism or the resurgence of Nazism.

7.3 Past Hate as a Yardstick for Future Genocide Denial Laws

The past hate theory also helps explain why even some of those—such as Deborah Lipstadt—who take a libertarian approach to Holocaust denial nevertheless understand why Germany, Austria, and France might choose to ban Holocaust denial. At the other extreme, there are clearly some facts whose denial—even if politically freighted—do not rise to the level of hate speech. The concept only covers hateful acts; no one is going to jail for making novel statements about the exploits of Alexander the Great. Nor, for that matter, is a denial of the Katyn massacre enough, by itself, for the past hate concept to apply, absent some link between that denial and some form of present hate.[120]

There are some closer cases, however, worth discussing. The first is a Europe-wide Holocaust denial law. Supporters of such a law could use the past hate theory to argue that the Nazi experience is largely a European one, and therefore, the connection between denial and anti-Semitism is present across Europe. Opponents could respond that in a number of countries, that connection is much weaker. This debate might ultimately wind up turning on how to best harmonize European laws: can a truly united Europe exist with a France that bans Holocaust denial and a United Kingdom that allows it?[121]

---

120. On the other hand, one could imagine a country in the former Soviet Union faced with a revanchist Russian movement making it illegal to deny Stalin's crimes.

121. For a discussion of the harmonization issue as it relates to laws banning denial of the Armenian genocide, *see* Sandrine Platteau, The criminalization of genocide denial in Europe: A growing threat for freedom of expression? The case of the Armenian genocide 76–82 (2008) (unpublished Master's Thesis from CEU and ELTE (Budapest)) (on file with author). From a U.S. perspective, one might note that while a number of states—mostly in the South—have laws banning Klan activity, others do not. Yet the difference in standards has not caused federalism-type problems. On the other hand, after Canada successfully prosecuted Ernst Zundel under an administrative hate speech law, he fled to

Regardless of how one answers this question, two points are important to keep in mind. First, even if Europe's past experience with Nazi hate necessitates Holocaust denial laws, this is still a relatively unique circumstance. Those who seek to ban denials of other genocides—and denials of other historical facts more generally—will have to show the same type of connection between past and present hate that the courts did in *Faurisson v. France*.

Second, there is nothing about the "past hate" theory that, by itself, directs a given country to enact a genocide denial law. The "past hate" theory simply highlights a judgment already made by courts and legislatures that, in at least some circumstances, denial of past hate can be as pernicious as direct face-to-face ethnic and racist insults. The recognition that "bare" Holocaust denial is a form of hate speech is—standing alone—not an argument that a state should ban it. The willingness of a given society to ban hate speech has varied across countries and time. The "past hate" concept will not change this. It might, however, lead to a situation where Holocaust denial is treated the same way as other forms of hate speech.

The second close case is the French proposal to ban denial of the Armenian genocide.[122] The key question here is one of nexus. There is little doubt that in a perfect world, the Turkish government, instead of promoting denial of the Armenian genocide, would take steps to combat it.[123] Were this to happen, it would follow the pattern of the Germans, Austrians, and French who—by banning denial—express a willingness to promote an open tolerant future through an honest evaluation of the past. Nor is there any doubt, even with the passage of time, that denial of the Armenian genocide has inflicted harm on survivors, their descendants, and the Armenian community more generally.[124]

The question raised by the French law is whether the "past hate" theory applies only where the society afflicted with the denial is the same society

---

the United States, where he took advantage of the broader speech protections to broadcast his views to supporters in Canada.

122. *See French lawmakers approve bill on Armenian genocide,* INTERNAT'L HERALD TRIB., Oct. 12, 2006, *available at* http://www.dailymail.co.uk/news/article-410066/French-lawmakers-approve-making-denial-Armenian-genocide-crime.html.

123. For a description of efforts by the Turkish government in the United States, *see* Roger W. Smith, Eric Markusen & Robert Jay Lifton, *Professional Ethics and the Denial of the Armenian Genocide, in* REMEMBRANCE AND DENIAL: THE CASE OF THE ARMENIAN GENOCIDE 271 (Richard G. Hovannisian ed., 1999).

124. For an overview, *see* MAUD. S. MANDEL, IN THE AFTERMATH OF GENOCIDE: ARMENIANS AND JEWS IN TWENTIETH-CENTURY FRANCE (2003).

that committed the original act. We have already seen how Garton Ash directly raised this concern in relation to the Armenian genocide, and it is implicit in Lipstadt's understanding of why Germany and Austria punish denial. This argument carries some weight. When the country of the perpetrators condones denial, others might ask if denial is the first step toward repetition. Under these circumstances, a law banning denial can be reassuring—especially when at least some of the deniers seek political rehabilitation of the wrongdoers.[125]

This argument, however, when applied to the Armenian genocide is too constricting. While France is not the land of the perpetrators, it has one of the largest populations in the Armenian Diaspora (second after the United States) and was the point of settlement of a large number of settlers of the genocide.[126] Moreover, in the Turkish successor state to the Ottoman Empire, genocide denial is not only tolerated, it is flourishing. The Turkish government's campaign of denial has imposed great suffering on the Armenian community in France, which, in response has mobilized and sued deniers under the same types of laws that Holocaust survivor Jews used against Faurisson in the days before the Gayssot law.[127]

In the end, we are left with a normative question: should the "past hate" concept apply when it is the country of the victims—or a country where a large number of victims reside—that does the punishing? This is the situation with the Armenians in France and, interestingly enough, with Holocaust denial in Israel.[128] In both cases, the political threat posed by denial is lessened. Even without the denial laws, Israel, for example, is probably the last

---

125. This was the case with Germany's decision in 1960 to pass a law targeting hate speech. KAHN, HOLOCAUST DENIAL, *supra* note 17, at 66.

126. For a discussion of survivor experiences, *see* Lorne Shirinian, *Survivor Memoirs of the Armenian Genocide in Cultural History*, *in* REMEMBRANCE AND DENIAL: THE CASE OF THE ARMENIAN GENOCIDE 165 (Richard G. Hovannisian ed., 1999).

127. The litigation came in response to a 1993 *Le Monde* interview in which historian Bernard Lewis asserted that the Armenian massacres did not constitute genocide. *See* Yves Ternon, *Freedom and Responsibility of the Historian: The Lewis' Affair*, *in* REMEMBRANCE AND DENIAL: THE CASE OF THE ARMENIAN GENOCIDE 237, 241 (Richard G. Hovannisian ed., 1999). Armenian groups in France sued Lewis both under the Gayssot Law, which was held not to cover other genocides, and under the French tort law used to show that Robert Faurisson, by falsifying history, had failed in his duties as a professional. *Id.* at 243–45. The latter lawsuit was successful but only resulted in nominal damages.

128. *See* Stephen J. Roth, *The Laws of Six Countries: An Analytical Comparison*, *in* UNDER THE SHADOW OF WEIMAR: DEMOCRACY, LAW, AND RACIAL INCITEMENT IN SIX COUNTRIES 177, 200 (Cyril Levitt & Louis Greenspan eds., 1993).

place in the world that needs to worry about neo-Nazis.[129] But the harm to the victims is every bit as real—perhaps more so on the part of the French Armenians who could read rejection into the failure of their adopted home to fight denial.

So while the nexus between the genocide and the country passing the laws is weaker in the French Armenian context than it was for France, Germany, and Austria—there still is a connection between the state and the act of past hate. This distinguishes the French-Armenian case from the situations discussed by Timothy Garton Ash and Roger Kimball in which a country with no connection to the historical events in question bans genocide denial.

8. Holocaust Denial Laws and Blasphemy

There is one final objection to genocide denial laws; some critics argue that these laws, by placing the Holocaust "off-limits," create a form of modern-day blasphemy. A version of this argument has been raised by the deniers themselves, who view the use of law as proof that as their arguments become "more scientific," the Holocaust becomes "more religious."[130] While the deniers' version of the argument is fairly easy to refute,[131] a more sophisticated version of the same general argument comes from Timothy Garton Ash, who views bans on Holocaust denial as reflecting a "taboo" that Europe can ill afford at a time that it is adapting to an increasingly multicultural world.[132] Proof of this last point is shown by the contrast made—at the height of the controversy over the publication of the cartoons depicting the Prophet

---

129. Holocaust denial among Israel's Arab and Muslim population is another matter. For an overview, *see* Robert A. Kahn, *Strange Bedfellows: Western Deniers and the Arab World, in* NOT YOUR FATHER'S ANTI-SEMITISM: HATRED OF THE JEWS IN THE 21ST CENTURY 191 (Michael Berenbaum ed., 2008) [hereinafter, Kahn, *Strange Bedfellows*].

130. This argument was made by Eric Delacroix, one of Faurisson's lawyers. *See* Kahn, HOLOCAUST DENIAL, *supra* note 17, at 114. He was convicted under the Gayssot law for making this statement in a book criticizing the law. *Id.*

131. For one thing, even if denial laws treat the Holocaust as a subject of "religious" reverence, this does not make deniers' arguments any more scientific. In this regard, deniers differ from the classic free speech martyr in their unwillingness to take the views of the scholarly community seriously. For more on the "pseudoscience" of denial, see MICHAEL SHERMER & STEVEN JAY GOULD, WHY PEOPLE BELIEVE STRANGE THINGS: PSEUDOSCIENCE, SUPERSTITIONS, AND OTHER CONFUSIONS OF OUR TIME 193–241 (2002).

132. Garton Ash, *supra* note 84.

Mohammed in a negative light—between state bans on Holocaust denial and the expectation that Muslims should become more thick skinned when it comes to satire directed at their religious beliefs.[133]

While there are some similarities between Holocaust denial laws and blasphemy—just as there are between hate speech and blasphemy—there is an essential difference between the Gayssot law and its close relatives and the traditional concept of blasphemy as it has existed in Europe since the Middle Ages. The medieval and early modern concepts of blasphemy were very broad: those who believed in another religion (or no religion at all) were often seen as blasphemous.[134] By contrast, the denial laws are very narrow. They do not prevent discussions about the meaning of the Holocaust, about whom or what social forces were ultimately responsible or its implications for the future. Under these laws, one can still argue that the Holocaust was an intentional act deriving from an eliminatory anti-Semitism or the functionalist result of in-fighting by Nazi elites without running afoul of the law.[135]

On the other hand, to the extent that blasphemy is viewed more narrowly as the showing of disrespect to the religious symbols of others, the concept is closer to both hate speech and denial laws. Take, for example, the 1978 *Gay News* case in the United Kingdom that involved a graphic poem about Christ's crucifixion.[136] While from a theological perspective, the poem was an offense against God, as a practical matter, the poem insulted practicing Christians.[137] The same applies to Salmon Rushdie's *Satanic Verses* and the cartoons depicting the Prophet Mohammed—while a modern secular society has no obligation to restrict speech on theological grounds, there is a duty to respect

---

133. For an overview, *see* Rudi Teitel, *No Laughing Matter: The Controversial Danish Cartoons Depicting the Prophet Mohammed, and their Broader Meaning for Europe's Public Square*, FINDLAW, Feb. 15, 2006, at http://writ.news.findlaw.com/commentary/20060215_teitel.html.

134. For an overview, *see* Levy, *supra* note 7, at 34 (describing how Christianity came to define blasphemy as "dissent from or defamation of Jesus' teachings").

135. *See* DANIEL GOLDHAGEN, HITLER'S WILLING EXECUTIONERS: ORDINARY GERMANS AND THE HOLOCAUST (1997); *see also* A.D. Moses, *Structure and Agency in the Holocaust: Daniel J. Goldhagen and His Critics*, 37 HIST. & THEORY 194 (1988). Note that this is not the only debate in the field of Holocaust studies that exists despite the presence of genocide denial laws.

136. For an overview of the *Gay News* case, *see* Levy, *supra* note 7, at 534–50.

137. For example, John Smyth, the prosecutor, described the poem as likely to outrage the feelings of Christians. *Id.* at 542.

the deeply held feelings of others, including those based on religion.[138] Moreover, protecting the dead from disrespect—a key goal of Holocaust denial laws—is a common feature across human societies. The same goes for showing respect to survivors. Therefore, even a modern secular society can justify a ban on Holocaust denial without wading into theology.

At first, the Danish cartoon controversy might seem to complicate the perspective here. After all, there have been no prosecutions of the *Jyllands Posten* editors for running the cartoons, nor has there been support among Europeans to tighten their blasphemy laws. From a legal perspective, however, the cartoon controversy shows how European Muslims faced the same problem that Jews and Holocaust survivors did in fitting a new type of offense into a set of outmoded categories. In particular, the main complaint the Danish Muslims had with cartoons was less the visual depiction of Mohammed—although there were some objections to that—and more the fact that some of the cartoons (especially the one featuring Mohammed with a bomb in his turban) made the suggestion that all Muslims were violent.[139]

In the ensuing debate, Muslims were often cast as supporters of blasphemy laws. And, as in the Rushdie controversy,[140] a number of Muslims made the argument that blasphemy laws only seemed outmoded because of an informal understanding among Europeans not to commit blasphemy against Christianity.[141] As a result, it was easy to characterize Muslims as

---

138. The distinction here is a critical one. To the extent religious defamation laws rest on an offense to the religion, they are hard to justify in a liberal society. *See* DAVID A. J. RICHARDS, TOLERATION AND THE CONSTITUTION 267–69 (1986) (arguing that religious conceptions about the criminality of abortion are not a sufficient reason for a liberal society to ban the practice). When, however, the offense is viewed as harming the believers themselves, some of the liberal objections should fade—at least in societies that have hate speech laws. For a theoretical justification of religious incitement laws, *see* David Norris, *Are Laws Proscribing Incitement to Religious Hatred Compatible with Freedom of Speech?*, 1 UCL HUMAN RIGHTS REVIEW 102, 102–06 (2008).

139. See Bent Nørby Bonde, *How 12 Cartoons of the Prophet Mohammed Were Brought to Trigger an International Conflict*, 28 NORDICOM REV. 33, 41 (2007).

140. For an overview, *see* Levy, *supra* note 7, at 551–67.

141. For a version of this argument in the Rushdie setting, *see* RICHARD WEBSTER, A BRIEF HISTORY OF BLASPHEMY: LIBERALISM, CENSORSHIP & "THE SATANIC VERSES" 25 (1992) (arguing that the sacredness of the Christian religion has been so profoundly internalized that the majority of British people would find it "psychologically difficult" to engage in "extreme or obscene" blasphemy "even in the privacy of their own imaginations[.]").

demanding a return to the full-bodied medieval blasphemy laws.[142] While some Muslims pushed for just that, others sought something much narrower—laws that criminalized religious incitement.[143] The same can be said of supporters of Holocaust denial laws. While critics see the erection of religious and historical "taboos," the laws themselves are much narrower.

Now this is not to say that Europe should prosecute the editors of the *Jyllands Posten* or the other papers that ran the Danish cartoons under Europe's hate speech laws. So far, the two attempts to do so have failed.[144] As mentioned above, a theory of hate speech can categorize speech acts, but it cannot itself say whether a given ban or prosecution is worth the trade-off. It can, however, break down the artificial distinction between hate speech and modern versions of blasphemy. Speech that attacks the core values of an ethnic, racial, or religious group harms society—and may on this ground be targeted as hate speech—regardless of whether it is also blasphemous.

9. Conclusion

This chapter has argued that "bare" Holocaust denial—the denial of the gas chambers, the six-million figure, and the Nazi policy of extermination—is, in those parts of Europe with direct experience with Nazi rule, a form of hate speech. It falls into this category for a number of reasons. First, there is a

142. The characterization of Muslims as advocates for medieval blasphemy laws fed into a larger tendency to see the cartoon controversy as a clash between an intolerant Islam and an explicitly European support for freedom of speech. For more, *see* Robert A. Kahn, *The Danish Cartoon Controversy and the Exclusivist Turn in European Civic Nationalism*, 8 STUD. IN ETHNICITY & NAT'LISM 524 (2008).

143. This is a gap in speech regulations of several European countries. For example, United Kingdom outlaws blasphemy but does not directly ban religious incitement. *See* Tariq Modood, *Muslims and European Multiculturalism*, OPEN DEMOCRACY, May 15, 2003, *at* http://www.opendemocracy.net/people-migrationeurope/article_1214.jsp.

144. In March 2006, the Danish office of public prosecutions issued a ruling explaining its decision not to go forward with prosecutions under Denmark's hate speech and blasphemy laws. The turban cartoon, while not "correct," was neither "scornful" enough to be blasphemous nor sufficiently directed at all Muslims to be hate speech. *See* Director of Public Prosecutions, *Decision on Possible Criminal Proceedings in the case of Jyllands Posten's article "The Face of Muhammed,"* No. RA-2006-41-0151, 7, Mar. 15, 2006, *available at* http://www.rigsadvokaten.dk/media/bilag/afgorelse_engelsk.pdf [hereinafter, *DPP Decision*"]. The following year, a prosecution brought by French Muslims against Charlie Hebdo for republishing the cartoons failed after a three-week trial that became a cause celebre for freedom of speech. *See French cartoons editor acquitted*, BBC NEWS, Mar. 22, 2007, *available at* http://news.bbc.co.uk/2/hi/6479673.stm.

well-organized movement on the extreme Right that uses Holocaust denial to rehabilitate Hitler and the Nazis. Second, in countries where descendants of the victims and perpetrators live together, denial—and state toleration of it—suggests that the agreement to treat May 1945 as "Ground Zero" is open to revision. This helps explain how even an advocate of free speech such as Deborah Lipstadt can hesitate when it comes to Germany and Austria. Finally, by ignoring the deaths of thousands of people, deniers separate the survivors from the rest of society, a separation that imposes the type of "aloneness" that Mari Matsuda sees as characteristic of traditional hate speech.

While the theoretical connections are many, the "legal career" of hate speech and Holocaust denial has been uneven. Early prosecutions faltered when prosecutors labored to show that Holocaust deniers also included direct anti-Semitic insults in their speeches. When, in response, a number of countries adopted laws that banned Holocaust denial as such, alarms were raised about the creation of state-enforced official truths that would soon devour all areas of historical inquiry. At this point, the European and international courts stepped in and supplied the missing piece of the puzzle. Genocide denial laws are permissible only when there is a connection between Holocaust denial and anti-Semitism (or, in Germany and Austria, the experience of Nazi rule).

This has been a clear advance in the sophistication of the legal campaign against denial. Instead of prosecutors having to prove on a case-by-case basis that a given Holocaust denier also made anti-Semitic utterances, now the European courts must prove that in a given country, Holocaust denial is anti-Semitic. The new approach, while smoother, does not resolve all the problems. For one thing, it raises questions about the future of Holocaust denial laws in a legally integrated Europe where denial is strongly linked to anti-Semitism in some countries (France) but not others (Britain). It also leaves open the question of whether a country can enact a law banning the denial of a genocide committed by a third nation. While the Armenians in France have made a strong case that—at least where a large survivor population resides in the host country—such laws are viable, the application of the principle to other situations is cloudier.[145]

Finally, the establishment of blanket Holocaust denial laws have given rise to charges that the laws create a modern-day blasphemy and—when viewed in the context of the absence of laws banning the Danish cartoons—reflect a

---

145. Nor do the laws necessarily end the legal and "didactic" challenges facing prosecutors at the trial level. *See* KAHN, HOLOCAUST DENIAL, *supra* note 17, at Chapter 5 (describing procedural difficulties facing prosecutors under the Gayssot law).

double standard. The first charge, however, relies on an outmoded view of blasphemy that overstates the amount of speech that Holocaust denial laws actually restrict. Meanwhile, the second charge downplays the similarities between Holocaust denial and the Danish cartoons—both combine a superficially neutral message with an embedded element of hate. The double standards argument also fails to recognize the limitations of hate speech theory as a justification for Holocaust denial laws. Hate speech theory can explain why a given speech act is offensive; it cannot however say definitively how a given society should weigh that act against the countervailing value of freedom of speech.

This brings us back to where we began. If hate speech theory is a "minor" province of censorship, Holocaust denial is an even smaller one. It has only recently arrived on the scene with the 1990 Gayssot law, and it is unclear how long it will last. But it is not unfamiliar territory and certainly not a new assault on freedom of speech. Rather, it is a recalibrating of the hate speech map to respond to a new situation.

FOUR

Defending Truth

Holocaust Denial in the Twenty-First Century[1]

–Kenneth Lasson

> The things i saw beggar description. I made the visit deliberately, in order to be in a position to give firsthand evidence of these things if ever, in the future, there develops a tendency to charge these allegations merely to propaganda.
>
> General Dwight D. Eisenhower after liberating a Nazi concentration camp[2]

From the still-burning embers of the Holocaust, we have come once again to learn the terrible truth—that the power of evil still lurks among the nations of the world and cannot be underestimated. Nor can the effect of the spoken and written word, which in modern times must be taken in tandem with the violence of terrorism.

It has been but a half-century since the liberation of Nazi death camps, a little more than two decades since the First International Conference on the Holocaust and Human Rights,[3] and a few short years since the United States Holocaust Memorial Museum first put on display its documentation of horror.[4]

---

1. Earlier analyses of this topic by Professor Lasson appeared in the journals *Current Psychology* (2007) and the *George Mason Law Review* (1997).

2. Eisenhower's words, written in a letter to Chief of Staff George C. Marshall on April 12, 1945, are etched in stone at the United States Holocaust Memorial Museum in Washington, D.C. Eisenhower went on to say that "[t]he visual evidence and the verbal testimony of starvation, cruelty, and bestiality were so overpowering as to leave me a bit sick. In one room, where there were piled up twenty or thirty naked men killed by starvation, George Patton would not even enter. He said he would get sick if he did so." *See* ALFRED D. CHANDLER, JR., THE PAPERS OF DWIGHT DAVID EISENHOWER: THE WAR YEARS 2616 (1970).

3. Sponsored by the Boston College Law School Holocaust/Human Rights Research Project and the Anti-Defamation League of B'nai Brith, the conference took place on April 17, 1986. *See* Debate, *Freedom of Speech and Holocaust Denial*, 8 CARDOZO L. REV. 559 (1987).

4. The museum opened in 1993.

Yet today, that form of historical revisionism popularly called "Holocaust denial" abounds worldwide in all its full-foul flourish—disseminated not only on Arab streets but in American university newspapers; not only in books, articles, and speeches but in mosques and over the Internet; and by heads of state.

"Israel must be wiped off the face of the map," declared Mahmoud Ahmadinejad, the elected president of Iran, in December of 2006. His primary justification—that the Jewish State's existence is predicated upon events that never happened—is echoed throughout the Muslim world. Ahmadinejad's true colors came through in a much ballyhooed international conference in Tehran, officially sponsored by the Iranian Foreign Ministry and billed as a "Review of the Holocaust: Global Vision."[5]

In a global environment increasingly dominated by mass media of manifold form and format, we have also begun to understand that what is printed on paper or broadcast on television or bytten into cyberspace affects everyone, actually or subliminally. Conversely, what is rejected or otherwise left out is doomed to a world of communication failure, ignorance, and misunderstanding.

Although Holocaust denial—one of the twenty-first century's fastest-growing forms of counterknowledge—is flourishing in the Arab world, many Western nations are wary of drawing attention to it for fear of upsetting Muslims.[6]

As the generation of survivors dwindles, whose words will win? Who decides what is to appear in the vast and burgeoning marketplace of ideas?

Many of these important choices are vested in editors and publishers, upon whom the United States Constitution confers almost unfettered discretionary authority. (Lesser but similar discretion is allowed in other Western democracies.) For the most part, journalists can write, say, depict, or ignore anything they want. Freedom of thought and expression is quintessentially American: one of our most hallowed liberties, limited only by circumstances where actual harm has been caused or is reasonably perceived as imminent. If a line can be drawn at all—between unfair suppression of

---

5. *International Conference on Holocaust Opens in Tehran*, BBC Worldwide Monitoring, December 11, 2006. Some insisted that Ahmadinejad's statement was a mistranslation of what he said—but the same quote was on the home page of the Iranian president.

6. Damian Thompson, *Fight Against Arab Holocaust Denial*, Telegraph.com, June 26, 2008, *available at* http://blogs.telegraph.co.uk/damian_thompson/blog/2008/06/26/fight_against_arab_holocaust_denial.

thought on the one hand and good editorial judgment on the other—it is sometimes exceedingly faint, often entirely arbitrary, and always fundamentally subjective. The greater the opportunity for excess in the exercise of the power of the press is, the more profoundly difficult are the consequences in the protection of civil liberties for individuals.

That axiom has been brought into sharp focus by Holocaust deniers, whose goal is both facilitated and confused by the aura of "political correctness," which nowadays surrounds a great deal of editorial decision making. Nowhere is this more pervasive than in academia. What should be the most receptive place for honest intellectual inquiry and discourse has instead become one where all assumptions are open to debate—even documented historical facts. This has had an unsettling effect on students (especially those editing university newspapers) who have long been subjected to the pressures of political correctness. When they become entangled in the black and nefarious thickets of Holocaust denial, their exercise of editorial discretion can be acutely conflicting psychologically and confounding intellectually.

So can the emotional pain suffered by victims of group libel. Remedies for that malady have not been clearly established in American law. Explored least of all is the effect upon a free society when the dissemination of demonstrably false ideas is constitutionally protected. Must writers and speakers who deny the Holocaust be guaranteed equal access to curricula and classrooms? Should the misrepresentation of historical fact be suppressed when it is motivated by nothing more than racial or ethnic animus? Should responsible libraries collect and classify work borne of blatant bigotry? Have survivors been injured when their victimization has been repudiated?

More profoundly, can we reject spurious revisionism or punish purposeful expressions of hatred and still pay homage to the liberty of thought ennobled by the First Amendment? Are some conflicts between freedom of expression and civility as insoluble as they are inevitable? Can history ever be proven as Truth?

This chapter attempts to answer these questions. Part I describes the background and nature of Holocaust denial, tracing the Nazis' adoption of a plan for the "Final Solution of the Jewish Problem" through the postwar Nuremberg Trials to the present day. Part II examines the tension between free speech and historical revisionism, presenting various arguments in deference to principles of liberty and opposed to group defamation. Part III addresses the quest for truth in a free society.

1. Holocaust Denial

> We will show you these concentration camps in motion pictures, just as the Allied armies found them when they arrived. . . . Our proof will be disgusting and you will say I have robbed you of your sleep. . . . I am one who received during this war most atrocity tales with suspicion and skepticism. But the proof here will be so overwhelming that I venture to predict not one word I have spoken will be denied.
>
> Sen. Thomas Dodd (1947)[7]

Both Eisenhower[8] and Dodd seriously understated the possibilities. In recent years, the contention that there was no mass extermination of Jews and no deaths in gas chambers at the hands of the Nazis has given rise to a pervasive (if predictable) revisionist industry. Holocaust denial books have made their way into academic and public libraries across the country and around the world, not to mention widespread dissemination over the Internet.

The Nazis themselves recognized that the sheer incredibility of what they had done would cast shadows of doubt upon any shocking eyewitness reports. Inmates at concentration camps testified that they were frequently taunted by their captors: "Even if some proof should remain and some of you survive, people will say that the events you describe are too monstrous to be believed; they will say that they are the exaggerations of Allied propaganda and will believe us, who will deny everything, and not you."[9]

Indeed, early newspaper accounts of the death camps were obscured by dispatches about the war's progress, if not questioned for their veracity.[10] That is why Eisenhower, after the Nazis were conquered, ordered every American soldier not committed to the front lines to bear witness to places like Auschwitz, Belsen, and Buchenwald.[11] "We are told that the American soldier does not know what he is fighting for," he said. "Now, at least, he will

---

7. Trial of the Major War Criminals Before the International Military Tribunal 2, 130 (1947). Senator Dodd served as the executive counsel to the American prosecutorial team.

8. Chandler, *supra* note 2.

9. Primo Levi, The Drowned and the Saved 11–12 (Raymond Rosenthal trans., 1989).

10. Both the *New York Times* and the *New York Herald Tribune* published limited reports of the camps as early as 1942. *See* Walter Laqueur, The Terrible Secret: Suppression of the Truth about Hitler's "Final Solution" 74, 93 (1980).

11. Robert H. Abzug, Inside the Vicious Heart: Americans and the Liberation of Nazi Concentration Camps 128 (1985).

know what he is fighting against."[12] This likewise explains why the International Military Tribunal at Nuremberg was so intent on documenting all of the atrocities found by the Allied liberators.

Without the past, without memory, without history, we are nothing—adrift. We place our destiny and dignity in the hands of the misfits and their projected psychoses. This movement is not an attack on the Holocaust but on the very notion of historical meaning. It is a revolt against reality, a threat not only to the past but to the future.[13]

1.1 The Nature of Denial

Holocaust deniers argue that the genocide of Jews and other minority groups during World War II either did not occur—that it was a deliberate Jewish hoax—or that it was a conspiracy to advance the interests of Zionism, or that it was greatly exaggerated. They maintain that the Nazi government never had a policy of deliberately targeting Jews, that many fewer than 6 million Jews lost their lives, and that there were no tools of mass extermination such as gas chambers or incinerators in the concentration camps.

Although such denial has been going on ever since the Holocaust occurred, as the years pass and the number of survivors diminishes, it has become more virulent. Many Holocaust deniers reject the term, describing themselves instead as "revisionists." But deniers can be differentiated from revisionists, who consider their goal to be historical inquiry using evidence and established methodology.[14]

1.2 Denial in the Twenty-First Century

There is abundant evidence that Holocaust denial is a global and growing phenomenon.

---

12. *See* Deborah Lipstadt's Blog, *Obama's Auschwitz Mistake [2]*, http://lipstadt.blogspot.com/(last visited Sept. 15, 2009) [hereinafter, Lipstadt, *Obama's Auschwitz Mistake*].

13. French historian Marc Bloch, *quoted in* James S. Robbins, *Adrift in Denial*, NAT'L REV. ONLINE, Dec. 13, 2006, *available at* http://article.nationalreview.com/300883/adrift-on-denial/james-s-robbins.

14. Holocaust deniers, on the other hand, argue that the Holocaust did not occur regardless of historical evidence. *See* DEBORAH E. LIPSTADT, DENYING THE HOLOCAUST: THE GROWING ASSAULT ON TRUTH AND MEMORY 183–208 (1993).

According to the Wyman Institute for Holocaust Studies, denial activity has substantially increased worldwide, following a temporary lull in 2006, possibly caused by the imprisonment in Austria of the revisionists' best-known figure, the British historian David Irving and the prosecution of the prominent activists Ernst Zundel and Gemar Rudolf in Germany.

Irving had been arrested while visiting Austria in November 2005 and prosecuted for speeches he had delivered in Austria in 1989. The appeals judge, Ernest Maurer, said the sentence should be reduced because the offending statements were made "a long time ago, 17 years," and because the judge did not expect Irving would repeat the crime.[15] But in January of 2007, Irving returned to the lecture circuit. He said in an interview on Italian television that Auschwitz "was a tourist attraction [which] did not have gas chambers." Two months later, in Budapest, he was promoting the Hungarian-language edition of his new book, which alleges that the defendants at the Nuremberg Trials did not receive fair ones.[16] In November, Irving spoke at the Oxford University Union debating society's Free Speech Forum.[17]

Zundel was born in Germany and lived in Canada from 1958 until 2005, when he was deported because of his Holocaust denial activity. That activity included hosting radio and television shows, publishing books and pamphlets, and managing a Web site.[18] In February of 2007, a German court sentenced Zundel to five years in jail; the country's highest appeals court upheld the conviction.[19]

Rudolf went on trial in a Mannheim court for denying the Holocaust. Rudolf had written an article in 1991 claiming the Nazis did not gas Jews in Auschwitz and was sentenced to fourteen months in prison in 1995. He fled Germany to avoid jail and sought political asylum in the United States. That request was rejected, and Rudolf was sent back to Germany in November

---

15. *See* Rafael Medoff & Alex Grobman, *Holocaust Denial: A Global Survey—2006*, Wyman Institute for Holocaust Studies, http://www.wymaninstitute.org/articles/HolocaustDenial2006.pdf. [hereinafter, Wyman 2006].

16. *See* Rafael Medoff & Alex Grobman, *Holocaust Denial: A Global Survey—2007*, Wyman Institute for Holocaust Studies, http://www.wymaninstitute.org/articles/HolocaustDenial2007.pdf. [hereinafter, Wyman 2007].

17. *See* "British Officials Boycott Oxford Debating Society over Speaking Invitation to Holocaust Denier," Associated Press, November 20, 2007.

18. Wyman 2006, *supra* note 15.

19. Wyman 2007, *supra* note 16.

2005 to serve his original sentence. During the trial's opening session, Rudolf declared that the Holocaust was "a gigantic fraud."[20]

Revisionists have also taken to late-night public-access television to assert that claims of Nazi genocide against the Jews during World War II are part of an elaborate hoax. Slickly produced videos purport to show that concentration camps like Auschwitz and Birkenau were recreational facilities, not death camps.[21] Holocaust deniers claim that archival materials concerning Nazi atrocities—voluminously detailed lists of victims, miles of gruesome film footage, and vividly remembered accounts of eyewitnesses—have all been forged.[22]

Meanwhile, as use of the Internet has burgeoned, its millions of subscribers provide a vast new target audience for the efforts of numerous hate groups. Catering to white supremacists, antigovernment survivalists, militiamen, and would-be terrorists, Holocaust deniers have set up enough new sites on the World Wide Web to reach a larger potential constituency than any revolutionaries in history.[23]

In recent years, incidents of Holocaust denial have proliferated around the world. In Australia, an Islamic cleric named Sheik Taj Din al-Hilali called the Holocaust "a Zionist lie." Mel Gibson and his father both support the Australian League of Rights, a group that denies the Holocaust. In Denmark, Al-Jazeera Television broadcast a meeting between Arab and Danish student groups, following the controversy over cartoons about Muhammad. During the meeting, Arab Students Union Chairman Ahmad Al-Shater referred to the Holocaust as "the imaginary Holocaust." In France, George Theil, a 65-year-old former adviser to the extremist National Front Party, was convicted of denying the Holocaust for having said on French Television that the Nazi gas chambers were "a fantasy." Robert Faurisson was convicted by a Paris court in October 2006 of Holocaust denial, after

---

20. *Holocaust denier goes on trial in Germany,* REUTERS, Nov. 14, 2006, http://www.reuters.com/article/idUSL1491246520061114.

21. *See* Alan Dershowitz, *It's Time for a Holocaust Video,* TIMES-UNION, Sept. 4, 1995, at A6.

22. For a detailed analysis of the use of film as evidence of the Holocaust, *see* Lawrence Douglas, *Film as Witness: Screening Nazi Concentration Camps before the Nuremberg Tribunal,* 105 YALE L.J. 449 (1995). The principal film described by Douglas also has been used to prove the falsity of Holocaust denials. *See* Leonidas E. Hill, *The Trial of Ernst Zundel and the Law in Canada,* 6 SIMON WIESENTHAL CENTER ANN. 165, 184 (1989).

23. *See* Greg Beck, *Hate War's New Battleground: The Internet,* SAN FRANCISCO EXAMINER, June 10, 1996, at A1; *see generally* Michael Shermer, *Proving the Holocaust,* 2 SKEPTIC 32 (1994).

he said on Iranian Television that no gas chambers were used by the Germans to kill Jews.[24]

Holocaust denial in the United States is not a popular phenomenon, even though America remains the lone Western democracy to protect it as free speech. But it does occur. In January of 2006, Sheik Fadhel as Sahlani, the leader of a prominent mosque in Brooklyn, asserted that the Holocaust "has been exaggerated." In April, Holocaust denier Larry Darby, a candidate for the Democratic nomination for attorney general of Alabama, was a featured speaker at a conference organized by the neo-Nazi National Vanguard in Elmwood Park, New Jersey. (The event included a performance by the neo-Nazi Holocaust-denying teenage singing duo "Prussian Blue.") In June, Darby won 44 percent of the vote in the Alabama race. Darby claims the figure of 6 million Jews murdered by the Nazis was concocted by "the Holocaust industry," insisting that no more than 140,000 Jews were killed and most of those by Typhus.[25]

The Institute for Historical Review (IHR) held its major event of the year at an unnamed restaurant meeting room in Arlington, Virginia, in July of 2006. IHR Director Mark Weber spoke about "the Jewish Zionist role in determining American foreign policy" and praised the recent study about the "Israel Lobby" by Stephen Walt and John Mearsheimer. Paul Fromm, director of the extremist Canadian Association for Free Expression, focused on the imprisonment of David Irving in Austria and Zundel in Germany.[26]

The summer 2007 issue of *IHR Update*, published by the Institute for Historical Review, included an article by Daniel McGowan, which came to the defense of Zundel, Rudolf, and Faurisson and also claimed that "[t]he Holocaust narrative . . . has been an important tool to drive the United States into Iraq and now into Iran."[27]

1.3 Denial in the Middle East

But all of these were relatively isolated incidents compared to what is happening in the Middle East. Holocaust denial has grown rapidly in Muslim countries, including American allies Egypt, Qatar, and Saudi Arabia—all of which receive significant U.S. economic and military aid. Members of the

24. *See generally* Wyman 2006, *supra* note 15; Wyman 2007, *supra* note 16.

25. *Id.*

26. *Id.*

27. Wyman 2007, *supra* note 16.

Syrian and Iranian governments, as well as Hizbollah and the Palestinian political group, Hamas, openly publish and promote such claims.[28]

In his 1982 doctoral dissertation, Mahmoud Abbas, a cofounder of Fatah and the current president of the Palestinian Authority, wrote: "It seems that the interest of the Zionist movement . . . is to inflate this figure [six million deaths] in order to gain the solidarity of international public opinion . . . . Many scholars have [determined] the number of Jewish victims at only a few hundred thousand." That claim was repeated in Abbas's 1983 book, *The Secret Connection Between the Nazis and the Leaders of the Zionist Movement.*[29]

As Israeli Cabinet Minister Isaac Herzog noted, Abbas's view "is not a matter that can be brushed under the carpet, because at issue is a moral question whose importance cannot be overstated."[30]

Islamic deniers appear to be inflamed by the attention given to Jewish victimization, which in their view has caused them to pay the price for Europe's treatment of the Jews. They thus seek to delegitimize both Europe (pluralistic and tolerant, committed to human rights and human dignity) and Israel (which sees itself as the legacy of the Nazis' victims and the antidote to another Holocaust). They also denigrate any country (especially the United States) where the Holocaust has come to occupy a prominent place in the moral discourse of the people.[31] Abbas is well known for waffling in consideration of the current political situation; in a March 2006 interview with Ha'aretz, Abbas stated: "I have no desire to argue with the figures. The Holocaust was a terrible, unforgivable crime against the Jewish nation, a crime against humanity that cannot be accepted by humankind. The Holocaust was a terrible thing and nobody can claim I denied it."[32] But at a

---

28. *Id.*

29. *See* Rafael Medoff, *A Holocaust-Denier as Prime Minister of Palestine*?, WYMAN INSTITUTE FOR HOLOCAUST STUDIES, Mar. 2003, http://www.wymaninstitute.org/articles/2003-03-denier.php.

30. Edward I. Koch & Rafael Medoff, *What Can Be Done About Holocaust Deniers?* JERUSALEM REPORT, Jan. 8, 2007, *cited in* EDWARD I. KOCH & RAFAEL MEDOFF, THE KOCH PAPERS: MY FIGHT AGAINST ANTI-SEMITISM 210 (2008).

31. Berenbaum suggests that it would be wise for the West to distinguish between Holocaust denial in the Islamic world and that elsewhere. Michael Berenbaum, *Holocaust Denial: Iranian Style,* BRITANNICA BLOG, Apr. 19, 2007, http://www.britannica.com/blogs/2007/04/holocaust-denial-iranian-style/.

32. Akiva Eldar, *Interview with Mahmoud Abbas,* HA'ARETZ, March 30, 2006.

rally in Ramallah in early January of 2007, Abbas said: "The sons of Israel are mentioned [in the Quran] as those who are corrupting humanity on earth."[33]

No such waffling from Ahmadinejad, who has become the world's most visible denier. "As to the Holocaust," he said in a *Time Magazine* interview, "I just raised a few questions. And I didn't receive any answers to my questions. I said that during World War II around 60 million were killed. All were human beings and had their own dignities. Why only six million?" A fair question, perhaps, when taken out of the context in which it was uttered—that Israel is the cause of the world's problems. Here are the official translations of some of Ahmadinejad's other statements:

> "The real cure for the conflict is elimination of the Zionist regime." "The way to peace in the Middle East is the destruction of Israel." "Like it or not, the Zionist regime is heading toward annihilation."[34]

Ahmadinejad's rhetoric was given its first showpiece at his Holocaust denial conference in Tehran in December of 2006. Officially sponsored by the Iranian Foreign Ministry and billed as a "Review of the Holocaust: Global Vision," it was a well-orchestrated group polemic attended by delegates from thirty countries, including former Ku Klux Klan leader David Duke, French revisionists Robert Faurisson and Georges Thiel, and Australian denier Frederick Toben.[35] In addition, several members of the extremist anti-Zionist Jewish sect Neturei Karta were prominently featured participants.[36]

---

33. Jeff Jacoby, *Statehood for Palestine? Take A Good Look*, BOSTON GLOBE, Feb. 14, 2007, at A9, *available at* http://www.boston.com/news/globe/editorial_opinion/oped/articles/2007/02/14/statehood_for_palestine_take_a_good_look/. *See also* Rosie Dimanno, *No Guarantee This "Map" Leads Anywhere*, TORONTO STAR, May 1, 2003, at A10.

34. *See generally* Mark Mazzetti, *Some in G.O.P. Say Iran Threat Is Played Down*, N.Y. TIMES, August 24, 2006, at A1, *available at* http://www.nytimes.com/2006/08/24/washington/24intel.html?pagewanted=print. Later, at a UN conference in Rome, Ahmadinejad said that it would be in the interests of Western Europe if Israel did not exist, and he has blamed the food crisis on Zionists. *See* Lipstadt, *Obama's Auschwitz Mistake*, *supra* note 12.

35. Anti-Defamation League, *Iran Hosts Anti-Semitic Hatefest in Tehran*, Dec. 14, 2006, *available at* http://www.adl.org/main_International_Affairs/iran_holocaust_conference.htm?Multi_page_sections=sHeading_5. In fact, there were several Arab commentators who condemned the conference. *See* Middle East Media Research Institute, *Criticism of Tehran Holocaust Denial Conference in Arab and Iranian Media* Special Dispatch Series—No.1425, Jan. 16, 2007.

36. *Id.* at 35. *See also* Bill Hutchinson, *Rabbi Among the Rabble-Rousers*, N.Y DAILY NEWS, Dec. 13, 2006, at 7.

All of the representatives were said simply to be "exercising their rights of free speech" in questioning the facts of World War II. In so doing, they were treated to an exhibit of photographs of dead Jews labeled "Myth" and "Typhus Victims" and of smiling Holocaust survivors under the heading of "Truth."[37] In addition, the conference enabled the Iranians to score propaganda points about Western hypocrisy—preaching free speech but disallowing "dangerous" views.[38]

In fact, many Holocaust revisionists claim their work falls under a "universal right to free speech" and seek to rely on Article 10 of the European Convention on Human Rights, which guarantees freedom of expression when faced with criminal sanctions against their statements or publications.[39] But the European Court of Human Rights, for one, has consistently declared that such arguments are without merit. According to Article 17, nothing in the convention may be construed so as to justify acts that are aimed at destroying any of the very rights and freedoms contained therein. Invoking free speech to propagate denial of crimes against humanity is, according to the court, contrary to the spirit in which the convention was adopted. Reliance on free speech in such cases would thus constitute an abuse of a fundamental right.[40]

Iran also announced plans to establish an institution to conduct ongoing "research" concerning the Holocaust. Additional support is likely by virtue of the creation of the new English-language division of the Qatari government-funded Al Jazeera television network, which broadcasts remarks by Holocaust deniers.[41]

In an address at Columbia University in September of 2007, Ahmadinejad asked:

> [W]hy is there not sufficient research that can approach the topic from different perspectives? There are researchers who want to push the topic

---

37. *Id.* at 35. *See also* Katrin Bennhold, *Ties Cut With Iran Institute Over Holocaust*, N.Y. TIMES, Sep. 16, 2006, at A9.

38. James S. Robbins, *Adrift on Denial: The Threat from Iran*, NAT'L REV., Dec. 13, 2006 ("[n]ot that speech in Iran is particularly free—I am waiting for the conference that brings together those who deny the divinity of the Koran.").

39. *See* D. D. Guttenplan, *Should Freedom of Speech Stop at Holocaust Denial?* INDEX OF FREE EXPRESSION 2005.

40. *Id.*

41. Wyman 2006, *supra* note 15.

> from a different perspective. Why are they put into prison? . . . My question is, why isn't it open to all forms of research? . . . Why don't we encourage more research on a historical event that has become the root, the cause of many heavy catastrophes in the region in this time and age? . . . If it is a reality, we need to still question whether the Palestinian people should be paying for it or not. . . .[42]

In October of 2007, Ahmadinejad made the following assertions on Iranian television:

> The leaders of several Western superpowers comprise the Zionist party. They are the ones who pull the strings. They created something called Zionism, and invented the so-called "oppression" of the Jews. They themselves created the background for this, and today as well, it is they who are running the show. . . . After World War II, they invented the so-called "genocide of the Jews." . . . By means of propaganda and a certain psychological atmosphere, and by using the issue of the so-called "crematoria," they created the sense that the European Jews were oppressed. They used the pretext that some Jews were oppressed and were harmed during World War II and by the wave of anti-Judaism in order to lay the foundations for the establishment of the Zionist regime.[43]

In September of 2009, prior to his appearance at the opening of the 64th General Assembly of the United Nations, Ahmadinejad once again stoked the fires by repeating his belief that the Holocaust was a myth. He questioned whether the Holocaust was "a real event," calling it instead a pretext used by Jews to trick the West into backing the creation of Israel. The Jewish state, he said, was created out of "a lie and a mythical claim."[44] He appeared to relish the controversy. Asked about widespread condemnation of such remarks, he replied, "The anger of the world's professional killers is (a source of) pride for us."[45]

---

42. Wyman 2007, *supra* note 16.

43. *Id.*

44. *See* Nasser Karimi & Lee Keath, *Ahmadinejad: Holocaust Denial A Source of Pride*, HUFFINGTON POST, Sept. 21, 2009, http://www.huffingtonpost.com/2009/09/21/ahmadinejad-holocaust-den_n_293083.html.

45. *Id.*

Shortly thereafter, Israel's Prime Minister, Binyamin Netanyahu, responded with his own speech before the UN Holding aloft a copy of Hitler's plan for a "Final Solution" to the Jewish problem—the detailed minutes of the infamous Wannsee Conference on January 20, 1942, in which the Nazis issued precise instructions on how to carry out the extermination of the Jews—he asked, "Is this a lie?" With the original construction blueprints for the Auschwitz-Birkenau concentration camp in his hand, he asked, "Is this too a lie?" Netanyahu recalled the agreement within the UN to create the Jewish state and expressed astonishment at what he had witnessed a day earlier in that organization's great hall. He commended those who boycotted Ahmadinejad's speech but condemned those who allowed it, scolding the UN for giving the Iranian president "legitimacy" just six decades after the Nazi scourge. "To those who gave this Holocaust denier a hearing, I say on behalf of my people: Have you no shame? Have you no decency? What a disgrace," Netanyahu said. "What a mockery of the charter of the United Nations."[46]

Meanwhile, back in Israel, denial has become part of the Palestinian landscape. A public opinion poll conducted by Haifa University in March of 2007 found that 28 percent of Israeli Arab citizens "say they do not believe the Nazi genocide took place." Among younger Israeli Arabs, the percentage was higher: 33 percent of Israeli Arabs of school age deny the Holocaust.[47]

Later that year, the Arab Institute for Holocaust Research and Education, a museum in Nazareth that teaches Israeli Arabs about the Holocaust, compared Israel's policies to those of the Nazis. According to the Jewish Telegraphic Agency (JTA), the museum "juxtaposes the Holocaust with the Israeli-Palestinian conflict by placing pictures of Nazis threatening or killing Jews next to pictures of Palestinian refugees, Palestinian victims of violence and the Palestinian flag." The JTA quoted several teenage Israeli-Arab visitors to the museum as saying, "[t]he Jews are doing the same that was done to them."[48]

Such perceptions, as one might suspect, are nurtured by Palestinian leadership. A new series of Palestinian Authority schoolbooks describe a World War II without the Holocaust. Instead, they teach about the "race theory" of the Nazi movement and even mention the trials of Nazi war

---

46. For a video and full text of Netanyahu's speech, *see* http://www.examiner.com/x-12837-US-Headlines-Examiner~y2009m9d25-Netanyahu-speech-at-UN-General-Assembly-counters-claims-regarding-Holocaust-by-Ahmadinejad—video.

47. Wyman 2007, *supra* note 16.

48. *Id.*

criminals at the end of the war, but they don't teach why they were on trial. The Palestinian Authority's official radio station, Voice of Palestine, aired a quiz that depicted the life of Adolf Hitler in a favorable light and omitted any mention of the Holocaust.[49]

In the countries bordering Israel, denial is no less visible. For instance, in October of 2007, Lebanese television aired a program on drug abuse that included this statement:

> Drugs were the Jews' method of wearing down the German people, which led to the Nazi extremism, in which the Jews themselves played a role. In addition, they carried out widespread drug dealing in Czarist Russia, from the 17th century. This was in accordance with the Jewish Talmud, which says that the Jews must devote their greatest efforts to prevent other nations from ruling the land, so that the rule would be in the hands of the Jews alone.[50]

1.4 Confronting Denial

In January of 2007, the United Nations General Assembly passed a resolution (to coincide with International Holocaust Commemoration Day) condemning Holocaust denial. The resolution—passed by general consensus, with only Iran explicitly dissenting—called on all 192 UN member states to "unreservedly reject any denial of the Holocaust as a historical event, either in full or in part, or any activities to this end."[51] UN Secretary-General Ban Ki-moon expressed "his strong desire to see this fundamental principle respected both in rhetoric and in practice."[52] In October, the United Nations Educational, Scientific, and Cultural Organization (UNESCO) passed a resolution urging efforts to promote Holocaust education and combat Holocaust denial. Seventy-two UNESCO member states cosponsored the resolution. Egypt and other Arab states, and also Iran, attempted to change the wording of the resolution but were unsuccessful.[53]

---

49. *Id.*

50. *Id.*

51. Judy Aita, *United Nations Condemns Denial of the Holocaust*, AMERICA.GOV, Jan. 26, 2007, *available at* http://www.america.gov/st/washfileenglish/2007/January/20070126160123eaifas0.887356.html.

52. *Id.*

53. State Department news release, Nov. 4, 2007; Roth Institute for the Study of Contemporary Anti-Semitism and Racism, Tel Aviv University.

There were also several hopeful developments: two prominent Muslims, the former prime minister of Indonesia and the president of the Islamic Society of North America, both condemned Holocaust denial; the United Nations General Assembly and UNESCO both passed resolutions opposing Holocaust denial; and the European Union urged all its member states to adopt legislation prohibiting Holocaust denial.

1.5 The Academic Voice

The gradual ascension of Holocaust revisionism into academic respectability is perhaps shocking only to those unfamiliar with the excesses of modern scholarship.[54] Group defamation in the academic voice persists to this day, most notoriously in the form of the infamous "blood libels," which claim that Jews kill Christian children for ritual purposes. Such myths are occasionally aided and abetted by "historical" accounts (not one of which has ever been buttressed by facts).[55]

Over time, in high schools and colleges across the United States, a number of teachers have come to tell their students that the Holocaust was a myth, while professors write "scholarly" articles, and school newspapers print denial advertisement/essays saying the same thing.[56] By 1995, the Anti-Defamation League had reported numerous incidents on American campuses concerning Holocaust denial.[57]

In recent years, one of the difficult decisions facing college or university newspapers has involved the controversial question of whether to publish a paid advertisement denying the existence of the Holocaust.[58] Most of these

---

54. *See* Kenneth Lasson, Trembling in the Ivory Tower: Excesses in the Pursuit of Truth and Tenure (2003).

55. The most famous of the modern blood libels is *The Protocols of the Elders of Zion*, first published in Russia in 1905 and still in widespread circulation today. A detailed account of the book's evolution is on display at the United States Holocaust Museum in Washington, D.C. Three new books on Jewish ritual killings have been published in the past year by Jewish scholars themselves. *See* Hillel Halkin, *Bloody Jews?*, Commentary, May 2007, *available at* http://www.commentarymagazine.com/viewarticle.cfm/bloody-jews—10873?search=1; David Abulafia, *The Blood Libel, Then and Now*, Times Literary Supp., Mar. 2, 2007.

56. *See generally* Kenneth S. Stern, Holocaust Denial (1993).

57. *See Anti- Defamation League Audit of Anti-Semitic Incidents 1995*, U.S. Newswire, Feb. 28, 1996, *available at* LEXIS, USNWR File [hereinafter ADL Audit].

58. *See* Bob Keeler, *Assault on History*, Newsday, Feb. 24, 1994, at 68. *See generally* Lipstadt, *supra* note 14, at 183–208.

advertisements are promulgated and paid for by the Committee for Open Debate on the Holocaust, which claims to "encourage scholarly discussion about the Holocaust."[59] In the 1980s, this committee began to place small notices in college newspapers with its address and telephone number. By the 1990s, these paid advertisements had become long essays, written in the academic voice, arguing that Holocaust statistics were vastly overstated and that allegations of Nazi gas chambers were frauds aided by doctored photographs.[60]

A private college or university newspaper is not a state actor (and therefore not protected by First Amendment guarantees), but is subject to the scrutiny of school administrators and bound by school policies. Although most colleges and universities adopt policies that are compatible with expressing and testing new ideas, they retain the power to impose prior restraints that could prohibit publication of certain material based on its content.

The primary issue to be determined in cases involving a state-supported college or university newspaper is whether school administrators are involved in the editorial decisions of the student paper. Where the newspaper is free from the control of the administration, its actions are viewed as being independent of the state and not subject to constitutional scrutiny. It follows in such cases that there has been no state action where an author of proffered material is denied access to the paper based on the material's content.

In short, the campus newspaper of a state-supported university is entitled to the First Amendment's freedom of the press protection—including the freedom to exercise subjective editorial discretion by rejecting a proffered article, editorial, or advertisement.[61] Thus, editors of a state college or university newspaper have a right to editorial discretion, and school administrators do not.

1.6 Books

Many of the Holocaust denial books are published by the so-called Institute for Historical Review, a once-obscure revisionist think tank which also

59. *See* Jeff Ristine, *Ad Questioning Holocaust Takes Aim at Students*, SAN DIEGO UNION-TRIBUNE, Jan. 11, 1992, at A1. *See also* LIPSTADT, *supra* note 14, at 183–208; *see* Leon Jeroff, *Debating the Holocaust*, TIME, Dec. 27, 1993, at 83.

60. *See* LIPSTADT, *supra* note 14, at 183–208. Some campus papers published the advertisements on free speech grounds, while others refused to do so. Apparently in response to Smith's campaign, classes on the Holocaust have been increasing. *Id.*

61. *See* Associates & Aldrich Co. v. Time Mirror Co., 440 F.2d 133, 135 (9th Cir. 1971).

produces a glossy periodical called the *Journal of Historical Review.*[62] The institute was founded by a notorious anti-Semite, Willis Carto,[63] and for years operated out of Newport Beach, California, and was headed by a nonacademic named Bradley Smith.[64] Among its most popular tracts are *The Hoax of the Twentieth Century*[65] by Northwestern University Professor Arthur Butz and *Debunking the Genocide Myth*[66] by Paul Rassinier. Both present the now-familiar argument that reports of the systematic killing of Jews in Nazi concentration camps were myths propagated by Zionists in an effort to create support for a Jewish State in Palestine.[67]

1.7 Holocaust Denial and Political Correctness

Political correctness may be on the run in the pop culture of talk radio, but it is no laughing matter in the Ivory Tower. Though scarcely reported by the media, hundreds of American colleges and universities—from the backwoods of Appalachia to the august quadrangles of Ivy League law

62. A self-described "historical revisionist society," the Institute for Historical Review supports the idea that the Holocaust was a distortion of history. *See* ENCYCLOPEDIA OF ASSOCIATIONS 1, 9 (Sandra Joszczak ed., 31st ed. 1996); *see also* LIPSTADT, *supra* note 14, at 105; Geri J. Yonover, *Anti-Semitism and Holocaust Denial in the Academy: A Tort Remedy*, 101 DICK. L. REV. 71, 76 n. 30 (1996).

63. *See* Doreen Carvajal, *Extremist Institute Mired in Power Struggle*, L.A. TIMES, May 15, 1994, at A3, *available at* http://articles.latimes.com/1994-05-15/news/mn-57997_1_staff-member. Carto had already organized the Liberty Lobby, a Washington-based group considered to be one of the most active anti-Semitic organizations in the country. *Id.*

64. See LIPSTADT, *supra* note 14, at 185; *ADL Report Reveals Split in Holocaust Denial Movement that is as Hateful as Their Anti-Semitic Propaganda*, BUSINESS WIRE, *available at* LEXIS; National Brief, HOUSTON CHRON., Jan. 25, 1992, at A12, *available at* http://www.chron.com/CDA/archives/archive.mpl/1992_1032765/national-briefs.html.

65. ARTHUR BUTZ, THE HOAX OF THE TWENTIETH CENTURY (1976). Noontide Press and the Institute for Historical Review are closely related. *See* LIPSTADT, *supra* note 14, at 152–53; *see also* Liberty Lobby, Inc. v. Dow Jones & Co., Inc., 838 F.2d 1287, 1296 (Bork, J.) (D.C. Cir. 1988) (describing the relationship as the "Liberty Lobby/Legion/Noontide/IHR network"). In 2006, Butz, a tenured professor of electrical engineering at Northwestern, wrote a column in the campus newspaper expressing support for the Holocaust denial activities of Iranian President Mahmoud Ahmadinejad. *See* Jodi S. Cohen, *NU Rips Holocaust Denial, President Calls Prof an Embarrassment but Plans No Penalty*, CHICAGO TRIB., Feb. 7, 2006.

66. PAUL RASSINIER, DEBUNKING THE GENOCIDE MYTH (1978); *see also* LIPSTADT, *supra* note 14, at 51–64.

67. *See* Donna Prokop, *Note, Controversial Teacher Speech: Striking A Balance Between First Amendment Rights and Educational Interests,* 66 S. CAL. L. REV. 2534, 2564 (1993). *See also* LIPSTADT, supra note 14, at 123–36, 51–65.

schools—are currently engaged in an entrenched battle over both the nature of the standard curriculum and the freedom of speech on campus.[68]

Fifty years ago, when the Holocaust was still a new and searing cataclysmic event, the bramble bush of political correctness was mere stubble in the wasteland of academic politics. Now, universities are pushing various political correctness agendas by way of curricular reform and the promulgation of speech and conduct codes. Orthodoxies of all kinds are being challenged. Eurocentric doctrine (including that of modern Jewish history) is subjected to "deconstruction," with the underlying theory that all opinions are valid. Facts are said to be nothing more than received opinions. This phenomenon has enabled Holocaust deniers to elevate their cause into the realm of academic debate.

Thus, when American adults were asked in 1993 if they thought it possible that the Holocaust never really ever happened, 20 percent of them answered in the affirmative.[69] Almost fifteen years later, a Haifa University survey found that more than a quarter of Israel's Arab citizens believed the Holocaust never happened; the percentage rose to a third for college and high school graduates.[70]

Such a response is not the concern of constitutional scholars, whose abiding interest in political correctness has always been the stifling effect on civil liberties and academic freedom of the restrictive speech and conduct codes that have become commonplace in the Ivory Tower.[71] Even though not one such code has been able to withstand constitutional scrutiny, both students and professors (as well as administrators) look and listen nervously over their shoulders for fear of offending mushrooming numbers of special interest groups.[72]

---

68. *See* Jenish D'Arcy & William Lowther, *War of Words: Academics Clash Over "Correctness,"* MACLEAN'S, May 27, 1991, at 44.

69. Deborah Lipstadt, *False "Reasoning" on the Holocaust,* NEWSDAY, July 23, 1993, at 61.

70. Poll Shows Israeli-Arab Holocaust Denial, Support for Hizbullah, ISRAEL FAXX, Mar. 19, 2007; Holocaust Denial, ISRAEL FAXX, Mar. 30, 2007.

71. *See* Robert Hawkins, *Some Imprints Left as 1991 Fades. . . Art-Censorship Battles Loom as Pressure Increasing From All Viewpoints,* SAN DIEGO UNION-TRIBUNE, Dec. 27, 1991, at C1.

72. *See generally* Kenneth Lasson, *Political Correctness Askew: Excesses in the Pursuit of Minds and Manners,* 63 TENN. L. REV. 689 (1996). The pernicious nature of political correctness is most clearly revealed by the absurd extremes encouraged by some campus conduct codes. Though many of them have never been tested in court and continue to be broadly implemented—some to the destruction of careers and reputations—not one of them to date has been found constitutional. *See* Kenneth Lasson, Trembling in the Ivory Tower (Bancroft Press, 2003).

What the Founding Fathers envisioned as vigorous disagreement in a free and open marketplace of ideas—even if some of those thoughts are abhorrent to the civil temperament—has been quashed at the very places that such debates are supposed to occur most freely.[73] What should be one of the richest and most receptive places of honest intellectual inquiry and discourse has instead become one of the most intolerant. The university has become a decidedly unwelcome nesting place for people with traditional points of view or ways of presenting them. What were once noble and defensible goals—intellectual curiosity and sensitivity toward others—have been forged into bludgeons of moral imperatives.[74]

In an academic environment charged with political correctness, the choice of campus speakers appears to be highly subjective. In the 1990s, noted figures who have uttered anti-Semitic words—Louis Farrakhan,[75] Tony Martin,[76] Khalid Abdul Muhammad,[77] and

---

73. *See* Stephen Reese & John D.H. Downing, *Holocaust Ad Poisons Public Debate*, AUSTIN-AMERICAN STATESMAN, May 1, 1992, at 1.

74. The rules regarding harassment have iced over into the first icy patch on the slippery slope to repression of unpopular ideas. They deter not only genuine misconduct but also harmless (and even desirable) speech, which in higher education is central both to the purpose of the institution and to the employee's profession and performance. Legislative remedies should not be necessary, but they are. In 1993, California saw fit to enact a new law guaranteeing "students. . . the same right to exercise their free speech on campus as they enjoy when off campus." CAL. [Schools and School Districts] CODE § 4(b) (West 1997). The clear line to be drawn between academic freedom and actionable harassment is the same as that between speech and conduct. The former is almost always protected by the First Amendment; the latter can be constitutionally proscribed.

75. *See ADL Quotes Farrakhan One Year After Million-Man March*, U.S. NEWSWIRE, Oct. 9, 1996; Richard Cohen, *Why the Silence on Farrakhan*, WASH. POST, July 26, 1985, at A25; *The Farrakhan Show*, WASH. POST, Aug. 1, 1984, *available at* 1984 WL 2024765; Garry Wills, *Perot's Anti-Semitic Company*, TIMES-UNION, Aug. 15, 1996, at A15.

76. *See* Ken Ringle, Of History and Politics: A Classicist at War, INT'L HERALD TRIB., June 12, 1996; Text of ADL Report on Writings of Professor Tony Martin, U.S. NEWSWIRE, Oct. 12, 1995; *see also* Selwyn R. Cudjoe, *Academic Responsibility and Black Scholars*, BALTIMORE SUN, Mar. 23, 1994, at 19A.

77. *See* Nat Hentoff, *The Return of Khalid Muhammad: "Hitler Used the Same Words About Jews,"* THE VILLAGE VOICE, Nov. 26, 1996, at 10 (*quoting* Jesse Jackson's characterization of Khalid Muhammad's Kean College speech as "racist, anti-Semitic, divisive, untrue, and chilling"); Stephen A. Holmes, *Farrakhan Is Warned Over Aide's Invective*, N.Y. TIMES, Jan. 25, 1994, at A12; Jon Nordheimer, *Divided by a Diatribe: College Speech Ignites Furor Over Race*, N.Y. TIMES, Dec. 29, 1993, at B1, *available at* http://www.nytimes.com/1993/12/29/nyregion/divided-by-a-diatribe-college-speech-ignites-furor-over-race.html?pagewanted=1; Steven Lubet, *That's Funny, You Don't Look Like You Control the Government: The Sixth Circuit's Narrative on Jewish Power*, 45 HASTINGS L.J. 1527, 1527–28 (1994); *Speech: "The Secret Relationship Between Blacks and Jews,"* N.J. L.J., Jan. 24, 1994, at 17 (entire text of Khalid Muhammad's Kean College speech).

Leonard Jeffries[78]—were regularly invited by student groups to appear on protected campus venues. When challenged, the sponsors often claim that they and their guests are exercising their First Amendment rights, the same argument that was used to justify the Holocaust denial conference in Iran in 2006.[79]

The pervasive atmosphere of the political correctness current in the university today complicates the question of Holocaust revisionism. In seeking to challenge traditional culture, the guardians of political correctness have been tellingly inconsistent. While they would be quick to condemn a historian who denied the evils of slavery, they have been reluctant to spurn Holocaust denial. Perhaps this is because their agenda is essentially anti-Western, anti-white, and anti-imperialist; Jews are not viewed as an endangered minority; Zionism is seen not as a liberation movement but as racism.[80]

Pressure to be politically correct has generated a backlash against political correctness as well. The combination of the two has had an unsettling effect on student editors. Can those who would voice alarm at the modern political correctness movement's exclusion of Eurocentric culture at the same time call for exclusion of revisionists and deniers? Students might find it difficult to condemn both the excesses of political correctness and the promulgation of Holocaust denial literature. Here, after all, is where two principles—the freedom of speech in the quest for truth and the suppression of racism in the quest for equality—are sometimes in conflict.

2. Historical Aspects of Free Expression: Framers and Revisionists

> If by the liberty of the press, we understand merely the liberty of discussing the propriety of public measures and political opinions, let us have as

78. *See* ADL Audit, *supra* note 57; Joseph Berger, *College Chief Calls Jeffries "Racist," But Defends Keeping Him*, N.Y. TIMES, Nov. 5, 1991, at B1; Prokop, *supra* note 67, at 2536; Jacques Steinberg, *CUNY Professor Criticizes Jews*, N.Y. TIMES, Aug. 6, 1991, at B3; Wills, *supra* note 75. *See also* Yonover, *supra* note 62, at 83 n. 75.

79. *See, e.g.*, Michael W. Sasser, *Speakers Find Cozy Home at Universities*, PALM BEACH JEWISH J., July 23, 1996, at 1.

80. Some teachers have dropped references to the Holocaust studies altogether, so as to avoid offending children of certain races or religions. *See* Alexandra Frean, *Schools Drop Holocaust Lessons To Avoid Offence*, THE TIMES (London), April 2, 2007, at 8, *available at* http://www.timesonline.co.uk/tol/news/uk/education/article1600686.ece. *See also* Abraham Cooper & Harold Brackman, *You Can't Teach History Without The Holocaust*, GLOBE & MAIL (Canada), Apr. 16, 2007, at A13.

much of it as you please; but, if it means the liberty of affronting, calumniating, and defaming one another, I own myself willing to part with my share of it whenever our legislators shall please to alter the law; and shall cheerfully consent to exchange my liberty of abusing others for the privilege of not being abused myself.

Benjamin Franklin[81]

2.1 Principles of Liberty

Franklin's view may have been civil and proper, but the Founding Fathers were motivated by a much more libertarian philosophy when they drafted the Bill of Rights.[82] The First Amendment not only protects the media from government interference but grants the press almost absolute power to print whatever it wishes.[83] Freedom of the press, often characterized as "the mother of all our liberties,"[84] had "little or nothing to do with truth-telling.... Most of the early newspapers were partisan sheets devoted to attacks on political opponents. . . ." Back then, freedom of the press meant "the right to be just or unjust, partisan or non-partisan, true or false, in news column or editorial column."[85] That same freedom also allows newspapers to reject any matter, editorial or advertising.

Constitutional interpretation often begins with speculation about the intent of the Founding Fathers.[86] As to the First Amendment, much has been

---

81. BENJAMIN FRANKLIN, FEDERAL GAZETTE (Phil.), Sept. 12, 1789, at 2.

82. *See e.g.*, Jeffrey A. Smith, *Prior Restraint: Original Intentions and Modern Interpretations,* 28 WM. & MARY L. REV. 439, 457–58 (1987).

83. "Congress shall make no law . . . abridging the freedom of speech, or of the press." U.S. Const. Amend. I.

84. Adlai E. Stevenson, *The One-Party Press, in* THE PAPERS OF ADLAI E. STEVENSON 75, 78 vol. 4 (Walter Johnson ed., vol.4, 1974) ("The free press is the mother of all our liberties and of our progress under liberty."). *See also* Junius, *Dedication to the English Nation* (1772), *in* THE LETTERS OF JUNIUS 7, 8–9 (John Cannon ed., 1978) ("Let it be impressed upon your minds, let it be instilled into your children, that the liberty of the press is the palladium of all the civil, political, and religious rights . . . ."); Edmund Randolph, *Essay on the Revolutionary History of Virginia, reprinted in* 44 VA. MAG. OF HIST. & BIOGRAPHY 43, 46 (1936) (stating that freedom of the press was one of "the fruits of genuine democracy and historical experience[.]").

85. Charles Beard, *St. Louis Post-Dispatch Symposium on Freedom of the Press* 13 (1938) *quoted in* COMMISSION ON FREEDOM OF THE PRESS, A FREE AND RESPONSIBLE PRESS 131 (1947).

86. The ideas expressed in this section were originally presented in Kenneth Lasson, *Group Libel Versus Free Speech: When Big Brother Should Butt In,* 23 DUQUESNE L. REV. 77, 97–101 (1984).

made of Thomas Jefferson's libertarian perspective on free speech: the best way to deal with error is to permit its correction by truth.[87] "The bar of public reason,"[88] said Jefferson, "will generally provide the remedy for abuses occasioned by the unfettered dissemination of information. Only when security and peace are threatened should the discussion of political, economic, and social affairs be restrained."[89] James Madison, often called the architect of the Bill of Rights, thought likewise: freedom of speech and press, he wrote in *The Federalist*, would engender a reasoned citizenry that would, in turn, keep the government in check.[90]

It can also be argued that the Framers would not have wanted to protect racial defamation, which deliberately exacerbates group tensions and plays negatively upon the heterogeneous, pluralistic character of American society.[91] The goal of casting contempt on an ethnic group is not to participate in political debate founded on the principle of pluralism but to destroy it. In this sense, racial defamation is subversive speech. Unlike political extremism in which (however distorted its form) the Framers' principle of self-government is evident, the principle underlying racial defamation is pure-form discrimination.[92]

---

87. *See, e.g.*, WILLIAM O. DOUGLAS, AN ALMANAC OF LIBERTY 362 (1954) and David N. Mayer, THE CONSTITUTIONAL THOUGHT OF THOMAS JEFFERSON 166–84 (1994).

88. Thomas Jefferson, *First Inaugural Address* (Mar. 4, 1801), *in* THE LIFE AND SELECTED WRITINGS OF THOMAS JEFFERSON 297, 300 (Adrienne Koch & William Peden eds.,1993).

89. *See* Douglas, *supra* note 87, at 362. Justice Douglas naturally interpreted Jefferson's meaning as in accord with his own absolutist stance. But the argument made by the state in favor of any given abridgment of speech is always that social peace and security is being threatened.

90. John Finnis, "Reason and Passion": The Constitutional Dialectic of Free Speech and Obscenity, 116 U. PA. L. REV. 222, 229 (1967). *See also* David A. Anderson, *The Origins of the Press Clause*, 30 U.C.L.A. L. REV. 455 (1983).

91. The stirring up of racial or ethnic "fears, hate, guilt and greed" is fundamentally opposed to the Framer's intent to ensure cooperative social pluralism. DERRICK A. BELL, RACE, RACISM AND AMERICAN LAW 59 (1973).

92. The positive intent of the Framers to found a nation based on pluralism should not, therefore, be distorted to tolerate the free rein of vindictive attack, which is unrelated, except in appearance, to any constitutional or national purpose. *See, e.g.*, BENJAMIN R. EPSTEIN & ARNOLD FORSTER, THE RADICAL RIGHT 40 (1967); Brendan F. Brown, *Racialism and the Rights of Nations*, 21 NOTRE DAME L. REV. 1, 13 (1945). Note also that invidious racial and ethnic discrimination has been rejected as antithetical to American national policy. *See* Bob Jones Univ. v. United States, 461 U.S. 574 (1983).

Other historians, however, conclude that there was no clear "intent" underlying the First Amendment.[93] Rather, the Framers perceived issues of individual rights as concerns to be addressed not by the newly established general government but by the respective states. In fact, not all freedoms were easily recognized by the drafters of the Constitution. On the final day of the Constitutional Convention, for example, a provision that "the liberty of the Press should inviolably be observed" was proposed but was promptly voted down because (said the delegates), "it is unnecessary—the power of Congress does not extend to the Press."[94] Eventually, say some historians, the Bill of Rights was adopted less as an additional guarantor of liberty[95] than as a bargaining chip to procure state ratification.[96]

Thus, one should not expect that understanding the intent of the Framers will resolve the question of precisely what they sought to protect by the First Amendment. There appears to have been no extensive carefully considered debate on the subject of individual freedom.

For some constitutional scholars, the principle of self-government sufficiently identifies the parameters of the First Amendment: Congress is forbidden from abridging the freedom of a citizen's speech whenever it has anything to do with political, economic, and social issues.[97] Put more succinctly, the Founding Fathers envisioned "the free and robust exchange of ideas and political debate."[98] The federal-state system of checks and balances was devised to prevent government tyranny.[99] Similarly, the various guarantees of the Bill of Rights effectively prevent a "tyranny of opinion" from being concentrated in any one institution or person and serve to ensure social,

---

93. *See* JAMES MACGREGOR BURNS, THE VINEYARD OF LIBERTY 60–62 (1982); Lillian R. BeVier, *The First Amendment and Political Speech: An Inquiry Into the Substance and Limits of Principle*, 30 STAN. L. REV. 299 (1978); Franklyn S. Haiman, *How Much of Our Speech Is Free?*, 2 CIV. LIB. REV. 111, 113 (1975).

94. Burns, *supra* note 93, at 62, 539–40.

95. Jefferson *supra* note 88, at 403, 405 (quoting from a letter to James Madison, Dec. 20, 1787, "a bill of rights is what the people are entitled to against every government on earth, general or particular").

96. Burns, *supra* note 93, at 542–43; *see also* Alexander Meiklejohn, *The First Amendment is an Absolute*, 1961 SUP. CT. REV. 245, 264.

97. *See* Meiklejohn, *supra* note 96, at 255. To Meiklejohn, the goal appears to be the acquisition by voters of "intelligence, integrity, sensitivity, and generous devotion to the general welfare"—a weighty purpose indeed for speech to play.

98. Miller v. California, 413 U.S. 15, 34 (1973); *see also* Finnis, *supra* note 90, at 238.

99. Burns, *supra* note 93, at 60–61.

political, and religious pluralism; it should be virtually impossible for popular self-government to be defeated by consolidation of control.[100] The Framers may have perceived government to be a necessary evil,[101] but it is probably more accurate to suggest that they drafted the Constitution to make the cooperation of competing interests the price for protecting the liberty of each. The guarantee of free speech enabled the citizens to express their will to a representative government.[102] Thus, the narrowest historical interpretation of the free speech clause would limit its protection to the expression of purely political ideas.[103] The broadest interpretation would allow for an absolutist intent on the part of the Framers. The Supreme Court, however, has adopted neither extreme. Instead, it has identified political speech as merely the central value to be protected. Such an evaluation logically requires a consideration of content: that is, what the speaker wants to say.[104]

The Founding Fathers' debate on the First Amendment was brief, for they recognized that the rights of free expression were inherent and belonged to the people.[105] "There are rights," wrote Thomas Jefferson in March of 1789, "which it is useless to surrender to the government, and which yet, governments have always been fond to invade. These are the rights of thinking and

---

100. *Id.*

101. *See* PETER USTINOV, MY RUSSIA 204, 209 (1983).

102. The free speech guarantee is thus a means to the end, not the end in itself. *See* FREDERICK F. SCHAUER, THE LAW OF OBSCENITY (1976) (claiming that "free speech is seen as an instrument of good, not as a good in itself"). *See also* Burns, *supra* note 93, at 62 ("[t]he issue that would become the grandest question of them all—the extent to which government should interfere with some persons' liberties in order to grant them and other persons more liberty and equality—this issue lay beyond the intellectual horizons").

103. For example, the Supreme Court's willingness to protect the wearing of a jacket with offensive words lettered on it or black armbands in school can be explained by the political nature of resistance to the unpopular war in Vietnam. *See* Schauer, *supra* note 102, at 13–14.

104. The motivation behind particular protected speech as a basis for regulation cannot be questioned. *Cf.* Eastern R.R. Presidents Conf. v. Noerr Motor Freight, 365 U.S. 127, 138 (1961) (holding that protected speech aimed at elimination of competition did not violate antitrust laws); Henrico Prof. Firefighters Assoc. v. Board of Supervisors, 649 F.2d 237, 245 n.12 (4th Cir. 1981) (holding that a speaker's motivation is irrelevant to First Amendment analysis). Any analysis of a speaker's motivation would necessarily scrutinize both the sincerity of his belief in certain ideas and his reasons for expressing them. *See* Young v. American Mini Theaters, 427 U.S. 50, 64–66 (1975); Finnis, *supra* note 90, at 222–23.

105. ANNALS OF CONGRESS, VOL. 1, 731–32 (Joseph Gales et al. eds., 1790), *reprinted in* BERNARD SCHWARTZ, THE BILL OF RIGHTS: A DOCUMENTARY HISTORY 1029 (Chelsea House Publishers 1971).

publishing our thoughts by speaking or writing; the right of free commerce; the right of personal freedom."[106]

Nevertheless, Jefferson's conception of the inalienable rights of speech and press was not absolute. In his draft constitution for Virginia, he had proposed freedom of the press "except so far as by commission of private injury cause may be given of private action."[107] In a letter to James Madison in August of 1789, Jefferson proposed to qualify what would become the First Amendment as follows: "The people shall not be deprived or abridged of their right to speak or to write or otherwise to publish any thing but false facts affecting injuriously the life, liberty, property, or reputation of others . . . ."[108] In short, interpreting the First Amendment to mean that suppression of ideas is not a legitimate governmental purpose is but one of several readings equally well rooted in language and history.[109]

2.2 The Right of Access

Regardless (or because) of interpretations of the Framers' intent, clear law has evolved around the right of access to newspapers, limitations on government interference with them, and the characterization of public forums. While for the most part individuals may be guaranteed freedom from government regulation of their privately owned presses, citizens have never had the right of access to someone else's printed pages. The Constitution does not grant a print forum to those without the wherewithal to start up their own newspapers, nor has Congress.[110]

Is there any difference between the First Amendment rights afforded a privately owned commercial newspaper and one sponsored by a private college or university? Is a public college or university newspaper any less protected by the Constitution?

Since newspapers have limited publishing space (and funds), editors must use their subjective judgment on a regular basis to determine exactly what

106. Jefferson, *supra* note 88, 428, 429 (quoting from a letter to Col. David Humphreys, Mar. 18, 1789).

107. Mayer, *supra* note 87, at 169.

108. *Id.* at 171 (quoting from a letter to James Madison, Aug. 28, 1789).

109. *See* David S. Bogen, *The Origins of Freedom of Speech and Press*, 42 MD. L. REV. 429 (1983).

110. Congress has recognized the unfairness of broadcast monopolies, which are regulated by the Federal Communications Commission and subjected to various egalitarian measures such as equal-time requirements in political campaigns.

will be published and what will not. A paper may refuse to print certain editorial material because of its content or due to lack of space or—in the case of advertising—out of financial considerations. While rejection based on space or financial considerations does not constitute an infringement on free speech, a content-based rejection may. The constitutionality of editorial discretion depends on the status of the publication—that is, whether it is an instrumentality of the state (in the language of the law, a "state actor") or is privately owned, funded, and operated.[111]

Editors always make choices about what to publish, nurturing a bond of trust between them and their readers. That trust is violated if they knowingly disseminate historical lies like Holocaust denial advertisements. With the power to publish comes the responsibility to seek truth, as well as to avoid defamatory propaganda.[112]

The Supreme Court has held that a private newspaper had a constitutional right to determine whether or not to publish a specific article, editorial, or advertisement. In *Miami Herald Publ'g Co. v. Tornillo*, the Court rejected a Florida statute requiring newspapers to publish replies to political editorials. Its decision was based upon the First Amendment's guarantee of freedom of the press and freedom of speech; "the clear implication [of precedent] has been that any . . . compulsion to publish that which 'reason' tells editors should not be published is unconstitutional."[113]

In essence, the Court held that editorial discretion under the First Amendment is almost absolute. Newspapers have a right to publish or refuse to publish whatever they choose: articles, editorials, or advertisements. Even if the newspaper is the only one in town, or the biggest, or the most widely read, it can still print or reject practically anything. That an individual or group has the wherewithal to pay for an advertisement does not guarantee access to a newspaper owned or operated by others. It can even discriminate against a particular advertiser if it so desires. In the absence of fraud or monopoly,[114]

---

111. *See* Leeds v. Meltz, 85 F.3d 51, 54–55 (2d Cir. 1996); Sinn v. Daily Nebraskan, 829 F.2d 662, 664 (8th Cir. 1987).

112. *See* Miriam Colton, *Leading Liberal Mag Yanks Ad Denying Holocaust*, FORWARD, April 30, 2004, *available at* http://www.forward.com/articles/5558/.

113. Miami Herald Publ'g Co. v. Tornillo, 418 U.S. 241, 256 (1974) (quoting Associated Press v. United States, 326 U.S. 1, 20 n.18 (1945)).

114. *See* Lorain Journal Co. v. United States, 342 U.S. 143, 144–57 (1951) (holding that publisher's policy of refusing to accept advertising from companies, which also placed ads with publisher's competitors. constituted a Sherman Act violation); *see also* Kansas City Star Co. v. United States, 240 F.2d 643 (8th Cir. 1957).

"it is immaterial whether such [discrimination] is based upon reason or is the result of mere caprice, prejudice or malice. It is a part of the liberty of action which the Constitutions, State and Federal, guarantee to the citizen."[115]

Prior restraints are seldom countenanced under the Constitution[116]—the rare exceptions relate to the publication of editorial matter advocating acts likely to incite imminent lawless action[117] or disclosing state secrets[118]—but newspapers may be punished after the fact for publishing libelous[119] or obscene[120] material. Thus, private commercial newspapers may be prohibited from publishing information deemed damaging to national security[121] and exhortations to violence or civil disobedience[122] and punished for publishing defamatory stories[123] and material considered obscene.[124]

While some limitations are imposed on publications, generally privately owned and operated newspapers have virtually unfettered discretion about what to publish and what not to publish. Just as editors are free to print almost anything, so can they decide what to reject. While the public might have a moral claim to have opinions expressed on editorial pages, it has no constitutional right of access to them.

---

115. Poughkeepsie Buying Serv., Inc. v. Poughkeepsie Newspapers, Inc., 131 N.Y.S.2d 515, 517 (N.Y. Sup. Ct. 1954). This position appears to be uniform among the states with one exception. In Uhlman v. Sherman, 22 Ohio N.P. (new series) 225 (1919), the court reasoned that the newspaper business was clothed with public interest and that a newspaper was in the class of a quasi-public corporation bound to treat all advertisers fairly and without discrimination. Courts in other states have expressly rejected *Uhlman*. *See, e.g., In re* Louis Wohl, Inc., 50 F.2d 254, 256 (E.D. Mich. 1931); Shuck v. Carroll Daily Herald, 215 Iowa 1276, 247 N.W. 813 (1933); Friedenberg v. Times Publ'g Co., 127 So. 345 (La. 1930). *See also* Zachary Berman, *Say What You Will: Not in My Newspaper*, N.Y. TIMES, Jan. 18, 1992, *at* A22, *available at* http://www.nytimes.com/1992/01/18/opinion/l-say-what-you-will-not-in-my-newspaper-271392.html?pagewanted=1.

116. *See* Near v. Minnesota, 283 U.S. 697 (1931).

117. *See* Brandenburg v. Ohio, 395 U.S. 444, 447 (1969).

118. *See* New York Times Co. v. United States, 403 U.S. 713 (1971).

119. *See* New York Times Co. v. Sullivan, 376 U.S. 254 (1964).

120. Newspapers may be punished for publishing material that offends contemporary community standards. *See* Miller v. California, 413 U.S. 15 (1973).

121. *See* New York Times v. United States, 403 U.S. at 713.

122. *See* Feiner v. New York, 340 U.S. 315 (1951).

123. Sullivan, 376 U.S. at 254.

124. *See, e.g.,* Miller v. California, 413 U.S. at 23 (1973) (defining obscenity as sexually explicit matter offensive to "contemporary community standards"); Roth v. United States, 354 U.S. 476, 487 (1957).

2.3 Arguments in Deference to Freedom of Expression

The traditional justification for viewing the First Amendment's guarantee of free expression as virtually absolute—the exceptions are few and narrow in scope—is to encourage an open and unfettered exchange of ideas.[125] Thoughts that are abhorrent to a free society, the argument goes, will wither when aired but fester if suppressed.[126] Moreover, who is to decide which ideas are abhorrent? Certainly not the government, reasoned the Constitution's Framers. Free speech is so precious and delicate a liberty, it must be preserved at great cost.[127] Thus, the depth of conviction in Voltaire's oft-quoted declaration: "I disapprove of what you say but I will defend to the death your right to say it."[128]

The interest that the First Amendment guards and gives it its importance, said Judge Learned Hand, presupposes that there are no orthodoxies—religious, political, economic, or scientific—that are immune from debate.[129] Others have pointed to the First Amendment's goal of ascertaining the truth—"[t]hrough the acquisition of new knowledge, the toleration of new ideas, the testing of opinion in open competition, the discipline of rethinking its assumptions, a society will be better able to reach common decisions that will meet the needs and aspirations of its members."[130]

A more current statement of jurisprudential philosophy justifying traditional First Amendment principle, particularly the notion that American concepts of tolerance are noble and defensible, was voiced by Lee Bollinger in his oft-cited 1986 book entitled *The Tolerant Society*.[131] Extolling the virtue of

---

125. *See* Whitney v. California, 274 U.S. 357, 372–80 (1927) (Brandeis, J., concurring); Abrams v. United States, 250 U.S. 616, 624–31 (1919) (Holmes, J., dissenting).

126. Whitney, 274 U.S. at 375–76.

127. *See* Lasson, *supra* note 86, at 78.

128. There is some doubt that Voltaire actually made this statement, although it is indicative of an attitude attributed to him. *See* BURTON STEVENSON, THE HOME BOOK OF QUOTATIONS 726, 2776 (10th ed., 1967) and S.G. TALLENTYRE, THE FRIENDS OF VOLTAIRE 199 (1907).

129. *See* International Bhd. of Elec. Workers Local 501 v. NLRB, 181 F.2d 34, 40 (2d Cir. 1950), *aff'd*, 341 U.S. 694 (1951).

130. Thomas I. Emerson, *Toward a General Theory of the First Amendment*, 72 YALE L.J. 854, 882 (1963). Professor Emerson's seminal article suggested three other First-Amendment values besides truth seeking: individual self-fulfillment; securing participation by members of society in political decision making; and maintaining a balance between stability and change.

131. LEE C. BOLINGER, THE TOLERANT SOCIETY: FREEDOM OF SPEECH AND EXTREMIST SPEECH IN AMERICA (1986).

magnanimity and the First Amendment's function in developing a capacity for tolerance, Bollinger claims that the toleration of verbal acts inculcates a "tolerance ethic," which he describes as "a general disposition of being able to put aside our beliefs, of overcoming the instinct to have things our own way, to control, to dominate. It is to live in a world of difference, and to do so comfortably." In essence, he says, "tolerance is to democracy what courage is to war."[132]

Among the most frequently cited arguments in favor of protecting offensive expression are to preserve legitimate scientific and scholarly inquiry, to document bigotry in all its forms, and to avoid the dangers of line drawing that censorship and criminalization often encumber. Both legitimate scientific method and traditional scholarly inquiry demand that all evidence be recognized, investigated, and analyzed before conclusions can be drawn. This standard applies not only to orthodox views but to unpopular (even offensive) ones as well.[133]

In a true democracy, the government may not dictate what is right or wrong, true or false. No matter how obvious the distinctions may appear to be between historical fact and racist theory—a differentiation perhaps best illustrated by Holocaust denial—only the people can reject the expression of any thought, whether spoken or written; and even then, only as a matter of individual choice.[134]

It follows that we should educate our children to tolerate the diverse views of a pluralistic society. Just as we countenance others who advocate different ways of looking at the world, even as we may disagree with them, our textbooks should reflect the existence (if not the soundness) of denial theories. Thus, if public schools teach the Holocaust as a historical event, they must also teach that it may not have happened; if parents object to what they consider a historical fabrication, their children should be excused from class; if a state university funds speakers, it must tolerate deniers. Just as Holocaust denial may be seen as a threat to the ultimate power of reason, belief in the ultimate power of reason requires recognition of denial theories.[135]

---

132. Lee C. Bollinger, *The Tolerant Society: A Response to Critics*, 90 COLUM. L. REV. 979, 986–88 (1990).

133. *See, e.g.*, ERNEST NAGEL, THE STRUCTURE OF SCIENCE: PROBLEMS IN THE LOGIC OF SCIENTIFIC EXPLANATION 1–14 (1961).

134. *See* Debate, *supra* note 3, at 588 (statement by Alan Dershowitz).

135. *See* Suzanna Sherry, *The Sleep of Reason*, 84 GEO. L.J. 453, 483–84 (1996). *But see infra* note 197 and accompanying text (suggesting the Holocaust is a crime that lies outside both speech and reason).

If reason is to prevail, the existence of racism in all its manifestations must be documented. This is true of both fact and fiction. If we are to learn from history, what is the difference between the Nazis' foul deeds and their descendants' denial of them? It is as important for later generations to witness the propaganda of genocide as to see its effects, to hear the statements of racism as well as to countenance its results. Why should we even seek to suppress Holocaust denial when we have the benefit of the Nazis' own diabolically meticulous record keeping as hard-core evidence of evil: the millions of personal effects they confiscated and itemized; the identification numbers branded into their victims' arms as if they were animals; the logs of scientific experiments in torture; and ultimately, the precise tallies of lives snuffed out? Both the propaganda and the facts reflect the personification of brutality. To expurgate either would blur the facts of history and blot out the memory of all those martyred because of their ethnicity and murdered because of their race.

Few Americans want the government to decide for them what they can hear on the street corner, read in the library, or see in the cinema. It is not difficult to find abuses in the name of fair play, especially in countries that (unlike the United States) permit censorship and criminalization of that which the government finds to be hate speech.[136]

Criminalization illustrates the difficulties of line drawing. For example, in 1995, the distinguished historian Bernard Lewis was found guilty by a French court for expressing doubts that the massacre of 1.5 million Armenians early in this century by the Ottoman Empire could be correctly termed "genocide."[137] In Germany, a 1985 law facilitated the legal proceedings against those who deny the Holocaust "or another violent and arbitrary dominance."[138] This

---

136. For a list of those countries, *see infra* notes 176–191 and accompanying text.

137. At first, several Armenian groups sought to have Professor Lewis prosecuted under France's criminal Holocaust denial law, but a court ruled that the statute applied only to the Nazi regime of terror. The groups were more successful before a subsequent civil tribunal, which found Lewis guilty and fined him $2,000 (while declining to rule on whether his opinion as expressed was right or wrong). *See "Hate Speech" Again, Abroad*, WASH. POST, Sept. 9, 1995, at A16 ("[w]hen a court is willing to punish a scholar—or anyone, for that matter, for expressing an "insulting" opinion on a historical matter, even when debate on the point in question has been raging worldwide for years, the absurdity and perniciousness of such laws is on full display").

138. *See* Eric Stein, *History Against Free Speech: The New German Law Against the "Auschwitz"—and Other—"Lies,"* 85 MICH. L. REV. 277, 280 nn. 9–11 (1986) (translating Art. 194 StGB). Germany also recently used its presidency of the European Union to replicate its strict laws prohibiting Holocaust denial. *See* David Charter, *EU Declares Trivializing Genocide A Crime*, NSW COUNTY EDITION, April 21, 2007, at 14.

clause became quite contentious, the resulting controversy centering around the issues of restricting historical facts, promoting national consciousness, attributing collective guilt, and identifying the role of courts in punishing lies. Should denial of other known events, for example, the violent expulsion of Germans from Soviet-occupied East Germany, or the annihilation of millions of Cambodians by Pol Pot, or the ethnic cleansing in Bosnia, be equally punishable? In other words, was the Holocaust a unique phenomenon?[139]

If Auschwitz is unique, the argument goes, then the phrase in the German statute, "or another violent and arbitrary dominance," should have been eliminated; this addition renders the Holocaust unjustifiably relative and offends both the memory of those murdered and the sensibilities of survivors.[140]

In addition, experience with earlier legislation shows that hate-speech defendants, almost without exception, remain convinced, if not strengthened, in the truth of their contentions. Not only is deterrence unlikely, there is a real danger of backlash. The lie may be forbidden, but the liars remain. The judicial process cannot carry the burden of education that should fall to family, school, and political discourse. To the contrary, the German courts have become forums for neo-Nazi propaganda.[141]

Moreover, the task of drawing a line between "good" and "bad" is exceedingly difficult. Every year in the United States, all kinds of books are banned by public libraries—from Thomas Paine's *The Age of Reason* and John Steinbeck's The *Grapes of Wrath* to Charles Darwin's On the *Origin of the Species* and Hergé's *Tintin in the Congo*.[142] In recent years, the growing influence of the religious Right has been reflected in challenges to books about the occult, homosexuals, and racial minorities.[143]

In Canada, customs officials issue a list of imported materials that are reviewed for their potential to stir up racial hatred. Of the ninety titles on a

---

139. See Letter from Herbert A. Strauss to Eric Stein in *Correspondence, On the "Auschwitz Lie,"* 87 MICH. L. REV. 1026, 1031 (1989).

140. *Id.* at 1030.

141. *See* Stein, *supra* note 139, at 315.

142. *See* Rekha Basu, *Banned Books Given Spotlight*, DES MOINES REG., Sept. 29, 1995, at 1; Alison Leigh Cowan, *A Library's Approach to Books That Offend*, N.Y. TIMES, Aug. 19, 2009, *available at* http://cityroom.blogs.nytimes.com/2009/08/19/a-librarys-approach-to-books-that-offend/.

143. For example, in Queens, N.Y., a book about Martin Luther King was opposed by a school board member who viewed him as a "leftist hoodlum with significant Communist ties." *Id.* at 1.

recent list, only four were banned, including the standard anti-Semitic text, *The Protocols of the Elders of Zion*; Henry Ford's *The International Jew: The World's Foremost Problem*; and Arthur Butz's The *Hoax of the Twentieth Century*. Those that were not banned included Neal Gabler's An *Empire of Their Own: How Jews Invented Hollywood* and a compact disk entitled *Aryan Outlaws in a Zionist Police State*.[144] There is little evidence that banning hate speech and literature serves to inhibit it. On the other hand, line drawing has proven virtually impossible.[145]

2.4 Arguments in Favor of Regulating Hate Speech

A persistent American shibboleth is that the First Amendment is virtually absolute: the Constitution guarantees everyone the freedom of self-expression, and anything that restricts this right is a step on the road toward tyranny. In the vernacular, "It's a free country and I can say whatever I want."[146]

That it is difficult to draw a line between acceptable and nonacceptable expression and hard to allocate responsibility for deciding what speech should be restricted, is too facile a rationale to justify a rule of absolute construction. The carefully drawn exceptions to the rule of free speech are based on logical demonstrations that there are certain utterances that must be limited even (if not especially) in a democratic society.[147]

The very existence of the doctrines in exception—"fighting words," "clear and present danger," "captive audience," "legitimate time, place, and manner restrictions"[148]—belies the simplistic popular understanding of free speech.[149]

144. *See* Carol Berger, *Hate Book Sparks Debate of Freedom*, EDMONTON J., Jan. 24, 1995, at A7.

145. For a recent learned article arguing why democratic principles of free speech should trump laws that prohibit Holocaust denial, *see* Peter R. Teachout, *Making Holocaust Denial a Crime: Reflections on European Anti-Negationist Laws from the Perspective of U. S. Constitutional Experience*, 30 VT. L. REV. 655 (2007).

146. Justices Hugo Black and William O. Douglas generally took the First Amendment literally to mean that Congress could make no law abridging free speech "without any 'ifs' or 'buts' or 'whereases.'" Beauharnais v. Illinois, 343 U.S. 250, 275 (1952) (Black, J., dissenting); *see also* Columbia Broadcasting Sys., Inc. v. Democratic Nat'l Comm., 412 U.S. 94, 156 (1973) (Douglas, J., concurring) ("[t]he First Amendment is written in terms that are absolute. . . . The ban of "no" law that abridges freedom of the press is in my view total and absolute.").

147. Lasson, *supra* note 86, at 79.

148. For a comprehensive discussion, *see* RODNEY A. SMOLLA, SMOLLA & NIMMER ON FREEDOM OF SPEECH 10, 32–34 (3d ed. 1996).

149. *See generally* Kenneth Lasson, Racial Defamation as Free Speech: Abusing the First Amendment, 17 COLUM. HUM. RTS. L. REV. 11, 20–30 (1985).

Such contextual limitations are joined by those which regulate content like obscenity and pornography,[150] matters of national security,[151] and threats against the president.[152] It is unarguable that there should be absolute freedom to think what one wants; it does not follow—either legally, logically, or philosophically—that one may openly express whatever one thinks, whenever and wherever one desires.[153] A majority of civil libertarians continue to advocate the First Amendment ideology that no orthodoxies should be immune from debate and dispute, but a growing number of constitutional scholars have begun to argue that that view should be "bemoaned and resisted rather than accepted or celebrated."[154]

Those in favor of regulating hate speech are often held to a higher standard (if not regarded in lower esteem) by First Amendment purists. For example, historian Leonard Levy's sponsors refused to publish his conclusion that (contrary to his earlier beliefs), the Framers of the Constitution had a far narrower conception of free speech and press.[155] Other arguments in support of regulating hate speech are often stigmatized by the widely accepted ideology that urges courts to offer even greater protections of free speech.[156]

Even Professor Bollinger concedes that "tolerance has its limits" and that different societies must of necessity treat hate speech differently.[157] The slippery slope theory, so often invoked by civil libertarians—dubbed by one doubter as "trickle-down chilling"—has not materialized in any other

---

150. *See, e.g.,* New York v. Ferber, 458 U.S. 747 (1982); Young v. American Mini Theaters, 427 U.S. 50 (1976); Roth v. United States, 354 U.S. 476 (1957).

151. *See, e.g.,* Dennis v. United States, 341 U.S. 494 (1951); Debs v. United States, 249 U.S. 211 (1919); Frohwerk v. United States, 249 U.S. 204 (1919).

152. *See, e.g.,* Watts v. United States, 394 U.S. 705 (1969).

153. *See* Mayer, *supra* note 87, at 171–72 (discussing Jefferson's views on the liability of publishers for false facts printed, despite freedom of the press and criminal acts dictated by religious error as punishable despite guarantee of free exercise of religion); *see generally* Lasson, *supra* note 149, at 97.

154. Frederick Schauer, *The First Amendment as Ideology*, 33 WM. & MARY L. REV. 853, 854 (1992).

155. *See generally* LEONARD LEVY, LEGACY OF SUPPRESSION: FREEDOM OF SPEECH AND PRESS IN EARLY AMERICAN HISTORY (1960); and Schauer, *supra* note 154.

156. *See generally* Schauer, *supra* note 154.

157. Bollinger, *supra* note 132, at 995. In Germany, for example, as long as the Holocaust remains part of recent memory, it will be difficult not to punish the expression of Nazi ideology. *Id.* at 990.

Western democracy. Yet all Western democracies but the United States have laws prohibiting the dissemination of hate speech.[158]

Traditional libertarians also argue that if one government can officially stipulate that the Holocaust occurred, then another government somewhere, sometime, can declare that it did not occur. Others say, "the grander the truth, the bigger the lie."[159] But such arguments are rendered speculative and facile, and ultimately meritless, when placed in the real-life context of what happens elsewhere.

A number of legal scholars have asserted that the harm of hate speech matters. Whatever form such speech takes, its purpose and effect are to deny the humanity of a group of people, making them objects of ridicule and humiliation so that acts of aggression against them, no matter how violent, are taken less seriously.[160] Meanwhile, the targets of such behavior often respond to it with fear and withdrawal; the more they are silenced, the deeper their inequality becomes; many suffer post-traumatic stress disorders of varying degrees.[161]

Hate speech may be analyzed as the first stage in a continuum of increasing violence and intimidation, followed by avoidance, discrimination, attack, and extermination. As illustrated by the history of the Third Reich, each stage is dependent upon the preceding one: it was Hitler's vocal anti-Semitism that led Germans to avoid their Jewish neighbors and friends; which, in turn, enabled easier enactment of the blatantly discriminatory Nuremberg laws; which, in turn, made synagogue desecration and street mugging more acceptable; which, in turn, allowed for creation of the killing fields in the death camps.[162]

The capacity of speech to cause injury in diverse ways is often viewed as a price that must be paid to ensure a truly free and democratic society. But even free societies must allocate the cost of injuries. If we permit individuals to recover damages for defamation, why not permit groups to prove that they (i.e., their members) have suffered injury from hate speech?[163]

---

158. Schauer, *supra* note 154, at 867.

159. Debate, *supra* note 3, at 571, 582–83.

160. *See* Kathleen E. Mahoney, Hate Speech: Affirmation or Contradiction of Freedom of Expression, 96 U. ILL. L. REV. 789, 792 (1996).

161. *See generally* Richard Delgado, *Words That Wound: A Tort Action for Racial Insults, Epithets, and Name-Calling*, 17 HARV. C.R.-C.L. L. REV. 133 (1982); Mari M. Matsuda, *Public Response to Racist Speech: Considering the Victim's Story*, 87 MICH. L. REV. 2320 (1989).

162. *See* Gordon W. Allport, *The Nature of Prejudice* 14–15 (1954).

163. *See* Lasson, *supra* note 149, at 108–28.

The argument that it is too difficult to draw the line between what is acceptable speech and what is not often fails to countenance the idea that the entire history of law could be described in terms of reasonable line drawing. This has also been true in First Amendment cases, such as those involving false advertising,[164] offensive pornography,[165] state secrets,[166] and defamation.[167] People who feel they have been grievously hurt by someone else's words—such as Holocaust survivors whose suffering has been denied[168]—ought to have a civil remedy. Free speech should not mean speech without cost.[169]

A tort action for intentional infliction of emotional distress would seem to be an appropriate remedy for racial insults, but courts have generally limited recovery to plaintiffs who suffered some physical injury caused by "extreme and outrageous conduct."[170] In many instances, racial insults would fall short of that standard, particularly if they were simply statements of opinion. Calls to establish another tort—one specifically aimed at combating racial insults—have thus far fallen on deaf ears.[171]

The few plaintiffs who have been awarded damages for emotional distress caused by hate speech have not been challenged on First Amendment grounds.[172] If they had been, however, good counterarguments could be

---

164. *See, e.g.,* Virginia State Bd. of Pharmacy v. Virginia Citizens Consumer Council, Inc., 425 U.S. 748 (1976).

165. *See, e.g.,* New York v. Ferber, 458 U.S. 747 (1982); Miller v. California, 413 U.S. 15 (1973).

166. *See, e.g.,* Nixon v. Administrator of Gen. Servs., 433 U.S. 425 (1977); New York Times Co. v. United States, 403 U.S. 713 (1971).

167. *See, e.g.,* Gertz v. Robert Welch, Inc., 418 U.S. 323 (1974); New York Times Co. v. Sullivan, 376 U.S. 254 (1964).

168. *See* Skokie v. National Socialist Party of America, 373 N.E.2d 21 (Ill. 1978) (allowing neo-Nazis to march through residential area largely inhabited by Holocaust survivors).

169. *See* Debate, *supra* note 3, at 576 (quoting Arthur Berney).

170. RESTATEMENT (SECOND) OF TORTS § 46 (1965). *See also* Stephen Fleischer, *Campus Speech Codes: The Threat to Liberal Education,* 27 J. MARSHALL L. REV. 709, 724–25 (1994). *But see* Geri J. Yanover, *Anti-Semitism and Holocaust Denial in the Academy: A Tort Remedy,* 101 DICK. L. REV. 71 (1996) (arguing strongly for the viability of intentional infliction of emotional distress as a remedy for Holocaust denial).

171. *See* Delgado, *supra* note 161, at 252. Professor Delgado notes, however, that although his call for establishment of a tort for racial insults has not been heeded, over the years since his article first appeared, a number of courts have recognized various causes of action to redress racist slurs. Telephone conversation with Richard Delgado, professor of law, UCLA Law School (Sept. 11, 1996).

172. *See* Delgado, *supra* note 161, at 172; *see also* Wiggs v. Courshon, 355 F. Supp. 206 (S.D. Fla. 1973); Agarwal v. Johnson, 603 P.2d 58 (Cal. 1979); Alcorn v. Anbro Eng'g, Inc., 468 P.2d 216 (Cal. 1970); Contreras v. Crown Zellerbach, Corp., 565 P.2d 1173 (Wash. 1977).

made that such speech does not fall within any of the classic categories of values said to be protected by the Constitution: individual self-fulfillment, truth seeking, securing participation by members of society in social and political decision making, and maintaining a balance between stability and change. Bigotry stifles, rather than enhances, moral and social growth. If truth seeking is to achieve the best decisions on matters of interest to all, most racial insults can be distinguished: a call for genocide can hardly be characterized as the best decision for all. Rather than to allow all members of society to voice their opinions, racial insults contribute to a stratified society. Finally, rather than contribute to a balance between stability and change, racial insults foment discord and violence.[173]

2.5 The Experience Elsewhere

The Convention on the Elimination of All Forms of Racial Discrimination requires the condemnation and criminalization of "all propaganda. . . based on ideas or theories of superiority. . . or which attempt to justify or promote racial hatred and discrimination in any form."[174] The European Commission on Human Rights has found such laws to be justifiable limits on the freedom of expression.[175]

In fact, every Western democracy with the exception of the United States has laws that punish various forms of hate speech, and a number of them specifically prohibit Holocaust denial; the debate elsewhere is not whether to control hate speech but how.

1. Canada

Canada, England, France, and Sweden are most notable among the countries whose values of social liberty are similar to those in the United States. While Canada's Charter of Rights and Freedoms[176] provides a comprehensive

---

173. *See* Emerson, *supra* note 130, at 879–86. This function of the First Amendment has been viewed by some as limited to political ideas. *See* Delgado, *supra* note 161, at 175–79; *see generally* Alexander Meiklejohn, Political Freedom (1960).

174. Convention on the Elimination of All Forms of Racial Discrimination, 660 U.N.T.S. 194, 3 I.L.M. 164, 166–67.

175. *See* Stephen J. Roth, The Legal Fight Against Anti-Semitism: Survey of Developments in 1993 at 23–26. (1995)

176. Canadian Charter of Rights and Freedoms, 1 S.C. V (1982).

guarantee for free speech with language even broader than that of the First Amendment, the country also has a number of other laws that effectively seek to regulate hate speech. A criminal statute prohibits three types of hate propaganda: (a) advocacy of genocide, (b) communications inciting hatred against an identifiable group where a breach of the peace is likely to follow, and (c) public and willful expression of ideas intended to promote hatred against an identifiable group.[177]

In addition, Canada's Human Rights Act prohibits use of the telephone to record hate messages.[178] The Broadcasting Act authorizes standards for radio and television and prohibits abusive comments likely to expose individuals or groups to contempt on the basis of their race, ethnicity, religion, sex, color, age, or mental or physical disability.[179] The Customs Act prohibits importation of hate propaganda.[180] Using these laws, Canadian courts have held that hate speech does not belong in any category of expression that deserves constitutional protection. Interestingly, one Canadian court expressly supported that principle by extensive references to American cases, especially *Beauharnais v. Illinois*.[181]

Although the most famous test case in Canada was that of Zundel (noted earlier),[182] which claimed that the Holocaust was in fact a Zionist swindle, equally pertinent was another challenge to the statute prohibiting Holocaust denial. There, a Canadian high school teacher was charged with violating the Criminal Code for teaching his students that the Holocaust was a hoax, and that Jews were responsible for all the world's problems; if the students' exams reflected his view, they received good grades; if not, poor ones. He argued that the law infringed upon his guaranteed right to free expression.[183]

In upholding the legislation, the Supreme Court of Canada linked the psychological and emotional harm caused by hate propaganda to the

177. Criminal Code, R.S.C., ch. C-46, 319 (1985) (Can.).

178. Canadian Human Rights Act, R.S.C., ch. H-6 (1985) (Can.).

179. Broadcasting Act, R.S.C., ch. B-9, 3 (1985) (Can.).

180. Customs Act, R.S.C., ch. 1, 181 (1985) (Can.).

181. Beauharnais v. Illinois, 343 U.S. 250 (1952) (holding that defamation of groups may be treated the same way as libel of individuals); *see* R. v. Keegstra [1990] S.C.R. 697, 707, 739–41 ("[c]redible arguments have been made that later Supreme Court cases do not necessarily erode [*Beauharnais*'] legitimacy" (*see, e.g.*, Lasson, *supra* note 149)).

182. R. v. Zundel [1987] 7 W.C.B.2d 26, *aff'd*, [1990] 9 W.C.B.2d 238, *rev'd*, [1992] 17 W.C.B.2d 106. *See supra* notes 21ff. and accompanying text.

183. *See* R. v. Keegstra [1990] 3 S.C.R. 697.

target group's constitutional right of equality. The court found that hate propaganda against particular groups must be prevented if multiculturalism is to be preserved and enhanced; that its "truth value" is marginal; that it denies citizens meaningful participation in the democratic process; and that its contribution to self-fulfillment and human flourishing is negligible.[184]

2. England

England has sought by statute to restrict racist expression since 1936, when the Public Order Act was passed to combat anti-Semitic fascist demonstrations.[185] The act banned the wearing of uniforms during public demonstrations and broadened the state's power to prohibit a march or demonstration deemed likely to lead to a breach of the peace. The law was periodically strengthened, so that by 1963, the burden was placed on the speaker to prove that his words were not likely to provoke a breach of the peace.[186] Subsequent acts prohibited the display of any threatening signs and racial incitement by spoken or written words.[187]

3. France

In France, more than one famous figure has faced charges for negating crimes against humanity, which there, is deemed a criminal offense. Most recently, the French author Roger Garaudy was cited for denouncing what he called Jewish "Shoah business" and claiming that Israel has exploited the Holocaust to put itself "above all international law."[188]

---

184. *Id.* at 744–68. *See also* Canadian Human Rights Comm'n v. Taylor [1990] 3 S.C.R. 892 (denying protection to a group prosecuted for operating a telephone service that played prerecorded messages denigrating Jews); R. v. Andrews [1990] 3 S.C.R. 870 (refusing to extend constitutional protection to leaders of a white supremacist group for publishing an anti-Semitic newspaper that stated the Holocaust was a Zionist hoax). A Canadian group also proposed that Ahmadinejad be indicted for advocacy of genocide. *See* Irwin Cotler, Speech to Target Iran for Genocidal Policy, CTV Television, Inc., Jan. 23, 2007.

185. Public Order Act, 1936, 1 Edw. 8 & 1 Geo. 6, ch. 6 (Eng.).

186. Public Order Act, 1963, ch. 52 (Eng.).

187. Race Relations Act, 1965, ch. 73 (Eng.); *see generally* Kenneth Lasson, *Racism in Great Britain: Drawing the Line on Free Speech*, 7 B. C. THIRD WORLD L.J. 161 (1987).

188. *See* Reports from the Cordoba OSCE Conference on Anti-Semitism and Other Forms of Intolerance, Internet Centre Anti-Racism Europe (ICARE), June 8–9, 2005, *available at* http://www.icare.to/cordoba/uk/.

In 1990, Jean-Marie Le Pen, leader of France's right-wing National Front Party, referred to the Nazi gas chambers as "a detail of history." Outraged survivors joined in a lawsuit against him, and a local court found Le Pen guilty of trivializing the Holocaust and fined him a symbolic one franc. But Le Pen appealed the ruling, claiming his freedom of expression was being denied. A court of appeals not only upheld the decision but increased the fine to 900,000 francs (about $180,000).[189]

4. Sweden

While Sweden specifically guarantees its citizens a number of liberties (including the freedoms of expression, press, and assembly), its Instrument of Government also sets explicit limits. For example, the Riksdag (Sweden's governing body) may restrict various freedoms of expression in order to achieve "a purpose which is acceptable in a democratic society."[190] With the same purpose, the Swedish Penal Code prohibits racial defamation.[191]

5. United States

In the United States—by way of stark contrast from certain European countries—the only jurisprudential remedy against Holocaust denial has been via contract law. In 1980, the aforementioned Institute for Historical Review offered a $50,000 reward for proof that Jews were gassed at Auschwitz. A Holocaust survivor named Mel Mermelstein claimed the reward, submitting as proof declarations by other survivors who witnessed friends and relatives being taken away to their deaths by the Nazis. His own testimony described how he watched his mother and sister led to gas chambers. When the institute told him the offer had been withdrawn because there had been no takers, he sued. The court, finding "the fact that Jews were gassed at Auschwitz is indisputable," ordered the reward paid.[192]

---

189. *See Comeuppance for a Bigot*, TIME, Apr. 1, 1991, at 50. It was not until 1995 that France publicly admitted responsibility for deporting almost 70,000 Jews to Nazi death camps—only 2,800 of whom returned. *See* Gail Russell Chaddock, *Cleric's Comments Ignite the Fury of French Media*, CHRISTIAN SCI. MONITOR, July 25, 1996, at 5.

190. IG 2:12–2:14.

191. Penal Code ch. 16, 8 (1972).

192. Mermelstein v. Institute for Historical Review, No. C356 542 (Cal. Super. Ct. July 22, 1985). The case was settled when the institute agreed to pay the $50,000 plus $100,000 for Mermelstein's pain and suffering caused by the revoked offer. *Id. See also Lawsuit Over*

3. The Quest for Truth in a Free Society

The devastating truth about the Holocaust is that it was a fact, not a dream. And the devastating truth about the Holocaust deniers is that they will go on using whatever falsehoods they can muster, and taking advantage of whatever vulnerabilities in an audience they can find, to argue, with skill and evil intent, that the Holocaust never happened. By being vigilant to these arguments we can all fight this second murder of the Jews–fight it, and weep not only for the victims' mortality but also for the fragility, and mortality, of memory.

Sen. Orrin Hatch (1995)[193]

Without the past, without memory, without history, we are nothing, adrift. We place our destiny and dignity in the hands of the misfits and their projected psychoses. This movement is not an attack on the Holocaust, but on the very notion of historical meaning. It is a revolt against reality, a threat not only to the past but to the future.

James S. Robbins[194]

Veritas vos liberabit.

(The truth shall make you free.)

3.1 Ignorance and Education

In a free society, it is up to the people to determine the facts of history. Courts and governments should not be arbiters of the truth, even of whether or not a monumental event indeed occurred.[195] But trying to prove a crime as monstrous as genocide serves to expose the law's limits. The capacity of the

---

Proof of Holocaust Ends with Payment to a Survivor, N.Y. TIMES, July 25, 1985, at A12, *available at* http://www.nytimes.com/1985/07/25/us/lawsuit-over-proof-of-holocaust-ends-with-payment-to-a-survivor.html.

193. 141 Cong. Rec. S16853 (daily ed. Nov. 9, 1995) (statement of Sen. Hatch) (quoting Dr. Walter Reich, executive director, United States Holocaust Memorial Museum).

194. Robbins, *supra* note 38.

195. As Justice Felix Frankfurter put it, "Courts ought not to enter this political thicket." Colegrove v. Green, 328 U.S. 549, 556 (1946). Even more to the point is Alan Dershowitz: "I am categorically opposed to any court, any school board, any governmental agent taking judicial notice about any historical event, even one that I know to the absolute core of my being occurred, like the Holocaust. I don't want the government to tell me that it occurred because I don't want any government ever to tell me that it didn't occur." Debate (above n. 3) 566.

Nuremberg Tribunal to comprehend Nazi atrocities in conventional terms of criminality was an overwhelming challenge, which may have contributed to an inability to grasp fully the nature and meaning of the Nazis' effort to exterminate the Jewish population of Europe.[196]

The argument that the Holocaust is a unique crime whose enormity puts it beyond traditional norms of trial and punishment cannot be easily dismissed. The world of Auschwitz has often been said to lie outside both speech and reason.[197] Can that rationale, however, explain why ignorance about the Holocaust is so widespread? A 1992 survey found that 38 percent of American high school students and 28 percent of American adults did not know what the Holocaust was.[198] A 2005 poll by the British Broadcasting Corporation found that 60 percent of women and people under 35 years of age had never heard of Auschwitz, the most notorious of all Nazi death camps.[199] Even supposedly well-educated people have difficulty identifying historical events related to the Holocaust. Many law students, for example, have never heard of Kristallnacht.[200] Law professors, on the other hand, have a special responsibility to educate law students about those who would polarize by preaching doctrines of hatred, which logically and inevitably lead to acts of persecution.[201]

---

196. *See* Douglas, *supra* note 87, at 453. Douglas also notes that by translating evidence of unprecedented atrocity into crimes of war, the Nuremberg prosecution was able to create a coherent and judicially manageable narrative of criminality that seemed to defy rational and juridical explanation. *Id.* at 454.

197. *See* GEORGE STEINER, LANGUAGE AND SILENCE 118, 123 (1967). If Auschwitz is unique, denying other violent and arbitrary dominance should be outside the purview of punishment.

198. The 1992 Holocaust poll was by Roper. *See* Jeroff, *supra* note 59. A poll by the same company in 2000 found that as many as 8 percent of Americans may be deniers. Michael Berenbaum, *The Growing Assault on the Truth of Absolute Evil*, L.A. TIMES, Jan. 28, 2000, at B7, *available at* http://articles.latimes.com/2000/jan/28/local/me-58733.

199. David McLoughlin, *Understanding the Holocaust*, DOMINION POST (Wellington, New Zealand), April 16, 2005, at 13. *See also* Alan Crawford, *Look to Germany to Learn Lessons of Holocaust*, SUNDAY HERALD, Jan. 23, 2005, at 11.

200. "The Night of Broken Glass," Nov. 9, 1938, called by many the beginning of the Holocaust. *See* 141 Cong. Rec. S16853 (Nov. 9, 1995). Every year, the author asks his civil liberties students (all of whom are upperclassmen) if they have ever heard of Kristallnacht. Few answer in the affirmative.

201. This responsibility was recognized at the 2007 Silberman Seminar for Law Faculty, The Impact and Legacy of the Holocaust on the Law, sponsored by the Center for Advanced Holocaust Studies of the United States Holocaust Memorial Museum, June 4–15, 2007, in Washington, D.C. *See also* Bruce Levine, *An Education in Law—For What Purpose?*, 34 WASHBURN L.J. 516 (1995).

The environment that enabled the Holocaust to happen has been described as the time "where technology was married to evil."[202] The Internet provides electronic forums called newsgroups—one of which is devoted to revisionist history, which due to its enormous size, is virtually impossible to monitor for hate speech.[203]

The need to remember the Holocaust is made all the more critical by the existence of well-known political figures who at various times express sympathy for accused Nazi war criminals or doubt the extent of the Holocaust. The most notable current examples in the United States are recent presidential candidate Patrick Buchanan[204] and Nation of Islam leader Louis Farrakhan.[205]

There can be little doubt that Holocaust denial will gain strength once there are no more victims alive to supply eyewitness testimony about Nazi atrocities.[206] Meanwhile, though, it has become less and less difficult for Holocaust deniers to find gullible converts among the growing numbers of young people with but a tenuous grasp of basic history. Much can be learned by way of a well-produced video or film, documenting in irrefutable detail the historical record of the Holocaust. Archival footage of the death camps themselves can be juxtaposed with statements by historians, victims, perpetrators, and liberators. Nazi records, Hitler's recorded speeches, and transcripts from the Wannsee Conference (at which the genocide was carefully planned) should also be made available. This kind of presentation should be unimpeachable and widely distributed, especially to college campuses.[207]

---

202. Robert Trussell, *Couple Brings Reality of Holocaust Home to Younger Viewers with "Anne Frank,"* KANSAS CITY STAR, Mar. 15, 1996, at Preview 18 (quoting Mark Weitzman of the Simon Wiesenthal Center).

203. Recent patrons have included Bradley Smith's Holocaust-denying Institute for Historical Review. "The Holocaust story," says Smith, "is closed to free inquiry in our universities and among intellectuals. The Internet represents a huge potential audience at minimal cost." Beck, *supra* note 23, at A1. *See also* Allison Sommer, *Free Speech Advocates and Opponents Move Their Battle to the Net*, JERUSALEM POST, Feb. 9, 1996, at 7.

204. *See* LIPSTADT, *supra* note 14, at 5–6; David A. Nacht, *Book Note*, 90 MICH. L. REV. 1802, 1808 (1992) (reviewing Alan Dershowitz, *Chutzpah*); William F. Buckley, Jr., *In Search of Anti-Semitism*, NAT'L REV., Dec. 30, 1991, at 20.

205. In France, the highly respected cleric Abbé Pierre lent credence to author Roger Garaudy's book, *The Founding Myths of Israeli Politics*, which sought to trivialize the Holocaust.

206. *See* Judith Miller, Erasing the Past: Europe's Amnesia About the Holocaust, N.Y. TIMES MAG., Nov. 16, 1986, § 6, at 30.

207. *See* Dershowitz, supra note 21, at A6.

3.2 Liberty and Responsibility

At the very least, if Holocaust denial is allowed to avoid the limitations we have come to put on obscenity, defamation, state secrets, and other forms of expression not accorded First Amendment protection, certain fundamental principles should be clearly recognized.

Holocaust deniers may self-publish their theories, but they are entitled to no greater access to the general press than anyone else. Their editorial and advertising matter can be constitutionally treated like that of defamers and pornographers. Moreover, it can be rejected at will by publishers who choose to do so for arbitrary reasons of ideology, space, financial considerations, or even caprice.

Additionally, there is no need that public libraries carry all books and journals that are available. Indeed, they cannot. Even university research libraries must choose from among the vast amounts of resources procurable. Thus, while accepting material that is patently racist may be important in order to demonstrate that it exists, few serious libraries would similarly carry a complete collection of pornography simply to satisfy a scholar's desire to analyze the difference between pornography and erotica. This same rationale should apply when assessing whether libraries should carry racist materials.

In its most-perfect form, speech is exercised freely in an open marketplace of ideas and serves to promote the quest for truth. In its least-perfect form, it suppresses ideas, stifles social discourse, and provokes violence. Thus there is an interdependence between the right to speak and the responsibility to speak honestly. In so doing, the dignity of the target of the speech must be preserved. If the relationship between the right of free speech and the responsibility for free speech is ignored, the traditional justification for protecting it—that it promotes the quest for truth—is denied.[208]

Holocaust denial is not an attempt at free inquiry but at distortion. Universities are places where students are supposed to think critically; they have no moral responsibility to provide a platform for bigots whose sole purpose is to stir up hatred.[209] It is arguable that in the long run, being offended by insensitive language or even outright bigotry might be a small price to pay

208. *See generally* Leon E. Trakman, Transforming Free Speech: Rights and Responsibilities, 56 OHIO ST. L.J. 899 (1995).

209. *See* Miller, *supra* note 206, at 30.

for the freedom of thought and expression. And there is nothing wrong with reevaluating history; offering new interpretations of old events—in fact, challenging entrenched dogma of all kinds—is central to the academic enterprise. Historians should be allowed to investigate any aspect of the events that have come collectively to be called the Holocaust with the same rigorous and impartial methods they would apply to any other historical event and publish freely the results of their research. "To forbid this is itself a form of denial."[210] But discarding past culture because it is deemed "white" or "patriarchal" or "Eurocentric" can hardly be understood as the honest scholar's quest for truth. Nor can denying the documented facts of history.

3.3 Toward a More Responsible Press

Various writers, commissions, and task forces have suggested new standards by which the press should be held more accountable. One of the most notable was the Hutchins Commission, which in 1947 published a report entitled *A Free and Responsible Press*.[211] Uncomfortable with the characterization of a free press offered by Charles Beard,[212] the commission recommended a number of initiatives, including a truthful comprehensive account of events in a meaningful context, a forum for the exchange of differing opinions, a means of presenting social values, and a way to reach "every member of the society by the currents of information . . . which the press supplies." The report warned that the press must become more responsible or face government regulation: "The legal right will stand if the moral right is realized or tolerably approximated."[213]

Others have urged adoption of legally enforceable codes of journalistic ethics, greater access to the press by those without realistic expectations of disseminating their views, stronger laws to protect privacy and reputation, and more meaningful restrictions on hate speech and pornography. The ultimate goal of a free press should be the presentation and clarification of the goals and values of society.[214]

---

210. Peter Simple, *Denial*, LONDON DAILY TELEGRAPH, Apr. 12, 1996 at A1.

211. THE COMMISSION ON FREEDOM OF THE PRESS, A FREE AND RESPONSIBLE PRESS (Robert D. Leigh ed., 1947). The Commission on Freedom of the Press was chaired by Robert Maynard Hutchins.

212. *See* above note 83 and accompanying text.

213. A Free and Responsible Press, *supra* note 85, at 1, 20–21, 131.

214. Smolla, *supra* note 148, at 184.

A majority of colleges and universities seek to guarantee their student newspapers the same freedom of the press that the Constitution confers upon the private commercial media. Problems arise when student editors and school administrators interpret the First Amendment too broadly, as part of an implicit obligation to foster an open and vigorous marketplace of ideas, which, in turn, should guarantee access by anyone (students or the general public) to editorial and advertising pages.

Such a constitutional perspective is both mistaken and misplaced. Too often overlooked is the simple logic of a free press: while a newspaper has a First Amendment right to publish what it pleases, it also has a First Amendment right to reject what it deems gratuitous or offensive. Such a rejection can be based on content, limited space, or financial considerations.

While philosophers may argue that there are no demonstrably false ideas, and while scientific propositions can never be proven absolutely true, a theory whose predictions fail the test of experimentation can and should be rejected—particularly if its acceptance and application would clearly cause injury.

Unless we are willing to brand nonsense as just that, the notion of truth itself becomes blurred. Both sides of an issue need to be presented only when there are two sides. When verifiable falsehoods become subjects for debate, then nonsense such as Holocaust denial cannot be effectively dismissed, and democratic society is imperiled as much by this as any other single threat, regardless of whether the origins of the nonsense are religious fanaticism, simple ignorance, or personal gain.[215]

4. Summary and Conclusion

The Holocaust falls into that unique category of criminal malevolence whose enormity puts it beyond the purview of traditional standards of law and reason. Yet, ignorance of its ever having happened is widespread: the tortured cries from the graves of the millions murdered out of madness, unheard.

---

215. Lawrence Krauss, Opinion, *Equal Time for Nonsense*, N.Y. TIMES, July 29, 1996, at A19. Krauss is chairman of the physics department at Case Western Reserve University. He goes on to cite favorably the advice passed on by Arthur Hays Sulzberger (publisher of the *New York Times* from 1935–1961): "I believe in an open mind, but not so open that your brains fall out."

Indeed, as eyewitnesses to survivors of Nazi atrocities themselves pass away, Holocaust denial has gained growing acceptance.

Thus, it is increasingly important that the expression of such thought need not be condoned in a free society. Group libel laws are viable even as civil liberties are fully protected. Tort actions can be pursued for intentional infliction of emotional distress; to that end, American courts should adopt the Canadian view, linking the psychological and emotional harm caused by hate propaganda to the target group's constitutional right of equality.

Racial hatred may be an inevitable facet of the human condition, but even under the First Amendment, demonstrably false ideas can be prohibited and punished. At the very least, if Holocaust denial is allowed to avoid the limitations we have come to put on obscenity, defamation, disclosure of state secrets, and other forms of expression excluded from First Amendment protection, certain fundamental principles should be clearly recognized. Holocaust deniers are not constitutionally entitled to access someone else's press. Nor do public libraries need to carry their books and journals.

Holocaust denial should be recognized not as an attempt at free inquiry but as an exercise in distortion. Universities should be regarded as places with the moral responsibility of training students to think critically, not of providing platforms for bigots whose sole purpose is to stir up hatred. Allowing them to discard the documented facts of history can hardly be understood as the honest scholar's quest for truth.

When perpetrated in an academic environment, Holocaust denial is a particularly pernicious form of hate speech. On American campuses, regardless of whether a student organization is privately or publicly funded, rejection of its right to sponsor a Holocaust denial speaker need not be viewed as suppression of free speech. Nor has freedom of the press been infringed when an advertisement denying the Holocaust is spurned by a student newspaper. Editorial discretion in a free society allows for—indeed, requires—the ability to reject as well as to accept material submitted by outside sources.

Holocaust deniers, often motivated by base anti-Semitic impulses, will always find ways to disseminate their views. Honest scholars have an obligation to confront, challenge, and when necessary, condemn them.

FIVE

The Criminal Protection of Memory

Some Observations About the offense of Holocaust Denial

–Emanuela Fronza

1. Law as Protection Against Oblivion: Punishing Holocaust Denial as Part of a General Trend

Denial of holocaust has a growing presence in our society. Its dissemination is even more insidious today since text as well as images can easily circulate on the Web. Propaganda denying, justifying, or minimizing the Holocaust,[1] other genocides, and crimes against humanity[2] surreptitiously complicate and augment the landscape of racist phenomenologies that manifest themselves through acts or words.

For this reason, most European legislators (on a national and supranational level) have introduced *ad hoc* criminal laws punishing acts of denial into their legal systems. This essay aims to investigate this reality. The laws examined have been challenged in a series of legal proceedings before domestic trial courts, constitutional courts, and the European Court of Human Rights. Analyzing denial as a crime means having to deal with the limits that criminal law imposes on freedom of expression and the question of whether

1. The Holocaust continues to be the main target, even if other acts of genocide and atrocity have met similar attempts of denial, minimization, or justification.

2. For denialism in a historical perspective, *see* Ginzburg, C., *'Beweis, Gedächtnis, Vergessen'* in *Memory o Werkstatt Geschichte* 30, (2002), 50–60 ; Vidal Naquet, P. , *Assassins of Memory: Essays on the Denial of the Holocaust* (New York: Columbia Univ. Press 1992); Poggio, P. P., *Nazismo e revisionismo storico,* (Roma: Manifestolibri, 1997); *Négationnistes: Les chiffoniers de l'histoire* (Paris: Syllepse 1997); Lipstadt, D., *Leugnen des Holocaust* (Zürich: Rio Verlag, 1994); Bailer-Galanda, B. Benz W., Neugebauer (eds.), W. *Wahrheit und Auschwitzlüge: Zur Bekämpfung "revisionistischer" Propaganda* (Wien: Verlag Deuticke, 1995); Tiedemann, M., *In Auschwitz wurde niemand vergast* (Mülheim an der Ruhr: Verl. an der Ruhr, 1996); Bastian, T., *Auschwitz und Auschwitzlüge* (München: Beck, 1997); Ternon, Y., *Du négationnisme: mémoire et tabou* (Paris: Desclée de Brouwer, 1998); Shermer M., & Grobman, A., *Denying History: Who Says the Holocaust Never Happened and Why Do They Say It?* (Berkeley: University of California Press, 2000). On the world of denial and the witness's importance, *see* Coquio, C. (ed.), *L'Histoire trouée, négation et témoignage* (Paris: Atalante, 2004).

the law and criminal trials can become the primary instrument for protecting and constructing memory. Indeed, maintaining the memory of the Holocaust has been identified as an antidote to future tragedies.

Before examining the provisions punishing Holocaust denial, it is my opinion that legislators' decisions to introduce such provisions is to be considered within a much broader trend, which we could define as "malaise de la mémoire."[3] In fact, the appearance and importance of memory in all spaces of public life are increasingly evident in Western societies. "We must remember" so that the memory of crimes of historical significance—often foundational moments in democratic societies—is not gradually and inevitably weakened.

Law and especially criminal law appear to be the most powerful instruments in embedding the memory of the Holocaust into society, even symbolically. The use of these instruments would thus satisfy the needs of narrating and reasserting *shared* memories, thus creating respect for a past that should never be forgotten. As part of this trend, many European states have turned to the law as an instrument of memory.

1.1 Les "Lois Mémorielles" and the Crime of Denial

Law and memory[4] intersect in a variety of forms; the intersection is not limited to issues of criminal law. For instance, the provisions instituting a "day of memory" or establishing a reconstruction of historical facts (the so-called *lois mémorielles*) do not employ criminal law. In this case, a law is passed that marks a day on the calendar for remembrance; one example is the Italian law—Law 211 of July 20, 2000—which officially made January 27th a day dedicated to the "memory" of "the Holocaust, racial laws, and all those who opposed inhumanity" and not a holiday or general commemoration day.[5]

Germany, Belgium, and France have also passed similar legislation. France acknowledged the Armenian genocide with the law of January 29, 2001, and

---

3. *See* Rousso, H., *Le Syndrome de Vichy de* 1944 à *Nos Jours* (Paris: Seuil, 1987); Rousso, H., *La Hantise du Passé* (Paris: Éd. Textuel, 1998).

4. Law and memory have been chosen instead of law and history because the concept of memory covers the whole social process of reprocessing the past. Despite a few differences, the concept of memory is generally considered as broader and more inclusive and dynamic than historical and historiographical investigations.

5. *See* www.parlamento.it and www.sissco.it for the law and debate in Parliament.

passed the same year a statute called *Loi Taubira*—a law that recognizes that the African slave trade and slavery constitute crimes against humanity.

In 2005, the French again passed a commemorative law; the *Loi Mekachera* on French colonialism expresses its gratitude "to women and men who participated in the activities carried out by France in the former French *Départements* in Algeria, Morocco, Tunisia and Indochina and in the other territories previously under French sovereignty." Art. 4 of the law states that academic research should recognize the history of the French presence abroad—especially in North Africa—and that school curricula should acknowledge its "positive role." This particular provision has been the source of much controversy; in fact, the second subsection of Art. 4 was repealed at the end of January 2006.

In 2005, the UN also created an International Day of Commemoration. With the adoption of Resolution 60/7 entitled "Holocaust Remembrance" on November 1, 2005, the General Assembly decided that the UN would designate January 27th—the anniversary date of the liberation of the Auschwitz concentration camp—as an International Day of Commemoration in memory of the victims of the Holocaust.[6] These national and international laws of commemoration define memory through the realm of legislation and outside the judicial sphere.

On October 31, 2007, Spain passed another type of "memory law," recognizing and enlarging the rights of victims of the civil war and dictatorship and establishing measures in their favor (*Ley de Memoria Histórica*).[7]

In addition to passing commemorative legislation, lawmakers have begun to turn to criminal law when instilling a collective memory on society. Criminal law acts as a harder and more invasive instrument because, in addition to the legislative instance, it implies a *punitive* aspect that may lead to the sacrifice of personal freedom. From a mere day of commemoration (soft legislative model), the relationship between law and memory may evolve into the creation of a criminal offence (hard legislative model).[8] Lawmakers may decide to punish conduct that challenges a specific memory based on a

---

6. *See* G.A. Res. 60/7, U.N. Doc. A/RES/60/7 (Nov. 1, 2005), *available at* http://www.un.org/french/holocaustremembrance/.

7. For an in-depth study and bibliographical references, *see* Gil Gil, A., La *Justicia de Transición en España: de la Amnistía a la Memoria Histórica* (Barcelona: Atelier, 2009).

8. For the distinction between this type of "penalizing" memory and a "celebrative" memory *see* Marquard O., & Alberto Melloni, A., *La storia che giudica, la storia che assolve,* 40-1 (Bari: Laterza, 2008), 40-1 (2008).

certain reconstruction of the past. The binomial expression law and memory is thus expanded into a trinomial one: law, memory, and punishment.

In the case of crimes of historical significance (like genocides and crimes against humanity), the criminal trial is viewed as a theater—with a highly evocative potential—in which instructive reenactment of history[9] may be staged in order to revive a generally accepted memory of the past. Punishment serves an additional purpose here: to strip historical facts from the natural process of being metabolized by memory and place them in an eternal and unchangeable present in an effort to combat manipulation of the past or the blurring memory of dramatic events.

Thus, more so than any other instrument, criminal law satisfies the needs of narrating and reaffirming a shared and *set* memory in an effort to protect a past that should never be forgotten. In this specific case, the punishment called for by the law is provided as retribution for violated memory.

Historically "the imperatives of memory" are not a new phenomenon.[10] In many other periods, those with political power have imposed legislation mandating a certain collective history. Political leaders forbade publicly remembering of the serious crimes committed in Athens during the Thirty Tyrants dictatorship, which were subsequently pardoned in 403 BC; the existence of these ancient dictates demonstrates how far back in history that law has been used in relation to memory.

All that leads to a basic question: can memory be successfully protected by criminal law? If historians and philosophers have constantly stressed memory's importance, the fact that it garners attention in the juridical arena (in connection with the larger scheme of the "fight against oblivion") sheds light on an element that lies deep in post-World War II society. The memory of historical facts—in particular, the history of World War II—has been considered, especially over the last decade, as meriting legal protection. Considering the importance of collective memory within a political and social system, the question arises as to what the best instruments are for protecting that memory.

9. Osiel, M:, *Politiche della Punizione, Memoria Collettiva e Diritto Internazionale, in* Baldissarra, L. Pezzino, P. (eds.) *Giudicare e Punire,* (Napoli: L´ancora del Mediterraneo, 2005), 106.

10. *See* Lollini, A., *Constitutionalism and Transitional Justice in South Africa* (Alexandra Tatiana Pollard trans., Cambridge: Berghahn, 2010).

In reality, the issue of law and memory is closely connected to the rethinking of the relationship between criminal law and ethics. There is no doubt that positive law includes protecting values among its functions: by criminalizing acts, criminal laws outline societies' fundamental values, and they therefore constitute one of the means of protecting what is socially held to be worthy of criminal law protection. Nevertheless, it can be observed that in our particular case, legislators go even further, imposing *a* memory and penalizing those who do not respect that provision. The activity of remembering the past in a particular way is considered a value worthy of legal protection and hence a significant moment in the political and social life of a community. This is demonstrated, not only by laws introducing the offence of denial but also by other legal means; judges also formulate and establish the "right to the truth"[11] and the "duty of memory."[12]

As mentioned before, here we will examine only legislation punishing denial. These laws dramatically express the ambiguity and complexity of the dialogue between law and memory and constitute a compelling paradigm for examining and understanding dynamics that have significant implications—not only from a juridical point of view but also from a historical, social, and political one.

Denial phenomena demand dealing with tragic events that are not so distant and, unfortunately, still relevant if we consider racism in its many new forms. As shall be seen in the rest of this article, questioning the criminalization of denial in no way implies acceptance of denialist theories. These are two completely separate positions. Discussing denial as an offence is one thing, while exploring in detail the debate, the validity and the content of denialist theories is another. This article sets out only to analyze the former, that is, the criminalization of denial conduct and not the larger issue of denial as a phenomenon. As for the latter, the value system I uphold connotes total disapproval of the ideas advocated by deniers.

All efforts should be made to stop similar experiences from repeating themselves and prevent the ideologies behind these atrocities from gaining

---

11. For the right to truth and other bibliographical references see Pastor, D., *Processi penali solo per conoscere la veritá? L´esperienza argentina*, in Fronza, E. , Fornasari G. (eds.), *Il superamento del passato e il superamento del presente. La punizione delle violazioni sistematiche di diritti umani nell'esperienza argentina e colombiana* (Trento: Collana del Dipartimento, 2009) 102–09 .

12. For more information and other bibliographical references, *see* Eiroa P. D., Otero, J. M., *Memoria y Derecho Penal* (Buenos Aires: Placido ed.2008).

power and legitimacy. The urgency of a serious and comprehensive challenge to denialism requires that we address how to respond to it and the effectiveness of the instruments that have been chosen.

2. Denial as an Offence

From a legal point of view, examining and contemplating legislation against Holocaust denial[13] raises rather delicate issues: the response to racist phenomena as well as the intervention of criminal law in relation to freedom of expression and freedom of historical research.

There are many important angles for the criminal law scholar that will not be analyzed here, such as respecting the harm principle and the decision to limit a fundamental (though not absolute) right (protected by international and national law) such as the freedom of expression. Thoughts here on denial as an offence will mostly examine in depth criminal law as an instrument protecting *a* memory and the implications arising from that choice. For this reason, analysis will focus on the need, function, and legitimacy of a law that criminalizes such a conduct.

The concept and territory of denialism should be clearly defined before proceeding with an examination of it as an offence. First, it should be distinguished from revisionism, which indicates a historiographical process that reviews established historical opinions in light of new information and knowledge and makes it possible to reinterpret and rewrite history. In this

---

13. For a comparative examination of denialism as a crime, *see* Kahn, R., Holocaust Denial and the Law: a Comparative Study (New York, NY: Palgrave Macmillan, 2004); Fronza, E., 'Profili penalistici del negazionismo', *Rivista italiana di diritto e procedura penale*, 3 (1999), 1034 ; and the special issue of *Revue Trimestrièlle des droits de l'homme* on the comparative analysis of antiracism legislation, *Revue Trimestrielle des Droits de l'Hommes*, 12/46 (2001). *See also* Roxin, C., *Was darf der Staat unter Strafe stellen?, in* Studi in onore di Giorgio Marinucci (Dolcini E., & Paliero C. E. (eds.) , Milano: Giuffré, 2006), 731; Visconti, C., *Aspetti penalistici del discorso pubblico* (Turin: Giappichelli, 2008), 236–42; Canestrari, S., *Laicità e diritto penale nelle democrazie costituzionali, in Studi in onore di Giorgio Marinucci*, (cit.148); Di Giovine, A., 'Il passato che non passa: "Eichmann di carta" e repressione penale', *Diritto pubblico comparato ed europeo*, I (2006), XIV–XVIII, which considers introducing a similar legislative provision in Italy plausible; Romano, M:, 'Principio di laicità dello Stato, religioni, norme penali',*Rivista italiana di diritto e procedura penale*, 2–3 (2007), 493 ; *see also* Manes, V., 'Attualità e prospettive del giudizio di ragionevolezza in materia penale', *Rivista italiana di diritto e procedura penale*, 2–3(2007), 739 ; concerning the legal responses of various liberal democracies toward hate speech and other forms of extreme expression. *See* Hare I., Weinstein J., (eds.) *Extreme Speech and Democracy* (New York: Oxford University Press, 2009).

sense of the word, every historian and scholar cannot help but be a revisionist since his activity entails a succession of different theoretical paradigms and models.

Reviewing previous historiographical reconstructions is an inevitable part of historiographical work. It is especially important to distinguish denialism from revisionism when it comes to World War II studies. The latter aims to redistribute accountability for the war and limit Hitler's responsibility, relativizing mass extermination but not denying the indisputable fact of the Holocaust. In contrast, deniers reject that the Holocaust ever took place. The term denialism refers to radical doctrines that argue that the genocide of the Jews, gypsies, and other "subhuman" categories at the hands of Nazi Germany never existed and belongs to the sphere of myth, lies, and deception[14]; these doctrines are to be distinguished from historical approaches that look at the Holocaust in a relative and historical perspective or criticize conventional interpretations of it.

The main tenets of denial works are the negation of the existence of the gas chambers; the dispute over the number of victims; the claim that the final solution was not mass extermination but simply emigration; and finally, the claim that the Nuremberg Military Tribunal was a victors' court; hence its outcome is not very reliable. Denialism first appeared in the late 1970s, in a context of historical revisionism. The movement fed off the same political and cultural background of historical revisions but took it to an extreme and fought an ideological battle; deniers claimed that there are no more certain facts; everything is a construction and a falsification.[15]

The geographical origins of denialism lie mostly in Germany and the United States with the Institute for Historical Review—an important enter for authors supporting these arguments and for formulating and organizing denialist strategies. Denialism has also had notable developments in France, Austria, Belgium, and Switzerland (and to a lesser extent in Italy).[16]

---

14. *See* Vidal Naquet, P. *Les assassins de la mémoire*, cit. 108 et seq.

15. *See* Poggio, P., *Nazismo e revisionismo storico*, cit., 104.

16. We do not have the space here to go into the "geography" of denialism. An interesting inquiry may be provided by examining attitudes toward denialism in the Middle East through the work of various Palestinian authors. *See, e.g.*, Vidal-Naquet, P., 'Qui sont les assassins de la mémoire?', *Réflexions sur le génocide: Les Juifs, la mémoire et le présent*, III (1995), 271–91. On cases of denialism outside Europe, *see* Kahn, *R.*, 'Who Takes the Blame? Scapegoating, Legal Responsibility and the Prosecution of Holocaust Revisionists in the Federal Republic of Germany and Canada', Glendale Law Review 16 (1997), 17; Hill, L. E., 'The Trial of Ernst Zundel. Revisionism and the Law in Canada', *Simon Wiesenthal Center*

Proponents of denialism have succeeded in creating an industry with books, magazines, and videocassettes, and its distribution network is international and facilitated by new technology. Authors frequently come from the extreme Right or the extreme Left. They share an ideological platform: anti-Semitism.[17] There is not just a single historiographical paradigm used by the "assassins of memory"[18]; denialist methods are linked to the following strategies: minimization, justification, and negation of crimes. The main argument—as mentioned before—focuses on denial of the Holocaust, though other genocides (like, for example, the Armenian genocide[19] or, more recently, the Rwandan genocide[20]) have also been discussed.

It would be impossible to undertake here a comparative analysis of how each legal system configures the crime. However, briefly describing the common elements of these criminal offence is useful for our analysis. Denialism has manifested itself to varying extents in different European countries, which have dealt with the issue in different eras and with diverse responses.

Annual, 6 (1989), 165 ; Kiernan, B., 'Le communisme racial des Khmers rouges. Un génocide et son négationnisme: le cas du Cambodge', *Esprit*, 252 (1999), 93–127; Rocha de Assis Moura, M. T., Zilli Coelho M., Montecoraonrado Ghidalevich, F. G., *Jurisprudencia latino americana sobre direito penal internacional. Relatorio Brasil, in* Ambos, K., Malarino E., Elsner G. (eds.), *Jurisprudencia latinoamericana sobre derecho penal internacional* (, Montevideo: Konrad Adenauer Stiftung, 2008), 95. See also the decision of South Africa's Constitutional Court on *Islamic Unity Convention v. Independent Broadcasting Authority et al.* of 11 April 2002..

17. Poggio, P., *Nazismo e revisionismo storico*, cit., 97.

18. The expression was coined by Yosef Yerushalmi and was used by Pierre Vidal Naquet at the title for his well-known essay on denialism.

19. In 2001 France passed a law (n. 70 of Jan. 29, 2001) entitled "*Loi relative à la reconnaissance du génocide arménien de 1915*" that recognizes the Armenian genocide, see Rapport fait au nom de la commission des affaires étrangères[(1)] sur la proposition de loi de m. didier migaud et plusieurs de ses collègues (n. 895), relative à la reconnaissance du génocide arménien de 1915 of May 28, 1998 at http://www.assembleenationale.fr/11/rapports/r0925.asp#P358_44916. For more information on the genocide and additional bibliographical references see Dadrian, V. N., *Histoire du Génocide Arménien* (Paris: Stock, 1996); Ternon, Y., *Les Arméniens* (Paris: Seuil, 1996); Chaliand G., & Ternon, Y., *1915 le génocide des Arméniens* (Paris: Éditions Complexe, 2002).

20. SeeBizimana, J. D., *L'Eglise et le génocide au Rwanda: les Péres blancs et le négationnisme* (Paris: L'Harmattan, 2001).

Holocaust denial is outlawed in most Western European countries. It is expressly punished in Germany,[21] France,[22]

21. See § 130, IV of the German criminal code entitled "Volksverhetzung." The Law of October 28, 1994, changed § 130 StGB . This provision today represents the general law against racial discrimination. For commentary and bibliographical and jurisprudence references see *Strafgesetzbuch, Leipziger Kommentar, 12. Auflage* (Berlin: De Gruyter, 2009), 445–513; Hochhuth, M., 'Schatten über der Meinungsfreiheit–den Babycaust-Beschluss des BverfG', *Neue Juristische Wochenschrift*, 4 (2007), 192; Bertram, G., ‚Kollateralschäden einer 'wehrhaften Demokratie', *Neue Juristische Wochenschrift* (2006), 2967; Böhm, M., 'Verteidigerfremdes Verhalten"–Neue Wege zur Ausschließung lästiger Strafverteidiger?', *Neue Juristische Wochenschrift*, 33 (2006), 2371; Kühl, K., *Auschwitz-Leugnen als strafbare Volksverhetzung? in Bernsmann K., Ulsenheimer K.*, (eds.), *Bochumer Beitrage zu aktuellen Strafrechtsthemen* (, Cologne: Heymanns Verlag, 2003) 103; Wandres, T., *Die Strafbarkeit des Auschwitz-Leugnens* (Berlin: Duncker und Humblot Verlag, 2000); Giles, G. J., *Blind in the Right Eye: German Justice and Holocaust Denial, in* Hayes, P. (ed.), *Lessons and Legacies III: Memory, Memorialization and Denial* (Evanston: Northwestern University Press, 1999), 248; Jahn, J., *Strafrechtliche Mittel gegen Rechtsextremismus: die Änderungen der §§ 130 und 86a StGB als Reaktion auf fremdenfeindliche Gewalt im Lichte der Geschichte des politischen Strafrechts in Deutschland* (Frankfurt: Lang, 1998); Werle G., and Wandres T., *Auschwitz vor Gericht: Völkermord und bundesdeutsche Strafjustiz: mit einer Dokumentation des Auschwitz-Urteils* (Munich: Beck, 1995); Dahs, H., ‚Das Verbrechensbekämpfungsgesetz vom 28.10.94–ein Produkt des Superwahljahres", *Neue Juristische Wochenschrift* (1995), 553; Wehinger, M., *Kolletivbeleidgung–Volksverhetzung: der strafrechtlicher Schutz von Bevölkerungsgruppen durch die 185 ff. und 130 StGB* (Baden-Baden: Nomos Verlag, 1994); Werle, G.,'Der Holocaust als Gegenstand der bundesdeutchen Strafjustiz', Neue Juristische Wochenschrift(1992), 2530; Jung, H., ‚Strafrechtliche Maßnahmen gegen die "Auschwitz-Lüge" *JuS* (1986), 80.

22. The offence of denialism (Art. 24 bis), entitled "*Contestation des crimes contre l'humanité*" was introduced as part of the law on freedom of the press n. 90-602 (*Loi Gayssot*) on July 13, 1990. See Beignier, B., '*De la langue perfide délivre-moi–Réflexions sur la loi du 13 juillet 1990 dite loi Gayssot*', *Pouvoir et liberté. Etudes offertes à Jacques Mourgeon* (Brussels: Bruylant, 1998), 497; CCohen, C., 'Le négationnisme: du ressort de l'Histoire ou des Tribunaux?', *Gaz. Pal.*, 25 and 27 March 2001, 28; Cammilleri A.-Subrenat,'L'incitation à la haine et la Constitution', *RID comp.*, 2 (2002), 513–48; Dreyer, E.,'Le fondement de la prohibition des discours racistes en France', *Légipresse*, II (2003), 19; Feldman, J.P., 'Peut-on dire n'importe quoi sur la Shoah?', *RID comp.*, (1998), 229; Feldman, P., 'Le délit de contestation de crimes contre l'humanité et la 17e chambre du Tribunal de grande instance de Paris', *Dalloz*, 1999, chron. 8; de Gouttes, R., 'À propos du conflit entre le droit à la liberté d'expression et le discours raciste ou révisionniste', *Pouvoir et liberté*, 497; Troper, M.,'Droit et négationnisme. La Loi Gayssot et la Constitution', *Annales*, Histoire, Sciences sociales, November-December (1999), 1239; Korman, C., 'Le délit de diffusion d'idées racistes', *Juris Classeur Pénal*, I (1989), 3404; Korman, C., 'La lutte contre le négationnisme, bilan et perspectives de la loi du 13 juillet 1990', *Actes du colloque du 5 juillet 2002 à la Cour d'appel de Paris* (2003); Lévinet, M., 'La fermeté bienvenue de la Cour européenne des droits de l'homme face au négationnisme, obs. à la décision du 24 juin 2003, Garaudy c/France,' *Revue Trimestrielle des Droits de l'Hommes* (2004), 653; Massias, F. 'La liberté d'expression et le discours raciste ou révisionniste,' *Revue Trimestrielle des Droits de l'Hommes* (1993), 183; Massias, F., 'Le droit face à la montée du racisme et de la xénophobie,' *Revue Trimestrielle des Droits de l'Hommes*, 46 (2001); Pech, L., 'Conflit entre différentes conceptions de la liberté d'expression sur l'internet: vers une lex americana en matière de lutte

Austria,[23] Belgium,[24] Spain,[25]

---

contre le discours raciste et négationniste?,' *Légipresse*, II (2002), 5; Roumelian, O., 'Un délit d'opinion au service des droits de l'homme?,' *Petites affiches*, 21 (1996), 10; Schaus, A., 'Le délit de presse raciste,' in *Mélanges P. Lambert*, (Brussels: Bruylant, 2000), 735; Tracol, X., 'L'affaire Faurisson devant le Comité des droits de l'homme des Nations-Unies,' *Légipresse*, II/141 (1997), 57; Véron, M., *Le renforcement du dispositif répressif contre la discrimination et le racisme. Présentation des lois des 12 et 13 juillet 1990*, Dr. pénal 1990, chron. 1; Frangi, M., 'Les «lois mémorielles» : de l'expression de la volonté générale au législateur historien,' *Revue de Droit pénal*, 1 (2005).

23. See par. 3 introduced by law of February 26, 1992 (*Bundesverfassungsgesetz vom 6 Februar 1947 über die Behandlung der Nazionalsozialisten*). It was in Austria, on February 20, 2006, that David Irving–who admitted he was guilty–was sentenced to three years in prison with probation for several lectures held in Vienna that disputed the existence of gas chambers. For the Irving trial in England, *see* Guttenplan, D., *The Holocaust on Trial: History, Justice and the David Irving Libel Case* (New York : W.W. Norton & Company, 2001); Lipstadt, D., *History on Trial: My Day in Court with David Irving* (New York: HarperPerennial, 2005); Van Pelt, R.J., *The Case for Auschwitz: Evidence from the Irving Trial* (Bloomington, IN: Indiana University Press, 2002).

24. Law of March 23, 1995, n. 31, amended by law of May 7, 1999, n. 57. The text was published in *Moniteur Belge* on March 30, 1995. *See* Batselé, D. Hanotiau M., Dourmont, O., 'La lutte contre le racisme et la xénophobie, mythe ou réalité?,' *Revue trimestrielle des droits de l'homme*, 7 (1991), 319 and 8 (1991), 435; Batselé, D., 'Racisme et liberté d'expression. Examen de la législation et de la jurisprudence belges,' *Revue trimestrielle des droits de l'homme, Numéro spécial. Le droit face à la montée du racisme et de la xénophobie* (2001) 321 et seq.; Ringelheim, F., 'Le négationnisme contre la loi,' *Revue trimestrielle des droits de l'homme*, 29 (1997), 118; Blero, B., 'La répression légale du révisionnisme,' *Journal des Tribunaux*, 32 (1996), 333; Van Drooghenbroeck, S., *La Constitution de la Belgique et l'incitation à la haine*, http://www.ddp.unipi.it/dipartimento/seminari/brisbane/Brisbane-Belgio.pdf; Centre pour l'égalité des chances et la lutte contre le racisme, *La loi du 30 juillet 1981 tendant à réprimer certains actes inspirés par le racisme et la xénophobie: Jurisprudence* (Brussels: SFI, 1999); Dumont H., Tulkens, F., 'Les activités liberticides et le droit public belge,' in Dumont, H., Mandoux, P., Strowel A., and Tulkens F.,(eds.), *Pas de liberté pour les ennemis de la liberté? Groupements liberticides et droit* (Brussels: Bruylant, 2000), 219–318. Siegfried Verbeke was convicted for denialism in Belgium in April 2005; see http://www.expatica.com/be/news/local_news/belgian-holocaust-denier-held-at-schiphol-22551.html.

25. See the last subsection of Art. 607 of the criminal code regarding the crime of genocide. It should be noted that the Spanish *Tribunal Constitucional* (see following pages) declared Art. 607.(2) partially unconstitutional and specifically Holocaust denial as criminal offence. *See* Quintero Olivares G.-Valle-Muniz, J. A., *Comentarios al nuevo Código Penal* (Pamplona, Aranzadi, 2008); Landa Gorostiza, M. "Nuevos' crímenes contra la humanidad: el nuevo delito de lesa humanidad (artículo 607 Bis CP 1995) desde una perspectiva intrasistemática,' *Eguzkilore: Cuaderno del Instituto Vasco de Criminología*, 17 (2003), 105-119; Gómez Navajas, J. 'Apología del genocidio y provocación a la discriminación en el código penal de 1995: (Algunas reflexiones al hilo de la sentencia del Juzgado de lo Penal núm. 3 de Barcelona, de 16 de noviembre de 1998),' *La Ley: Revista jurídica española de doctrina, jurisprudencia y bibliografía*, 3 (1999), 1839-1852; Cuerda Arnau, M.L. ,'El denominado delito de apología del genocidio: Consideraciones constitucionales,' *Revista del poder judicial*, 56 (1999), 63-118. For criminal law limitations on the freedom of speech see Rebollo Vargas, R., *Aproximación a la jurisprudencia constitucional: libertad de expresión e información y límites penales*,

Portugal,[26] and Switzerland[27] and is punishable by fines (and) or detention. Norms that deal with provisions punishing denialism can also be found in Sweden, the Czech Republic, Slovakia, Poland, Romania, and Israel. Italy is one of the few countries that decided not to designate denial as an offence.[28] Italy, along with Canada, the United Kingdom, and Poland punishes denial as conduct that can be considered to constitute other offences, like incitement to hatred.

While there is a shared decision to punish denial on a national level, the configuration of its prohibition does differ. Some countries have included it in their criminal code (this is the case for Germany, Spain, Portugal, and Switzerland), whereas others made it part of a law *extra codicem* passed for this specific purpose (Belgium) or already in existence (France and Austria).

As for specific individual acts, laws tend to punish denial, trivialization, and justification. There are, however, some variants: for example, in Belgium only flagrant minimization is punishable. Some legal systems view acts of revision as punishable instead of denial of facts: the German code speaks of "approving" or "justifying," whereas the French code condemns "contesting" the facts.

What is denied, minimized, or justified also changes. Some countries—like France, Germany, and Belgium—exclusively designate the Holocaust, while others—like Spain, Switzerland, and Portugal—include other genocides and crimes against humanity.

The interest protected is also subject to variation. For example, in Germany, public peace is protected; while in France, public order and human

(Barcelona: PPU, 1992) and the interesting *Tribunal Constitucional* court decision dated November 11, 1991 on the "Grenelle" case, *Jurisprudencia Constitucional*, 31, 444 et seq.

26. See Art. 240 of the criminal code: "Racial or Religious Discrimination," especially subsection 2(b).

27. See Art. 261 bis of the criminal code introduced by law of June 18, 1995. See Guyaz, A., *L'incrimination de la discrimination racial* (Bern: Stämpfli, 1997); Niggli, M. A. *Rassendiskriminierung, Ein Kommentar zu art. 261 bis StGB und art. 171c MStG* (Zürich: Schulthess, 1996);Kunz, K. L., 'Zur Unschärfe und zum Rechtsgut der Strafnorm gegen Rassendiskriminierung,' *Rivista Penale Svizzera*, 2 (1998), 223.

28. Italy does not have an ad hoc offenceprovision, although it does have laws on freedom of expression and on non discrimination (Art. 21 Const. and Art. 3 Const.) and many instruments for combating racist phenomena. See laws 962/67, 654/75 and especially Art. 3, 223/90, and the legislative decree 122/93 "*Misure urgenti in materia di discriminazione razziale, etnica e religiosa*" and Art. 43 of legislative decree 286/98, as well as law 85/2006 reforming speech crimes . Also see *Norme sulla sensibilizzazione e repressione della discriminazione razziale, l'orientamento sessuale e la identità di genere. Riforme della legge n. 654 del 13 ottobre 1975*, approved by the Council of Ministers in January 2007; concerning the italian current debate on punishing Holocaust denial see the article of Prosperi, A.:http://www.repubblica.it/cronaca/2010/10/16/news/shoah-negazione_reato-8109041/index.html?ref=search.

dignity are protected. A common element of these criminal offence, however, is the public nature of the act. Finally, it should be noted that the scope of the norm's application also varies from country to country. In Germany, for example, the norm's scope of application is limited by the requirement that the acts in question be capable of disturbing public peace.

Supranational instruments for challenging denialism are a separate issue. International law includes an elaborate normative system against racist phenomena. European rules also demonstrate a tendency to punish denial phenomena. The European Union has a strong influence on national criminal laws. As is well known, criminal policy guidelines that also regard individual national legal systems are increasingly determined on a European level.

Important European measures regarding denial include the *Joint Action* of 1996[29] and the framework decision, on combating certain forms and expressions of racism and xenophobia[30], which expressly asks that European states take the legislative steps necessary for punishing "condoning, denying or grossly trivializing" crimes against humanity and crimes of war as defined by Articles 6, 7, and 8 of the Statute of the International Criminal Court (Art. 1(1)(c)). The decision also asks European states to punish for the crimes defined in Art. 6 of the Charter of the International Military Tribunal appended to the London Agreement of August 8, 1945 (Art. 1(1)(d)), "directed against a group of persons or a member of such a group defined by reference to race, colour, religion, descent or national or ethnic origin when the conduct is carried out in a manner likely to incite to violence or hatred against such a group or a member of such a group." Thus, at the European level we find a request for more criminal law similar to the trend of overcriminalisation that we can observe at a national level.

Two observations should be made about this latter provision. Just like some of its national counterparts, the European legislator demonstrates concern about limiting a fundamental right such as the freedom of expression;

---

29. *See* "Joint Action of July 15, 1996 adopted by the Council on the basis of Art. K.3 of the Treaty on European Union, concerning action to combat racism and xenophobia," *Official Journal of the European Community*, L/185, 24 July 1996, 5.

30. *See Council Framework Decision 2008/913/JHA of 28 November 2008 on combating certain forms and expressions of racism and xenophobia by means of criminal law.* . See Renauld, B., *La décision-cadre 2008/913/JAI du Conseil de l'Union Européenne : du nouveau en matière de lutte contre le racisme ?*, Revue trimestrièlle des droits de l´homme, 2010, number 81, 119 -140.

it therefore added—as a balancing measure—a danger clause according to which Member States may punish only conduct "carried out in a manner likely to disturb public order or which is threatening, abusive or insulting." On the one hand, the European Union establishes a threshold of criminal liability; on the other hand, the states are given a margin of freedom, permitting the creation of varying parallel normative systems.

Furthermore, the *Framework Decision* provides that the crimes be those set out by the Statute of the International Criminal Court or of the Nuremberg Tribunal. But who decides that a specific historical event falls under the definitions in Articles 6, 7, and 8 of the International Criminal Court's Statute? Is it the legislator or the judge? What about a genocide that has not been defined as such or that has not been subject to legal proceedings and therefore not qualified as an international crime? Would it for this reason alone not be considered as the object of a crime of denialism? Differently stated, a law configured in this way could cause *selective criminalization* of genocide denials because it only contemplates mass extermination in connection with historical events defined as such by the courts or legislator. Moreover, this choice does not appear to be very practical for building a *shared memory* since there is ample room for different opinions in the definition of historical events.

The Council of Europe—especially the decisions of the European Court—also allows for limiting the exercise of freedom of expression (protected by Art. 10 of the European Convention) to repress denialism; we will return to this particular issue when analysing *Garaudy v. France.*

3. Deniers on Trial

Denial offences have been the subject of numerous decisions made by national courts[31] and constitutional courts[32] in deciding the compatibility

31. Some examples are the trials against Robert Faurisson and Roger Garaudy (in France) or David Irving (in Austria and in England).

32. The Spanish decision *Tribunal Constitucional*, STC, November 7, 2007, n. 235, cuestión de inconstitucionalidad núm. 5152-2000; German court decision, BVG German Federal Constitutional Court, April 13, 994, in *Neue Juristische Wochenschrift*, 1994; commented on inKommers, D.P., *The Constitutional Jurisprudence of the Federal Republic of Germany*, (Durham, NC: Duke University Press, 1997), 382; and the Belgian court decision of the *Cour d'arbitrage*, July 12, 1996, n. 45, Revuc universelle des droits de l'homme, 1997, 106 with commentary by Ringelheim, F., 'Le négationnisme et la loi', *Journal des tribunaux*, 1997, 95.

with the right to freedom of expression and the European Court and Commission.[33]

We will analyze some of the decisions that are representative of the problematic issues arising from criminalizing denial not only because it is an offence involving speeches or writing but also because it protects a specific memory.

3.1 History as *Res Judicata*: the Holocaust as a "Historically Established Fact" and Garaudy v. France

The jurisprudence of the European Court of Human Rights provides interesting terrain for examining some crucial aspects of denial as a crime that imposes limits on freedom of expression—generally protected by Art. 10 of the European Convention of Human Rights (hereinafter ECHR)—to be limited.[34]

Garaudy v. France,[35] a court decision often referred to in other cases, should be analysed. In this decision, the court ruled that the claimant's

33. See ECHR, *Witzsch v. Germany (2)*, (dec.) December 13, 2005, n. 7485/03; ECHR, *Garaudy v. France*, (dec.), June 24, 2003, n. 65831/01; ECHR, *Witzsch v. Germany (1)*, (dec.), April 20, 1999, n. 41448/98; ECHR, *Lehideux and Isorni v. France*, September 23, 1998, n. 24662/94; *D. I. v. Germany*, (dec.), June 26, 1996, n. 26551/95; ECHR, *Pierre Marais v. France*, (dec.), June 124, 996, n. 31159/96; ECHR, *Nationaldemokratische Partei Deutschlands v. Germany*, (dec.) November 29, 1995, n. 25992/94; ECHR, *Remer v. Germany*, (dec.), September 6, 1995, n. 25096/94; ECHR, *F. P. v. Germany*, (dec.), March 29, 1993, n. 19459/92; ECHR, *T. v. Belgium*, July 14, 1983, (dec.), n. 9777/82; ECHR, *X. v. Federal Republic of Germany*, (dec.), July 16, 1982, n. 9235/81. For commentary, see Oetheimer, M., "La Cour européenne des droits de l'homme face au discours de la haine,' *Rev. trim. droits de l'homme*, 69 (2007), 63; Wachsmann, P., 'Liberté d'expression et négationnisme,' *Rev. trim. droits de l'homme*, 46 (2001), 590 ;Roscini, M:, 'La libertà di esprimere dichiarazioni razziste e blasfeme nella giurisprudenza della Corte europea dei diritti dell'Uomo,' *Riv. int. dir. umani*, 1, (1998), 95 ; Massias, F., 'La liberté d'expression et le discours raciste ou révisionniste,' *Rev. trim. droits de l'homme*, 13 (1993), 183 et seq; Cohen Jonathan, G., "sub Art. 10," in *La Convention européenne des droits de l'homme* (Pettiti, L. E., Decaux E., Imbert P. H. (eds.), Paris: Economica, 1999), 386, 393, and 395. On a supranational level, see UN Human Rights Committee: Human Rights Committee, *Faurisson v. France*, November 8, 1996; Revue universelle des droits de l'homme, 1997, 46 and commentary of Cohen Jonathan, G., "Négationnisme et droits de l'homme', *Revue Trimestrièlle des droits de l'homme*, 32 (1997), 571.

34. Also see ECHR, *Pierre Marais v. France*, *Lehideux and Isorni v. France*, September 23, 1998; Cohen Jonathan, G. "L'apologie de Pétain devant la Cour européenne des droits de l'homme,' *Revue universelle des droits de l'homme*, 38 (1999), 366 et seq.

35. ECHR, *Garaudy v. France*, June 24, 2003. This judgment has been cited in various cases before the court; regarding denial, see ECHR, *Witzsch v. Germany*, December 13, 2005,

application was inadmissible and by doing so, imposed limitations on freedom of expression. Roger Garaudy had been convicted in France for "*contestation des crimes contre l'humanité, diffamation publique raciale*" and "*provocation à la haine raciale*" because he published a book called *The Founding Myths of Modern Israel.*

Summarizing or analysing all of the aspects touched on by the decision would be impossible here. What is important to note is not so much the court's solution, as much as some elements of the court's analysis, which is particularly significant because it accounts for problems associated with the prohibition of denial and the choice of law and criminal trial as the instruments for responding to this alarming phenomenon.

When faced with applicants who claim a violation of freedom of expression, the court makes a distinction between "clearly established historical facts—like the Holocaust"[36]—and facts that are part of "an ongoing debate among historians about the events in question and their interpretation."[37]

The issue of limits on the historical debate relating to World War II events is thus examined. Though the court considers it necessary for any country to have open and peaceful debate about its own history,[38] the court rejects the notion that Art. 10 ECHR protections allow for revising or denying the Holocaust's existence. According to this interpretation, it is up to the court to evaluate whether or not historical facts are being denied by analyzing the aim pursued, the method used, and the content.[39]

Based on this reasoning, the court rules that the claimant's application is inadmissible: the book published by *Garaudy* aimed to deny the Holocaust because it advocates denialist ideas. The purpose of the work was not a search for truth but to falsify history in order to rehabilitate the National-Socialist regime and, in turn, accuse the regime's victims of falsifying history.[40]

(dec.), 7485/03, § The law 3 (which applies Art. 17 ECHR even if the defendant—in a private letter—did not deny the Holocaust or the gas chamber but an "equally significant and established circumstance of the Holocaust").

36. See ECHR, *Lehideux and Isorni v. France*, par. 53 and 47; ECHR, *Garaudy v. France*, par. 28.

37. ECHR, *Lehideux and Isorni v. France*, par. 47.

38. Ibid., par. 55.

39. ECHR, *Garaudy v. France*, par. 26, quoting ECHR, *Lehideux and Isorni* v. *France*, par. 53.

40. ECHR, *Garaudy v. France*, par. 29. The trend of punishing denial claims already appeared in ECHR, *Remer v. Germany*, September 6, 1995 (n. 25096/94, D.R. 82-a, p. 117); ECHR, *Pierre Marais v. France* (n. 31159/96, D.R., 86-A, 184); ECHR, *DI c. Allemagne*, June 26, 1996;

Holocaust denial publications undermine "[T]he values on which the fight against racism and anti-Semitism are based and constitutes a serious threat to public order. Such acts are incompatible with democracy and human rights because they infringe the rights of others. Its proponents indisputably have designs that fall into the category of aims prohibited by Art. 17 of the Convention".[41]

Denial claims go against justice and peace—fundamental values of the ECHR expressly stated in its Preamble[42]—and for this reason, they are not protected by Art. 10 of the ECHR.

3.2 History on Trial: "the Correct Method" and the Theil Case

Another court decision worth examining is the one made by the Court of Lyon on January 3, 2006. Like our analysis of *Garaudy v. France*, we will only look at the elements that are important when thinking about denial as a criminal offence.

In France, the denial phenomenon has had a significant presence. The offence of denialism was introduced as part of the Law on the Freedom of the Press of 29 July 1881: Art. 24 bis, entitled "*Contestation des crimes contre l'humanité*," provides:

"Seront punis . . . ceux qui auront contesté l'existence d'un ou plusieurs crimes contre l'humanité tels qu'ils sont définis par l'article 6 du statut du Tribunal militaire international annexé a l'Accord de Londres du 8 août 1945 et qui ont été commis soit par les membres d'une organisation déclarée criminelle en application de l'article 9 du dit Statut, soit par une personne coupable de tels crimes par une juridiction française ou internationale".

To limit the risk of excessively reducing freedom of expression and to avoid entrusting courts with the task of pursuing historical truth, denial was limited to the Nazi genocide and the crimes judged by a national or

---

Nationaldemokratische Partei Deutschlands of November 29, 1995 (n. 25992/94, D.R. 84-A, 149).

41. ECHR, *Garaudy v. France*, par. 29.

42. ECHR, *Garaudy v. France*, par. 29. See also ECHR, *Pierre Marais v. France*, 191, and *Remer v. Germany*, September 6, 1995.

international Tribunal. Based on this provision, denials of other genocides (like the Armenian one) are not punishable.

The court decision of *Tribunal de Grande Instance* in Lyon sentenced George Theil to six months in prison and a fine of 10,000 euros for "*contestation des crimes contre l'humanité*" (under Art. 24 bis) because in a television interview, he denied that the gas chamber existed.

The judges expound on the *ratio legis* and scope of Art. 24 bis within a broader discussion of *querelle des mémoires* or *mémoires abusives*. They cite all the T*ravaux Préparatoires*, expressing the need for providing an offence punishing act condoning Nazism and anti-Semitism; simultaneously, they call attention to the importance of not transforming judges into guardians of an official historical truth because it would impede historical research from being carried out in good faith. From their reading of the T*ravaux Préparatoires*, the judges obtain useful indications about the protected interest, which is identified as equal human dignity for all people regardless of ethnic group, nation, race, or religion. Protecting this interest requires combating against every insult to the memory of victims of the crimes against humanity covered by Art. 6(c) of the Charter of the International Military Tribunal of Nuremberg. Art. 24 *bis*, therefore, is supposed to counter all forms of memory denial that conceal anti-Semitism.

For solving the specific case in question, the judges delineate certain criteria. The most important of these is the historian's use of the *correct method*. In line with the European Court's of Human Rights jurisprudence, which insist on evaluating context, aims, method, and content, the judges argue that analysing the ideas advocated by *Theil* is not as important as analysing his method. In order to do so, they must verify if the historian followed a procedure in good faith, bearing in mind the sources used, respecting a certain hierarchy among them, and the use of sufficient documentation.

The court of Lyon made its decision on Art. 24 *bis* based on these legal arguments. The court supported its holding with previous French court judgements, decisions of the European Court of Human Rights(especially *Lehideux* and *Isorni v. France* and *Garaudy v. France*),[43] and some studies on denialism (especially Papadopoulos's "Pénalisation du négationnisme et premier Amendement"[44]).

---

43. See p. 28 and 29 of the decision.

44. See p. 30 of the decision.

This case not only demonstrates the general trend toward punishing denialist conduct, but it also reveals a dangerous implication of this legislation offence: judges can go *as far as* determining the correct method for a historian. As a result, their work goes beyond the law, invading the terrain of historians. But what is the method? Moreover, how can a judge establish the correct method for historians?

3.3 Claims About Facts and Claims About Values: the Spanish Tribunal Constitucional's Judgement of Partial Unconstitutionality

In this last section, we will look at the judgement made by the Spanish *Tribunal Constitucional* regarding the constitutionality of denial as a criminal offence. The crime of denial is codified in the last subsection of Art. 607 of the Criminal Code and is associated with freedom of speech protected under the Spanish Constitution.[45] The judges outline a distinction, which is not crystal clear, between the actof denial—ruled as not being in contrast with the Constitution—and act of justification, which may be punished although within specific limits.

The issue of constitutionality was raised on September 14, 2000, by *Seccion III* of the *Audiencia provincial* of Barcelona during the *Varela* appeal. *Varela* was the owner and manager of a bookstore that distributed and sold books and documents denying the Holocaust.

---

45. *Tribunal Constitucional*, November 7, 2007, 235/2007. See the dissenting opinions appended to the decision. For commentary on the decision, see Landa Gorostiza, J. M., '*La llamada "mentira de Auschwitz" y el "delito de provocación" a la luz del "caso Varela": una oportunidad perdida para la cuestión de inconstitucionalidad*', *Actualidad Penal*, 36 (1999), 709; Ramos Vázquez, J. A., 'A declaración de inconstitucionalidad del delito de "negacionismo" (artículo 607.2 del código penal)', *Revista penal*, 23 (2009), 120-137; de la Rosa Cortina, J. M. 'Negacionismo y revisionismo del genocidio: perspectiva penal y constitucional', *Diario La Ley*, 6842 (2007), 6842; Bilbao Ubillos, J. M., 'La negaciòn de un genocidio no es una conducta punible (comentario a la STC 235/2007)', *Revista espanola de derecho constitucional*, 2009, n. 85, 322; Visconti, C., *Aspetti penalistici del discorso pubblico* cit., 228–36. It is interesting to compare this decision with the aforementioned *Bundesverfassungsgericht* decision of 1994, which reached the opposite conclusion: according to the German court constitutional protection of the freedom of speech does not cover denial because they are untrue claims about "facts." For a comparison, see Visconti, C., *Aspetti penalistici del discorso pubblico*, cit., 224 et seq. See also the judgement of the *Bundesverfassungsgericht:* http://www.bundesverfassungsgericht.de/entscheidungen/rs20091104_1bvr215008.html

According to the applicant, incitement to conduct offending fundamental rights or human dignity is punishable based on other legal provisions. As a result, prohibiting denial is neither necessary nor constitutional because it limits freedom of speech and therefore runs counter to Art. 20(1) of the Spanish Constitution (*Antecedente de hecho* n. 3).

The *Tribunal Constitucional* responded by declaring (not unanimously) the unconstitutionality of criminalizing the dissemination of ideas that deny the genocide because "criminally vacuous" ("*penalmente inane*"); however, it accepted that, in a restricted form, a criminal offence of justifying those crimes was compatible with the Constitution.

The *Tribunal Constitucional*'s reasoning begins by stressing the importance of the freedom of expression (pp. 21–22 of the Judgement). This fundamental right may be exercised even when the opinions expressed are disturbing, unsettling, dangerous, or wrong. The court found this freedom to be consistent with the pluralism a society needs in order to be democratic. Freedom of expression protects even opinions running counter to the spirit of the Constitution itself unless those opinions infringe upon other constitutionally protected interests, in which case they may be limited and considered an offence. Thus, the issue becomes whether disseminating ideas that deny or justify genocide imposes on a constitutionally protected interest and would therefore be punishable.

The Tribunal proceeds to quote old precedents. In 1991, the *Tribunal Constitucional* ruled that opinions about historical facts are covered by freedom of expression in so much as they are "subjective opinions regarding historical facts" (p. 23 of the Judgement).

The Spanish constitutional court notes that Art. 607(2) of the criminal code punishes simply the dissemination of ideas without requiring damage to other constitutionally important interests and therefore represses conduct protected by freedom of expression, academic freedom (Art. 20(1) Constitution) and freedom of thought (Art. 16 Constitution). Because criminal law may not interfere with the constitutionally protected content of those rights–even in the case of odious ideas against human dignity—the Spanish constitutional order does not allow lawmakers to punish mere dissemination of ideas (*Fundamento Juridico* 6 of the judgement). However, freedom of expression shall not be protected for hate speech that directly incites violence against citizens in general or against specific races or groups (citing jurisprudence of the European Court of Human Rights[46]).

---

46. Hate speech is defined referring to ECHR, *Erdogdu v. Turkey*, 8 July 1999.

The court then proceeds to examine the provision in question by looking at the international legislation against Holocaust denial. The Tribunal examines Art. 22 of the International Covenant on Civil and Political Rights and Art. 5 of the Genocide Convention as well as Art. 615 and Art. 510(1) of the criminal code, crimes against honour, and other provisions regarding the exercise of fundamental rights.

At this point, the Tribunal provides that there is a distinction between *denial* and *justification*. This distinction is a central part of the Tribunal's reasoning and the creation of different solutions for the two types of conduct: the former being legal while the latter is not.[47]

> Denial is defined as merely expressing a point of view on certain facts claiming that these facts were realized in such a way as not to be qualified as genocide. Justification, on the other hand, does not imply total denial that a specific crime of genocide took place but its relativization or denial of its unlawfulness, starting with a certain identification of the perpetrators.

The two offences provided by Art. 607(2) of the criminal code comply with the Constitution if they constitute directly inciting violence against specific groups or contempt for the genocide victims. While conduct justifying the Holocaust satisfies this condition, mere denial, as such, does not meet the threshold of danger criteria (namely the direct incitation to violence against specific groups).

The other fundamental aspect for the Tribunal´s decision is the connection of denial to "hate speech." Denying genocides is not ascribable to this concept because "merely stating conclusions about whether certain facts took place or not without judging those facts or their unlawfulness falls within the scope of academic freedom," which receives broader protection in the Constitution than freedom of expression and information (p. 30 of the Judgement). In support of this claim, the *Tribunal Constitucional* cites one of its own decisions—n. 43 of March 23, 2004—in which the Tribunal rules that historical research "by definition is argumentative and debatable since it centers around claims and judgements, the objective truth of which is impossible to attain with full certainty." This "uncertainty consubstantial with historical debate represents the most important element, which should be

47. Legal basis n. 7 of court decision.

respected and protected for the fundamental role played by the formation of a historical conscience commensurate with the dignity of the citizens of a free and democratic society" (*Fundamento Juridico* 4 of the Judgement).

Mere denial of the crime—as compared to other conduct implicating advocating the values of a crime by expressing a positive opinion about it—is innocuous ("criminally vacuous"), and making it an offence is therefore unconstitutional. This conduct does not objectively pursue (nor is it apt to pursue) the creation of a hostile social environment toward the victims of those crimes.

Denial is a step behind the instance in which criminal law may intervene; in fact, it does not even constitute a potential danger for the interests protected by the law in question, with a violation of Art. 20 of the Spanish Constitution. Discussing the facts of the past is therefore legal and receives protection on two levels: in reference to the freedom of opinion and the freedom of historical research.

Different reasoning and solutions are provided for the provision punishing justification, which is deemed constitutional: in fact, it is a value judgment about the crime containing an element that objectively pursues creating a hostile environment toward the people belonging to the same groups that were victims of genocide. In these cases, legislators may punish the conduct as long as the justification takes places publicly and indirectly incites committing genocide, a crime defined as particularly odious and endangers the spirit of our society (*Fundamento Juridico* 9 of the Judgment).[48]

4. The Judge as Historian?

The Spanish decision demonstrates some of the many problematic issues that an ad hoc criminal provision for denial may cause. Behind the *Tribunal Constitucional*'s deny/justify dichotomy is a fact/value distinction. According to the judges, justifying genocide—which is not limited to merely denying a historical fact—goes against the values set forth by the Constitution. However, the Tribunal's distinction does not seem to stand up to a more careful scrutiny. The protected legal interest, in fact, is the same in both cases as is the threshold of danger. Indeed, no higher degree of danger seems to be required of the offence of justification.

---

48. For this decision's contradictions see Vasquez Ramos, J. 'La declaracion de incostitucionalidad'

The Spanish judgement—just like the European Framework Decision—signals a significant change in the debate on making denial an offence. In fact, this debate no longer hinges upon the expediency of punishing or not punishing such conduct as much as on the need to distinguish punishable instances of denial from non punishable ones. In my opinion, it would be opportune to punish forms of direct incitement to serious racist conduct; however, national legal systems already contain multiple provisions to this end, like those relating to racial defamation or hate crime laws. Based on the same legal argument, the *Tribunal Constitucional* could have also declared justification unconstitutional.[49]

In the preceding pages of this article, a distinction was made between *Lois mémorielles* and the criminal offence of denial. Aside from the traditional problems related to opinion offence, denial as a crime raises specific issues arising from the profound relationship between criminal trials and memory processes, and it risks transforming the judge into an arbiter of history.[50]

Since the end of World War II, the legal instrument has been increasingly utilized for establishing historical memory; in addition to historical research and memory produced by testimony, literature, and film, memory has been established through a legal approach in which the figures of the judge and the historian may overlap. More recently, there is a growing trend of turning to criminal justice not only for punishment but also for reconstructing events from a *historical* point of view. The court and the trial thus become a space for building and imposing a memory of particular historically significant facts and the judge the fundamental actor of this process, with the additional distortion that in these instances, the main function is to send a message to the public and to *"establish* historical facts."[51]

---

49. Vasquez Ramos, J. 'La declaracion de incostitucionalidad'., cit.

50. For the risks and dangers of entrusting courts with deciding on history and not law, see Vidal Naquet, P., *Les assassins de la mémoire*, cit., 183, according to whom making a decision on history would mean supporting the idea that there are two schools of thought on history and that one can defeat the other. The overlapping of law and historical truth clearly entails mixing ethics and law, even if just a question of "shared, definite and definitive interpretation," since historical truth cannot be a legally protected interest. In this direction, see Canestrari, S., 'Laicità e diritto penale nelle democrazie costituzionali', in *Studi in onore di Giorgio Marinucci* cit., 148. Against the introduction of a criminal provision on Holocaust denial, see also Donini, M.,"Danno" e "offesa" nella c. d. tutela penale dei sentimenti (note su morale e sicurezza come beni giuridici a margine della categoria dell"offense' di Joel Feinberg), *Rivista italiana di diritto e procedura penale*, n° 4 (Ott.-Dic. 2008), 1587-1588.

51. On denialism as an example of *symbolic criminal law (symbolische Strafgesetzgebung)*, see also Canestrari, S., 'Laicità e diritto penale', cit., 149; Roxin, C. 'Was darf der Staat unter

Law and criminal proceedings have a very specific language and way of functioning.[52] Trials are based on much different rules than those employed by the historian: the court must investigate only the facts contested by the prosecuting body; if the court is not absolutely convinced, it must acquit the defendant in accordance with the principle *in dubio pro reo*; investigations are completed in a period of time respecting the principle of reasonable length of proceedings. Moreover, the criminal trial, which ends with a judgment, is defined by its dividing nature, juxtaposing black and white, innocent and guilty, and culminating in a final irrevocable judgement.A court decision drastically ends an issue and is powerful in the short run, which is another reason why it cannot be an act of constructing memory as a founding element of a society. Historical judgement, conversely, allows one to return to a previous interpretation of facts; it is an unending process of reading and interpreting facts. Unlike the process of analysing history, once a judgement is made by the courts, it is final, and judges may not undertake revision.[53]

Punishing denial—minimization and justification—of the Holocaust (or other serious crimes of genocide or against humanity) mixes these two methods and may cause dangerous distortions. There are a number of risks from an historical point of view, including instrumentalizing truth; elevating it to the status of a legal truth[54]; transforming historical truth into an official truth;[55] and, in this way, giving credit to the idea that only one school of

---

Strafe stellen?', cit. 731. Attention is drawn to the powerful criminal law resources regarding symbolic communication in which criminal law becomes an arena of conflict between socioethical concepts. See Stortoni, L. in Bertolino M., Cadoppi A. (eds.), *Commentario delle «Nuove norme contro la violenza sessuale L. 15 febbraio 1996, n. 66»* (, Padua: Cedam, 1996), 475.

52. Transmitting memory, according to the well-known dynamics of selection, rests more on monumental history. Carlo Ginzburg notes that evidence (in a legal sense) cannot protect the memory of the Shoah from the forces that threaten to erode it. See Ginzburg, 'Beweis, Gedächtnis, Vergessen."

53. The diverging roads taken by the historian and the judge are stressed in C. Ginzburg, *Il giudice e lo storico. Considerazioni a margine del processo Sofri* (Turin: Einaudi, 1991), 108–10.

54. The truth is the truth; it does not need to be a legal truth. Moreover, when it becomes a legal truth, there is the suspicion that it could be instrumentalized. See P. Vidal Naquet, Interview in *Le Quotidien de Paris*, May 9, 1998. Though in reference to certain trends in international criminal justice, M. Damaska is of the same opinion and claims: "The pressing need to carry out historical research cannot be met by the judges' capacity to do so . . . Res judicata in relation to historical issues is thus nothing more than an absurdity." Damaska, M., 'L'incerta identità delle Corti penali internazionali', *Criminalia*, 1 (2006), 17.

55. "Disputing the Shoah's existence should not be outlawed because historical truth should never become official truth." Ginzburg, C., 'Beweis, Gedächtnis, Vergessen," 1.

historical thought exists.[56] In addition to the risks that emerge from the decisions mentioned above, it is the judge who identifies "*historically established facts*," therefore admitting that history may be *settled* or *established*. When legislators introduce the criminal offence of denial, judges are "forced" or "inclined" to investigate both the content and research methods of history.

All that is a dangerous turn away from the rules that should govern criminal trials, of which the main objective is not to reconstruct and narrate history but rather to ascertain individual responsibility in relation to clearly identified facts.[57]

5. Denial as an Attack on the Founding Ethical Pact and the Need for a *Long Road* of Memory

With legislation that criminalizes denial conduct, the criminal law scholar faces a paradox—an aporia—about the legal system. On the one hand, there is the danger and seriousness of these deplorable ideas; on the other, there is the question whether responding with criminal law is necessary—more so than opportune—for blocking or at least containing this serious phenomenon.

After the end of World War II, the world witnessed a recodification—new constitutions of different European states—and the creation, on an international level, of documents and bodies protecting fundamental rights and expressing a direct disapproval of the atrocious facts and the acceptance of new values. All of the values that characterized the postwar period were incorporated in the whole system of ethics and law that has developed since 1945 (constitutions, national legislation, and international binding and

56. Vidal Naquet, P., *Les assassins de la memoire*, cit., 183. Hence such legislation would not be secular because the judge's evaluation hinges less upon the reconstruction of the facts and more on the examination of claims that interpret those facts. In fact, the court must rule on the denial and trivialization of justification of those events. Even if totally share, definite and definitive, the law cannot protect an interpretation nor repress statements that challenged it because, in this particular case, it would be defending an ideological issue. Identifying a historical interpretation among the many possible as a legally protected interest does not appear be acceptable; those claims are punishable only if they threaten the interest or right of others or if they are offensive to a group.

57. Pierre Vidal Naquet also stresses that the law may be used (and in this case he refers to laws on defamation and racist activities). However, he adds that the court must be asked to rule on only law and not on history. Vidal Naquet, P., *Les assassins de la memoire*, cit.,183.

nonbinding documents), and represent the reaction to the nefarious ideas behind the murderous actions of totalitarian regimes.

Denialism rejects the facts that are the source of this reaction and therefore denies the ethical-political universe created after World War II. This phenomenon does not strike at the constituted powers and structures created; it strikes hardest at the *ethical pact*, that is, the unconditional disapproval of the dynamics that dragged Europe into the horror of war and totalitarianism. The "ethical pact" is defined here as the common commitment to undoing the codification of the founding event: the Nazi genocide—an event that made a decisive contribution to changing the face of constitutions and the international legal system. This is proven by the object of the offence of denialism, confined, in most cases, to the Holocaust. Racism and denialism thus shake the ethical and legal basis of postwar reconstruction.[58] This memory has public importance and is not merely a cultural fact.[59] The deniers are aware of the significance of this memory and its meaning in relation to the *genetic* components of our society, and thus, they use freedom of speech as rhetoric. Case-law of the European Court of Human Rights seem to recognize the *subversive* effect of denialist ideas—claiming that denialism runs counter to the ideas underlying the convention—as does the European Union, which in its Framework Decision sets forth that this act infringes upon principles of freedom, democracy, and respect for human rights. These are principles upon which the European Union is founded and that are shared by Member States (recital 1).[60]

Nevertheless, analysis of legislation and jurisprudence points to the problematic implications of the Spanish and French "models" of denialism. Not even the German model, which is more in line with the harm principle—in that it has a public peace danger clause—seems adequate.

---

58. Every political institution, whether tyrannical or democratic, bases its own legitimacy on some abstract and concrete taboos, founding myths that must be protected. European democracies were founded on the condemnation of the Holocaust, and the historical truth of those events is a foundation that must be defended. *See* Buratti, A., "L'affaire Garaudy di fronte alla Corte di Strasburgo. Verità storica, principio di neutralità etica e protezione dei "miti fondatori" del regime democratico', *Giurisprudenza italiana*, 12 (2005), 2247.

59. *See* Lollini, A., *Constitutionalism and transitional justice in South Africa, cit.*.

60. Less sensitivity to the issue and therefore less criminalization may be observed in countries that have not directly experience those atrocities (for example, Scandinavian countries in Europe, or South American or African countries).

We are, in fact, looking at a highly complex situation. The problem that denial and its dissemination pose—and that justifies the social alarm it has created—seems to be first of all of a *political* nature. As stated above, the denialist method shakes the ethical foundations of European states, ignoring the ethics of the scientific method; it willingly aims to damage the foundation of all European democratic orders of pluralism, tolerance, and equality. Denying the Nazi genocide means not only denying the mass extermination, it also means negating the premises and fundamental principles upon which modern states were formed. So that more than a criminal aspect it involves a political and ethical sphere.

Denial attacks the democracy's *constituent* moment rather than its institutions.[61] Here we again encounter an aporia: the attack is deep, it is serious, and touches upon a constituent moment, and yet criminal law is not considered adequate for facing this phenomenon.[62] In the event that these opinions degenerate into instigation, legal systems may turn to other criminal offences (incitement or dissemination of racist ideas). In my opinion, it is not a question of expediency or of whether to punish denialism in a specific form or at all.[63] Producing criminal laws and confirming a *single* truth using a legal instrument appears to be problematic when it comes to denialism.

Italian historian Carlo Ginzburg's notes on the matter seem fitting. Referring to a central rhetorical question in Yerushalmi's essay on the uses of oblivion: "Is it legitimate to think that the opposite of 'oblivion' is not 'memory'

61. Constituent power is defined here as the moment in which a specific political framework is created, both previously—hence the resistance movement in Italy and France was a constituent power of the future republic—and internally, no institution or policy cannot "live" without support and participation, if citizens do not believe or participate in the law. In this sense, the moment of supporting and sharing the law translates into collective conduct.

62. On the principle of subsidiarity, according to which criminal law should be used as *ultima* and not as *prima ratio*, and for other bibliographical references, see Donini, M., *Il volto attuale dell'illecito penale* (Milan: Giuffré, 2005), 85.

63. Defining the distinction between expressions of "mere" Holocaust denial, justification or minimization from "specific" ones—a more offensive form—is fundamental for understanding the perplexity of introducing an *ad hoc* criminal offence that criminalizes denialist conduct. The latter, in fact, make of denial claims—which on their own are not instigative in scope—as an instrument of incitement to hatred or racial, ethnic, religious, or national discrimination. While most criminal legislation prohibit such conduct under the category of "hate speech," that is not the case for mere denial (simple denial), which consists in demonstrating one's own historical conviction without incitement to violence or intolerance. Therefore, when there is discussion about the need to introduce this criminal offence, prohibiting the basic, simple form is referred to, since its specific form is usually punished as a method of realizing incitement to hatred and to racial discrimination.

but justice?"[64] Ginzburg argues that when oblivion is pitted against court justice, oblivion has won.[65]

Criminal legislation against denialism is a false solution, a *short cut*, which risks following the same path as the wrong to be combated, with the additional risk of transforming victims into martyrs of freedom of expression and subject to special legislation criminalizing dissent.[66] The mechanism of victimization has always been an essential part of the strategy in question; in fact, the main denial issues—denying gas chambers and genocide—are presented not just as claims of truth but also as censored and rejected because they unmask (in their opinion) an official historical lie. Repressing such theories may thus be a factor in generating approval of the very phenomenon to be challenged, hence obtaining the opposite result of the one desired. Furthermore, other offences could be used for punishing offensive conduct. Thus, it is not necessary to introduce new ones that would also comply with the principle of *extrema ratio* that governs criminal law.

A specific separate prohibition of denialist conduct does not seem necessary or opportune. Additionally, it creates multiple complications in the spheres of history and law. The function of criminal law is not to counter these phenomena, or, as the German criminal lawyer Claus Roxin says, "historical truth should be able to maintain itself on its own without criminal law."[67]

A response and a commitment of a political nature are needed "against the agents of oblivion, against those who tear documents to shreds, against the assassins of memory, and the editors of Encyclopedias, against the conspirators of silence, against those . . . who can erase a man from a picture leaving only his hat behind."[68] A *long road* of memory, a long-term solution is necessary, not a short one that is achievable by criminal prosecution.

---

64. Yerushalmi, Y., *Usi dell´oblio*, in Yerushalmi, Y., Loraux, N., Mommsen, T., Milner, B. Vattimo, G., *Usi dell´oblio* (Parma: Pratiche editrice, 1990), 24.

65. Ginzburg, C., 'Beweis, Gedächtnis, Vergessen', cit.,.

66. For considerations in this direction regarding the situation in Germany see Bailer-Galanda, Benz, and Neugebauer (eds.), *Wahrheit und Auschwitzlüge*, cit., 246–47.

67. Roxin, C., 'Was darf der Staat unter Strafe stellen?',cit., 731.

68. Yerushalmi, Y., 'Usi dell´oblio', cit., 23–24.

PART THREE

Ruling Denial Prohibition

SIX

The Law of Holocaust Denial in Europe

Toward a (qualified) EU-wide Criminal Prohibition

–*Laurent Pech**

WHEN THE EUROPEAN COMMISSION issued its Proposal for a Council Framework Decision on combating racism and xenophobia in November 2001,[1] only a minority of EU Member States (ten out of twenty-seven[2]) had national laws explicitly aimed at punishing the denial of the Holocaust and/or other genocides and crimes against humanity. Some European countries, while not possessing legal provisions specifically addressing Holocaust denial, were nonetheless willing to punish such utterance on the basis of general provisions dealing with what may broadly be described as "hate speech."[3] As a result, and contrary to a prevalent belief in countries where Holocaust denial is subject to specific criminal sanctions, while all EU Member States have legislation outlawing hate speech, a majority of these countries have long considered the fundamental right to freedom of expression *inter alia* to preclude the criminalization of Holocaust denial per se. By contrast to this

---

* The writer is grateful for the input of Professor William Schabas. Thanks for research assistance are due to Richard Lee. The usual caveats apply.

1. Proposal for a Council Framework Decision on combating racism and xenophobia, COM(2001) 664, OJ C 75 E, March 26, 2002, p. 269.

2. In 2001, those ten countries were Austria, Belgium, the Czech Republic, France, Germany, Lithuania, Poland, Romania, Slovakia, and Spain. For an outline of all national legal provisions dealing with Holocaust denial in Europe, *see* M. Whine, *Expanding Holocaust Denial and Legislation Against It, in* EXTREME SPEECH AND DEMOCRACY (I. Hare & J. Weinstein eds., New York: Oxford University Press, 2009), 540 et seq.

3. As noted by T. McGonagle, the term hate speech, although it enjoys widespread and largely uncontested currency nowadays, does not lend itself easily to legal definition. The European Court of Human Rights has referred to it for the first time in 1999 but is yet to precisely define it. T. McGonagle, *International and European Legal Standards for Combating Racist Expression: Selected Current Conundrums, in* The European Commission against Racism and Intolerance (ECRI), *Expert Seminar: Combating Racism While Respecting Freedom of Expression*, Strasbourg, November 16–17, 2006, 2007, 42–44. In this paper, "hate speech" is used as a shorthand to refer to all legal provisions, such as criminal provisions on insult or defamation, incitement to hatred, etc., that may be relied on to punish racist utterances.

"liberal" practice, public authorities in countries still haunted by their "dark pasts" or faced with the resurgence of extreme-Right forces have shown less reluctance to enact legislation aimed at Holocaust deniers.

As this paper will demonstrate, the full implementation of the recently adopted EU *Framework Decision on combating certain forms and expressions of racism and xenophobia by means of criminal law* (hereinafter the EU FD on racism) will radically alter the legal landscape in Europe.[4] The militant democracies' camp, however, did not completely triumph. While the EU FD on racism considerably harmonizes the law of Holocaust denial in Europe by compelling all EU Member States to punish it, along with other genocides—another striking change—several provisions of the EU FD on racism offer a series of legal options enabling any Member State to limit the scope of national provisions criminalizing "genocide denial."[5] Yet it remains that all EU Member States are now under the legal obligation to criminalize genocide denial when it is carried out either in a manner likely to incite to violence or hatred or in a manner likely to disturb public order or which is threatening, abusive or insulting.

Before offering a critical review of the EU FD on racism and arguing that the political necessity of laws punishing genocide denial and the legal need for an EU-wide prohibition may be questioned seriously, it is essential to first review why and to what extent national approaches on the question of Holocaust denial have diverged. This review will help determine the national model(s) the drafters of EU FD on racism sought to emulate. It also will prove, on the one hand, that scholars were not entirely right to oppose an American approach to a European model regarding hate speech—if one agrees to include Holocaust denial in this category[6]—and, on the other hand, that even among

---

4. OJ L328/55 [2008]. Member States shall take the necessary measures to comply with the provisions of the EU FD on racism by November 28, 2010.

5. "Holocaust denial" or "genocide denial" will be used as shorthand to describe any utterance that denies, downplays, or trivializes crimes of genocide or crimes against humanity.

6. The existence of a clear "philosophical" divide between the United States and most European democracies cannot, however, be denied when one compares the modern case law of the U.S. Supreme Court to the case law of the European Court of Human Rights and national constitutional courts. To put it concisely and at the risk of oversimplification, the case law in Europe generally reflects, when it comes to reviewing restrictions on "extremist speech," the rejection of the presuppositions inherent to what may be labeled the Holmesian approach, which is dominant in the United States and according to which (i) "the ultimate good desired is better reached by free trade in ideas—that the best test of truth is the power of the thought to get itself accepted in the competition of the market,"

EU Member States with criminal provisions aimed at punishing Holocaust denial, these provisions have been drafted diversely and interpreted. What is striking, however, is that national courts, in militant democracies, with the exception of the Constitutional Court of Spain in a 2007 judgment, invariably have upheld the compatibility of Holocaust denial laws with the right to freedom of expression. This paper will argue that the legal reasoning developed by German and French courts is far from being entirely convincing. It will argue further that the European Court of Human Rights should have refrained from labeling the Holocaust a clearly established historical fact for which denial constitutes ipso facto an "abuse of right." To that extent, one may welcome the fact that the EU FD on racism preserves the right of each Member State to decline to apply this jurisprudence and punish genocide denial "only" where genocide deniers directly incite to violence or hatred. One cannot completely rule out, however, the possibility that EU legislative intervention might either result in the eventual criminalization of denial of crimes committed by communist regimes at EU level and/or tempt national legislatures to use the force of the law to ban alternative interpretations of particular historical events in order to gain the favor of some vocal minorities.

I. The Situation Before 9/11[7]: United in Diversity

Most EU Member States have long lacked *specific* criminal provisions aimed at Holocaust deniers. This obviously shows that there is "no unanimity among

250 U.S. 616 (1919), 630 (Holmes, J., dissenting); and (ii) "[N]o danger flowing from speech can be deemed clear and present, unless the incidence of the evil apprehended is so imminent that it may befall before there is opportunity for full discussion. If there be time to expose through discussion the falsehood and fallacies, to avert the evil by the processes of education, the remedy to be applied is more speech, not enforced silence," 274 US 357 (1927), 377 (Brandeis and Holmes, JJ., concurring). For further analysis, *see, e.g.,* L. Pech, *La liberté d'expression et sa limitation* (Paris: LGDJ, 2003); E. Barendt, *The First Amendment and the Media, in* IMPORTING THE FIRST AMENDMENT: FREEDOM OF SPEECH AND EXPRESSION IN AMERICAN, ENGLISH AND EUROPEAN LAW (I. Loveland ed., Oxford: Hart Publishing, 1998) 29; S. Douglas-Scott, *The Hatefulness of Protected Speech: A Comparison of the American and European Approaches,* 7 WM. & MARY BILL RTS. J. 305 (1999); M. Rosenfeld, *Hate Speech in Constitutional Jurisprudence: A Comparative Analysis,* 24 CARDOZO L. REV.1523 (2003); R. KROTOSZYNSKI, THE FIRST AMENDMENT IN CROSS-CULTURAL PERSPECTIVE: A COMPARATIVE LEGAL ANALYSIS OF THE FREEDOM OF SPEECH (New York: New York University Press, 2006).

7. It may seem curious at first to link the 9/11 terrorist attacks in the United States to EU legislative development. Yet this tragic event quickly convinced most, if not all, national

Member States on the issue of the incrimination of the conduct of publicly condoning, denying or grossly trivializing crimes of genocide, crimes against humanity, and war crimes."[8] In fact, only in those countries that one may describe as militant democracies was the denial of the Holocaust expressly criminalized.

1.1 The Principle: The Lack of Criminal Provisions Prohibiting the Denial of the Holocaust

In an exhaustive report on *Combating Racism and Xenophobia through Criminal Legislation*, the EU Network of Independent Experts on Fundamental Rights distinguishes between countries with *specific* criminal provisions incriminating Holocaust denial and countries where *general* criminal provisions can be used to sanction this conduct.[9] The report lists Finland, Hungary, Italy, Ireland, Latvia, Greece, Malta, Poland, the Netherlands, Sweden, and the United Kingdom as examples of countries where "revisionist ideologies" could be punished under general criminal provisions dealing with the maintenance of public peace or provisions dealing with statements and behaviors motivated by racist intent. For instance, in the United Kingdom, denying the Holocaust, while not an offense under British law, might be prosecuted nonetheless if—and only if—it is done in a manner that also constitutes incitement to racial hatred as defined under British law.[10] In contrast, in the

---

governments of EU Member States to push for the adoption of numerous laws and regulations in the area commonly known as Justice and Home Affairs. With respect to this paper's topic, it may be sufficient to cite the Commission's proposal to give an idea how tragic external events sometimes influence or motivate the adoption of legislation for which there was little consensus beforehand: "Furthermore, the conclusions and the plan of action adopted by the Extraordinary European Council meeting held on 21 September 2001 to analyse the international situation following the terrorist attacks in the United States, expresses the European Union's commitment with the international community to pursue the dialogue and negotiation with a view to building at home and elsewhere a world of peace, the rule of law and tolerance. In this respect, the EU emphasizes the need to combat any nationalist, racist and xenophobic drift," Proposal for a Council Framework Decision on combating racism and xenophobia, COM(2001) 664, OJ C 75 E, March 26, 2002, p. 269.

8. EU Network of Independent Experts on Fundamental Rights, *Combating Racism and Xenophobia Through Criminal Legislation: The Situation in the EU Member States*, Opinion no. 5-2005, November 28, 2005, p. 79.

9. *Ibid.*

10. *Ibid.*, p. 66. To the best of our knowledge, no Holocaust denier has ever been successfully prosecuted in the UK on the basis that his speech constituted racist propaganda likely to

Netherlands, the Supreme Court has authorized the sanction of Holocaust denial when it amounts to insult or defamation of Jews.[11]

There are also countries in which the right to freedom of expression, as interpreted by the national constitutional court, appears to exclude any criminalization of Holocaust denial per se. While the report previously mentioned refers to Italy or Greece as examples of countries where general criminal provisions could be used to sanction Holocaust deniers, other studies suggest that this would not be constitutionally conceivable unless their conduct poses a "clear and present danger" of violence.[12] It also would appear evident that in countries such as Denmark and Hungary, where the case law clearly reflects the strong influence of First Amendment jurisprudence, that freedom of expression excludes the sanction of revisionist views as such. Yet, as will be shown in this paper's final section, EU legislative intervention means that all EU Member States will eventually have to criminalize genocide denial. Notwithstanding the EU FD on racism, some countries have already had to amend their criminal codes following their decisions to ratify the Council of Europe's *Additional Protocol to the Convention on cybercrime concerning the criminalisation of acts of a racist and xenophobic nature committed through computer systems*. This explains, for instance, why Slovenia and Cyprus recently passed legislation criminalizing the distribution, through a computer system, of material that denies, grossly minimizes, approves, or justifies acts constituting genocide or crimes against humanity.[13]

---

stir up racial hatred. This seems to explain why a member of the House of Commons thought it useful to introduce a bill to make it a criminal offense to claim, whether in writing or orally, that the policy of genocide against the Jewish people committed by Nazi Germany did not occur on the basis that such utterance is always animated by the intent to stir up racial hatred. *See* HC Deb., January 29, 1997, vol. 289 cc. 370–72.

11. *Ibid.*, p. 81. The Report refers to a judgment of the *Hoge Raad* issued on November 25, 1997.

12. *See* the Greek and Italian national reports in Table Ronde "Constitution et Liberté d'Expression," *Annuaire International de Justice Constitutionnelle*, vol. XXIII–2007, Economic-PUAM, 2008, 265 and 327 respectively. The Italian Report further indicates (p. 332) that, in 2007, a bill aimed at criminalizing Holocaust denial was introduced by the ministry of justice but was later withdrawn following strong opposition from historians who feared for their academic freedom.

13. *See Report on Combating Racism and Xenophobia Through Criminal Legislation* (above n. 8) 81–82.

1.2 The Exception: The Express Criminalization of Holocaust Denial in "Militant Democracies"

The long and difficult gestation of the EU FD on racism was essentially a reflection of the fact that only a minority of European countries had clearly opted for a "militant" stance on the issue of Holocaust denial. What one may call the weight of the past explains, if not justifies, why in countries such as Germany, Austria, and the Czech Republic, the dissemination of such views is expressly subject to criminal sanctions. Following the contemporary resurgence of extreme-Right parties and groups in a context of growing immigration, countries such as France, Belgium, and Spain also felt the need to enact criminal sanction legislation in the 1990s. In both cases, however, public authorities appear to have been clearly inspired by the ancient philosophy famously espoused by the French revolutionary Saint-Just, "*pas de liberté pour les ennemis de la liberté*" (no freedom to the enemies of freedom). The fear is that as past historical episodes would allegedly demonstrate, any tolerance for antidemocratic speech may endanger the very existence of democratic regimes. This, in itself, reveals how the denial of the Holocaust is generally understood: as a type of speech or conduct motivated by a racist *as well as* antidemocratic intent. As a result, it may be prohibited without violating the deniers' fundamental rights and, in particular, their right to freedom of expression. This reasoning has naturally been subject to recurrent judicial challenges. These challenges invariably have failed, with the exception of a recent judgment of the Spanish Constitutional Court. Before examining this controversial case, the German and French laws and relevant case law will first be considered in order to emphasize the relative diversity of the criminal provisions in force at the national level before recent international and European interventions.

1. Punishing the "Auschwitz Lie" in Countries Haunted by Their Dark Past: The Example of Germany

Germany is often described as the archetype of the "militant democracy"; in other words, a country whose constitution is based on the principle of a "democracy capable of defending itself" (*streitbare Demokratie*).[14] Essentially,

---

14. *See, e.g.*, D. Oberndörfer, *Germany's militant democracy: An attempt to fight incitement against democracy and freedom of expression through constitutional provisions. Historical*

this refers to the fact that the framers of the 1949 Basic Law, mindful of what happened under the Weimar Republic, decided to include provisions that allow public authorities to prevent individuals or groups wishing to abolish Germany's "free democratic constitutional order" from abusing the rights and freedoms guaranteed by the Constitution.[15] More generally, two key ideas largely explain why the German Federal Constitutional Court has ruled consistently that criminal convictions for denying the Holocaust are fully compatible with the fundamental right to freedom of expression:[16] On the one hand, German democracy must be ready to defend itself against those who wish to subvert its free and democratic constitutional system, and, on the other hand, freedom of expression must be interpreted in light of the cardinal value on which the constitutional system is based, i.e., the principle of respect for human dignity.

Before dealing with the court's case law, it may be useful to look briefly at the criminal provisions on the basis of which Holocaust deniers have been prosecuted and, in most cases, sanctioned. In what may come as a surprise, the German Criminal Code lacked any specific provision aimed at punishing the so-called Auschwitz lie (*Auschwitzlüge*) until 1994. A previous attempt in 1985 failed to expressly criminalize this act. It was agreed, however, and to simplify, to insert a new provision (Section 130) aimed at

---

and overall record, in FREEDOM OF SPEECH AND INCITEMENT AGAINST DEMOCRACY (D. Kretzmer & F. Kershman Hazan eds., The Hague: Kluwer, 2000), 237. Germany, however, is far from being the only example of a democracy where the long-term survival of democratic institutions has been used as a rationale to justify short-term deprivation of political rights to antidemocratic actors. *See, e.g.*, G. Fox & G. Nolte, *Intolerant Democracies*, 36 HARV. INT'L L.J. 1 (1995).

15. To give a single example, Article 21 of the Basic Law hence authorizes the banning of political parties who pursue "anticonstitutional" aims. It follows from the Constitutional Court's judgment on the banning of the former Communist Party (KPD), that political parties must not, for instance, advocate the dictatorship of the proletariat or approve recourse to force in order to overthrow the constitutional system. *See, e.g.*, BVerfGE 5, 85; BVerfGE 39, 334.

16. *See* Article 5 of the Basic Law:
"(1) Everyone shall have the right freely to express and disseminate his or her opinions in speech, writing and pictures and freely to obtain information from generally accessible sources. Freedom of the press and freedom of reporting on the radio and in films shall be guaranteed. There shall be no censorship.
(2) These rights shall be subject to the limitations laid down by the provisions of the general laws and by statutory provisions aimed at protecting young people and to the obligation to respect personal honour.
(3) There shall be freedom of art, science, research and teaching. Freedom of teaching shall not release citizens from their duty of loyalty to the Constitution."

punishing incitement to hatred against segments of the population.[17] This obviously does not imply that Holocaust deniers, before 1985, could not be prosecuted and sanctioned. Numerous successful prosecutions were conducted, not only on the basis of general criminal provisions dealing with breaches of public order,[18] insult or defamation,[19] or the disparagement of the memory of deceased persons[20] but also on the basis of provisions of the civil code.[21] This proved satisfactory until a controversy erupted about a decision of the Federal Supreme Court—not to be confused with the Federal Constitutional Court—holding that publication of another person's denial of the Holocaust could not constitute incitement to racial hatred. As a result and as previously mentioned, a new Section 130 was inserted into the German Criminal Code in 1985 to more effectively punish incitement to hatred. For symbolic more than legal reasons, Holocaust denial finally was clearly outlawed in 1994, although the Holocaust is yet not explicitly mentioned and singled out. Section 130(3) now states that "whoever, publicly or at a meeting, approves of, *denies or trivializes an act committed under the regime of National Socialism . . . in a manner likely to disturb the public peace*, shall be liable to imprisonment up to five years or a fine" (our emphasis). The criminal law arsenal was further strengthened in 2005. According to the new Section 130(4), "whoever, publicly or at a meeting, disturbs the public peace in a manner that violates the dignity of the victims by approving of, glorifying, or justifying National Socialist rule of arbitrary force shall be liable to imprisonment of not more than three years or a fine."

These provisions call for several remarks. Firstly, the *denial* as well as the *trivialization* of the Holocaust, or any of the crimes against humanity

---

17. For further analysis and references, *see* E. Stein, ***History Against Free Speech: The New German Law Against the 'Auschwitz' -and Other -'Lies'*** 85 MICH. L. REV. 277 (1986).

18. *See* Section 130(1): "Whosoever, in a manner capable of disturbing the public peace incites hatred against segments of the population or calls for violent or arbitrary measures against them; or assaults the human dignity of others by insulting, maliciously maligning, or defaming segments of the population, shall be liable to imprisonment from three months to five years."

19. *See* Sections 185 and 186 of the Criminal Code.

20. *See* Section 189 of the Criminal Code: "Whosoever defames the memory of a deceased person shall be liable to imprisonment of not more than two years or a fine."

21. For a good example, see the European Commission of Human Rights' decision in the case of X v. Germany, no. 9235/81, Commission decision of July 16, 1982, DR 29, p. 194 (the applicant was subject to civil and criminal proceedings following the display of pamphlets denying the Holocaust).

committed by the Nazis, may be punished. The notion of trivialization (or of downplaying), being far from self-evident, has naturally required further judicial clarification. In practice, courts have interpreted it in a broad fashion in order to guarantee the sanction of those who seek, for instance, to play down the number of victims of Nazi gas chambers or to qualify the responsibility of Nazi officials. This raises difficult questions as far as freedom of expression is concerned. By contrast, the fact that Section 130(4) also punishes speech approving, glorifying, or justifying Nazi crimes or rule is both conventional and uncontroversial. Secondly, the sole crimes committed by the Nazis are expressly mentioned.[22] Accordingly, it would seem that one can publicly deny the existence of the Armenian genocide as this horrendous episode did not take place under the rule of the National Socialist regime. It goes without saying that statements of this nature could, nonetheless, be prosecuted if the speaker were to violate provisions on incitement to hatred, defamation, etc. Finally, it is worth emphasizing that the sanction of Holocaust denial, formally speaking, is subject to one restrictive condition: statements denying or trivializing Nazi crimes must be made in a manner capable of disturbing public peace. One can, however, easily deduce from the case law that German courts operate on the presumption that any utterance denying or downplaying Nazi crimes invariably poses, in itself, a threat to public peace. In dramatic contrast with the American standard of "clear and present danger," the mere existence of a potential and abstract threat is sufficient.[23] As for the position adopted by the Federal Constitutional Court

---

22. Similarly, in Austria, the 1945 National Socialist Prohibition Act, as amended in 1992, specifically and exclusively targets the crimes committed by the Nazis. Anyone who publicly denies, grossly trivializes, approves, or seeks to justify the National-Socialist genocide or other National-Socialist crimes against humanity, may be punished by a prison sentence of between one and ten years. A different historical experience explains why the Czech Republic possesses a criminal provision (Section 261A of the Criminal Code) that punishes not only those who publicly deny, dispute, approve, or attempt to justify Nazi genocide or other crimes against humanity committed by Nazis but also those who publicly deny, dispute, approve or attempt to justify Communist genocide or other crimes committed by Communists.

23. In the United States, following the decision Brandenburg v. Ohio, 395 US 444 (1968), it is commonly held that hate speech can only be constitutionally proscribed if likely to lead to imminent disturbance of public peace. In this particular case, the Supreme Court ruled that the right to free speech does not allow "a State to forbid or proscribe advocacy of the use of force or of law violation except where such advocacy is directed to inciting or producing imminent lawless action and is likely to incite or produce such action," *ibid.*, p. 447. The so-called "fighting words" doctrine, expressions which by their very utterance are said to inflict injury or to incite an immediate breach of the peace, follows a similar

on the question of whether the criminalization of Holocaust denial is compatible with freedom of expression, one may also describe it as quite "absolutist."

While space constraints preclude any comprehensive overview of the Constitutional Court's case law on freedom of expression,[24] it is sufficient to stress here that the court has referred to freedom of expression in eloquent terms:

> The fundamental right to free expression of opinion is, as the most direct expression of human personality in society, one of the foremost human rights of all (one of the most precious of the rights of man according to Article 11 of the Declaration of the Rights of Man and of the Citizen). For a free democratic State system, it is nothing other than constitutive, for it is only through it that the constant intellectual debate, the clash of opinions, which is its vital element, is made possible. It is, in a certain sense, the basis of every freedom whatsoever, "the matrix, the indispensable condition of nearly every other form of freedom" (Cardozo).[25]

This is not to say that freedom of expression as a constitutional right is an absolute right. In all legal systems, the nonabsolute character of freedom of expression is an understandable and unavoidable consequence of the existence of other fundamental rights and competing public interests. In Germany, this is made clear, for instance, by Article 5(2) of the Basic Law, which states that freedom of expression and the right to information "are subject to limitations in the provisions of general statutes, in statutory

---

logic but its scope of application has also been severely restricted by the Supreme Court. *See* RAV v. St. Paul, 505 US 377 (1992).

24. For a stimulating overview and the argument that the Constitutional Court's case law since the early 1990s demonstrates that freedom of expression is a "preferred freedom" in the German constitutional order, *see* E. Eberle, *Public Discourse in Contemporary Germany,* 47 Case W. Res. L. Rev. 797 (1997). While it is undeniably accurate to contend that the Court's contemporary case law on Article 5 of the Basic Law has moved German law in the direction of its American counterpart, some striking exceptions remain and in particular, as regards Holocaust denial.

25. *Lüth*, BVerfGE 7, 198, p. 208. The quote from Justice Cardozo is taken from the case of Palko v. Connecticut, 302 US 319 (1937), p. 327. The Court's leading decisions with respect to Article 5 of the Basis Law are available in English. See Decisions of the Bundesverfassungsgericht (Federal Constitutional Court) of the Federal Republic of Germany, Volume 2: Freedom of Speech (1958–1995) (Baden-Baden: Nomos Publishers, 1998).

provisions for the protection of the youth, and in the right to personal honour." As a result, public authorities can and do regularly restrict freedom of expression. While a case-by-case analysis is almost always required to assess precisely the constitutionality of these public interferences, the court has articulated some general principles of interpretation that greatly clarify how public authorities should balance freedom of expression with other rights and/or interests when they enter into conflict with each other.

With respect to the denial of the Holocaust, the basic legal distinction is the one made between opinions and factual utterances.[26] A well-settled principle is that opinions, being at the heart of the individual right to express oneself, cannot be interfered with because public authorities view them as unfounded, emotional, worthless, or dangerous. Demonstration of their truth or untruth is simply impossible, and there is no need for anyone, as a matter of principle, to provide verifiable arguments in order to be able to freely speak one's mind. Furthermore, the court has held repeatedly that freedom of expression also extends to the form of the statement, which means that opinions can be formulated in a sharp or hurtful manner. Another important and protective principle is that where a value judgment contributes to the intellectual battle between opinions on a question of public interest, German courts must operate under a presumption favorable to free speech. By contrast, and this is the most decisive point as far as Holocaust denial is concerned, Article 5 of the Basic Law does not protect the dissemination of a factual statement that the speaker knows to be false or when the speaker relies on a fact that has been proven to be false. In other words, incorrect or untruthful statements of facts do *not* fall within the area of protection guaranteed by Article 5. The Constitutional Court's main argument is that statements of this nature do not contribute anything to the formation of public opinion. This argument includes the important caveats that ordinary courts may nonetheless interpret what appears to be a factual utterance as a statement of opinion, or hold that the factual utterance serves as a prerequisite for the formation of opinions, or is irremediably linked to a statement of opinion.

It follows from these general principles that it would not be constitutionally permissible to sanction Holocaust denial on the basis of its false nature, were the court to agree to view it as an opinion. A statement of opinion may,

---

26. See case law referred to in the *Auschwitzlüge* (Holocaust Lie) Case, Decision of April 13, 1994, BVerfGE 90, 241, p. 247.

nevertheless, be sanctioned if, for instance, it takes the form of an insult. However, for the court, those denying the Holocaust do not express opinions, even abusive ones, but rather offer factual assertions if the assertions' notoriously untrue nature has been established beyond any doubt, thanks to countless testimonies of eyewitnesses and documents, the evidence collected in numerous previous criminal proceedings, and the findings of historical scholarship.[27] As a result, a statement denying or trivializing the Holocaust cannot enjoy constitutional protection.[28]

The Constitutional Court's reasoning in the so-called Holocaust Lie case, while clear and sophisticated, is not always entirely convincing. First and foremost, the court draws a rather subjective distinction between statement of opinions on historical events, which cannot be reduced entirely to statements of facts,[29] and "pure" statements of facts. Statements denying the Holocaust are said to fall within the latter category. The difficulty is that this distinction goes against a long-established and extremely generous interpretation of the concept of opinion and the principle, regularly recalled by the Constitutional Court, that ordinary courts must do their utmost to interpret litigious statements in a nonpunishable manner.[30] Accordingly, some scholars, convincingly in my view, have made the case that even the "simple denial of the Holocaust"—when the denial is not accompanied by a normative judgment or call for action—should be recognized as an "opinion."[31] That being said, it is obvious that an "opinion" expressing the view, for instance, that

---

27. *Ibid.*, 249.

28. In practice, this meant that municipal (preventive) orders instructing an association to be ready to interrupt or terminate the conference it was planning to organize if any statement denying or putting into question the persecution of the Jews in the Third Reich was expressed, are compatible with the applicant's right to freedom of expression. This plainly demonstrates that German courts do not demand that public authorities demonstrate the likelihood of a disturbance to public peace on a case-by-case basis. The association subsequently lodged a complaint with the European Commission of Human Rights. *See* Nationaldemokratische Partei Deutschlands v. Germany, no. 25992/94, Commission decision of November 29, 1995, DR 84, p. 149. This decision is examined *infra*.

29. *See* "Historical Fabrication" Case, Decision of 11, January 1994, 90 BVerfGE 1 (1994). For the Court, the denial of German guilt and responsibility at the outbreak of the Second World War is not only an "opinion" but one that is protected by Article 5 of the Basic Law.

30. *See* the "Soldiers are murderers" controversy (or Tucholsky Case), Decision of October 10, 1995, BVerfGE 93, 266.

31. W. Brugger, *The Treatment of Hate Speech in German Constitutional Law*" (Part II) (2003) 4 GERMAN L.J. 1, para. 65: "The rationale used to refuse simple Holocaust denial the character of "opinion" under Art. 5 (1) BL is not convincing."

Jews profit from distorting the historical records of the Holocaust, could always be punished on the basis of provisions dealing with incitement to hatred or insult.

Second, the court felt required to stress that even if the statement that "the Nazis did not persecute Jews" is considered a prerequisite for the formation of opinions and may therefore fall within the area *covered* by Article 5 of the Basic Law, this provision does not *protect* a right to deny the Holocaust, as such a statement violates the criminal provisions that protect the Jews living in Germany from insult.[32] This point may seem superfluous as the court previously, and authoritatively, held that the Auschwitz lie is not an opinion but rather a statement of fact whose untrue nature has indisputably been established. Yet as the distinction between fact and opinion is not an easy one to work out in theory and in practice,[33] the court might have felt obliged to underline strongly that the denial of the Holocaust, regardless of the opinion-fact distinction, is never acceptable.[34] Indeed, for the Constitutional Court, relying heavily on a previous judgment of the Federal

32. BVerfGE 90, 241, p. 254. The Constitutional Court here refers to a well-known judgment of the Federal Court of Justice. Reversing a judgment of a lower court, the Federal Court of Justice held on the one hand, that the Jews living in Germany, on the basis of the fate to which the Jewish population was exposed under the Nazis, form a specific group and, on the other hand, that the denial of the Holocaust can be construed as an insult inflicted on this group. See Judgment of September 18, 1979, BGHZ 75, 160. This judgment has been criticized on the ground that it overstretches the standard definition of what may constitute an insult within the meaning of the Criminal Code. Furthermore, it justified the legal standing of the plaintiff, a German of Jewish origin whose grandfather had died in the Auschwitz concentration camp and who initiated defamation proceedings against the person who displayed pamphlets denying the Holocaust, on the basis of a particular historical context. This meant that each person belonging to the Jewish community may feel defamed by any statement denying the Holocaust, irrespective of whether he has personally suffered from persecution during the period of the Third Reich, or whether he has lived during that time.

33. An eminent free speech scholar described the distinction opinion-fact as "deeply obscure" and one which "has proved resistant to most analytic attempts at clarification," R. Post, *The Constitutional concept of public discourse*," 103 HARV. L. REV. 601 (1990), 649–50.

34. According to D. Grimm, the judge rapporteur of the 1994 judgment, the Court's finding that Holocaust denial constituted a false statement of fact, whose falsehood was undoubtedly established at the time when the NPD wanted to hold its assembly, should have ended the case. He offers the interesting suggestion that "the Court continued its examination, perhaps to avoid the impression that it had chosen an easy way to circumvent the crucial question, or maybe because it was aware of the difficulty of clearly distinguishing between opinions and statements of fact." Dieter Grimm, *The Holocaust Denial Decision of the Federal Constitutional Court of Germany, in* EXTREME SPEECH AND DEMOCRACY (I. Hare & J. Weinstein, eds.), above n. 2, 558.

Court of Justice,[35] Holocaust denial constitutes an intolerable affront to the dignity of German Jews in a society whose "dark past" justifies a special moral responsibility on the part of its fellow German citizens when it comes to guaranteeing the collective self-perception, dignity, and security of Jews living in contemporary Germany. Above all, it would seem that for the Constitutional Court, it is this special *moral* responsibility that explains, regardless of the sometimes Byzantine *legal* justifications put forward in its judgment, why the criminalization of the Auschwitz lie is compatible with the German Constitution.[36] Viewed in this light, one may wonder why countries lacking the kind of special moral responsibility, as they did not engage in crimes comparable to those committed by the Nazis, have decided in the past two decades to criminalize Holocaust denial. The rationale advanced by public authorities in countries such as France slightly differs from the reasons put forward by German authorities. Rather than focusing on the notoriously untruthful nature of the Auschwitz lie, French authorities have relied mostly on the argument that Holocaust denial must be proscribed because Holocaust deniers pursue racist as well as antidemocratic aims.

2. Punishing Holocaust Denial in a Context of Extreme-Right Resurgence: The Example of France

As in most European democracies, the ratification of the 1966 International Convention on the Elimination of All Forms of Racial Discrimination was followed swiftly in France by the adoption, in 1972, of the first significant piece of legislation dealing with "hate speech."[37] The ancient and venerable French 1881 Law on Freedom of the Press was hence amended to explicitly outlaw all racist, anti-Semitic, or xenophobic acts, but no provision explicitly outlawed the denial of the Holocaust. It would be wrong, however, to believe that Holocaust deniers could not be subject to criminal sanctions. Indeed, and similar to the situation in Germany until the 1994 revision of the German Criminal Code, "negationist"[38] statements could be criminally punished only

35. *See* BGHZ 75, 160, p. 162.

36. It is therefore far from certain that the German Constitutional Court, in the absence of a special moral responsibility, would find compatible with the Constitution a law proscribing, for instance, the denial or downplaying of the Armenian genocide.

37. *See* Act no. 72-546 of July 1, 1972.

38. Those who deny the Holocaust are often referred to in France as "negationists" rather than "deniers" or "revisionists."

when they infringed provisions on racial insult or defamation, incitement to hatred, or condoning of crimes against humanity. Civil proceedings were also an option.[39] The analogy with Germany does not cease here. The decision to criminalize Holocaust denial as such is directly linked to the intense media coverage of a sinister incident.[40] This event, in the context of increasing popularity of the National Front,[41] convinced the French government of the need to proscribe the denial of the Holocaust explicitly. Soon afterwards, the so-called "*Loi Gayssot*" (from the name of the MP who sponsored the bill) inserted a new provision (Section 24 *bis*) into the 1881 Freedom of the Press Act, which reads as follows:

> Anyone who disputes[42] the existence of one or more crimes against humanity as defined in Article 6 of the Statute of the International Military Tribunal annexed to the London agreement of 8 August 1945 which have been committed either by the members of an organisation declared criminal under Article 9 of the Statute or by a person found guilty of such crimes by a French or international court shall be liable to [one year's imprisonment and a fine of €45,000, or one of those penalties only].[43]

If one compares Section 24 *bis* with Section 130(3) of the German Criminal Code, one common element and two essential differences can be noted. In both countries, the law solely refers to crimes committed by persons associated

39. The leading civil case is the case of *Ligue internationale contre le racisme et l'antisémitisme et autres c/Faurisson*, TGI Paris, July 8, 1981, *Recueil Dalloz*, Jurisprudence, 1982, 61 (holding that the defendant, a notorious Holocaust denier, failed to observe, in his work on the Holocaust and the existence of gas chambers, the obligations of prudence, objective circumspection and intellectual neutrality which must be observed by all academics).

40. In May 1990, in the southern city of Carpentras near Avignon, a Jewish cemetery was desecrated. Six years later, four individuals, known for their neo-Nazis sympathies, were finally convicted.

41. The National Front's leader, Jean-Marie Le Pen, was also known for regularly expressing offensive views on the Holocaust. For instance, in 1987, he argued that the mode of extermination used in Nazi concentration camps was "a minor point" in the history of World War II. He was subsequently successfully prosecuted on the basis of Article 1382 of the Civil Code.

42. Most English translations use the verb "to deny" to translate the French verb "*contester*." Yet rather than the denial of the Holocaust, Section 24 *bis* prohibits anyone from "disputing" the existence of the Holocaust. The restriction on freedom of expression is therefore, theoretically speaking, greater.

43. Section 24 *bis* of the Freedom of the Press Act added by Law no. 90-615 of July 13, 1990.

with the Nazi regime, with the additional temporal restriction in France that the crimes must have been committed between 1939 and 1945. This means, for instance, that the denial of the Armenian genocide cannot, under current laws, be criminally sanctioned and explains why some proposals to extend the temporal and material scope of the Gayssot Act have been made by both scholars and MPs.[44]

By contrast with the German provision, the Gayssot Act does not formally punish the act of downplaying the crimes committed against the Jews, unlike subsequently passed and better-worded legislation in countries such as Belgium[45] and Switzerland.[46] French courts, however, have interpreted the notion of "denial" in a very broad manner. For instance, one may be punished if the denial of the Holocaust is disguised, presented in terms expressing doubts, or by insinuation. The offense is also made out where, on the pretext of attempting to ascertain an alleged historical truth, one expresses doubts on the number of victims or grossly minimizes, in bad faith, the number of victims.[47] This judicial extension of the scope of the prohibition, while having the merits of closing any potential loophole, is nonetheless difficult to reconcile with the cherished and ancient principle that criminal provisions must be strictly construed. Another difference between the French and German provisions, which remains a rather theoretical difference considering German case law, is that the French Section 24 *bis* does not require any demonstration that the denial is done in a manner capable of disturbing the public peace (or in a manner capable of inciting to hatred for that matter). In other words, Section 24 *bis* takes the form of a pure "content-based" restriction on

44. For further discussion, see La lutte contre le négationnisme, bilan et perspectives de la loi du 13 juillet 1990 (Paris: Documentation française, 2003), 89 et seq.

45. In Belgium, Article 1 of the Law of 23 March 1995 on the denial, minimization, justification, or approval of the genocide perpetrated by the German National Socialist Regime during the Second World War, punishes whoever, in the circumstances described in Article 444 of the Penal Code denies, grossly minimizes, attempts to justify, or approves the genocide committed by the German National Socialist Regime during the Second World War.

46. In Switzerland, Article 261 *bis* punishes, since January 1, 1995, whoever publicly grossly minimizes or attempts to justify any genocide or other crimes against humanity when the intent is to attack the human dignity of a person or group of persons because of their race, ethnic affiliation, or religion.

47. *See* Cour de Cassation, chambre criminelle, June 17, 1997 in *Recueil Dalloz*, 1998, jurisprudence, p. 50, case note J.-Ph. Feldman.

freedom of expression.[48] Indeed, a particular viewpoint is prohibited in all circumstances because of its content. The rather exceptional nature of this legislative limitation explains that the Gayssot Act, unlike the criminal provisions that sanction the *apology* of crimes against humanity, has been extremely controversial from the outset. To give a single example, the French Senate rejected the bill not once but three times on the grounds that it instituted an official historical truth in violation of freedom of expression, and that current legal provisions on "hate speech" were adequate to effectively deal with revisionist utterances. For the government, however, the bill pursued legitimate aims, such as the fight against anti-Semitism and the need to punish behavior that seriously threatens public order and/or damage the reputation and honor of individuals. The government further claimed that the Gayssot Act was compatible with the Constitution, and in particular, Article 11 of the 1789 Declaration of the Rights of Man and of the Citizen ("Any citizen may therefore speak, write and publish freely, except what is tantamount to the abuse of this liberty in the cases determined by law") as the denial of the Holocaust constitutes an abusive use of freedom of expression.

Regrettably, the French Constitutional Council did not get the opportunity to rule on the constitutionality of the Gayssot Act as all major political parties agreed not to submit the bill to its attention.[49] Ordinary courts nonetheless had jurisdiction to rule on the compatibility of the Gayssot Act with

48. In U.S. First Amendment doctrine, a key distinction is made between content-based and content-neutral restrictions on free speech. Content-based restrictions, i.e., public regulations that interfere with particular viewpoints because of their sole content, are viewed with suspicion by the Supreme Court as it "raises the specter that the Government may effectively drive certain ideas or viewpoints from the marketplace," Simon and Schuster, Inc. v. Members of New York State Crime Victims Bd., 502 US 105 (1991), p. 116. Accordingly, content-based regulations are subject to a strict degree of judicial scrutiny, which essentially means that they must be justified by a compelling public interest, be narrowly tailored and the public authorities must prove that there are no least restrictive alternatives. In practice, it is extremely difficult for a public regulation, once classified as a content-based restriction, to survive judicial scrutiny. *See, e.g.*, RAV v. St. Paul, 505 US 377 (1992) (a city cannot prohibit hate speech on the sole basis of its content).

49. Until a series of amendments made to the French Constitution in July 2008, constitutional review of statutes exclusively operated on an *a priori* basis. As private parties have gained the right to challenge the constitutionality of any statute, legal scholars expected the Constitutional Council to be finally offered the opportunity to authoritatively rule on the constitutionality of the Gayssot Act. The *Cour de cassation*, however, recently refused to refer an application for a priority preliminary ruling of the constitutionality of the Gayssot Act to the Constitutional Council on the ground that the application did not raise any legal issue of "a serious nature" (Cour de cassation, May 7, 2010, no. 09-80.774).

the right to freedom of expression as guaranteed by Article 10 of the European Convention on Human Rights (ECHR). On several occasions, the *Cour de cassation*, as well as the *Conseil d'Etat*, held that convictions or sanctions adopted of the basis of the Gayssot Act were fully compatible with Article 10 ECHR.[50] The legal reasoning put forward by French courts is invariably the same; Article 10 ECHR, which guarantees freedom of expression, nevertheless provides in its second paragraph for certain restrictions or penalties, as are prescribed by law, which constitute necessary measures in a democratic society for the prevention of disorder and the protection of the rights of others. These aims are said to be precisely the aims pursued by Section 24 *bis*, and this provision, it is argued, protects the rights of the Nazis' victims in terms of ensuring and safeguarding the respect due to their memory and safeguarding the peaceful coexistence of persons in the French State. Therefore, any conviction pronounced on that basis is invariably held to constitute a measure necessary in a democratic society. To justify this conclusion further, courts sometimes additionally refer to Article 17 ECHR in order to hold that freedom of expression does not protect the public denial of facts that have been the subject of a final ruling by the Nuremberg International Military Tribunal. Under Article 17, none of the provisions of the ECHR may be interpreted as implying any right to engage in any activity or perform any act aimed at the destruction of the rights and freedoms set forth in the ECHR. Indeed, statements of this nature are said to relate to events that are totally incompatible with the values of the Convention. In other words, Holocaust denial constitutes an abuse of right within the meaning of Article 17 ECHR because the revisionist ideology represents a threat to any democratic society as it seeks to rehabilitate or justify the Nazi regime.[51]

While French courts wisely have avoided defending the criminalization of the Holocaust denial on the basis that freedom of expression does not protect a right to utter untruthful statements on clearly established historical facts, the legal reasoning they have developed may nevertheless be found wanting. In particular, French courts continue to apply the requirement of "necessity" in a very superficial manner. This, however, reflects a more widespread failure to carefully scrutinize public interferences with freedom of

50. For further references, *see* B. de Lamy, "Révisionnisme," *Juris-Classeur Communication* (LexisNexis), Fascicule 3160.

51. This rationale has also influenced the Belgian Supreme Court. See Cour d'arbitrage de Belgique, July 12, 1996, in *Revue trimestrielle des droits de l'homme*, 1997, p. 111, case note F. Ringelheim.

expression in light of the methodology patiently elaborated by the European Court of Human Rights over the years.[52] Yet, as will be shown *infra*, the European Court of Human Rights has exercised its supervisory jurisdiction in a highly deferent manner with respect to national convictions for Holocaust denial.

Regardless of the European Court's case law, the Gayssot Act may be questioned on political and legal grounds. For instance, some irreproachable individuals such as Simone Veil, an eminent politician and former member of the *Conseil constitutionnel* whose family, including herself, was tragically deported to Auschwitz, have voiced their unease with the Gayssot Act as it appears to transform a historical truth into an unchallengeable state-sponsored truth. As for the (legal) arguments put forward by the French courts to justify the punishment of Holocaust deniers, they do not appear entirely convincing when it comes to justifying a pure and overbroad content-based restriction on freedom of expression.[53] If one may certainly agree that Holocaust deniers are generally animated by anti-Semitism intent and that Holocaust denial harms the reputation and honor of the Jews as a group, it seems wiser to rely on "standard" provisions dealing with racial insult and defamation to prosecute them. Furthermore, it may not be prudent to rely on the principle of human dignity and/or the principle of respect due to the memory of victims of Nazi crimes, as these principles subject legal analysis to eminently vague notions and have naturally led other groups, whose ancestors have been victims of what we would now describe as genocides or crimes against humanity, to lobby for the inclusion of these crimes into the category of historical events that cannot be disputed. Public order considerations are hardly

52. For historical and cultural reasons, French courts have been extremely reluctant to strike down legislative limitations to freedom of expression on the basis of Article 10 ECHR. As a result, France has been found to have violated this provision on numerous occasions. For further analysis, see L. Pech, *Fondements du droit de la presse et des médias, in* TRAITÉ DU DROIT DE LA PRESSE ET DES MÉDIAS (B. Beignier et al., eds., Lexis Nexis, 2009), para. 96 et seq.

53. *See contra* S. Garibian, *Taking Genocide Seriously: Genocide Denial and Freedom of Speech in the French Law*, 9 CARDOZO J. OF CONFLICT RESOLUTION 479 (2008). In this interesting study, the author argues that the Gayssot Act merely punishes those who, under the cover of academic legitimacy, spread, in bad faith, an ideology grounded on racist or anti-Semitic propaganda with the likely effect of producing dangerous or harmful effects in a democracy. Yet Garibian fails to mention that the Gayssot Act does not require any proof of the speaker's racist intent or the likelihood of any *concrete* disturbance to the public peace. Besides, the case law requires that bad faith be established only where one seeks to grossly minimize the number of victims of the Holocaust. It is also difficult to agree with the author's point that the criminalization of Holocaust denial is only one limitation of free speech among many others like defamation or insult.

more persuasive. French courts, indeed, do not demand that public authorities prove that Holocaust deniers' utterances are likely to incite anti-Semitism or produce anti-Semitic acts because, in most cases, it would be extremely difficult to do so. Furthermore, in practice, and to mention a controversial example, pro-Palestinian speech has proved more likely to lead to civil unrest and anti-Semitic attacks, yet it is not subject to a specific and preventive prohibition. It is also difficult to be convinced by the argument that Holocaust deniers pose a real and present danger to the French constitutional order. No evidence of an actual and imminent danger to the democratic system is ever required by courts. In reality, the Gayssot Act punishes a particular viewpoint because of the exceptional nature of the Holocaust. To put it differently, the Holocaust—being an incomparable event from so many points of view[54]—it may at least reasonably be argued that a legal regime *d'exception* is justified even though this regime cannot easily be reconciled with what is normally constitutionally permissible. Rather than the harm suffered by descendants of Nazis crimes' victims, which may be relatively diffuse and indirect when Holocaust deniers do not specifically target them or the *potential* dangers mentioned by public authorities, it is the quasi-unanimous public abhorrence for these horrendous crimes that fundamentally explains legislative action and why any attempt to deny or downplay the Nazi crimes continues to be viewed as morally intolerable. This also appears to explain why most recent legislative initiatives aimed at punishing the denial of "other" genocides have been met with fierce resistance.

In addition to the 2001 law which formally acknowledged the existence of the Armenian genocide,[55] another controversial law passed in 2001 describes the slave trade as "a crime against humanity."[56] More controversial, as the view defended is less "politically correct," is a provision of a 2005 law (later repealed) that also required school history teachers to stress the "positive aspects" of French colonialism.[57] Last but not least, a 2006 bill sought to punish, by a prison sentence of up to one year and/or a fine of up to €45,000,

---

54. For further discussion, *see* A. Margalit and G. Motzkin, *The Uniqueness of the Holocaust*, PHIL. & PUB. AFFAIRS, Vol. 25(1), (Winter 1996), p. 65.

55. *See* Act no. 2001-70 of January 29, 2001.

56. *See* Act no. 2001-434 of May 21, 2001.

57. *See* Act no. 2005-158 of February 23, 2005. Its Article 4, paragraph 2 reads: "School courses should recognize in particular the positive role of the French presence overseas, notably in North Africa." A vast controversy ensued. It ended thanks to an opportunistic decision of the Constitutional Council (decision no. 2006-203 L), which allowed for this provision

anyone who denies that the mass murder of Armenians committed in Turkey between 1915 and 1917 constitutes a genocide,[58] i.e., the enforcement of a concerted plan aimed at the partial or total destruction of a national, ethnic, racial, or religious group or of a group determined by any other arbitrary criterion.[59] The Armenian genocide bill has so far failed to become law following the continuous opposition of the government and the mobilization of academic historians and lawyers against what became known as the *lois mémorielles* or memory laws,[60] i.e., laws that promote and at times forbid people from challenging state-sponsored historical interpretations of past events. Space constraints preclude any exposition of the pragmatic arguments that one may raise against the Armenian genocide bill.[61] The most significant aspect of the academic mobilization is that numerous critics went as far as to advocate the repeal of the Gayssot Act while others argued, convincingly in my view, that the denial of the Holocaust cannot be (legally) compared with the denial of the Armenian genocide as the sole Holocaust deniers are clearly animated by racial hatred.[62] The intensity of the public controversy finally led the French Parliament to spell out clearly that it did

---

to be repealed by mere administrative decree (see Decree no. 2006-160 of February 15, 2006).

58. See Parliamentary Bill no. 610 (Proposition de loi tendant à réprimer la contestation de l'existence du génocide arménien), adopted on first reading, October 12, 2006.

59. *See* Article 211-1 of the French Penal Code.

60. *See, e.g.*, M. Frangi, *Les « lois mémorielles » : de l'expression de la volonté générale au législateur historien*, REVUE DE DROIT PUBLIC 241 (2005); P. Fraissex, *Le droit mémoriel*, 67 REVUE FRANÇAISE DE DROIT CONSTITUTIONNEL 483 (2006). For the argument that these laws violate the principles of equality, legal certainty and freedom of expression, see B. Mathieu, *Les « lois mémorielles » ou la violation de la Constitution par consensus*, RECUEIL DALLOZ 3001 (2006). On his initiative, sixty Law Professors signed a petition arguing against these laws. See *JurisClasseur Périodique* 2006, Actualité, 2201.

61. *See* L. Pech, *"Genocide-denial laws: A misguided attempt to criminalize history," NUI Galway Faculty of Law Conference Papers*, 7 LAW CPS 2006, translated into Turkish and published in *Ifade Özgürlügü* (Istanbul: Iletisim, 2007), 159.

62. See, however, the ruling by the Tribunal Fédéral Suisse, ruling of December 12, 2007, X. v. Y., 6B.398/2007. In this ruling, the Court found the defendant (a politician with a doctorate in law) guilty of racial discrimination for having denied that the massacres and deportations of Armenian people in Turkey in 1915 constituted genocide and argued that these actions were, in any event, justified by the necessities of war and national security. For the Court, as the defendant's public statements were motivated by racist intent—a conclusion drawn up from the fact that the defendant described the Armenian people as the aggressor in 1915—he violated the Swiss criminal provision that punishes anyone who denies or downplays any genocide or other crimes against humanity.

not intend to enact any additional "*loi mémorielle*" in the foreseeable future.[63] At last, the controversy over the Armenian genocide bill had the merit of illustrating how delicate it is to reconcile criminal provisions on genocide denial with the right to free speech. In a striking contrast to the reasoning developed by German or French courts, the Spanish Constitutional Court actually found it impossible to satisfactorily reconcile them.

3. Decriminalizing the Denial of the Holocaust in a "Non-Militant" Democracy: The "Surprising" Judgment of the Spanish Constitutional Court

In 1995, the Spanish Parliament, not insensitive to legislative developments taking place outside of the country's borders, decided to amend the Criminal Code in order to punish Holocaust denial explicitly, as well as incitement to discrimination, hatred, or violence against groups or entities when motivated, in particular, by racist or anti-Semitic intent. With respect to genocide denial, Section 607(2) of the Criminal Code punishes by imprisonment for one to two years the dissemination of ideas and doctrines that *deny or justify* genocide or that purport to rehabilitate regimes or institutions responsible for these crimes. This provision was first applied in the context of legal proceedings initiated against the owner of a bookshop where Holocaust denial literature was sold. Convicted in the first instance,[64] the defendant appealed the ruling before the Provincial Court of Appeal of Barcelona. Uncertain of whether Section 607(2) was compatible with Article 20(1) of the Spanish Constitution, which guarantees freedom of expression, the appeal court

63. *See* Assemblée Nationale, *Rapport de la mission d'information sur les questions mémorielles*, Rapport d'information no. 1262, November 18, 2008, p. 181. While the report accepts that the Parliament plays its role when enacting laws aimed at fighting racism and xenophobia, it concedes that laws are not the most appropriate instruments when the Parliament seeks to qualify historical facts or to express views on particular historical events, especially when these laws are accompanied by criminal sanctions. The report suggests that legislative resolutions should instead be used. In doing so, the French Parliament would emulate U.S. practice. *See, e.g.,* House Resolution no. 106, "Affirmation of the United States Record on the Armenian Genocide Resolution," 110th Congress, January 30, 2007. The resolution calls upon the president "to accurately characterize the systematic and deliberate annihilation of 1,500,000 Armenians as genocide."

64. In first instance, the bookshop owner was sentenced to two years in prison for genocide denial and another term of three years in prison for incitement to discrimination, racial hate, and violence against groups or entities by racist and anti-Semitic motives (Section 510.1 of the Criminal Code).

submitted a "question of unconstitutionality" to the Constitutional Court. In the Ruling 235/2007, a majority of the court (eight judges out of twelve) answered this question negatively and ruled that the criminalization of the "mere" denial of any genocide is not compatible with the constitutional right to free speech.[65]

In light of the German and French case law previously analyzed, this outcome may seem particularly surprising. The key legal explanation is that a majority of the Spanish Constitutional Court refused to accept the classic argument according to which the dissemination of Holocaust deniers' views poses, in all instances, a general threat not only to the security of some minority groups (public order argument) but also to the constitutional and democratic order as a whole (abuse of right argument). In Germany and France, courts have accepted this rationale easily, without ever requiring from public authorities any concrete evidence that Holocaust deniers' speech actually poses a tangible and present danger. However, for the Constitutional Court of Spain, a content-based restriction on freedom of expression cannot be justified on the basis of a mere abstract or potential danger.

Interestingly, the court justifies this interpretation by reference to Spanish history and also refers to U.S.-inspired philosophical presuppositions when it comes to protecting freedom of expression in a democratic society. With respect to the court's historical views,[66] the most interesting point raised by the court is that Spain, unlike Germany or France, is not a "militant democracy," which means that the exercise of fundamental rights cannot be restricted on the grounds that they may be used for anticonstitutional purposes. The court actually notes that there is no equivalent to Article 17 ECHR in the Spanish constitutional system.[67] Another general and decisive point developed by a majority of the court is that public authorities cannot, in a democratic regime in which cornerstones are the value of pluralism and the free exchange of ideas, control, select, or seriously undermine the public circulation of ideas or doctrines even if these ideas or doctrines are repulsive to the majority or incompatible with the principle of respect of human dignity.[68]

---

65. On this ruling, *see* P. Salvador and A. Rubi, "Genocide Denial and Freedom of Speech. Comments on the Spanish Constitutional Court's Judgment 235/2007, November 7th" (2008) 4 *Review of the Analysis of the Law* (available at: www.indret.com). The judgment is available in English on the Court's Web site (www.tribunalconstitucional.es).

66. *See* Judgment 235/2007, para. 4.

67. *Ibid.*, para. 5.

68. *Ibid.*, para. 6.

This is clearly reminiscent of the American "marketplace of ideas" paradigm from which is derived the principle that public authorities cannot prohibit "the expression of an idea simply because society finds the idea itself offensive or disagreeable."[69] The court, nonetheless, carefully explains that freedom of expression is not, of course, an absolute right. This means, for instance, that hate speech can be punished because in this instance, there is generally a clear connection between racist utterances and effective harms on the rights of others.

These general principles of interpretation enunciated, the court then proceeds to assess the constitutionality of Section 607(2). At this stage, however, the reader can be forgiven for thinking that these general principles will make it extremely difficult, if not impossible, to reconcile freedom of expression and the criminalization of the "mere" denial of past genocides. And indeed, after recalling the "international origin" of Section 607(2) and explaining that Germany, among other countries, decided to punish Holocaust denial as a result of tragic historical circumstances, the court ruled that the right to freedom of expression in Spain cannot tolerate that "the mere transmission of ideas to be classified as a crime, not even in cases where those ideas are truly execrable, being contrary to human dignity," even though human dignity is "a precept which forms the basis of all the rights included in the Constitution."[70]

In other words, as Section 607(2) neither requires proof of *mens rea*—no specific malicious intent is required contrary to what is required for the crime of inciting to commit a genocide—nor "positive" actions of racist or xenophobic proselytizing or even indirect incitement to commit genocide. The criminalization of the mere denial of a genocide is not compatible with freedom of expression. By contrast, and unsurprisingly, the court does not raise any objection to the criminalization of the act of publicly justifying a genocide—which includes the act of condoning, glorifying, or inciting to the crime of genocide—or those responsible for this type of crime. The essential

---

69. Texas v. Johnson, 491 US 397 (1989), p. 414. Interestingly, in his dissenting opinion, Jorge Rodríguez-Zapata explicitly deplores the influence of U.S. doctrine on the Court before arguing in favor of the European free speech model as it gives primacy to the principle of human dignity.

70. Judgment 235/2007, para. 6.

difference between denying and justifying the crime of genocide is that the latter conduct does create a clear and present danger.[71]

In light of previous case law, this ruling, while controversial, is not utterly startling. Indeed, the court had indicated previously and clearly that the right to free speech includes the right to express subjective and biased opinions on historical facts, even those opinions clearly mistaken or lacking in substance, unless the opinions are expressed with the *intentional* objective of inciting to racial discrimination or hatred, pose a real risk to the pacific coexistence among citizenry, or violate the dignity of persons, which, similar to Germany, is one of the key values on which the Spanish constitutional order is said to be based.[72] Yet, Ruling 235/2007 does seem to go plainly against the spirit—but not the letter, as will be shown in the last section of this paper—of the EU FD on racism (not yet adopted at the time of the judgment), a point emphasized by all the dissenting judges.[73] In my view, the majority also relied on a challengeable understanding of the case law of the European Court of Human Rights and, in particular, the European Court's interpretation of Article 17 ECHR.[74] This is not to say that the ruling is not convincing. The Spanish Court's insistence that public authorities can punish the denial of a genocide only where there is a clear and present danger to public peace or when it is directly linked to "hate speech" seems to me perfectly reasonable in principle, but it fails to properly appreciate the Strasbourg Court's case law on Holocaust denial.

---

71. In March 2008, the Appeal Court of Barcelona found Mr. Varela guilty of the crime of justifying genocide. He was sentenced to seven months in prison.

72. *See* judgments 214/1991 (León Degrelle case) and 176/1995 (Hitler-SS comic case).

73. All dissenting judges defended the "legitimacy" and "necessity" of Article 607(2) on the basis of three main arguments: This provision complies with the letter and spirit of the EU FD on racism; past tragic historical experiences in Europe demonstrate that genocide deniers are motivated by antidemocratic as well as racist intent; finally, there is a clear casual link between the denial of past genocides and the present commission of racist acts of violence. These last two points have been largely accepted by German and French courts.

74. For the Spanish Constitutional Court, quoting *Refah Partisi v. Turkey* (nos. 41340/98, 41342/98, 41343/98 and 41344/98, ECHR 2003-II) and *Ždanoka v. Latvia* (no. 58278/00, 17 June 2004), Article 17 ECHR may only be used where there is evidence of damage and further requires from public authorities that they prove the defendant's intention to rely on freedom of expression to destroy freedoms and pluralism, or to attack the freedoms recognized in the Convention. The Spanish Court is nonetheless right to point out that there is no legal obligation for Spanish authorities to apply Article 17 ECHR-type of analysis to genocide deniers residing in Spain. See Judgment 235/2007, para. 6.

2. Holocaust Denial Laws Before the European Court of Human Rights: From a Low Standard of Scrutiny to the Absence of any Scrutiny

In the well-known case of *Handyside*, the European Court eloquently stressed that freedom of expression "constitutes one of the essential foundations of a democratic society, one of the basic conditions for its progress and for each individual's self-fulfilment."[75] With respect to Holocaust denial, however, the court has come to adopt a very restrictive stance: freedom of expression does not protect a freedom to deny "clearly established historical facts." As a result, Holocaust deniers have been unable to rely on Article 10 ECHR to challenge national criminal convictions.[76]

2.1 The Principle: The Freedom to Express Offensive, Shocking, or Disturbing Information or Ideas

In line with national constitutional provisions in Europe, Article 10 ECHR first provides an extensive definition of the right to freedom of expression before describing the circumstances in which (national) public authorities may legitimately interfere with the exercise of this right:

> 1. Everyone has the right to freedom of expression. This right shall include freedom to hold opinions and to receive and impart information and ideas without interference by public authority and regardless of frontiers. This Article shall not prevent States from requiring the licensing of broadcasting, television or cinema enterprises.
> 2. The exercise of these freedoms, since it carries with it duties and responsibilities, may be subject to such formalities, conditions, restrictions or penalties as are prescribed by law and are necessary in a democratic society, in the interests of national security, territorial integrity or public safety, for the prevention of disorder or crime, for the protection of health or morals, for the protection of the reputation or rights of others, for preventing the

75. December 7, 1976, Series A no. 24, para. 49.

76. Holocaust deniers have also sought to rely on Article 6 ECHR (right to a fair trial) but to no avail.

disclosure of information received in confidence, or for maintaining the authority and impartiality of the judiciary.

Article 10 therefore makes clear that the multiple freedoms covered by the label "freedom of expression" are protected insofar as their exercise does not conflict with other fundamental rights or objectives of general interest. In more technical terms, Article 10 is not violated as long as the national public interference is "prescribed by law" (i.e., is the relevant legal rule accessible and foreseeable?), pursues a legitimate public objective (one of the aims provided for in Article 10(2)), and is "necessary in a democratic society." In practice, the European Court of Human Rights almost always exclusively focuses on the "necessary" nature of the public interference. The adjective "necessary" essentially means that in order to survive judicial scrutiny under Article 10, national authorities (including national courts) must demonstrate that a fair balance was struck between the applicant's freedom of expression and the relevant competing individual rights or public interests.[77] To put it differently, national authorities must convince the European Court that the litigious interference is proportionate to the legitimate aims pursued, and that the reasons advanced to justify it are relevant and sufficient. To complicate things further, in exercising its supervisory jurisdiction, the court also takes into account the so-called "national margin of appreciation" when it comes to assessing whether a "pressing social need" exists or whether the litigious interference is proportional to the aim(s) pursued. Indeed, as a matter of principle, the court's task in exercising its supervisory function is not to take the place of the national authorities but rather to review the decisions they have adopted pursuant to their power of appreciation. The notion of margin of appreciation, being rather open ended, has been diversely and not always clearly applied by the court. From its case law, one can nonetheless conclude that the court "modulates" the intensity of its scrutiny depending on the nature of the speech involved. For instance, national interferences, when political speech is at issue or when the press is involved,

77. Strictly speaking, in the context of Article 10 ECHR, the Court never faces a direct conflict between fundamental rights, as paragraph 2, through a sequence of "interests," exhausts all hypothesis of conflict. If a conflict occurs, the Court would have to reconcile freedom of expression with a public interest protected by law that may, in turn, protect an individual fundamental right such as reputation or privacy. It is also important to note that applicants can only claim a violation of Article 10 ECHR in relation to an action or omission of the "State."

will be strictly scrutinized. This results in the *de facto* annihilation of the margin of appreciation. However, when "sensitive" speech is at issue—for example, racist or blasphemous speech—the court normally assumes that national authorities are better placed to determine precisely the appropriate limits on freedom of expression and also that these limits do not have to be identical from country to country.

It would be an exaggeration, however, to argue that the court's case law is unpredictable. While it is true that the circumstances of each case ultimately determine whether freedom of expression shall prevail, one can easily deduce a general framework of guiding principles or "philosophical" presuppositions from a "transversal" analysis of the case law. To put it concisely, the court's invariable starting point is that freedom of expression, as previously quoted, "constitutes one of the essential foundations of a democratic society, one of the basic conditions for its progress and for each individual's self-fulfilment."[78] The court also has emphasized repeatedly that freedom of expression includes the right to disseminate information or ideas that some may regard as offensive, shocking, or disturbing, because such are the demands of that pluralism, tolerance, and broadmindedness without which there is no democratic society. And if freedom of expression, as enshrined in Article 10, is subject to exceptions, these exceptions must be narrowly interpreted, which essentially means that the necessity for any public interference must be convincingly established.

Unsurprisingly, these guiding principles have led the European Court to develop a very protective case law so much so that it is not unusual to see the court being sharply criticized for "importing" the First Amendment into Europe, in contradiction, allegedly, with more "balanced" national constitutional traditions.[79] While it would be interesting to address this point, it is sufficient to say here that not all of the court's guiding principles are favorable to freedom of expression. In particular, the court regularly stresses that the exercise of this right involves "duties and responsibilities." This means, for instance, that the scope of one's freedom of expression may be diversely interpreted, depending on one's profession. It is on this basis that civil servants do not benefit from an ample freedom of expression or that historians

78. Handyside v. the United Kingdom, December 7, 1976, Series A no. 24, para. 49.

79. *See recently, e.g.*, L. François, *La protection de la réputation ou des droits d'autrui et la liberté d'expression. Etude de la jurisprudence de la Cour européenne des droits de l'homme*, Légipresse (2006), n. 230, II-41, 45; E. Derieux & A. Granchet, Droits des médias (Paris: LGDJ, 2008) 12 n. 15.

may have to demonstrate compliance with the "ethics" of scholarly research in order to be protected by Article 10. As for those who seek to promote "revisionist" theories in the name of historical research, they face another hurdle as the European Court has ruled that freedom of expression does not include a right to deny "clearly established historical facts."

2.2 The Holocaust Denial Exception: No Freedom to Deny "Clearly Established Historical Facts"

In ways reminiscent of the German case law, the European Court of Human Rights has "neutralized" any protection that the right to freedom of expression may have conferred on "revisionist historians" by labeling the Holocaust a clearly established historical fact, the denial of which constitutes an abuse of right. This approach, however, is rather recent and does not entirely reflect the previous and, dare I say, more reasonable approach adopted by the European Commission of Human Rights.

1. The Initial Approach: A Minimalist Degree of Scrutiny Under Article 10 ECHR Interpreted in Light of Article 17 ECHR

For procedural reasons, the (now-defunct) European Commission of Human Rights had long been the sole institution reviewing applications from those convicted at the national level for Holocaust denial. The Commission constantly found the applications inadmissible on the basis of the following reasoning: While the relevant national judgments were found to constitute an interference with the applicants' freedom of expression, the interference was always held to be "necessary in a democratic society" within the meaning of Article 10.

Two essential points can be made. Firstly, the Commission's decisions reflect a readiness to grant national authorities an extremely ample "margin of appreciation," even though the Commission never failed to mention that national restrictions must always be justifiable in principle as well as proportionate. In the absence of any real explanation and justification from the Commission as to why it chose not to double guess the reasons put forward by national authorities to justify the conviction of Holocaust deniers, one may understand this policy of self-restraint as essentially motivated by a desire to pay due respect to the specific historical past of each country. As an external human rights body, the Commission might have had no other choice but to exercise its subsidiary supervision in a conciliatory manner. In practice, this meant that public authorities from a country with a "dark past" could expect to be given a free rein whenever they sought to limit the diffusion of ideas inspired by National Socialist ideology. A previous experience with Nazism was enough to justify any content-based restriction as an objective, reasonable, and proportionate one.[80]

Second, and contrary to German practice, the right to freedom of expression was not, however, entirely "neutralized." Applications were dealt with under Article 10(2) rather than under Article 17, which deals with "abuse of rights" and reads as follows:

> Nothing in this Convention may be interpreted as implying for any State, group or person any right to engage in any activity or perform any act aimed at the destruction of any of the rights and freedoms set forth herein or at their limitation to a greater extent than is provided for in the Convention.

This provision prevents anyone from taking advantage of the provisions of the Convention to engage in any *activity* or perform *acts* aimed at destroying the rights and freedoms that the Convention guarantees.[81] When found

---

80. *See, e.g., B.H., M.W., H.P. and G.K. v. Austria,* no. 12774/87, Commission decision of October 12, 1989, DR 62, p. 216: "Insofar as National Socialist activities are treated differently in Section 3g from those of other political groups, this has an objective and reasonable justification in the historical experience of Austria during the National Socialist era, her treaty obligations, and the danger which activities based on National Socialist thinking may constitute for the Austrian society." The European Court also plainly accepts to consider the historical circumstances specific to each country when assessing the "necessary" character of an interference with freedom of expression. *See, e.g., Vogt v. Germany,* September 26, 1995, Series A no. 323, para. 59. Reviewing the dismissal of a civil servant for belonging to a political party pursing anticonstitutional aims, the Court accepted the principle that it should take into account "Germany's experience under the Weimar Republic and during the bitter period that followed the collapse of that regime up to the adoption of the Basic Law in 1949" and "Germany's position in the political context of the time," when reviewing how the duty of political loyalty imposed on civil servants is applied by German authorities. In the present case, but only by ten votes to nine, the decision to dismiss the civil servant from her post as secondary school teacher was found disproportionate to the legitimate aim pursued, and therefore in violation of Article 10 ECHR. For the dissenting judges, Germany's "special history" should have led the Court to consider the decision as falling with the national margin of appreciation.

81. Similar provisions can be found, for instance, in the UDHR (Article 30) or in Article 18 of the German Constitution.

applicable, Article 17 has a dramatic impact as the applicant is then precluded from relying on any of the rights and freedoms guaranteed by the ECHR, to challenge national measures. Yet, and contrary to the prevalent view,[82] the Commission never *directly* applied Article 17 to deal with applications from Holocaust deniers. It is true that the Commission easily accepted that statements denying the Holocaust run counter to one of the basic ideas of the Convention, namely justice and peace, and that Article 10 may not be invoked to protect activities that, if admitted, would contribute to the destruction of the Convention's rights and freedoms. However, the Commission essentially relied on Article 17 to guide its interpretation of the sphere that ought to be protected by Article 10. To put it differently, the Commission applied the "standard" Article 10 step-by-step analysis (Is the restriction prescribed by law? Does it pursue a legitimate goal? Is it necessary in a democratic society?), before deciding on whether there was a breach of Article 10.

As previously noted, the question of whether a public interference is "necessary" is almost always the decisive question. It is also a delicate question, as it involves balancing freedom of expression with competing rights or interests. However, in the case of statements denying the Holocaust, the Commission constantly referred to a series of public interests (i.e., the prevention of crime and disorder and, in particular, the need to secure "the peaceful coexistence" of the population; the protection of the Jews' reputation and rights) before promptly concluding that the public interests outweigh the applicants' freedom to express their views as one can see from this brief synopsis of the Commission's most important decisions:

> *X v. Germany*[83]: A civil conviction for defamation of all Jews following the public display of pamphlets denying the Holocaust is found "necessary in a democratic society," within the meaning of Article 10(2), as the pamphlets failed to observe the principles of tolerance and broadmindedness on which such a society rests;

82. *See, e.g.*, F. Tulkens, "Freedom of expression and racism in the case law of the European Court of Human Rights," in The European Commission against Racism and Intolerance (ECRI), *Expert Seminar: Combating Racism While Respecting Freedom of Expression*, Strasbourg, November 16–17, 2006 (2007) 54.

83. No. 9235/81, Commission decision of July 16, 1982, DR 29, p. 194.

T. v. Belgium[84]: Although this decision does not directly deal with Holocaust denial, it is worth noting as the applicant's conviction and confiscation of pro-Nazi material pamphlets is found proportionate and necessary for the prevention of disorder as well as for the maintenance of the authority of the judiciary;

H., W., P. and K. v. Austria[85]: The promotion of pamphlets suggesting that the killing of six million Jews by the Nazis was a lie can be described as an activity inspired by National Socialist ideas and the ensuing criminal convictions of the applicants' can be justified as being necessary in a democratic society in the interests of national security and territorial integrity as well as for the prevention of crime;

Honsik v. Austria[86]: A criminal conviction for having denied in several publications the systematic mass extermination of certain groups of the population in gas chambers of Nazi concentration camps can be considered as "necessary in a democratic society";

Nationaldemokratische Partei Deutschlands v. Germany[87]: A city's decision obliging the applicant organisation to ensure that, in the context of a conference, Nazi persecution of Jews is not denied constitutes a "necessary" interference. The Commission further stresses that the public interests in the prevention of crime and disorder in the German population due to incriminating statements denying the persecution of Jews under the Nazi regime, and the requirements of protecting the reputation and rights of Jews, outweigh the freedom of the applicant organization to hold a meeting without being obliged to take steps in order to prevent such statements;

Irving v. Germany[88]: The criminal conviction of the applicant, a British national and notorious "revisionist," for insulting and blackening the memory of the deceased following a speech in which he denied *inter alia* that gas chambers had ever existed in Auschwitz, can be considered as "necessary in a democratic society";

---

84. No. 9777/82, Commission decision of July 14, 1983, DR 34, p.158.
85. No. 12774/87, Commission decision of October 12, 1989, DR 62, p. 216.
86. No. 25062/94, Commission decision of October 18, 1995, DR 83-A, p. 77.
87. No. 25992/94, Commission decision of November 29, 1995, DR 84, p. 149.
88. No. 26551/95, Commission decision of June 29, 1996.

Marais v. France:[89] The criminal conviction of the applicant, another notorious Holocaust denier, for complicity in the denial of crimes against humanity following the publication of an article in which he denied that gas chambers had existed or has been used to commit genocide can be considered "necessary in a democratic society."

Overall, the Commission's approach seems both reasonable and persuasive. Rather than adopting an "absolutist" position whereby any statement denying the Holocaust is dealt with as an abuse of right, the Commission distinguished between the sphere covered by Article 10 and the sphere protected by the same provision. In other words, while the Commission found Article 10 to be applicable, it also held that freedom of expression does not protect the dissemination of views that go against the basic ideals on which the Convention is based. Faced with a continuing wave of applications from Holocaust deniers, the European Court of Human Rights has, unfortunately in my view, decided to adopt a more radical approach.

2. A More Radical Approach: Holocaust Denial as an Abuse of Right

The Court's more radical approach was consolidated on two occasions. In the 1998 case of *Lehideux and Isorni*, the Court, on the basis of the German-inspired notion of established historical fact, held that the negation or revision of clearly established historical facts such as the Holocaust is *entirely* removed from the protection of Article 10 by Article 17. In other words, those found guilty of Holocaust denial by national courts cannot merely invoke Article 10 before the court as this type of "speech" is said to constitute an abuse of rights. As if concerned by its own audacity, the court did not seek to apply this new jurisprudence immediately.[90] In 2003, in the case of *Garaudy*,

---

89. No. 31159/96, Commission decision of June 24, 1996, DR 86, p. 184.

90. *See, e.g., Witzch v. Germany* (dec.), no. 41448/98, April 20, 1999: For having denied the existence of gas chambers and the mass killing therein, the applicant was convicted of disparaging the dignity of the deceased pursuant to section 189 of the German Penal Code. Having regard to Article 17, the Court held that the applicant's conviction can be regarded as necessary and stressed that "the public interest in the prevention of crime and disorder due to disparaging statements regarding the Holocaust, and the requirements of protecting the interests of the victims of the Nazi regime, outweigh, in a democratic society the applicant's freedom to impart views denying the existence of gas chambers and mass murder therein."

the court crossed the Rubicon and held that the applicant, a former politician and the author of a book entitled *The Founding Myths of Modern Israel*, in accordance with Article 17, could not rely on the provisions of Article 10 regarding his conviction for denying crimes against humanity.[91]

While the Commission also previously equated "revisionism" with ideas running counter to the fundamental values of the Convention and also emphasized that "revisionists" are attempting regularly to rely on Article 10 for ends that are contrary to the text and spirit of the Convention, the court took a more absolute stance in *Garaudy*: (i) It first denied the quality of historians to those denying the reality of clearly established historical facts, such as the Holocaust, as their goal is not a quest for historical truth but rather the rehabilitation of the National-Socialist regime; (ii) It equated "revisionism" with the "the most serious forms of racial defamation of Jews and of incitement to hatred of them" as well as "a serious threat to public order"; and (iii) it logically concluded, on the basis of these premises, that the denial or rewriting of this type of historical fact are "acts" incompatible with democracy and human rights that fall into the category of aims prohibited by Article 17.

This reasoning is not entirely above reproach. First, the European Court's analysis in *Garaudy* hardly can be reconciled with the logic espoused by the court in relation to all other historical events and according to which it is not the task of the court to settle historical debates. And in a case where the French applicants were prosecuted for questioning who was responsible for the policy of collaboration with Nazi Germany, the court went as far as to state that

> [e]ven though remarks like those the applicants made are always likely to reopen the controversy and bring back memories of past sufferings, the lapse of time makes it inappropriate to deal with such remarks, forty years on, with the same severity as ten or twenty years previously. That forms part of the efforts that every country must make to debate its own history openly and dispassionately.[92]

The *Chauvy* and *Monnat* judgments further made clear that Article 10 includes the right to seek historical truth and reemphasized the principle

91. Garaudy v. France (dec.), no. 65831/01, ECHR 2003-IX.

92. Lehideux and Isorni v. France, 23 September 1998, para. 55, Reports of Judgments and Decisions 1998-VII.

that it is not the court's role to arbitrate historical debates.[93] The court also reiterated that the principle according to which freedom of expression covers offensive, shocking, or disturbing ideas also applies to historical debate, "a sphere in which it is unlikely that any certainty exists and in which the dispute is still ongoing."[94] It is true, however, that the court is always careful to state that these principles apply to questions that are still part of a "continuing debate" between historians. Yet on the basis that the Holocaust belongs to the German-inspired category of clearly established historical facts, these liberal principles are sidelined.

This is the second problematic aspect of the court's jurisprudence. While the court uses the plural, the sole Holocaust has been found to constitute a clearly established historical fact, and the court has yet to precisely explain when exactly a historical fact does become "clearly established." In *Garaudy*, the court notes that the applicant questions "the reality, extent and seriousness" of historical events "that are not the subject of debate between historians, but—on the contrary—are clearly established."[95] This precision is of little help as the question then becomes: how can a court determine when a debate between historians has ended? One option may be to defer to the national legislature's "historical expertise" and hope that it has the ability to distinguish between undeniable historical facts that cannot be challenged and those facts which still are debated among well-intentioned historians. This was, for instance, the road followed in France with respect to the Armenian genocide, and this is a road full of dangers. To put it concisely, genocide denial laws raise *line-drawing problems* and increase the danger of a *slippery slope effect*. Indeed, once you accept that public authorities can legislate historical truths and ban alternative interpretations of particular historical events, multiple and diverse groups will inevitably attempt to use

---

93. Chauvy and Others v. France, no. 64915/01, para. 69, ECHR 2004-VI; Monnat v. Switzerland, no. 73604/01, para. 57, ECHR 2006-X.

94. In light of these principles, the Court, in *Monnat*, unanimously held that sanctioning a journalist for denouncing in a TV program the "myth" of Switzerland's courageous resistance to Nazism without suggesting that there were differing views among historians is not compatible with Article 10 ECHR because the journalist acted in good faith and his "report was indisputably based on historical research." By contrast, in *Chauvy*, a conviction for defamation, following the publication of a book on two members of the French anti-Nazis resistance in which it was argued that they betrayed their leader, was found compatible with Article 10 ECHR on the ground that more than half a century after the events, there was still a risk that the honor and reputation of these two persons would be seriously tarnished by a book that raised the possibility of their betrayal.

95. Garaudy v. France (dec.), no. 65831/01, ECHR 2003-IX.

the force of the law to protect their own historical narratives from any challenge. This is, for example, what happened in France where legislative proposals to criminalize the denial of the Armenian genocide have rapidly led some MPs to put forward bills aimed at criminalizing the denial of the alleged Vendean genocide of 1793–1794[96] or of the Ukrainian genocide of 1932–1933.[97]

An important point is that the European Court is nevertheless unlikely to agree to view the Armenian, Vendean, or Ukrainian genocides as "clearly established historical facts," the negation or revision of which would be removed entirely from the protection of Article 10 by Article 17.[98] Indeed, the European Court has linked Holocaust denial with the notions of racial defamation and of incitement to hatred constantly. As it is highly doubtful that those questioning the Armenian genocide, for instance, are animated by a racist intent or hatred of the Armenian people, it would be ill advised to apply the *Garaudy* jurisprudence. Furthermore, there is no objective of rehabilitating a regime comparable to the National-Socialist regime. The only justification left is the eventual theoretical threat to the public order that such "speech" could cause. Yet any legislation criminalizing the denial of the Armenian genocide on this sole ground would have to be assessed under Article 10 rather than Article 17. As a result, the "necessary" character of any public interference, in any country other than Turkey, may well be impossible to demonstrate convincingly.

Rather than relying on the notion of "clearly established historical facts," a better and more traditional option may be to focus on the goal pursued by "revisionist historians." In *Garaudy*, the European Court agrees with the assessment made by the national courts that the applicant's goal is not a quest for historical truth but rather the rehabilitation of a criminal regime. This assessment is motivated essentially by the applicant's nonrespect for the research standards that academics must comply with. But this judicial method used to distinguish between "legitimate" historians and biased ones is not infallible. For instance, a renowned American academic, who specializes in

96. Proposition de loi no. 3754, February 21, 2007.

97. Proposition de loi no. 254, October 9, 2007.

98. To the best of my knowledge, only in Switzerland did the Federal Court agree to interpret the criminal provision punishing the denial of any genocide as covering the Armenian genocide. The Court further held that the Armenian genocide, like the Holocaust, is *a historical* fact recognized as clearly established by the Swiss legislator. *See* Tribunal fédéral suisse, ruling of 12 December 13, 2007, X. v. Y., 6B.398/2007.

the history of the Middle East, was prosecuted for remarks he made in an interview to the newspaper *Le Monde* and in which he expressed doubts as to whether the term "genocide" could accurately describe the atrocities inflicted on the Armenians by Ottoman Turkey in 1915–1917. While the criminal action was dismissed on the ground that French law incriminated the sole denial of the Holocaust,[99] the professor nevertheless was held liable for damages (for a symbolic amount) by a civil court on the ground that he failed to express his views with "objectivity and prudence" as elements counter to his thesis were not alluded to.[100] This last judgment is far from convincing, if only for the reason that one cannot be expected to express oneself with objectivity and prudence in the context of a journalistic interview. A judicial assessment of the scientific character of the revisionists' writings on a case-by-case basis, therefore, seems preferable to overbroad legislative bans whose chilling effect is undeniable.

A third problematic aspect of the European Court's jurisprudence is that the court too rapidly concludes that Holocaust denial is a type of speech that falls entirely—and one may add almost automatically—outside Article 10 ECHR. True, this is not without precedent at the national level. The German Constitutional Court also held that Holocaust denial does not fall within the scope of Article 5(1) of the Basic Law. The German Court nonetheless justified this conclusion by stressing that Holocaust denial does not reflect the expression of an opinion but must be categorized as untrue factual statements. By contrast, the European Court excludes Holocaust denial from the scope of Article 10 ECHR because it is said to constitute an abuse of right.[101] In doing so, the court's de facto allows national authorities to impose pure content-based restrictions on freedom of expression. It may have been preferable to carefully distinguish between "Article 10 coverage" and "Article 10 protection." In other words, the sphere covered by the right to freedom of expression does not to have to be identical to the sphere that this right protects. The European Commission of Human Rights' past jurisprudence, whereby national authorities were given a large margin of appreciation and convictions for Holocaust denial were assessed

99. Tribunal correctionnel de Paris, October 14, 1994, unreported.

100. Tribunal de grande instance de Paris, June 21, 1995: *Juris-Data* no. 044058.

101. As a result, it may be said that the *Garaudy* jurisprudence "goes even farther than the German Constitutional Court's jurisprudence," D. Grimm (above n. 34) 559.

under Article 10, itself interpreted in light of Article 17, may be found more reasonable.

Finally, the Court's reliance on Article 17 is also problematic as the court too easily assimilates the mere public dissemination or promotion of "opinions" with "acts" falling within the scope of this provision. Yet a strict reading of Article 17 excludes its application to "pure speech"—even when the views expressed can be described as seditious—as it is expressly aimed at *activity* or *act* undertaken with the objective of destroying the Convention's rights and freedoms or limiting them to a greater extent than is provided for in the Convention. It does not seem correct, therefore, to interpret Article 17 as allowing public authorities to subject to criminal sanctions those who merely *express ideas* contrary to the text and the spirit of the Convention.[102] Even assuming that Article 17 does cover "acts" such as the publication of a book, and even when it does not include calls for illegal actions but merely disseminates ideas incompatible with democracy and human rights or ideas likely to destroy the rights and freedoms of others, the court nonetheless should offer, on a case-by-case basis, some reasoning as to *how* such a book may contribute to the destruction or limitations of the rights guaranteed by the Convention. And while the principle of a "democracy capable of defending itself" definitely justifies the existence of provisions such as Article 17 as long as they are implemented under strict conditions, it does not seem wise to enable public authorities to prohibit certain ideas on the sole grounds that they undermine some cherished values (rather than the rights and freedoms of others) and/or represent in all situations a serious threat to public order, even if this threat is purely theoretical. In any case, it seems hardly logical to apply Article 17 to Holocaust denial views while refusing to sanction racist speech under the same provision.[103]

---

102. *See, e.g.,* Witzch v. Germany, no. 7485/03, December 13, 2005: "The Court observes that the general purpose of Article 17 is to make it impossible for individuals to take advantage of a right with the aim of promoting ideas contrary to the text and the spirit of the Convention."

103. *See, e.g.,* Soulas and Others v. France, no. 15948/03, 10 July 2008. This judgment shows that racist speech, even of the most offensive and dangerous nature as the applicants called in their book for a war of ethnic re-conquest, is still assessed by the Court under Article 10(2) ECHR on the basis that the disputed passages in the book are not sufficiently serious to justify the application of Article 17 ECHR in the present case. Yet no explanation is given as to when a particular utterance becomes sufficiently serious.

3. The Triumph of the Militant Democracies' Camp: The 2008 EU Framework Decision on Combating Certain Forms and Expressions of Racism and Xenophobia by Means of Criminal Law

While the European Court of Human Rights' case law on Holocaust denial may be criticized, it is important to realize that it never imposed any obligation to criminalize statements of this nature. Any attempt to do so would obviously be met with strong resistance. And indeed some countries were extremely concerned when the EU Commission proposed to harmonize national criminal provisions with a view of making genocide denial a criminal offense in all the Member States of the EU. This largely explains why seven years lapsed between the first Commission proposal and the adoption of the EU FD on racism, and why this last text contains a certain number of options on the basis of which Member States may decide to limit the scope of the provision requiring each EU country to punish the act of publicly condoning, denying, or grossly trivializing crimes of genocide, crimes against humanity, and war crimes.

3.1 The Lack of a Universal Consensus

The lack of consensus among European countries regarding the question of whether genocide denial must be criminally prohibited reflects, more generally, a lack of universal consensus. While "hate speech" has long been outlawed on the basis of specific provisions contained in several international instruments,[104] there is less clarity on the question of whether international law compels the criminalization of Holocaust denial. The 1948 Genocide

---

104. *See, e.g.,* Article 20(2) of the Covenant on Civil and Political Rights (Any advocacy of national, racial or religious hatred that constitutes incitement to discrimination, hostility or violence) and Article 4 of the 1966 International Convention on the Elimination of All Forms of Racial Discrimination (requiring *inter alia* that State Parties "declare an offence punishable by law all dissemination of ideas based on racial superiority or hatred, incitement to racial discrimination, as well as all acts of violence or incitement to such acts against any race or group of persons of another colour or ethnic origin, and also the provision of any assistance to racist activities, including the financing thereof"). The Convention has been ratified by all EU Member States, but some Member States have entered reservations on Article 4. For an exhaustive overview, *see* S. Farrior, *Molding The Matrix: The Historical and Theoretical Foundations of International Law Concerning Hate Speech"* 14 BERKELEY J. OF INT'L L. 3 (1996).

Convention, for instance, requires State Parties to punish "direct and public incitement to genocide" but does not refer explicitly to genocide denial as a potential crime.[105] In fact, the unique treaty that specifically requires the criminalization of the act of denying the Holocaust or any other genocide or crimes against humanity is the 2003 *Additional Protocol to the Convention on cybercrime, concerning the criminalisation of acts of a racist and xenophobic nature committed through computer systems.*

According to its Article 6 dealing with denial, gross minimization, approval, or justification of genocide or crimes against humanity, each Party to the Additional Protocol must adopt such legislative measures as may be necessary to criminalize genocide denial "when committed intentionally and without right." Genocide denial is further defined as the act of

> distributing or otherwise making available, through a computer system to the public, material which denies, grossly minimises, approves or justifies acts constituting genocide or crimes against humanity, as defined by international law and recognised as such by final and binding decisions of the International Military Tribunal, established by the London Agreement of 8 August 1945, or of any other international court established by relevant international instruments and whose jurisdiction is recognised by that Party.[106]

According to T. McGonagle, this provision "introduces a novel focus into international human rights treaty law"[107] as the scope of the offense has been extended, for the first time, to apply to genocides other than the Holocaust. And indeed, the Explanatory Report annexed to the Additional Protocol makes clear that "the drafters considered it necessary not to limit the scope of this provision only to the crimes committed by the Nazi regime during the 2nd World War and established as such by the Nuremberg Tribunal, but also to genocides and crimes against humanity established by other international

105. For further analysis, *see* W. SCHABAS, GENOCIDE IN INTERNATIONAL LAW. THE CRIME OF CRIMES (Cambridge University Press, 2nd ed., 2009), p. 319 et seq. After reviewing how the concept of direct and public incitement to commit genocide has been interpreted, the author concludes (p. 334) that "Holocaust denial and other forms of revisionism are forms of hate propaganda, and should generally be addressed within that context rather than as incitement to genocide."

106. Article 6(1).

107. T. McGonagle (above n. 3) 49.

courts set up since 1945 by relevant international legal instruments (such as UN Security Council Resolutions, multilateral treaties, etc.)."[108]

The Explanatory Report further states three major reasons why genocide denial must be criminalized: (1) "revisionists" inspire, and even stimulate and encourage racist and xenophobic groups; (2) the dissemination of revisionist views insults the memory of those persons who have been victims of such evil, as well as their relatives; and (3) genocide denial threatens the dignity of the human community.[109] To secure an agreement on the inclusion of this controversial provision into the Additional Protocol, it was decided that Article 6 would contain provisions allowing any party to the Protocol either (i) to require, through a declaration, that the denial or the gross minimization is committed with the intent to incite hatred, discrimination, or violence against any individual or group of individuals, based on race, color, descent, or national or ethnic origin, as well as religion; or (ii) to make use of a reservation by allowing a Party not to apply, *in whole or in part*, this provision.[110]

The last option strikingly illustrates the lack of universal consensus on the question of whether genocide denial should be criminalized. Furthermore, some countries remained unconvinced and took the view that making use of a reservation would not adequately answer their concerns.[111] For instance, and unsurprisingly, the U.S. government refused to become a Party to the Additional Protocol on the ground that the final version of the protocol is not "consistent" with the First Amendment.[112] The United States, however,

---

108. Explanatory Report to the Additional Protocol, para. 40.

109. *Ibid.*, para. 39.

110. Article 6(2).

111. Only a few countries made use of the options offered by Article 6(2). On the one hand, Lithuania and Ukraine declared that criminal liability for denial or gross minimization may only arise if it is committed with the intent to provoke hatred, discrimination or violence against any individual or group of individuals, based on race, color, descent, or national or ethnic origin, as well as religion if used as a pretext for any of these factors. On the other hand, Denmark and Norway declared that they reserve their right to fully or partially refrain from criminalizing acts covered by Article 6(1).

112. "The United States does not believe that the final version of the protocol is consistent with its Constitutional guarantees. For that reason, the United States has informed the Council of Europe that it will not become a Party to the protocol. . . . Thus, its authorities would not be required to assist other countries in investigating activity prohibited by the protocol," US Department of Justice, Computer Crime and Intellectual Property Section, "Council of Europe Convention on Cybercrime–Frequently Asked Questions and Answers," *available at* http://www.usdoj.gov/criminal/cybercrime/COEFAQs.htm#topicE.

is not the only major democracy that has refused to sign the Additional Protocol. So did an important number of EU Member States (Bulgaria, Czech Republic, Hungary, Ireland, Italy, Spain, and the United Kingdom) on the ground that it requires the criminalization of speech and conduct in a manner not compatible with the right to freedom of expression as protected by their respective constitution. This rather widespread opposition to the Additional Protocol, in addition to the possibility offered to State Parties not to apply Article 6 in whole or in part, have evidently constituted serious obstacles to the effective harmonization of substantive criminal law in the fight against Holocaust denial on the Internet. This is one of the reasons why some European countries promptly sought to push for EU legislative intervention.

3.2 A Long Time in the Coming: The 2008 EU FD on racism

In November 2001, the Commission brought forward its proposal for a Council Framework Decision on combating racism and xenophobia,[113] with the objective of replacing the 1996 Joint Action concerning action to combat racism and xenophobia.[114] Several reasons were offered to justify the need for a new piece of legislation: (1) a new EU text would present a strong signal by political leaders that can influence public perceptions, (2) it would send out the message to minority communities that they are a recognized and integral part of our societies, and (3) having an EU FD would have a positive impact on the implementation of law addressing racism and xenophobia in European societies.[115] These are noble but hardly pressing reasons when it comes to justifying EU legislative intervention. The key argument was a legal one. The Commission and supporters of its proposal often contended that although all EU Member States possess legislation addressing, to a large extent, the issues dealt with by the proposed FD on racism, the diversity and variation in the relevant criminal provisions allegedly highlighted the need

---

113. COM(2001)664, OJ C 75 E, p 269.

114. [1996] OJ L 185/5.

115. B. Winkler, Director of the EUMC, "Racism and Xenophobia in the EU Member States: Trends and Developments," Seminar on Combating Racism and Xenophobia, Vienna, 20 June 2006. Speech available at: http://eumc.europa.eu.

for an EU-wide approximation, i.e., harmonization, of national criminal law. Divergent views between national governments on the potential impact of this proposal on freedom of expression explain that no agreement was found in the EU Council of Ministers until April 2007. Following further consultation with the European Parliament,[116] the EU FD on racism was, at last, adopted in November 2008.[117]

By comparison to the 1996 Joint Action, the list of offenses is expanded, and there is also a change in the method of achieving approximation: while the Joint Action gave Member States the *option* either to incriminate certain conduct or to derogate from the principle of dual criminality, the Framework Decision *imposes*, for the first time, an express obligation on Member States to treat forms of racist and xenophobic conduct as criminal offenses, which can give rise to extradition or surrender. In another radical development, the EU Council of Ministers, at the insistence of countries such as Germany, France, and Luxembourg,[118] also agreed to punish those who deny or trivialize crimes of genocide, crimes against humanity, and war crimes on the basis of provisions that are "largely inspired by the German law, which incriminates not only the denial but also the trivialization of the crimes mentioned, if that is liable to disturb the public peace."[119]

According to Article 1(1) ("Offences concerning racism and xenophobia"), each EU Member State shall take the necessary measures to ensure that the following intentional conduct is punishable:

> (c) publicly condoning, denying or grossly trivialising crimes of genocide, crimes against humanity and war crimes as defined in Articles 6, 7 and 8 of the Statute of the International Criminal Court, directed against a group of persons or a member of such a group defined by reference

---

116. The compromise text agreed in April 2007 was submitted to the European Parliament for "re-consultation" given that the original text from 2001, for which the Parliament was previously consulted in 2002 (OJ C 271 E, 12.11.2003, p. 558), had since been subject to major amendments.

117. Framework Decision of November 28, 2008 on combating certain forms and expressions of racism and xenophobia by means of criminal law, OJ L328/55 [2008].

118. *See also* ECRI general policy recommendation N°7 on national legislation to combat racism and racial discrimination, December 13, 2002: "18. The law should penalise the following acts when committed intentionally: . . . e) the public denial, trivialisation, justification or condoning, with a racist aim, of crimes of genocide, crimes against humanity or war crimes."

119. Commission proposal, explanatory memorandum.

> to race, colour, religion, descent or national or ethnic origin when the conduct is carried out in a manner likely to incite to violence or hatred against such a group or a member of such a group;
> (d) publicly condoning, denying or grossly trivialising the crimes defined in Article 6 of the Charter of the International Military Tribunal appended to the London Agreement of 8 August 1945, directed against a group of persons or a member of such a group defined by reference to race, colour, religion, descent or national or ethnic origin when the conduct is carried out in a manner likely to incite to violence or hatred against such a group or a member of such a group.

These provisions have raised a certain number of concerns. First, the notions of "public condoning," "denial," and "gross trivialization" are not defined. The last one, in particular, is especially vague. French courts, for instance, decided to interpret the Gayssot Act liberally in order to punish the gross minimizing of Nazi crimes but formally require the demonstration that those engaged in such conduct acted in bad faith. No such requirement is explicitly mentioned in the EU FD.

Second, the EU FD is more open ended and broader than the 2003 Council of Europe's Additional Protocol on cybercrime. Indeed, Article 1(1)(c) of the EU FD remains silent as to *who* can establish the factual existence of a genocide contrary to what Article 6 of the Additional Protocol does. In addition, there is no *temporal* limitation, so it cannot be entirely excluded that countries may decide to describe as genocides historical events, such as the Armenian genocide, which took place before the concept of genocide was formalized.[120] The EU FD might also be interpreted as obliging countries, where the legislator has "merely" recognized the *existence* of a particular genocide, to introduce criminal provisions logically in order to punish the act of publicly condoning, denying, or grossly trivializing this genocide.

---

120. *See* R. LEMKIN, AXIS RULE IN OCCUPIED EUROPE: LAWS OF OCCUPATION, ANALYSIS OF GOVERNMENT, PROPOSALS FOR REDRESS (Washington: Carnegie Endowment for International Peace, 1944). As observed by D. Fraser, "one must ask if it is possible to apply this term retrospectively to events which pre-dated the concept of "genocide" itself. . . . In other words, in order to apply such general prohibitions to a denial of the Armenian genocide, a real issue in today's world, a court would first have to determine that events in Turkey in 1915 did in fact constitute genocide, a concept which by necessity would have to be applied retrospectively to the historical facts in order to impose criminal liability today?," D. Fraser, *'On the Internet, Nobody Knows You're a Nazi': Some Comparative Legal Aspects of Holocaust Denial on the WWW,* in I. Hare and J. Weinstein eds., (above n. 2) 512.

The scope of the EU FD also appears broader than the Additional Protocol as it is aimed at crimes of genocide, crimes against humanity, and *war crimes*. Furthermore, the notions of denial and gross trivialization are now to be applied to all genocides, crimes against humanity, and war crimes (as defined by the Statute of the International Criminal Court). By contrast, in its 2001 version, the EU FD only expressly punished the act of denying or grossly trivializing the sole Holocaust.[121] The drafters of the Commission proposal must have thought initially that the Holocaust is such an unprecedented crime that it must be the unique historical event, the denial or gross trivialization of which must be punished because of the implicit yet obvious racist and antidemocratic intent of those engaged in such "conduct." But rather than distinguishing among genocides on a case-by-case basis, the final version of the EU FD makes it also possible to criminally sanction those denying any genocide, crime against humanity, or war crime, while reserving a "special" provision regarding the Holocaust. In doing so, the EU FD allows for the continuing coexistence of the "genocide model" (see, e.g., legislation in Spain or Switzerland) as opposed to the "Holocaust denial model" (see, e.g., legislation in France or Germany) in Europe. Finally, it is important to stress that the scope of the EU FD may be broadened further. Indeed, Recital 10 provides that a Member State may decide to *extend* the application of Article 1(1)(c) and (d) to crimes directed against a group of persons defined by other criteria than the ones previously mentioned, such as social status or political convictions.

The broader scope of Article 1(1)(c) and (d), by comparison to the 2001 draft proposal issued by the Commission, and more generally, the mere presence of provisions punishing the denial or the trivialization of all genocides and other international crimes proved to constitute real stumbling blocks to the adoption of the EU FD. In order to secure a unanimous vote from all national governments, several concessions were offered to the countries that expressed concerns regarding the potential impact of the EU FD on freedom of expression.

---

121. "Member States shall ensure that the following intentional conduct committed by any means is punishable as criminal offence: . . . (c) public condoning for a racist or xenophobic purpose of crimes of genocide, crimes against humanity and war crimes as defined in Articles 6, 7 and 8 of the Statute of the International Criminal Court; (d) public denial or trivialisation of the crimes defined in Article 6 of the Charter of the International Military Tribunal appended to the London Agreement of April 8, 1945 in a manner liable to disturb the public peace . . ."

First, the Council agreed in 2007 that EU Member States will only be compelled to punish genocide denial "when the conduct is carried out in a manner likely to incite to violence or hatred"[122] against a particular group or a member of such a group. Yet some have expressed their disappointment with this new condition on the ground that trivialization of the crime of genocide is "a form of racism, and Member States should be able to punish it even where incitement to hatred or violence is not involved."[123] This would, however, likely conflict with Article 10 ECHR, as interpreted by the European Court of Human Rights, especially if the trivialization is not aimed at the Holocaust.[124] But similar to the option offered in relation to "hate speech," Member States can also opt to punish genocide denial "which is either carried out in a manner likely to disturb public order or which is threatening, abusive or insulting."[125] It would seem that this provision does not offer an additional "escape route" to those countries that are unwilling to prosecute genocide deniers but should be understood, on the contrary, as enabling the "militant democracies" to continue to punish the denial of the Holocaust when collective interests, rather than individual interests, have been harmed. In other words, the threshold, in this last hypothesis, is less difficult to satisfy. And since the EU FD does not define either "likely" or the notion of "public order," one can assume that national authorities, in countries such as France or Germany, remain free to decide when, for instance, a statement denying the Holocaust becomes likely to disturb public order.

The second major concession offered to the "liberal camp," Article 1(4), offers the additional opportunity for each country "to make a statement that it will make punishable denying or grossly trivialising the crimes referred to in paragraph 1(c) and/or (d), only if the crimes referred to in these paragraphs have been established by a final decision of a national court of this Member State and/or an international court, or by a final decision of an international court only." In doing so, the EU FD on racism emulates, but does not strictly follow, Article 6 the Council of Europe's Additional Protocol. This reservation may be welcome insofar as it enables any EU country to let

122. Article 1(c) and (d).

123. M. Roure MEP, Report on the proposal the proposal for a Council Framework Decision on combating certain forms and expressions of racism and xenophobia by means of criminal law, Committee on Civil Liberties, Justice and Home Affairs (A6-0444/2007), November 14, 2007, 14.

124. *See supra* Section 2.2.2.

125. Article 1(e).

national or international courts, rather than its own legislature, determine when a particular event can legally be described as genocide.

Despite these major concessions and contrary to what the Council of Europe's Additional Protocol offers, EU Member States are not granted the right not to apply, in whole or in part, paragraphs (c) and (d) of Article 1(1). Furthermore, the EU FD raises the distressing possibility of a person being extradited for having engaged in a conduct lawful in his/her country of residence but constitutive of a racist offense in another EU Member State. To put it differently, one cannot exclude the issuance of a European arrest warrant for behavior that is constitutionally protected in one country but prohibited in another one. Assuming, for instance, that a country decides to criminalize the denial of the Armenian genocide, a person living in a Member State where such conduct is lawful could be subject to a European arrest warrant for posting materials denying or trivializing the Armenian genocide on the Internet as these materials would then be accessible from the territory of other Member States. Some governments, however, have been keen to promise that they would not extradite anyone who has acted in a lawful manner under domestic law.[126]

As previously mentioned, concerns about freedom of expression largely explain why the EU FD on racism has not been welcomed unanimously, especially in countries where "simple" Holocaust denial (i.e., when the denial does not also constitute incitement to hatred) cannot be criminally sanctioned. As pointed out by *The Economist*, quoting Jacques Chirac, Holocaust denial may be "a perversion of the soul and a crime against truth. But that does not mean it should be a crime in law."[127] Yet it is important to stress that

---

126. For example, the UK government gave the House of Lords Select Committee on the EU the assurance that "no one who has acted in a lawful manner in this country would be extradited under an EAW to another Member State for a racism and xenophobia offence where the whole or a part of the conduct occurred in the UK," *The Proposed Framework Decision on Racism and Xenophobia–An Update*, Session 2002-03, 32nd Report, HL Paper 136, para. 14. This means, in practice, that "if a British citizen posted something on a Web site in the UK, for whatever reason, denying the Holocaust, and that was accessed by a German citizen and the German state wished to act on that and asked for extradition under the Extradition Bill to the United Kingdom, we would not do so because it is not an offence in Britain to deny the Holocaust and therefore we would not extradite in those circumstances," Lord Filkin, Parliamentary Under Secretary of State, Home Office, *quoted in* House of Lords, *The Proposed Framework Decision on Racism and Xenophobia–An Update*, *op. cit.*, Appendix 2: Explanatory Memorandum, Correspondence and Oral Evidence, Appendix 2002-03, question 38.

127. Charlemagne, *Slippery slope*, ECONOMIST, January 25, 2007.

the text of the EU FD on racism has been improved dramatically over time, so much so that some NGOs have criticized the efforts of those who attempted to limit the impact of the EU FD by putting "an overemphasis on the need to limit its scope in the context of freedom of speech."[128] These efforts were indeed not entirely unsuccessful. In addition to the different limitations and options previously outlined, the EU FD contains a provision (Article 7) on "constitutional principles and fundamental principles" which reads as follows:

> 1. This Framework Decision shall not have the effect of modifying the obligation to respect fundamental rights and fundamental legal principles, including freedom of expression and association, as enshrined in Article 6 of the Treaty establishing the European Union.
> 2. This Framework Decision shall not have the effect of requiring Member States to take measures in contradiction to fundamental principles relating to freedom of association and freedom of expression, in particular freedom of the press and the freedom of expression in other media as they result from constitutional traditions or rules governing the rights and responsibilities of, and the procedural guarantees for, the press or other media where these rules relate to the determination or limitation of liability.

Article 7(1) may be described as a standard and rather "toothless" reference to fundamental rights. It merely states the obvious point that the EU law always must respect the fundamental rights recognized by Article 6 TEU, which include the rights and freedoms protected by the European Convention on Human Rights. By contrast, Article 7(2) is more original but also less clear. It was devised by the Council of Ministers to meet ongoing concerns about media liability. One should note also that this provision was criticized by the Commission on the ground that it may be interpreted as authorizing certain Member States to set aside EU law were it to conflict with national procedural rules shielding the media from liability. Despite the potential threat to the primacy of EU law that it poses, Article 7(2) was maintained as it was considered of utmost importance by some countries. Intriguingly, a recital, which initially stated that Article 7(2) could not result in the exemption of

128. Response of the European Network Against Racism, Framework Decision on Racism and Xenophobia: "Europe cannot fail a third time," February 2007, 3.

the press from criminal liability, also disappeared from the final version. It remains unclear whether this should be understood as implying that Article 5 on "liability of legal persons" contains an implicit exemption as far as the media are concerned. One may hope that the Court of Justice soon will be given the opportunity to clarify how the notion of "constitutional traditions or rules," which may exempt media from criminal liability, should be interpreted.

Regardless of these multiple and rather confusing legal safeguards, one may remain legitimately unconvinced about the political necessity of laws punishing genocide denial and the legal need for an EU-wide prohibition. To follow the arguments neatly summed in an article published in *The Economist*,[129] the EU FD on racism seriously limits freedom of speech, one of the basic freedoms on which other liberties depend but more pragmatically is rather unclear about whether the proposed remedies aimed at stopping anti-Semitism would actually work. Furthermore, laws against genocide denial come up against the rule of unintended consequences. In practice, they tend to give more publicity to the views of genocide deniers. The slippery slope effect should also be taken into account. As the example of France shows, where multiple and diverse memorial laws have been voted or proposed, national authorities may find it difficult to resist the temptation also to criminalize expressions merely because they might cause ethnic or religious offense. Finally, it seems reasonable to argue that genocide denial laws are only understandable and *necessary* in countries where Nazism had indigenous roots. To these traditional arguments, one may want to add that the EU FD on racism also participates in this unfortunate trend, which leads to an inflationary use of the term genocide and to the "normalization" of the Holocaust as merely one among many other genocides.

However, at present, the most worrying development has to do with the slippery slope effect of the EU FD on racism. Indeed, while the EU FD was being negotiated, Latvia and other Baltic countries pushed to include condemnation of crimes committed during the Soviet occupation of their countries in the legislation. In order to accommodate the concerns of those Member States that wanted the EU FD to cover Stalinist crimes, the Council agreed to annex a declaration that deplores all totalitarian crimes.[130]

---

129. Charlemagne (above n. 127).

130. "The Framework Decision is limited to crimes committed on the grounds of race, colour, religion, descent and national or ethnic origin. It does not cover crimes committed on

Furthermore, it was also agreed (in the so-called "rendez-vous" clause) that the Commission will report to the Council within two years after the entry into force of the EU FD, with the purpose of determining whether an additional instrument was needed to cover public condoning, denying, or grossly trivializing of crimes directed against a group of persons defined by criteria such as social status or political convictions. The underlying idea was to allow for the eventual criminalization of the denial of crimes committed by communist regimes. In the meantime, the European Parliament, in a manner reminiscent of the French Parliament's "historical activism," decided it was time to refer to the great Ukrainian famine of 1932–1933 as a crime against humanity.[131]

While the objective to fight misinterpretations of history to lay the foundations for reconciliation based on truth and remembrance is a noble one, it cannot be excluded that the EU also decides, for reasons of political convenience, to punish *gulag* denial or those who refuse, for instance, to describe the Ukrainian or Irish great famines as crimes against humanity. For this author, public authorities should, however, resist the enticing temptation to use the force of criminal law to "sanctify" clearly established historical facts. This is not to say that nothing can and should be done to counter the genocide deniers' fallacies. The EU Member States should find inspiration in the Terezin Declaration. In other words, they would be well advised to focus their energy and resources on establishing and supporting research and education programs, not only about the Holocaust, but also about other genocides and crimes against humanity, as well as to encourage ceremonies of remembrance and support the preservation of memorials.[132]

---

other grounds for example by totalitarian regimes. However, the Council deplores all of these crimes," Council of the European Union, Annex Statements to be entered in the minutes of the Council, 16351/1/08, November 26, 2008.

131. European Parliament resolution of October 23, 2008 on the commemoration of the Holodomor, the Ukraine artificial famine (1932–1933) (P6 TA(2008)0523). In its resolution of April 2, 2009 on European conscience and totalitarianism (P6 TA(2009)0213), which calls for August 23 to become a Europe-wide day of remembrance for victims of twentieth-century Nazi and communist crimes, the European Parliament is nonetheless careful enough to stress that "official political interpretations of historical facts should not be imposed by means of majority decisions of parliaments" and that "a parliament cannot legislate on the past."

132. See the section on "Education, Remembrance, Research and Memorial Sites" in the *Terezin Declaration on Holocaust Era Assets and Related Issues* adopted by 46 countries on June 30, 2009, in Terezin (Czech Republic). The text is *available at* http://www.eu2009.cz/fr/news-and-documents/news/terezin-declaration-26319.

SEVEN

Denial of the Holocaust, Genocide, and Crimes Against Humanity

A Comparative Overview of Ad Hoc Statutes

–Martin Imbleau

1. Introduction

It is a common belief for members of their respective allegiances that historians and tribunals do not think alike and supposedly do not behave or establish facts the same way. Both deniers—or negationists—and scholars view judicial truth establishment as biased and limited, arguing that it shall never serve the purpose of historical truth establishment. Nor should tribunals be used for the protection of historical truth. But history is not the sole property of historians.[1] The functional artifice, we believe, cannot be a justification to ban legislation prohibiting the denial of the Holocaust and other genocides. As we will see, deniers are not only a subtle vector of racism but are truly hooligans: by publicly defending the indefensible, their goal is to provoke anti-Jewish sentiments. Through their denial, they aim to confound history. They pretend to be engaged in a legitimate scholarly effort and in a genuine attempt at historical interpretation. But denial propaganda is not interpretation: it is a tissue of lies and distortions. Denial literature and other forms of denial propaganda substitute truth with lies. Historians may engage in historical revision of past events when new evidence makes it sensible to think earlier interpretations over—but no new evidence exists that would allow deniers to question that the Holocaust occurred. The holocaust deniers' only true goal is a racist one. We hold the view that ad hoc statutes, such as those examined in this article, are justified and even required.

Important and striking historical events may have a substantial impact today. Thus, political and legislative forums often refer to such events for various reasons—whose in-depth analysis would go beyond the scope of

1. Alexandra Barahoma de Brito, *Truth, Justice, Memory and Democratization in the Southern Cone*, *in* THE POLITICS OF MEMORY—TRANSITIONAL JUSTICE IN DEMOCRATIZING SOCIETIES 160 (A. Barahoma de Brito et al. eds., 2001).

this text. Parliaments can act by different means to enter the forum of historiography. Legislative assemblies have adopted declarations and resolutions recognizing commonly known events as official facts under the law. Such texts are sometime defined as memorial laws.[2] In many instances, they invite members of the population to acknowledge the historical fact and incite them to remember it. For example, many countries have adopted resolutions enticing people not to forget the Holocaust or the Armenian genocide. Countries with no laws against denial, such as Canada, have also adopted such types of legislation.

Current political context can indeed be of influence. In some more controversial instances, memorial laws deal with historical events not universally supported. Legislative interventions can focus on the establishment of the historical event itself, as well as on its promotion. In France, the Taubira-Delannon Law recognizes past slavery as a crime against humanity and requires that the event be taught in that context.[3] A debate emerged recently, also in France, over a proposed act to amend school programs to promote the positive aspects of France in its colonies, notably to counterbalance the negative image of the country with regard to the Algerian conflict. This sort of intervention is also of declarative nature but implies a more direct acknowledgment of history for political motivations.

The third category of legislative intervention encompasses ad hoc statutes with effective legal measures, such as prohibition of the denial of a historical event. Such ad hoc statutes target denial of the Holocaust, genocide, and other crimes against humanity, either referring to denial of a specific event or in a broader context. This paper focuses on the scope, application, and interpretation of this category of legislative intervention.

Most countries facing active and influential denial movements—mainly Western European countries—have enacted specifically adapted legislation penalizing the denial of gross human rights violations. Other countries, like Canada, have relied on the prohibition of hate speech. In the United States, the First Amendment, which guarantees freedom of speech, is sacrosanct and—it is argued—cannot be subject to much limitation. For this reason, there is a relative absence of jurisprudence concerning Holocaust deniers in this country.

---

2. The term "memorial laws" stems from the French "lois mémorielles."

3. Loi no. 2001-434 du 23 mai 2001.

Over the past two decades, the international legal corpus on denial law has progressed significantly from a hate speech approach to quite specific and adapted ad hoc statutes prohibiting denial. In the 1980s and 1990s, ad hoc denial statutes focused, to a large extent, on the Holocaust. European countries have recently enacted laws to protect other genocides and crimes against humanity. There is also an increasing body of international instruments condemning the denial of such crimes, which has contributed to the formation of a soft-law corpus on the issue.

Different approaches have been adopted, and a variety of ad hoc statutes prohibiting the denial of the Holocaust, genocide, or other crimes against humanity have been enacted. Before assessing the scope of these ad hoc statutes, we will briefly look at the tactics and intentions of deniers, which will provide the necessary background for interpreting the legal provisions. We will examine the different events targeted by the statutes, as well as the spectrum of these provisions: they cover not only direct denial but also the gross minimization and apology of the crimes covered by these laws. This section will be followed by a discussion of the rules governing the evidence and of the establishment of the targeted events, as well as of the difference between direct legislative establishment of historical events and referring to the decision of an international tribunal. We will then provide a brief overview of the main ad hoc statutes. Looking at these statutes, we will focus on some provisions that have generated important jurisprudence, including the French Gayssot Law. As we discuss the standardization of ad hoc approaches among European countries to more consistently prohibit denial speech, we will cover the infringements, by those statutes, on freedom of speech, which, in these cases, are justified. Finally, future developments of ad hoc statutes will be examined.

2. Deniers' Intent and Tactics

As most ad hoc statutes criminalize not only the more direct and evident forms of denial, but also the justification or the minimization of the Holocaust and other genocides, it is necessary to understand the tactics employed by deniers. Many ad hoc statues require the demonstration of intent to attack a group of individuals for belonging to a racial or religious group. Understanding the intent of the deniers is thus a prerequisite.

Deniers of massive human rights violations engage in obsessive quests to demonstrate—via fallacious arguments, erroneous facts, and historical distortions—that the events in question never occurred or are grossly exaggerated. Ad hoc statutes are interpreted through the balance of rights between one's freedom of speech and the protection of minorities through human rights instruments. Denial speech, notwithstanding its effort to be perceived as a historical debate, is about contemporary political motivation and racism. It is an ideology, not a historical endeavor.[4] Deniers' conclusions precede their research and analyses. Their aim is not only to try to destroy the truth, which is per se indestructible, but to eradicate the awareness of the truth that prevents the resurgence of past criminal ideologies[5]—for example, by reshaping history to rehabilitate the reputation of the Nazis.[6]

Deniers attack, minimize, or try to justify many historical events. But the deniers' main focus is more on large-scale, state-sponsored crimes, precisely to negate the criminal intent of the regime. For instance, Srebrenica genocide denial Web sites as well as biased reports, including some submitted to the UN, in support of Milosevic, claimed that the Srebrenica massacre was prepared by the Muslims themselves.[7] Holocaust deniers argue that the Holocaust is a giant hoax, that the only creatures gassed at Auschwitz and Treblinka were lice. This subtler, but just as efficient form of racism aims at attacking the historical truth. It does so notably vis-à-vis the first official records of the violations in question, mostly those established by bodies such as the International Military Tribunal at Nuremberg (IMT). The deniers' intent is to justify the criminal behavior of regimes condemned by such bodies; to rehabilitate these regimes; and to eliminate, from public opinion, the barrier that those past events represent for the resurgence of criminal policies.

The most active—and doubtlessly the most pernicious—movement is that of the Holocaust deniers—or, as they erroneously refer to themselves—revisionists. The general philosophy behind statutes criminalizing the deniers' behavior is the protection of the veracity of the event. In this case, ad hoc statutes intend to block the deniers' attempts to eliminate the historical

---

4. Henry Rousso, Le syndrome de Vichy, De 1944 à nos jours 176 (2001).

5. Pierre Vidal-Naquet, Les assassins de la mémoire—"Un Eichmann de papier" et autres essais sur le révisionnisme 7 (1991).

6. Deborah Lipstadt, Denying the Holocaust—The Growing Assault on Truth and Memory 74 (1994).

7. *See* Letter for Dragomir Djokic of the Permanent Mission of Yugoslavia to the United Nations addressed to the Secretary General, U.N. Doc. A/48/177 and S/25835 (May 24, 1993).

fact as a whole and to rehabilitate Nazi philosophy; these statutes thus seek to prevent a new wave of anti-Semitism.

When facing deniers, the dilemma between prosecuting them and engaging in a dialog with them is a common one. Supporters of the latter method argue that if deniers are sued, they will claim to be victims, underlining the Jewish monopoly on politics and media. Consequently, some think that ad hoc statutes only provide deniers with a good forum. On the contrary, we feel that the absence of prosecution allows them to disseminate their views. A dialogue presupposes a common ground of facts and good faith. No such ground exists with deniers, and it is useless to try to convince them as their conclusions precede their research. According to Vidal-Naquet, the paper supplied by the Canadian forests would not suffice to refute deniers' assertions.[8]

Holocaust deniers have paved the way to the denial or patent minimization of other genocides and crimes against humanity. Holocaust denial can take many forms, use different faces, and invent multiple theories to explain—or justify—what happened to the Jews during the Second World War. Briefly reviewing the methods that deniers employ to falsify history will help understand the lack of merit of their position.

Initially, deniers used to attack the event directly. But recently, denying the most-marking elements of the Holocaust, which are also the most vivid ones in our memory, has become the most distinctive characteristic of the Holocaust denial movement, which focuses on denying the existence of the gas chambers and on challenging the validity of the claim that six million Jews were killed.[9] Deniers attack the event in different ways: they directly and bluntly deny the event or its main components (denial approach); they grossly minimize important aspects (minimization approach); they reverse the burden of proof by pretending that all main aspects are part of a giant conspiracy (conspiracy theory); and when they are out of arguments, they argue that even if crimes were committed, they were either perpetrated in the context of a war and are thus understandable or justifiable, or that both sides perpetrated evil actions, so both are equally morally responsible. Deniers of other genocides or large-scale crimes against humanity have copied these methods.

---

8. VIDAL-NAQUET, *supra* note 5, at 108.

9. Alain Bihr, *Les mésaventures du sectarisme révolutionnaire*, *in* NÉGATIONNISTES: LES CHIFFONNIERS DE L'HISTOIRE 125 (1997).

In *Irving v. Penguin Books Limited, Deborah E. Lipstadt*—a case in which famed Holocaust denier David Irving sued scholar Deborah Lipstadt for defamation—Professor Evans, the historian Ms Lipstadt had hired, provided a good summary of the Holocaust deniers' attacks, embracing four broad points:

i. Jews were not killed in most cases in gas chambers;
ii. The Nazis had no formal policy, thus did not attempt to systematically exterminate European Jewry, and deaths were the consequence of the acts of individuals not acting under any authority;
iii. The six million figure is outrageously exaggerated; the number of Jews murdered did not run into millions;
iv. The Holocaust is a myth invented by the Allied and Jewish propagandists to obtain financial support for the newly created State of Israel (conspiracy argument).[10]

Holocaust deniers question what is indisputable, volunteer false evidence while denying historical evidence detrimental to their thesis, dwell on details to reject all testimonies of survivors (*Falsus in uno, falsus in omnibus*), and hide behind claims of scientific or scholarly status without having any relevant scholarly background. Deniers plead the absence of specific written orders emanating from Hitler that would prove the genocidal intent. For deniers, the gas chamber is a myth. On this point, they rely heavily on false reports such as the ones produced by Arthur Butz, who claims that the Nazis lacked the technical capacity to build such chambers and those of the self-proclaimed engineer and witness in the Ernst Zundel trial, Fred A. Leuchter, who similarly claims that it would have been physically and chemically impossible for the Nazis to accomplish what they were accused to have done. Having dismissed the technical feasibility of the killing centers, deniers move on to claim that places such as Treblinka, Chelmno, Sobibor and—even more importantly for deniers—Auschwitz-Birkenau are propagandist fantasies created by the Jews. Thus, the six million victim figure cannot be true. Finally, they claim, the IMT was fraudulently set up by the Allies to obtain financial compensation for the Jews.

10. Irving v. Penguin Books Limited, Deborah E. Lipstadt [2000] EWHC QB 115 (April 11, 2000), par. 8.4.

By denying the Holocaust's most outstanding features, deniers achieve two overlapping goals. First, they remove the status and significance of the Holocaust as a point of reference. Deniers want to erase the educational value of the event, its prophylactic role. In other words, by eliminating the event from our conscience and our history, deniers hope to influence the present. When they don't simply deny the occurrence of the event, they argue that the Holocaust was only one in a long list of similar crimes. By putting aside the unique aspects of the Shoah and by minimizing the suffering of the Jews, deniers disavow the specific racist intent of the Nazis and deny the true nature of the crime. But it is pointless to indulge in claims of comparative pain and suffering; nor is it useful to enter into a competition over the head count of victims. By saying that all crimes are equal, deniers engage in historical distortion.[11] This is why they deny the existence of the gas chambers and the genocidal function of Auschwitz. The elimination of the monstrous instrument erases the uniqueness of the mass killing of the Jews. The utilization of the gas chambers is not just a different kind of technology employed in war—it has wider implications. The chambers were built with the specific intent of killing a mass of people and were used with the aim of total annihilation of a group. When deniers seek to expunge the gas chambers from history, they are denying not just a detail of the larger event but one of that event's defining concepts.[12] The deniers' agenda includes the rehabilitation of the Nazis' reputation: if such a crime was never committed, then there is nothing wrong with again pursuing Nazi policies. Second, if the Holocaust is a fraud, deniers are free to reiterate the claim that is the basis of their racist rationale: that Jews manipulated the world before World War II and still do so. The evidence of this ongoing manipulation, deniers claim, is the Jews' ability to impose a lie of such magnitude for so long. In any case, Jews are the targets.

3. Scope of Ad Hoc Statutes

3.1 Historical Events Targeted

Legislation prohibiting denial of massive human rights violations can apply to one specific event, plus to some or to all similar events. The Holocaust is

---

11. Lipstadt, *supra* note 6, at 213.

12. Don D. Guttenplan, The Holocaust on Trial 112 (2001).

the most common event subjected to denial prohibition. The evolution of ad hoc statutes can be summarized as follows. Before the massive introduction of ad hoc statutes, hate speech provisions were used to prosecute deniers. Subsequently, as far as the Holocaust goes, the prohibition of Nazi symbols (in Germany) was used against deniers. The first ad hoc statutes concentrated on the Holocaust, and the first such statutes prohibiting Holocaust denial were adopted by European countries that had been the most directly affected by the Nazis. Israel, the exception for evident considerations, was precursor with its law adopted in 1986. Austria amended in 1992 its act prohibiting the promotion and support of Nazi crimes by including a specific provision prohibiting the denial of the National Socialist genocide. Germany had dealt with Holocaust denial cases for a number of years when it adopted—in 1994—a law specifically criminalizing the denial of acts committed under the regime of National Socialism. In France, the Gayssot Law changed the dynamics of legal proceedings against deniers.

As we shall see, many approaches have been adopted to penalize denial speech. This variety of options opens the doors to criticism by deniers, who perceive them as improvisation and seek to show their lack of legal merit. From their standpoint, the absence of consistency in the approaches demonstrates the absence of the need for legal intervention on a historical ground.

Other statutes go beyond penalizing merely Holocaust denial. Many countries prohibit not only the denial of the Holocaust but also that of other crimes committed by the Nazis (Israel) or by similar movements (Slovak Republic). Some statutes target genocide in general, while others have an even broader scope as they include genocide and crimes against humanity, recognized or not (Switzerland) by an independent competent body or according to a definition under the Convention on the Prevention and Punishment of the Crime of Genocide—or Genocide Convention—or the IMT Charter (Luxembourg). Others have no such references as to definition.

The UK evaluated the introduction of an ad hoc provision in its Public Order Act, but the proposal failed to be adopted. The aim of the provision would have been the same as for other similar ad hoc statutes, but the proposed draft was awkward enough to generate a new debate about its scope. It proposed to criminalize as racial any hatred words, behavior, or material that purported to deny the existence of the policy of genocide against the Jewish people, and it also covered other similar crimes against humanity committed by Nazi Germany. One could only imagine the debates before courts of law about whether or not genocide was similar to the Holocaust or conversely about the uniqueness of the Holocaust that this approach would have triggered.

The denial of the Armenian genocide is a patent example of a state's denial of its own past.[13] The State of Turkey officially denies the genocide committed against the Armenian population. Turkey has tried for decades to deny the burden of guilt that the genocide represents for an emerging nation that is trying to build itself a different past. Here, the debate is created by the Turkish State itself: it revolves around the definition of genocide and its applicability to the crimes committed against the Armenians rather than on whether the massacres ever actually occurred.

Deniers of the Armenian genocide assert that the 1915 deportations and massacres in the Ottoman Empire against the Empire's Armenian inhabitants were not part of a state-organized genocide. The Republic of Turkey acknowledges that during World War I, many Armenians died but strongly denies that the Ottoman authorities attempted to eliminate the Armenian people. The international community, for the most part, acknowledges the existence of the Armenian genocide, but Turkey still threatens other states with diplomatic reprisals when the question of such recognition is debated. Deniers, in this case, argue that the event debated is the result of interethnic violence that was part of a wider conflict during World War I. In those circumstances, deniers allege, massacres were committed on both sides during the conflict, with many Turks dying as well. Throughout the world, many countries have adopted declarative laws recognizing the Armenian genocide.

The scope of the French law does not include the Armenian genocide. Switzerland, however, prohibits the denial or the gross minimization of any genocide or other crime against humanity. France and Belgium have debated the need to amend Holocaust denial law to include that of the Armenian genocide. Many deniers use that gap with an *a contrario* argument: denial of the Armenian genocide cannot be prohibited since this legislation was specifically enacted for a different genocide,[14] and states could have done the same for the

---

13. Yves Ternon, Du négationnisme:Mémoire et Tabou 8 (1999) [hereinafter, Ternon, Memoire].

14. See the Bernard Lewis cases before both the Civil and Criminal Court, which generated a controversy. When asked about the Armenian genocide, Lewis had answered that the use of this definition premised the acceptance of the Armenian version of the event. Lewis was unsuccessfully tried under the Gayssot Law. In its judgment, the court refused to extend the law to include the Armenian genocide. *See* Marc Nichanian, *The Truth of the*

Armenian genocide if that had been their intention. In this case, the denial is more of a state affair as the Turkish State is the instigator of the denial. For the majority, the scale of the massacre and the deportation is not in dispute. Moreover, the Armenian genocide or the Armenian massacres were not the result of a fundamental racist hate of the Armenians.[15] Thus, the spurious debate about this genocide is politically driven, not racially motivated.

In October 2006, the French Parliament adopted a proposal to penalize the denial of the Armenian genocide. This proposal was preceded by a 2001 law recognizing the genocide against the Armenians. But the 2001 legislation is of a declarative nature only: it limits itself to one provision stating that France publicly recognizes the Armenian genocide of 1915.[16] In the case of the Armenian genocide, the event does not benefit from prior establishment or acknowledgment by a third party. No internationally recognized body has done any work similar to that which the IMT accomplished on the Holocaust and that is referred to in the Gayssot Law. So contrary to the Gayssot Law—which does not per se recognize the Holocaust but still refers to facts considered by the IMT, while avoiding qualifying these facts and the conclusion of the IMT, the approach advocated for the Armenian genocide required a prior legislative inclusion. The proposal to include Armenian genocide legislation triggered opposition from historians, jurists, and intellectuals in France. The proposal, which only provided an autonomous provision prohibiting the "denial of the existence of the Armenian genocide of 1915," was presented to the French Senate but was not adopted.[17]

3.2 From Complete Denial to Moral Equivalence—The Spectrum of Ad Hoc Statutes

Over time, deniers have refined their position and have tried to introduce more subtle forms of denial. Holocaust trivialization has become more

---

Facts: About the New Revisionism, *in* REMEMBRANCE AND DENIAL: THE CASE OF THE ARMENIAN GENOCIDE 249 (Richard G. Hovannisian ed., 1999).

15. YVES TERNON, ENQUÊTE SUR LA NÉGATION D'UN GENOCIDE 218 (1989) [hereinafter, TERNON, GENOCIDE"].

16. Loi No. 2001-70 du 29 janvier 2001 relative à la reconnaissance du génocide arménien de 1915.

17. Proposition de loi tendant à réprimer la contestation de l'existence du génocide arménien, *Texte* no. 20 (2006–2007) transmis au Sénat le 12 octobre 2006.

frequent since direct and evident denial has become a criminal act. The double genocide excuse, for example, is now commonly used by deniers. This argument is called the moral-equivalence argument: deniers argue that Israel committed—and, to some extent, still commits—genocide against the Palestinians. Ad hoc statutes have dealt with direct denials but also with gross minimization. Spain, for instance, initially criminalized the denial but also the justification of such crimes and the intent that leads to them. The Constitutional Court felt, though, that Spain's denial section was unconstitutional.[18] Some countries' statutes criminalize justification or apology of the Holocaust or other genocides: for instance, the Austrian *Verbotsgesetz* punishes both the gross minimization and the justification of the event.

Section 6 (1) of the Additional Protocol to the Convention on Cybercrime, concerning the criminalization of acts of a racist and xenophobic nature committed through computer systems,[19] mentions that states shall adopt measures to establish—as a criminal offense—the act of making available to the public, via a computer system, material that denies, grossly minimizes, approves, or justifies acts constituting genocide or a crime against humanity (as defined by international law and recognized as such by final and binding decisions of the IMT, or of any other international court).

In some instances, this refinement of the deniers' tactics has triggered new debates about the need for courts to entertain evidence in prosecutions of deniers. For example, is minimization or gross minimization implicitly included in ad hoc statutes prohibiting denial? And at what level does a minimization become a gross minimization? France had to deal with this question. The Gayssot Law does not explicitly prohibit the minimization of any aspects of the Holocaust, nor does it address the justification of the Nazis' behavior. Still, the Gayssot Law has been interpreted in a relatively broad fashion, and courts have focused their attention on the objective of this law. In the case of Alain Guionnet, who faced justice for claiming that Auschwitz—the symbol of all death camps in public opinion—had been responsible for "only" 125,000 deaths, the Cour de cassation acknowledged that the debate over the number of Nazi victims did not per se constitute a punishable act under the law. The court felt, nonetheless, that a gross minimization on the number of

---

18. Tribunal Constitucional, Pleno. Sentencia 235/2007, de 7 de noviembre de 2007. Cuestión de inconstitucionalidad 5152-2000.

19. Strasbourg, 28.I.2003, STE 189.

victims, when done in bad faith, falls under the scope of the law and is punishable.[20]

We still feel that in this case, the court took an unwarranted detour in two senses: first, it could have interpreted the gross minimization as a form of denial; second, referring to the bad-faith concept is counterproductive when interpreting the Gayssot Law as that law precisely seeks to avoid the debate over the intent behind denial speech; opening the debate on good faith could produce undesired effects. Consequently, the determination of the burden of proof concerning bad faith is a key consideration. Should the establishment of bad faith be evidenced by a historical debate? Or should the effect of the denial speech be the evidence? The *Irving* case revolved around these very questions. However, the French approach quite dramatically changed the angle taken under hate-propaganda legislation regarding the requirement to demonstrate the intent and the effect of the denial speech. In our perspective, the merit of the Gayssot approach is to limit the debate over the material aspect of the crime—i.e., the denial—for the court to reach its verdict.

3.3 The Event and the Rules of Evidence

The general goal of ad hoc statutes is the criminalization of a specific form of hate propaganda. They do so by adopting a provision that avoids, to the largest extent possible, the need to establish the historical fact itself—which would otherwise require a confrontation between experts on the existence of the event and of its components. They also intend to limit the common requirement for infringements on the freedom of speech in order to establish, each time, the specific intent of the deniers to target a group of individuals for their racial or religious affiliation, as well as the impact of the denial speech on them.

Holocaust denial has become an important and active anti-Semitic movement in Canada and in the United States and more recently, in Middle-Eastern countries. But most of the Holocaust denial jurisprudence comes from Western Europe. Countries that had suffered from the Nazis' criminal actions were the first to enact ad hoc statutes prohibiting denial, mainly Holocaust denial.

20. FNDIR, UNADIF v. Guionnet, Cour de cassation, chambre criminelle, June 17, 2007, Bulletin criminel 1997 no. 236, 786.

Civil and common law countries have different views with regard to ad hoc statutes. The common law adversarial system and the civil law inquisitorial system are certainly different. We do not share the view, though, that there are more impediments under common law to implement ad hoc statutes than there are under civil law regimes. Differences lie notably in the evidentiary rules governing the respective systems.[21] However, for us, the main difference becomes apparent precisely because there are no ad hoc statutes in Anglo-Saxon common law countries; the courts of law of those countries thus need to entertain long and inefficient trials against deniers. While common law courts have yet to establish an ad hoc Holocaust denial law, nothing would preclude common law systems from establishing the Holocaust or other genocide as a fact under law and require tribunals to interpret the event in a similar fashion as if it were of judicial notice.

For both aforementioned systems, evidence can be established by different means before a court. The onus and rules of evidence can vary among different systems. Civil law courts create records from a different perspective than common law forums. Nonetheless, the events discussed in this article can be established and referred to under three main angles. Or, as Kahn puts it, the Holocaust can be put on trial in different fashions.[22] First, subtleties set aside, both systems can take judicial notice of an event. Second, courts can hear and accept all evidence on the events from both parties (this applies to both civil and criminal procedures). Without judicial notice or an ad hoc approach on events like the Holocaust, the trial turns into a debate on the weight of the evidence from both sides. In other words, the event can be put on trial and demonstrated by piles of facts. Parties may bring expert witnesses to explain the evidence filed, and the other side may counter by bringing their own expert. Judicial notice allows a judge to accept certain facts as indisputable evidence, but he or she still has to follow rules concerning evidence. Finally, courts can be compelled by law to consider events as factual. Such reasoning can be compared to a fact acknowledged by judicial notice, since the event is generally known. Over the years, the first two approaches have been used to prosecute deniers—almost exclusively Holocaust deniers—before civil and criminal courts. In recent years, parliaments have opted for the third option, limiting quite significantly the debate over the need for evidence of the Holocaust before the courts.

---

21. Robert A. Kahn, Holocaust Denial and Law—A Comparative Study 12 (2004).

22. *Id.*

In Germany, judicial notice jurisprudence of the Holocaust should not require plaintiffs to prove the event in each case. Still, it was not always clear that this prevented the accused from presenting evidence.[23] Though the Holocaust was a well-established fact, evidence questioning this event could still be presented. The controversial German Supreme Court decision in the *Günter Deckert* case, leader of the right-wing NDP (Nationaldemokratische Partei),[24] was rendered after the evolution of German jurisprudence increasingly limited the accused's ability to challenge the truth about the Holocaust. The court dismissed Deckert's claim that the mass murder of Jews in the gas chambers needed to be proven, and it established the event as one to be taken by all courts by judicial notice and imposed as a rule of law. As a result of this ruling, courts are allowed to reject defendants' motions to introduce evidence on the Holocaust.

In regard to the judicial notice approaches to consider the Holocaust as a fact before courts of law, the evolution of the French one differed from that of Germany mentioned above. The first Faurisson affair, in France, was not of a criminal nature. It was heard under Section 1382 of the French civil code covering civil responsibility. The court accepted the position of the plaintiffs, condemned Faurisson to a symbolic one franc sentence, and ordered the publication of the judgment against him. But the court acknowledged its limited authority in such debates. Indeed, it had to rely on the mere evidence supplied by both parties and felt that it was not within its mandate to decide on how the Holocaust, an event of such great importance, should be characterized.[25] According to France, the Gayssot approach was rendered necessary since other legislation commonly used to combat hatred or hate speech—an article on civil responsibility of the Civil code—was not adequate when dealing with Holocaust denial litigation.

Jean-Claude Gayssot, then a member of the French Parliament, proposed a way to avoid transforming courts of law into a historical forum at every

23. *Id.* at 19. Many holocaust denial cases of the 1980s were heard under other sections. Rules of evidence were debated, and consistency on judicial notice of the Holocaust did not really exist.

24. Bundesgerichtshof [BGH] Mar. 15, 1994; Reg. No 1 StR 179/93BHG, Mar. 13, 1994. The highest appeals court in *Deckert* case reversed the defendant's conviction on a charge of incitement to racial hatred. The court held the view that publicly repeating another person's denial of the Holocaust was not in itself enough to prove the charge. Deckert had translated and commented a speech of Fred Leuchter.

25. LICRA v. Faurisson, recueil Dalloz-Sirey, Jurisprudence D.1982.

occasion. The proposed approach intended to avoid the onus to establish the negated event. Ten years after the first Faurisson affair, the French court, using the Gayssot Law, confirmed the validity of this second legislative approach. The court concentrated its effort and judgment on the applicability of the recently passed legislation. The French Parliament, the court concluded, has the liberty to limit one's freedom of expression in order to protect the fundamental rights of others, including the protection against racial discrimination. The law was thus considered adequate. In the first Faurisson affair, the plaintiffs had the onus to establish, with a complete set of evidence on the Holocaust, that Faurisson was wrong. Under this second legislative approach, the court felt it was not up to judges to receive and evaluate evidence about the Holocaust: their only role is to apply the law. Many cases were heard since then under the Gayssot Law, and courts have limited the possibility to produce evidence on the Holocaust as the law imposed the event as judicial notice and actually made it part of the offense to deny it.

In a recent case in France, similar to the one between Irving and Lipstadt in the United Kingdom, Faurisson attempted to clean his reputation—and attract attention—by instituting a libel action against Robert Badinter, the former justice minister of France. On television, Badinter had said that Faurisson had previously been convicted for being a falsifier of history, referring to a previous conviction of Faurisson in 1981. Faurisson filed a petition for libel, arguing that the court had not used the word "falsifier." Faurisson lost his cause but forced Badinter to present the court with evidence and expertise on the said judgment and its interpretation. We view this case as another example of the need for ad hoc statutes. Otherwise, trials run the risk of being transformed into sterile historical debates on the veracity of the Holocaust, which is, ironically, what opponents to ad hoc statutes strive to avoid.

3.4 Formal Legislative Establishment and References to International Tribunal Decision

The Holocaust has a tremendous bearing on our lives. The event is *the* point of reference for evil acts. It is our society as a whole that is under attack when crimes of such magnitude, having affected us as human beings, are denied. It is the teaching of such events, their prophylactic role, that deniers want to erase and that ought to be protected. By eliminating the event from our consciousness and our history, deniers want to influence the present. Reality is that a fair-minded reader might unfortunately believe deniers' allegations. Therefore, as long as the event exists, public opinion represents an insurmountable hurdle for deniers. But if it does not exist, if the parapet disappears, nothing precludes the resurgence of racist measures.

Truth must have a point of reference. The Gayssot Law opted to refer to the IMT Charter and decision instead of unilaterally imposing history. For deniers, the result is the same. What allows for the rejection of the deniers' views and consequently for their prosecution is that the events are historical facts established by judicial bodies such as an international tribunal. Thus, they cannot be denied by anyone acting in good faith. This is the first—and remains the most important—obstacle facing those who deny historical facts like the ones mentioned herein. The Holocaust, for example, was established by the IMT judgment at Nuremberg[26] and by the other trials conducted under the Allied Control Council Law No. 10.

Large-scale, state-sponsored massacres or massive human rights violations should not be manipulated. Before engaging in any debate about who is responsible for what and who is to be held accountable, and before trying to understand the lessons learned from the past, it is necessary to know the facts. A transitional body, such as a court of law or a truth commission, aims at establishing that truth. The establishment of historical truth, which will serve as a point of reference, is one objective for such transitional bodies. Consequently, we are of the opinion that referring to decisions by such bodies is a warranted approach.

For more comprehensive and complex research in countries where massive human rights violations have occurred, historians genuinely depend on documentation accumulated during trials and by truth commissions. In fact, for events such as genocides or crimes against humanity, gathering evidence is not an easy task; thus, nearly all historical sources come from the judicial forum, at least during the initial period following the crime. The Nuremberg trial is a good example in this respect.[27] In the case of the Holocaust, the record of the event comes, to a large extent, from a judicial body. Such transitional bodies, including truth commissions, can legitimately generate this point of reference as they establish themselves as historical

26. France et al. v. Goering et al., (1946) 22 IMT 203.

27. *See* Florent Brayard, *Juges et Historiens—Sur un segment et deux triangles*, *in* LE GÉNOCIDE DES JUIFS ENTRE PROCÈS ET HISTOIRE, 1943–2000, *at* 14 (2000).

authorities and, to some extent, go beyond the more traditional legal aspects.[28]

For some authors and scholars, historical truth does not equal judicial truth since the latter faces only two possibilities: the guilty and the innocent. Courts are not the best places for establishing historical truth.[29] For courts, the image of the past results from the confrontation between the accusation and the defense and not from an elaborated account or an accumulation of evidence and arguments.[30] According to this vision, these forums are ill suited to establish a proper historical representation since they only offer a limited view and allow a limited examination of the facts. The trial, they argue, does not call upon science but instead uses the confrontation of different versions of history in a contradictory forum that must always respect any and all rights of the defense. In this context, to render justice is not simply to come to a logical conclusion but to exercise power. Judgment is then not a logical conclusion of the inquiry. For such critics, the difficulty lies in the structural parameters of the trial—which is a reduction of the past—as they are "based upon the need to establish the provable rather than the probable."[31] Thus, there is not only one version of the events but two or more, the tribunal inevitably endorsing one or another of the competing historical accounts.

The controversy is understandable but, in our opinion, remains academic. One must go beyond this perception and look at the real role and implications of trials. Judges always have the obligation to decide upon the facts that are being presented to them. The fact that the events are considered to be historical ones should not alter this process. Contrary to the allegations mentioned above, the conclusion reached by a trial is not opposed to that which historians would otherwise establish through their research. Just like historians, judges, before agreeing to an argument, must agree on the facts. The obstacles they meet in doing so are not fundamentally different from those encountered by historians.[32] In fact, comparing the roles of a judge to

---

28. *See* DONALD BLOXHAM, GENOCIDE ON TRIAL—WAR CRIMES TRIALS AND THE FORMATION OF A HOLOCAUST HISTORY AND MEMORY 221 (2001).

29. *See* Tzvetan Todorov, Mémoire du Mal Tentation du Bien, Enquête sur le siècle 301 (2000).

30. Michael R. Marrus, *L'Histoire et l'Holocauste dans le prétoire*, *in* LE GÉNOCIDE DES JUIFS ENTRE PROCÈS ET HISTOIRE, 1943–2000, *at* 43 (Florent Brayard ed., 2000).

31. BLOXHAM, *supra* note 28, at 221.

32. *See* Mark J. Osiel, *Making Public Memory, Publicly*, *in* HUMAN RIGHTS IN POLITICAL TRANSITIONS: GETTYSBURG TO BOSNIA 238 (Carla Hesse & Robert Post eds., 1999).

those of a historian allows us to define common denominators[33]: both have a third-party position with regard to the event and, if acting in good faith, both intend to establish the same truth. For the former, the research is carried out in court, whereas for the latter, it is done in archives and by plowing through records. The accounts provided by witnesses are essential elements for both professions in their quest for truth. The concern with the evidence and with the credibility of witnesses is also very much present in the two instances. Moreover, there are usually the same complementary aspects between the oral account provided by witnesses and the material evidence provided either by experts or independently, as well as the same perspicacity in trying to reveal and detect contradictions, inconsistencies, or improbabilities. Finally, the same attention is given to omissions, forgery, lies, and allusions.[34] When the evidence is not complete, both judges and historians must accept the risk of guessing following logical steps to conclusion.[35] In historical debates, one can sometimes avoid responding to a question in an adequate way. This is absolutely impossible before a tribunal and represents a fundamental aspect of transitional justice. Even if we doubt the absolute convergence between the methodology of the historian and that of the judge or of the commissioner, one must recognize that these parties inquire from similar perspectives. While the judge has to settle the question, this role does not justify the rejection of judicial processes for historical-truth establishment and as a point of reference for ad hoc statutes.

Furthermore, the court's role is not limited to fact finding. The idea is not merely to establish truth in a vacuum but to do so in a manner that it will be recognized as truth. The court's role—like the historian's role—is to clarify, among public opinion, the what, the how, and the why of acts. Courts of law are generally publicly accepted and authoritative fact finders,[36] which is a characteristic that historians lack as their research does not have an equivalent impact. The process leading to the truth, its acknowledgement by the public and its dissemination are key aspects because truth can be either contested or simply not known. Therefore, it is preferable that the process leading to truth recognition be handled by a recognized and unbiased third party. The importance and educational values of events dealt with in this article

---

33. *See* Paul Ricoeur, La Mémoire, L'histoire, L'oubli 413 (2000).

34. *See* Brayard *supra* note 27, at 14.

35. Oscar Handlin, Truth in History 119–20 (1979).

36. Osiel, *supra* note 32, at 223.

have to be maintained. Historical-truth establishment has to be done correctly and its process recognized by as many constituents as possible. Declarative memorial laws and ad hoc statutes referring to crimes with no linkage to a recognized fact-finding institution are in our opinion more likely to be attacked.

Memorial laws including ad hoc statutes run two very common but opposing risks that can create the impression of political truth making and thus lead to the rejection of the provision. On the one hand, it might be perceived that the states adopting such provisions are creating a myth about a certain version of the past. On the other hand, there is also a risk of doing the opposite by diluting the truth and the evils. The danger of creating a sacred event is an argument commonly voiced by opponents of ad hoc statutes. However, an event like the Holocaust is not unique or considered sacred because ad hoc statutes preclude its denial. Indeed, by making this claim, opponents are reversing cause and effect: it is the uniqueness of the event and its effects on today's society that ad hoc statutes intend to protect.

Holocaust deniers heavily rely on the fact that at Nuremberg, truth was established by one side only and thus ought to be rejected. Their objection is that there is too close a relationship between the construction of collective history and today's politics. When politics and history are closely intertwined, history is not only constructed for truth establishment purposes, and there might be attempts to create a myth[37] to promote a certain angle of history. Myth making favors the appearance of denial movements—and neither states nor courts of law are free from all suspicion about myth making.

While the Gayssot Law refers to the IMT Charter and to organizations that its judgment recognized as criminal, the IMT decision does not crystallize a myth—it is only the starting point, not the end point. Records like this one are neither definitive nor permanent with regard to facts. The partial picture of past repression implies a continued need for research, and accordingly, dozens of studies and books relating to the Holocaust are written and published each year. Referring in ad hoc to renowned international bodies such as the IMT does not impose the view—or even try to suggest—that a consensus exists on all aspects of the Holocaust. The truth it refers to may not be complete, but it is still an established record on which we keep relying. It forms the big picture: it is a macro-truth about the atrocities that has been established and that cannot be denied in good faith.

---

37. *See* RUTI G. TEITEL, TRANSITIONAL JUSTICE 70 (2002).

In a paranoid postmodernist world, there is never just one truth. In an era like ours, deniers know too well that truth is more easily accepted when all parties are blamed, and they take advantage of this situation. A common criticism of ad hoc statutes put forward by deniers is precisely that the history to which these statutes refer depicts only the oppressor's regime as the evil one, without concentrating too much effort on the actions of the alleged "other side." While certainly not desirable, this situation is understandable. Not many Americans, British, or Russians were prosecuted after the Second World War. Maybe the bombing of Dresden would have justified prosecution or public inquiry and an acknowledgment. But the bombing of Dresden by the Allied forces, although a terrible event, did not take on the scope of a continent-wide campaign designed to eliminate one group from the face of the earth. It is morally inadequate to put the two situations on the same level and to say that Jewish sufferance under the Nazi regime equaled the Allies' acts. This is not to create a billboard of sufferance but to qualify the events based on facts and legal definitions: putting both on an equal footing would have been the opposite of myth making. The danger or dilemma is to *force* the establishment of well-balanced or sanitized history. In short, moral equivalence is no better than myth making.

Patrice Boizeau—the editor of *Le choc du mois*—and Faurisson pretended that the judgment of the IMT, to which the Gayssot Law—under which Faurisson was prosecuted—refers, should be considered as hearsay. The judgment, they argue, could not be referred to since it was not available and not officially incorporated into French law. The Cour d'appel rejected that argument since the defendants were not prosecuted for crimes against humanity but for denying them, which is precisely the criminal act targeted and defined by the law. As for the judgment, it is available to all (in French), since it was filed with the International Court of Justice of The Hague.[38] The Cour de cassation came to the same conclusions in the case of Alain Guionnet, the editor of *Révision*.[39]

Maybe there is a limited risk of politicizing history to create either a myth or its moral equivalent. France debated the danger of generating even more controversy by giving the impression it was imposing an official version of

38. Association des Déportés v. Boizeau, Faurisson, Sarl les Éditions Choc, Cour d'appel [CA] [regional court of appeal] Paris, Dec. 9, 1992, Légipresse no. 103—III 90.

39. Guionnet, Arrêt du 23 février 1993, Bulletin des arrêts de la Cour de cassation, chambre criminelle, Journal officiel de la République française no. 1, janvier 1993, no. 86, 208, 209.

history, but it still adopted the Gayssot approach. The method that refers to international bodies, it seems to us, is the right one in that regard.

4. An Overview of Ad Hoc Statutes and Other Approaches

In this section, we will concentrate on countries that have generated an abundant amount of case law or that have provided for a distinctive approach. We will also look at jurisdictions without such legislation but with prominent deniers on their territory. The intent is to provide an overview of the spectrum of approaches; we do not pretend to present an exhaustive list.

4.1 Ad hoc Statutes in Europe

1. Germany

Article 130(3) of the German Penal Code (*Volksverhetzung*) criminalizes the acts of those who publicly deny, diminish, or approve of the acts committed under the regime of National Socialism in a way likely to disturb public peace. This is crime under any provision that resembles that provided by the Genocide Convention.

Paragraphs 1 and 2 of Section 130 prohibit the incitement of racial hatred against segments of the population or any calls for violent or arbitrary measures against them. They criminalize assaults on human dignity by insulting, maliciously maligning, or defaming segments of the population. These two paragraphs require that the action lead to an attack on human dignity and disturb or endanger peace in a concrete fashion. While paragraph 3—which deals specifically with denial—drops this requirement, a denier must still utter speech or act in a manner capable of disturbing public peace. It does not suffice that he or she speaks or acts in public—there needs to be a severe form of disrespect that is targeted at creating a hostile attitude toward the victim of the attack. German jurisprudence usually sees denial speech as an action capable of disturbing peace.

Section 130 prohibits the denial of an act committed by the Nazis that fits the definition of genocide. It clearly targets the denial of genocide against the Jews. To some extent, the German approach imposes obligations on the court to take the Holocaust, a crime recognized as genocide, as judicial notice. With this definition, a broader interpretation including other genocides committed by the Nazis is possible, though improbable. The provision does not seem to require prior recognition of such possible other genocides or crimes. In theory, the denial of other crimes, in order to be punishable, could then require the establishment, before the court, of the event debated and of the crime committed.

In a recent case, German courts had to deal with the following intent issue. Frederick Töben, an Australian citizen and founder/director of the Holocaust denial Adelaide Institute, a forum for deniers' ideas, was prosecuted and condemned under Section 130. Töben was responsible for Holocaust denial material put on an Australian Web server but available in Germany. The court again had to determine whether the publication constituted an incitement to racial hatred under paragraphs 1 and 2. The accusation was made also under paragraph 3, which is often done in similar cases. Töben was found guilty under the three sections. Concerning the demonstration of the concrete danger, the court found that it was sufficient to have concrete reasons to fear that the action would indeed disturb peace (by opposition to the "clear and present danger" concept discussed below). The court concluded that Töben intended to disturb peace in Germany even if the server was in Australia since the Web pages were accessible in Germany.[40] It felt there was good reason to believe that Töben's site would indeed disturb peace as it was attacking Jewish people, and that it could be interpreted as being addressed to German citizens. Töben was also found guilty under paragraph 3 of Section 130.

Recent developments in Germany involved prominent deniers Germar Rudolf and Ernst Zündel. Rudolf is a German citizen who fled to the United States to avoid justice but was expelled. The U.S. Immigration Services rejected Rudolf's application for political asylum and sent him back to Germany, where he was charged with incitement to racial hatred. Rudolf, a trained chemist, has a long history regarding Holocaust denial. Following Leuchter's footsteps, he published pseudo-scientific claims that it was impossible that Zyklon-B poison was used in the gas chambers at Nazi death camps.

---

40. R. v. Töben, Bundesgerichtshof [BGH] Urt, v, Dec. 12, 2000—1 StR 184/00 (LG Mannheim), *available at* http://www.jurpc.de/rechtspr/20010038.htm.

2. *France*

France is considered the birthplace of the denial movement, and Maurice Bardèche—and even more so, Paul Rassinier—are considered its fathers. Robert Faurisson, a literature professor at the University of Lyon, is its actual leader. Henri Roques, Roger Garaudy, and Jean-Marie LePen—the leader of the Front National (FN) Party that brought Holocaust denial into politics—are other prominent members of the movement. Other FN partisans are known as denial supporters: Bruno Gollnsich was charged and condemned in 2007 for publicly disputing the Holocaust and suspended from the University of Lyon. FN representative Georges Theil and FN supporter Martin Peltier, director of the *National Hebdo* (the party's unofficial journal) were also prosecuted and condemned in the last couple of years.

The Gayssot Law was adopted in 1990, in the midst of a wave of Holocaust denial cases. In the 1980s, the extreme right-wing movement—mainly the Front National—was gaining in popularity in France. The legendary "point de détail" comment (referring to the Holocaust as "a detail" of history) by Jean-Marie Le Pen brought Holocaust denial to the forefront of legislative debate. Article 24 *bis* of the amended *Loi du 29 juillet 1881 sur la liberté de la presse* makes punishable disputing the existence of one or more crimes against humanity defined in the IMT Charter and that were committed by members of an organization declared criminal in the judgment of that tribunal.[41] It was on the basis of this charter that Nazis were tried in Nuremberg.

As we have seen in many cases, ad hoc statutes still require the demonstration of some aspect of the event or the intent behind the deniers' words. The merit of ad hoc statutes such as the Gayssot Law precisely resides, we think, in the fact that it provides the missing link through legislative intervention. It clearly establishes the *actus reus* of the crime in the very denial of an event previously established by legislation and assumes that the denial was made with an illegitimate intent (the *mens rea*). It avoids the usual requirement under hate propaganda provisions to demonstrate the effect or the intent to attack the victims. The infraction is defined in clear terms. It avoids the debate between fact and opinion about internationally recognized genocide. It does not confer any power to courts to establish the event.

---

41. Those who were tried include the leadership of the Nazi party, the SS, the SD, and the Gestapo. *See* Bulletin officiel du Ministère de la Justice, no. 39 du 30 septembre 1990, circulaire CRIM 90-09 F1 du 27 août 1990, Application of Law No. 90-615 of July 13, 1990.

The task of the court is limited to the material aspect of the crime. Courts do not have to consider—and in fact, are precluded from considering—evidence on the negated event. Their only role resides in the application of a criminal provision, which in this case targets undisputable facts. The law does not limit the circulation of an opinion here, since the denier's expression is not an opinion; what is being limited is the expression of a lie, a lie made publicly with anti-Semitic intent.

Robert Faurisson was convicted in 1992 but challenged the legitimacy of the Gayssot Law before the United Nations Human Rights Committee. He argued that the decision violated his freedom of speech according to Section 19 of the International Covenant on Civil and Political Rights (ICCPR). The committee dismissed Faurisson's claims, but the reasoning for the dismissal remains ambiguous. The committee's concern revolved around the required *mens rea* for the crime. The provision, in the committee's opinion, did not clearly link criminal responsibility and intent. In addition, the committee felt that the objective of the law may have been reached otherwise, without establishing a legislative dogma about a historical event. Additionally, because the committee's role is not to judge *in abstracto*—even if preoccupied by the scope of the law—the committee ruled that in this specific case, the law was not incompatible with the ICCPR.[42]

France's past has been debated before the courts on many other occasions. The European Court of Human Rights for example, adjudged the Lehideux and Isorni affair. The case involved the promotion and defense of General Petain's era and the Vichy government. The accused were prosecuted and condemned by national courts under Section 24 of the *Loi du 29 juillet 1881 sur la liberté de la presse* and not under the Gayssot provision. Still, the merit of this controversial decision resides in the clear condemnation of Holocaust denial.[43]

The Additional Protocol to the Convention on Cybercrime, concerning the criminalization of acts of a racist and xenophobic nature committed through computer systems,[44] opted for an approach quite similar to the

---

42. Faurisson v. France, Communication No. 550/1993, U.N. Doc. CCPR/C/58/D/550/1993.

43. Lehideux and Isorni v. France, Sept. 23, 1998, Application No. 24662/94, 1998-VII, no. 92, para. 47 (European Court of Human Rights).

44. Additional Convention on the Protocol on Cybercrime, *supra* note 19.

Gayssot one. It explicitly—and through a binding obligation—requests that legislatures criminalize denial in a similar fashion to the Gayssot Law.

3. United Kingdom

In the United Kingdom, there is no legislation on denial of the Holocaust or other crimes against humanity. Contrary to the United States, though, the UK does not have the equivalence of the First Amendment impeding such legislative initiatives. For the past few decades, deniers have been relatively active in the United Kingdom. The most memorable example is the *Irving* defamation case mentioned above. Deborah Lipstadt described Irving as a Holocaust denier in her book, and the latter sued, claiming that she had damaged his reputation.

Considering the procedural vehicle taken by Irving, Lipstadt was forced to hire a historian, Richard J. Evans, to present a detailed expertise on the Holocaust and on the misrepresentations and bad faith of Irving's position. The long and mediated trial provided Irving with a spectacular tribune to present masses of evidence supposedly proving the inexistence of the Holocaust or its gross exaggeration. This decision is interesting because of the treatment of the amount of evidence rather than because the court's evaluation of the infringement of the freedom of speech. Justice Gray was ultimately persuaded by Lipstadt and rendered a long and detailed judgment addressing all the main arguments of Irving's view. The judgment refuted Irving's arguments in an exhaustive way probably to ensure that the judgment would not be attacked and that it would become a jurisprudential point of reference for similar cases.

During the trial, Irving persistently and deliberately misrepresented and manipulated historical evidence to portray Hitler in an unwarrantedly favorable light, principally in relation to his attitude toward the treatment of the Jews. The court agreed with Lipstadt that Irving was indeed an anti-Semite, a racist, and an active Holocaust denier. The conclusion of Justice Gray is worth citing:

> Irving displays all the characteristics of a Holocaust denier. He repeatedly makes assertions about the Holocaust which are offensive to Jews in their terms and unsupported by or contrary to the historical record . . . Irving has for his own ideological reasons persistently and deliberately misrepresented and manipulated historical evidence; that for the same reasons he has portrayed Hitler in an unwarrantedly favourable light, principally

> in relation to his attitude towards and responsibility for the treatment of the Jews; that he is an active Holocaust denier; that he is anti-Semitic and racist and that he associates with right wing extremists who promote neo-Nazism.[45]

It will be interesting to monitor future development in the UK with regard to the proposed framework decision on combating racism and xenophobia, which will be discussed below.

4. Austria

In Austria, the first version of the National Socialism Prohibition Law Act *(Verbotsgesetz)* was passed in 1945. It prohibited participation in the Foreign Organization of the National Socialist German Workers Party (NSDAP) and subjected anybody who still belonged to that party or who acted for it or its aims, to capital punishment. The act was amended several times, notably to define the criminal offenses in a more detailed way and to replace the general offense with more specific provisions.

Paragraph 3(h) of the *Verbotsgesetz*, added in 1992, makes Holocaust denial punishable. It provides that a person is liable if he or she denies, grossly minimizes,[46] approves or tries to excuse the Nazi genocide or other Nazi crimes against humanity in a print publication, broadcast, or other media. The legislature—and later the courts—made it clear that the mass extermination of Jews is accepted as an established historical fact that does not need to be proven.[47] The act covers explicitly the gross minimization but also the justification of the Nazis' criminal behavior. The law limits its scope to the Nazis but not to the Holocaust: an approach that can be explained by the country's history. It also prohibits the denial of other Nazi crimes against humanity. Potentially, this provision also covers crimes against the tsiganes, gypsies, homosexuals, or Jehovah's Witnesses if a court confirms the qualification of crimes against humanity.

---

45. Irving v. Penguin Books Limited and Lipstadt, [2000] EWHC Q.B.D. 115 (Eng), para. 13.167.

46. For more on the gross-minimization concept, *see* ECommHR, Sept. 9, 1998, Case No. 36773/97, Herwig Nachtmann v. Austria.

47. *See* Gerd Honsik v. Austria, req. No. 25062/94, 83-B D.R. 77.

5. Switzerland

Section 261*bis* of the Swiss Criminal Code prohibits words, writings, images, and gestures that have been uttered or made in public and that discriminate in a way that undermines the human dignity of a person or a group of people because of their race, their ethnic membership, or their religion. It also prohibits the denial, coarse minimization, and justification of genocides or other crimes against humanity when engaged in for the same reason. Basically, any genocide or crime against humanity falls under the scope of this broad ad hoc statute. This statute does not refer explicitly to a past decision like that of the IMT nor does it refer to an internationally approved definition (e.g., by the Genocide Convention) or to the statute of an internationally recognized body (e.g., the International Tribunal for Rwanda or former Yugoslavia, or the International Criminal Court). This approach leaves the legal definition of genocide open to debate before the court. Swiss courts have interpreted the statute in many occasions and extended its scope to the Armenian genocide. With this statute, Switzerland could be the turf for an expansion of the jurisprudence to other events.

6. Belgium

In Belgium, the Act of March 23, 1995 prohibits the negation, minimization, justification, or approval of the genocide committed by the Nazi regime in Germany. For the definition, the statute refers to the Genocide Convention. The Belgian approach resembles that of the Gayssot Law as it prohibits the crimes committed by the Nazis. However, unlike the Gayssot provisions, the Act of March 23 does not refer to the IMT Charter or to its judgment, which would directly link the crime to the definition. Rather, it refers to the definition of genocide under the Genocide Convention, which only came into force three years after the end of the Second World War, on Dec. 9, 1948. A debate over the extension of the statute to include the Armenian genocide recently took place in Belgium, but the proposed amendment was not adopted.

7. Spain

The Spanish denial provision has a broad application as it makes criminal the denial of the existence of genocide. Section 607 (2) of Spain's criminal code makes criminal the dissemination of ideas or doctrines that deny or justify the crime of genocide or that purport to rehabilitate regimes or institutions that advocate these crimes.

Spain offers an interesting perspective because of its case law. Léon Degrelle, a Belgian and an ex-Nazi, was sued by a Holocaust survivor. In a journal, Degrelle had expressed his doubts about the existence of the crematories and insulted the Jewish people by expressing his desire for the rise of another Führer. After a lengthy trial before inferior courts, the Constitutional Court finally recognized that denial speech initially fell under the constitutional protection of the freedom of speech. The court nonetheless viewed that Degrelle did not only express his doubts on the existence of the crematoria but actually formulated racist declarations when he referred to the desire for a new Führer and when he stated that "if today there are so many Jews, it is difficult to believe that they have escaped alive from the crematoria." Neither the liberty of ideology nor the freedom of speech protected by the Constitution can allow for such racist declarations. These declarations, the court concluded, are not only contrary to the right to honor but also to other fundamental constitutional principles, such as the protection of human dignity. Still, similar to the approach used by other national courts—like Canada's—or by international bodies such as the European Human Rights Court, the court felt that in this context, one's right to dignity should have predominance over another person's freedom of speech. The court felt that Degrelle's comments had an anti-Semitic and racist connotation and thus constituted anti-Jewish incitement, regardless of whether the Holocaust constitutes a historical fact.[48]

Following this case, the Spanish penal code was modified to introduce a provision prohibiting the denial of genocide and not only of the Holocaust. It criminalizes the diffusion of ideas or doctrines that deny or justify genocide or intend to rehabilitate regimes responsible for such a crime.[49] The constitutionality of the provision was interpreted in quite a unique way. In 2007, the Constitutional Court struck the denial aspect off the provision but by the same token confirmed that it was acceptable to prohibit the justification of the event.[50] In other words, deniers could deny the Holocaust but could not try to justify the event.

8. Other European Countries

In addition to the aforementioned statutes, denial of the Holocaust is also criminalized in other European countries including, for example, Lithuania.

---

48. STC, Nov. 11, 1991, (No. 214/1991 (Sala Primera), apartado 8).
49. Art. 607 del Codigo Penal de Espana, (C.P. 10/1995) para. 2.
50. STC, Nov. 7, 2007, (No. 235/2007) Cuestión de inconstitucionalidad 5152-2000.

In Liechtenstein, article 283 of the penal code prohibits public denial or trivialization of the Holocaust, genocide, or other crimes against humanity, as well as attempts to justify these events. In the Netherlands, article 137 of the criminal code contains a provision criminalizing defamation and religious and racial incitement which been interpreted as prohibiting Holocaust denial. In Portugal, article 240(2) of the Criminal Code punishes anyone who defames or insults an individual or a group of individuals on grounds of their race, color, ethnic, national, or religious origin, including through denial of war crimes and crimes against peace or humanity. The action is made criminal if it is carried out with the intent of inciting racial or religious discrimination. In the Slovak Republic, Section 261 of the criminal code punishes public sympathy with fascism or any other similar movement, as well as the public negation, expression of doubt, acceptance, or justification of fascist crimes or other similar movements. Romania punishes the promotion of persons who are found guilty of crimes against peace and humanity as well as of the promotion of fascist, racist, or xenophobic ideologies through propaganda. Romania also explicitly prohibits the negation of the Holocaust. Luxembourg adopted an ad hoc statute very similar to the Gayssot Law. Article 457-3 of the criminal code forbids publicly contesting, trivializing, justifying, or denying the existence of war crimes or crimes against humanity that are defined in the statutes of the IMT or the existence of a genocide.

Countries like Poland and the Czech Republic offer a different perspective as their statutes reflect their communist past. In Poland, denial is illegal under Article 256 of the criminal code. The definition is broader than in most statutes: it comprises Nazi crimes, crimes against peace, crimes against humanity, and war crimes. It is worth mentioning that the statute also covers communist crimes. Additionally, Poland's statute contains a time limitation: in order to make a claim; the crime in question needs to have been perpetrated between September 1, 1939, and December 31, 1989. In the Czech Republic, Article 261(a) of the Constitution has many similarities with the Polish statute.

4.2 North America

The North American approach is increasingly isolated as far as the Western Hemisphere goes. North America's "absolute freedom of speech" dogma—which is especially pervasive in the United States—seems to protect deniers and limits the courts' ability to protect those targeted by denial speech.

1. Canada

While, like the United States, Canada has no specifically adapted legislation prohibiting denial speech, it does have a comprehensive legal mechanism with regard to freedom of speech and hate propaganda. The Canadian Charter of Rights and Freedoms protects the freedom of speech but also recognizes that fundamental rights such as the freedom of expression are subject to limits that need to be reasonable, prescribed by law, and justified in a free and democratic society.

The Ernst Zündel case is an example of a Holocaust denial case that arose in Canada. Zundel was unsuccessfully prosecuted in Canada for spreading false news.[51] Through his publishing house, Samisdat Publishing, Zündel distributed a pamphlet with the title "Did Six Million Really Die?" It suggested that the Holocaust was a myth perpetrated by a worldwide Jewish conspiracy. The Supreme Court of Canada found that the scope of the provision that prohibits the spreading of false news was too broad to be applied here and, as a result, the limitation of the freedom of speech text was unjustifiable in this context.[52]

It is the Internet that provided Zündel with the audience that he had always looked for. It is also the Internet that led to his conviction and deportation to Germany when Canada finally succeeded in prosecuting him. His *Zündelsite*, webmastered by his wife and hosted by a service provider in United States, allowed him to disseminate his views regarding denial. As far as his Web site dedicated to Holocaust denial goes, Canadian courts found Zündel guilty of using telecommunication devices to spread heinous messages against minorities.[53] The Canadian Human Rights Act,[54] prohibiting hate propaganda communicated through telephone lines, was successfully used to prosecute Zündel. He was finally deported to Germany in 2005 after exhausting his appeal possibilities. As a welcome token, Zündel was prosecuted and convicted in Mannheim in February 2007.

The other main cases brought against deniers in Canada were under laws prohibiting hate propaganda. The Supreme Court upheld the constitutionality of Section 319 of the criminal code in the *Keegstra* case, which involved a

---

51. Criminal Code, R.S.C. c. C-46, s. 181.

52. *See* Q. v. Zündel, [1992] 2 S.C.R. 731 (Can.).

53. Sabina Citron et al. v. Ernst Zündel, [2000] 4 F.C. 255 (Can.).

54. Canadian Human Rights Act, R. S.C. 1985, c. H-6, s. 13.

teacher who had taught that Jews were "child killers" and "treacherous" and that the Holocaust was a myth.[55] The court found that the defendant, Keegstra, had abused his right to freedom of speech and recognized the role of the government in penalizing hate propaganda, which was perceived as being consistent with the commitment that Canada had made when ratifying the International Convention on the Elimination of all Forms of Discrimination (CERD). The court felt that hate propaganda harmed the targeted persons and groups—by humiliating and degrading them—and society as a whole. The court, in its decision, also emphasized the long-term harmful influence of propaganda, holding that denial propaganda was only tenuously connected with the values underlying the guarantee of freedom of expression—which is the quest for truth and the promotion of individual self-development. The court ruled that the prohibition of such propaganda did not unduly impair the right to freedom of expression.[56]

2. United States

The origin of a structured Holocaust denial movement in the United States originates in the late 1970s with the creation of the pseudo-academic organization, Institute for Historical Review (IHR). The IHR uses its *Journal of Historical Review* and conferences to disseminate its propaganda. Contrary to what its name suggests, the IHR is not engaged in historical research. It is a platform for racist publications and speeches. Members of the IHR include anti-Semitic propagandists such as Zündel, Irving, Faurisson, and Bradley Smith. It is also supported by self-proclaimed scholars such as Arthur Butz Smith. Along with of the Committee for Open Debate on Holocaust—an organization active in the 1990s—these revisionists placed paid advertisements in college newspapers inviting students to engage in "open debate" on the Holocaust, thereby implying that its very occurrence is subject to legitimate controversy.

The United States believes in an idealized free market of ideas in which all forms of expression should be allowed to compete. The approach puts hate speech on an equal basis with any other expression and considers the opposition between hate propaganda and counterargument as a legitimate debate. This method relies on the premise that truth and rationale will always

---

55. Q. v. Keegstra, [1990] 3 S.C.R. 697 (Can.).

56. Canada (Human Rights Commission) v. Taylor, [1990] 3 S.C.R. 892, 919 (Can.); Q. v. Andrews, [1990] 3 S.C.R. 870.

prevail over hate propaganda and that intolerance can be countered by more expression—which, as history has shown, is questionable.

The United States only allows for the narrowest and absolutely necessary restrictions of the freedom of expression. The First Amendment states that "Congress shall make no law . . . abridging the freedom of speech, or of the press." It does not provide any ground for government justifications of limitations of that freedom. For this reason, the United States hosts many of the Web sites of foreign deniers.

In most instances, U.S. jurisprudence does not recognize the link between propaganda and the harm it causes. Under the "clear and present danger" doctrine, only the present danger of imminent evil could justify the curtailment of the freedom of speech.[57] Restrictions can be justified only when there is a clear and present danger of eminent violence arising from the expression and that no other reasonable means of preventing the violence can be used. It is not sufficient to demonstrate that there is a probability for the expression to cause such a clear and present danger. "Imminent" was interpreted as likely to occur within a very short time span.[58] The First Amendment may allow legislation to prohibit hate speech advocating the use of force but only in the very narrow circumstances where such advocacy is directed at inciting or producing imminent lawless action and is likely to incite or produce such action.[59]

Suppression of expression based on content is generally prohibited and found unconstitutional. The Supreme Court extended this prohibition of content-based regulation and has made the control of speech targeting identifiable groups even more difficult to justify. It holds the view that only a prohibition of all fighting words would be justifiable and that the prohibition of racist hate speech and anti-Semitic speech or displays alone is unconstitutional.[60] The imminent threat test[61] and the total lack of recognition of the long-term effects of propaganda makes the prohibition of hate speech in the United States almost impossible.

While the United States has far broader free speech protections than certain European countries, it also has some interesting case law relating to

57. Abrams v. United States, 250 U.S. 616,628 (1919).

58. Hess v. Indiana, 414 U.S. 105, 108 (1973).

59. Brandenburg v. Ohio, 395 U.S. 444 (1969).

60. R.A.V. v. St.Paul, 505 U.S. 373 (1992).

61. Brandenburg v. Ohio, *supra* note 59.

Holocaust denial. In 1980, the IHR published an ad offering $50,000 to anyone who could "prove" that Jews were gassed by the Nazis at Auschwitz. Mel Mermelstein, a 65-year-old Holocaust survivor, filed an affidavit as the required evidence. He then sued the IHR and its director, William David McCalden, who had refused to pay the promised amount. McCalden, who had previously offered $25,000 to Simon Wiesenthal if he could prove that one single Jew had been gassed and that the diary of Anne Frank was authentic, admitted that the ad was just a means to attract publicity. The case was ultimately settled. However, the statement of record and the letter of apology to Mr. Mermelstein referred to the conclusion of Justice Thomas T. Johnson: "This court does take judicial notice of the fact that Jews were gassed to death at the Auschwitz concentration camp . . . it is not reasonably subject to dispute. And it is capable of immediate and accurate determination by resort to sources of reasonably indisputable accuracy. It is simply a fact."[62]

4.3 Israel

Israel adopted an ad hoc statute in 1986 (Law 5746-1986). It prohibits any statement denying or diminishing the proportions of the acts committed during the Nazi regime—defined as crimes against the Jewish people—but also other crimes against humanity committed by the Nazis. The action is prohibited if it is aimed at defending the perpetrators of those acts or at expressing sympathy or identification with them (Sections 2 and 3). Section 4 allows for the publication of a correct and fair report publication—otherwise prohibited—as long as it is not made with any intent to express sympathy with the perpetrators.

5. Standardization of Ad Hoc Approaches in Europe

We believe that the Gayssot Law provides a well-suited approach. As we have just seen, though, many other approaches have been adopted to prohibit denial speech. In that context, the Council of EU Justice Ministers

62. Statement of record and letter of apology to Mr. Mermelstein, in Mermelstein v. IHR (Institute for Historical Review) et al., No. C 356542 (Cal. Super. Ct. 1981).

reached an agreement on a framework decision on combating racism and xenophobia in 2007. This text allows for a binding minimum harmonization throughout Europe of the provisions of criminal liability for disseminating racist and xenophobic statements, including denial or gross trivialization of genocide out of racist or xenophobic motives. The text establishes that the following conducts will be punishable in all EU Member States:

- Publicly inciting to violence or hatred, directed against a group of persons or a member of such a group defined by reference to race, color, religion, descent, or national or ethnic origin;
- Publicly condoning, denying, or grossly trivializing
    - crimes of genocide, crimes against humanity, and war crimes as defined in the Statute of the International Criminal Court directed against a group of persons or a member of such a group defined by reference to race, color, religion, descent, or national or ethnic origin;
    - crimes defined in the IMT Charter and directed against a group of persons or a member of such a group defined by reference to race, color, religion, descent, or national or ethnic origin.

With regard to its application, the proposed framework offers Member States flexibility in many respects. Moreover, a compromise was reached between states with no criminal provisions on denial and that are thus reluctant to adopt them—and others with enacted laws already containing such offenses.

The suggested approach seems to adopt the French position but to adapt it in some regards. It suggests referring to the decision of an international tribunal as the fact-finding authority and as a point of reference for denial legislation. It refers states to definitions of genocide and crimes against humanity contained in the Statute of the International Criminal Court (ICC) and in the Charter of the IMT. However, it is still unclear which historical events fall under these definitions and which judicial instances will be empowered to decide which historical events will be considered as a crime. It seems that it will be up to national courts to determine whether a specific historical crime falls under these definitions. In the case of the Holocaust, for example, the Nuremberg Tribunal had already made these determinations, so the matter is easily settled.

Pursuant to the framework, Member States will also have the possibility to make criminal liability—dependent upon the determination, by a national or international court—that a historical event constituted genocide, a crime against humanity, or a war crime. A provision of the proposed framework provides Member States with the possibility to make a statement that it will make punishable the denial or the gross trivialization of the crimes referred to above only if these crimes have been established by both its own national court and an international court or by an international court alone. This will of course open a debate about what type of tribunal and what jurisdiction can be referred to.

States may choose to punish only conduct that is either likely to disturb public order or that is threatening, abusive, or insulting. This approach allows for the interpretation that denial or gross trivialization of genocide and other crimes against humanity can only be penalized if it can be demonstrated that these acts amount to racist or xenophobic agitation. Said otherwise, this way of linking denials to the potentially required demonstration of xenophobic agitation is similar to forcing the interpretation of Holocaust denial provisions via hate speech provisions with the same burden of proof that implies the immediate effect—or, as the U.S. courts put it—"a clear and present danger." However, this does not impede states from going beyond this interpretation and criminalizing the denial or gross trivialization of such facts even if the expression does not directly incite hatred and violence.

6. Requirements to Prosecute Denial as a Form of Hate Speech: Are Ad Hoc Statutes Justified Infringements of the Freedom of Speech?

Denial speech is analog to hate speech in both its intent and its effect. Contrary to hate speech, though, denial speech seeks to be perceived as a factual debate based on historiography. As we have seen, hate speech provisions have been of little help in prosecuting deniers. Deniers go beyond the spectrum of speech protected by the freedom of speech. The absence of value of such discourse removes it from the realm of freedom of speech and transposes it into the heresy of the racial superiority arena. As such, this kind of speech is condemnable. The limitation of the deniers' freedom does not per se target their speech; rather, it targets the denier's goal to attack the victims. Ad hoc statutes take those premises as a starting point, trying to avoid the trap of conferring the tasks of establishing or confirming history upon a tribunal.

The regulation of hate speech revolves around the interplay and the conciliation of two fundamental human rights: the freedom of expression and the right to equality. There is an international consensus that hate speech threatens democracy, justice, and equality, which encourages countries to prohibit it. The Genocide Convention declares direct and public incitement to commit genocide a punishable act, but it goes no further back up in the genocidal food chain, omitting hate propaganda in its list of crimes.[63] Subsequent international human rights instruments have filled that void.

Two international instruments go further and require states to penalize hate propaganda. Section 20 of the ICCPR states that any propaganda for war and any advocacy of national, racial, or religious hatred that constitutes incitement to discrimination, hostility, or violence shall be prohibited by law. The ICCPR Committee has affirmed the duty of states to restrict the freedom of expression in order to assure the protection of other people's rights.[64] In the *Faurisson* case, the committee expressed the view that the prosecution of defendant Robert Faurisson did not breach his fundamental right of freedom of expression. Article 4 of CERD is even more precise: state parties shall adopt positive measures to eradicate incitement to discrimination and shall declare a punishable offense all dissemination of ideas based on racial superiority or hatred; this mandate includes incitement to racial discrimination, as well as all acts of violence or incitement to such acts against any race or group of persons of another color or ethnic origin.

The European Convention of Human Rights (ECHR) does not contain any specific provision dealing with hate propaganda. In numerous cases, the defunct European Commission of Human Rights had nonetheless excluded hate propaganda from the protection of Article 10 safeguarding the freedom of speech.[65] For the Commission, hate propaganda is contrary to the text and spirit of the Convention and contributes to the destruction of the rights and freedoms of others.[66] Article 17 of the Convention enshrines that principle by stating that nothing in the Convention may be interpreted as implying any right to engage in any activity aimed at the destruction of any of the rights

63. William A. Schabas, Genocide in International Law—The Crimes of Crimes 162 (2000).

64. Ross v. Canada, Communication No. 736/1997, Views of Oct. 18, 2000, para. 11.5; J.R.T. and the W.G. Party v. Canada, Communication No. 104/1981 (declared inadmissible on April 6, 1983).

65. See notably Glimmerveen and Hagenbeek v. Netherlands App. Nos. 8348/78 and 8406/78, (1979) 18 D.R. 187; Kühnen v. Federal Republic of Germany, App. No. 12194/86, (1988) 56 D.R. 205; Marais v. France, App. No. 31159/96,(1996) 86-A D.R. 184.

66. See notably Honsik v. Austria, App. No. 25062/94 (1995), 83-A D.R. 77.

and freedoms set forth in the Convention. The Commission had generally ruled that deniers' complaints about limitation of their freedoms were manifestly ill founded. It has also determined that deniers seeking the destruction of the rights and freedoms of others are merely engaging in a campaign against peace and justice.[67]

The European Court of Human Rights made it clear that hate speech regulation was compatible with the Convention. Recognizing the utmost importance of the freedom of speech, the court nonetheless agreed that the Convention should be interpreted, whenever possible, in a way that is reconcilable with CERD, which, as we have seen, explicitly prohibits hate speech.[68] The negation of the Holocaust and the justification of pro-Nazi policies were also considered a form of hate and racist propaganda unprotected by Article 10 of the Convention.[69] The court has found that the freedom of expression guaranteed under Article 10 may not be invoked in conflict with Article 17, particularly, in cases concerning Holocaust denial and related issues.[70] The protection of the interests of the victims of the Nazi regime outweighs the freedom to impart views denying the existence of the gas chambers.[71] The court found that Holocaust denial was in direct contradiction with the fight against racism and anti-Semitism, thus constituting a serious threat to public order. The court also found that such acts were incompatible with democracy and human rights because they infringed on the rights of others.[72]

Today, there is also a broader international consensus condemning Holocaust denial. Recent international conventions or declarations have opted for a declarative approach such as memorial days. One instrument even goes farther than that, requesting states to implement denial prohibition within national legislation. Section 3 of the Declaration of the Stockholm International Forum on the Holocaust[73] invites signatories to uphold the terrible truth of the Holocaust against those who deny it, to strengthen the

---

67. Nationaldemokratische Partei Deutschlands, Bezirksverband München-Oberbayern v. Germany, App. No. 25992/94, (1995) 84-B D.R. 149.

68. Jersild v. Denmark, 298 Eur. Ct. H.R. (ser. A) (1994).

69. Lehideux and Isorni v. France, *supra* note 43.

70. Witzsch v. Germany, No. 7485/03 (Eur. Ct. H.R. Dec. 13, 2005).

71. Lehideux and Isorni v. France, *supra* note 43.

72. Garaudy v. France, No. 65831/01 (Eur. Ct. H.R. 2003).

73. Declaration of the Stockholm International Forum on the Holocaust, (January 28, 2000).

moral and political commitments of governments, and to ensure that future generations can understand the causes of the Holocaust and reflect upon its consequences. Section 4 invites them to promote education, remembrance, and research about the Holocaust.[74]

Recent UNESCO and United Nations General Assembly resolutions even more clearly stress the importance of actively disseminating the knowledge regarding the facts and moral lessons of the Holocaust, as well as their refusal to countenance any form of Holocaust denial.

On November 1, 2005, the UN General Assembly adopted Resolution 60/7 on Holocaust Remembrance, reaffirming that "the Holocaust, which resulted in the murder of one-third of the Jewish people, along with countless members of other minorities, will forever be a warning to all people of the dangers of hatred, bigotry, racism and prejudice." That resolution declared January 27th as an annual International Day of Commemoration of the Holocaust and urged Member States to develop educational programs to inculcate lessons of the Holocaust. Resolution 61/255 of January 26, 200 of the UN General Assembly on Holocaust denial was adopted on the eve of that commemoration day. The resolution condemns without any reservation any denial of the Holocaust and urged all Member States to reject any such denial. Furthermore, it welcomes the initiative by Member States to include, in their educational programs, measures to confront attempts to deny or minimize the importance of the Holocaust. It is worth mentioning that the resolution was proposed by the United States representative, who argued that denying the Holocaust reveals ignorance and moral failure and commended the Assembly to assert its moral authority and political will on that matter.

To give effect to the previous resolutions, the UNESCO General Conference adopted a resolution in 2007,[75] requesting UNESCO to consult with the United Nations Secretary-General as far as his or her outreach program goes,

---

74. For other resolutions, *see also* section 16 of the Resolution on Racism, Xenophobia and Anti-Semitism and the European Year against Racism, 1997 O.J. 17 (1997), European Parliament, B4-0045/97; Comm. of Ministers, *Declaration on the Follow-Up to the European Youth Campaign against Racism, Xenophobia, Anti-Semitism and Intolerance*, 98th Sess., Dec-03.05.96/1/3 (May 3, 1996); European Parliament Resolution on Remembrance of the Holocaust, anti-Semitism and Racism, EUR. PARL. DOC. PE 354.156 (2005); OSCE Permanent Council Decision on Combating Anti-Semitism, PC.DEC/607; Resolution on Combating Anti-Semitism and other forms of intolerance, Brussels Declaration of the OSCE Parliamentary Assembly, July 3–7, 2006; Declaration and Programme of Action of the World Conference against Racism, Racial Discrimination, Xenophobia and Related Intolerance, U.N. Doc. A/CONF.189/5 (2001).

75. UNESCO General Conference· 34th session, Paris, France, 34 C/49 (Oct. 8, 2007).

in order to explore what role it could play in promoting awareness of Holocaust remembrance, but also to combat all forms of Holocaust denial. The resolution was proposed by many states, including—once again—the United States.

As of now, only one international instrument compels states to prohibit denial while another one contemplates doing so. The Additional Protocol to the Convention on Cybercrime, requests—through a binding obligation—that the state implements legislation to criminalize denial. The EU Framework Decision on combating racism and xenophobia mentioned above, when fully implemented, will go in the same direction. This demonstrates more than a trend: we are now seeing a very large consensus on the requirement to criminalize the denial of events such as the ones examined in this text.

7. Future Developments: The Cases of Japan, Rwanda, and Former Yugoslavia

We expect the debate about what event deserves protection to continue, but if we feel that there is a clear justification for prohibiting Holocaust denial, the question remains open about expanding ad hoc statutes on denial to other events beyond the Armenian genocide.

Controversies on historical revisionism are becoming frequent in Japan. Radicals from the Japanese political Right reject historical accounts in which Japan is portrayed as being guilty of crimes against the Chinese population. They deny or outrageously minimize the aggression and atrocities committed by the Imperial Army in the first half of the twentieth century. One example of the massive human-rights abuses denied or minimized by the Japanese right is the Rape of Nanking, during which Chinese women were held in confinement to be used as sex slaves and tortured. Similar to Turkey in its intent, the Japanese denial movement aims not at perpetuating discriminatory behavior toward the Chinese but at exonerating Japan from its responsibilities concerning atrocities committed on behalf of the State.[76] Denial of events such as the Rape of Nanking has even been a phenomenon in schoolbooks recently. South Korea and China protested against the introduction of these books in the classrooms, and most public schools rejected them; as a

76. MICHAEL SHERMER & ALEX GROBMAN, DENYING THE HOLOCAUST–WHO SAYS THE HOLOCAUST NEVER HAPPENED AND WHY THEY DO SAY IT 231–37 (2000).

result, they were later withdrawn. Denial also recently found its way into Japanese comic books, or mangas. In those circumstances, South Korea, the Philippines, or China may debate the merit of ad hoc approach for these crimes.

The denial movement of the 1994 Rwandan genocide is still limited in size and influence. The proximity in time of the killings of approximately 800,000 Tutsis and moderate Hutus makes it difficult for deniers to claim that Tutsis were not targeted and killed. In this context, deniers focus more on the notion of "double genocide" than on the nonexistence per se of the genocide of the Tutsis. Extremist Hutus plead that genocide was committed against them by Tutsis and the FPR (Front patriotique rwandais). By doing so, they put the two events—the genocidal violence against Tutsis and the killing of Hutus—on an equal footing. However, the difference between the concepts of genocide and killings—or even slaughter—is not only etymological. By assimilating these concepts, Hutu deniers downplay the importance of the crime and its intent. They try to remove the stigma of killers from the Hutu extremists. Their argument suggests that since genocide was committed on both sides, there are no victims and no perpetrators, all being equal on the scale of crimes. Rwanda—and certain countries like France or Belgium with a large diaspora of Rwandans—have recently been the scene of debates about extending the scope of ad hoc statutes to cover this genocide. Pierre Péan was recently prosecuted in France for incitement to racial hatred. In his book,[77] Péan was of the view that the FPR knew what it was doing when it allegedly shot down the president's plane to provoke the spark that would lead to large-scale massacres of Tutsis, and that the number of Tutsis killed is grossly exaggerated. The Cour d'appel de Paris discharged Péan in November 2009.[78] In Canada, an ex-candidate to a provincial election in Québec, Robin Philpot was the center of a similar debate for a recently published book[79] in which he supports some of the arguments described above.

The Srebrenica massacre is a recent case of denial; some are suggesting that it was a hoax. More than 7,000 Muslims were killed in Srebrenica in July 1995; most of them were either rounded up and summarily executed or hunted down in the woods. Bosnian Serb General Radislav Krstic was convicted of genocide in relation to the Srebrenica massacre by the International

77. Pierre Pean, Noires fureurs, blancs menteurs: Rwanda, 1990–1994 (2005).

78. *See* Pierre Péan, *Rwanda: j'ai été injustement sali*, LIBÉRATION, Dec. 1, 2009.

79. Robin Philpot, Ça ne s'est pas passé comme ça à Kigali (2003).

Criminal Tribunal for the Former Yugoslavia (ICTY) in a decision that provided much detail about the event.[80] According to Former President of Serbia and Yugoslavia, Slobodan Milosevic, the massacre plot was elaborated during a meeting at the home of a Muslim municipal official and executed by Muslims, a mercenary unit, and the French intelligence services as a pretext for military engagement. The Serb government released a report stating that "only" between 2,000 and 2,500 Muslims had died in the massacre and that most of them were soldiers, suggesting that the Muslims had fabricated the massacre. Here, deniers are not reinventing the wheel; they only use techniques developed by Holocaust deniers. Milosevic's judgment would have been a key element in establishing the macro-truth, but the recent arrest of former politician Radovan Karadzic and the hopefully yet-to-come arrest of Ratko Mladic will help in truth establishment. Still, will all sides of the former-Yugoslavia conflict try to establish new ad hoc laws? Probably so. In this case, though, it will be important to monitor any possible manipulation.

8. Conclusion

All crimes are not equal and do not have the same impact or significance, and we all must try to learn from them. Wide-spread state-sponsored crimes against humanity such as genocide have therefore a prophylactic role. These events can be projected beyond themselves and in some instances govern the acts of the present. The protection of the Holocaust as a historical fact is necessary because its elimination has an objective: deniers wish to suppress the event's importance and as a result, revive the original criminal intent behind the event. The Holocaust is the reference point for state-sponsored genocide and mass-murder crimes. Tragic events like those crystallize an exemplary memory, one that is present in our lives and that keeps producing its effects by changing our points of reference and our behavior.

The eradication of six million people for the very reason that they formed a group will always bear a strong stigma in the face of humankind. Not only they were killed, but a complete, detailed, organized and costly machine was put in place—on a continent-wide basis—to seek, trap, arrest, transport, kidnap, and murder via a unique industrial killing process. The elimination

80. Prosecutor v. Radislav Krstic, Case No. IT-98-33-A, International Criminal Tribunal for the Former Yugoslavia (ICTY), April 19, 2004.

of the horrific, unique barbarian tools that the gas chambers represent is a prerequisite to the deniers' task. According to them, if the instrument did not exist, if it was a fabrication of the Jewish Diaspora, it confirms the Jewish conspiracy to control the world since they were capable of imposing such a belief on the world.

Those who still oppose the prosecution of deniers argue that everything can and should be debated and that truth ought not to be imposed by law. But avoiding deniers or not responding to their provocative action is not a solution. One would not think that racist attacks or the promotion of racial superiority could be freely diffused. The same is true for denial speech. Responding to each and every point is not the perfect solution either. Projects that try to confront deniers with research and counterarguments are certainly efficient. But the truth is that in a paranoid postmodernist world that likes to believe in conspiracies, human beings will still readily believe what is presented as a forgery or a myth.

The deniers' debate exists only because of such utopian protections. They are both the messengers and the message. By conveying messages of contempt against a group, deniers dehumanize those targeted, thus precluding them from participating equally in society. Denial speech, just like hate speech, impairs the right to fully and equally exercise one's human rights. It is not synonym of interpretations but of lies and forgeries. With denial messages, we are not in the sphere of opinions but in the sphere of facts, on a territory where facts oppose interpretation and where truth opposes lies. Historians may engage in a historical revision of past events. But among serious historians, no such debate exists on topics such as the very existence of the Holocaust. The deniers' goal is a racist one: attack the Jews a second time.

Denial is effective, thus dangerous. Otherwise, deniers would simply not be active. Generally accepted racial behavior takes time to develop. Even if it does not pose an immediate threat, propaganda is the first step toward extermination policies. It establishes the basis upon which genocide can unfold. Denial, like propaganda, may not be a clear and present danger, but it is a clear and future danger.[81] The mass killing of people of an identifiable group takes years to develop: Serbian-nationalist propaganda under Milosevic is one recent example. Propaganda prepares the crimes by making the messages that it is conveying acceptable to those systematically exposed

81. Guttenplan, *supra* note 12, at 77.

to them. The Holocaust and the Rwandan genocide are examples in which propaganda was allowed, tolerated, and supported, paving the way to tragic events. This contradicts the dogma that only speech posing an immediate threat or harm is dangerous enough to be circumvented. Hate propaganda does not simply go away by itself or because one can find counterarguments. The more society tolerates hate speech, the more frequent such speech is likely to become, thus increasing the probability of success of the message conveyed.

Some fear that prosecuting deniers will lead to imposing state-sponsored versions of historical truth. Such fears seem unjustified. Deniers are not prosecuted with the intent to impose a state-sponsored version of historical truth but rather to protect the historical record. Ad hoc statutes such as the Gayssot Law do not preclude research on the historical facts. They only set aside one historical fact—the very existence of the Holocaust—on the basis of authoritative evidence.

As discussed above, the argument about providing deniers with a platform when they are sued under ad hoc statutes is flawed. It is much more the absence of such statutes that provides a genuine opportunity for deniers to showcase their arguments. The *Zündel* and the first *Faurisson* cases in the 1980s, and more recently the *Irving* case in the UK, are good examples. In all three cases, the tribunal had to receive, evaluate, and judge historical evidence.

Solutions have varied considerably from one region to another, but the issue is always the same: balancing the deniers' rights to freedom of speech against the protection of the rights of the people targeted. Freedom of speech is indeed a basic element of any democratic society. Fundamental international, regional, and national laws protect it. Most of those instruments, however, reject the idea that freedom of speech is absolute and not subject to certain restrictions. Holocaust denial exceeds the limit of freedom of speech and is an act of racism.

A consensus exists on the effect of propaganda. Denial is a form of hate speech, but the effect cannot be demonstrated as easily. Ad hoc statutes dealing and penalizing Holocaust denial are thus required. Until an international consensus is reached and an international and binding instrument prohibits Holocaust denial—and potentially that of other forms of genocide or large-scale crimes against humanity—ad hoc statutes represent an appropriate *sui generis* response.

EIGHT

The Denier's Intent[1]

–*Thomas Hochmann*

AMERICAN TRIBUNALS SEEM TO CONFINE the prohibition on fortune-telling to instances in which the fortune-teller knows that he is conveying false information or that he has no power of seeing into the future.[2] Comparing deniers of crimes against humanity with fortune-tellers is certainly not felicitous. Describing what might happen in the future has little in common with denying what effectively did—even if one endorses the popular post-Holocaust aphorism that "those who cannot remember the past are condemned to repeat it."[3] Nevertheless, several questions can be raised concerning the denier's awareness of the falsity of his claims. I shall begin by showing the relevance of such questions for a legal study.

Not all legal systems agree on the sanction against hate speech, but the issue at hand is at least clear: can hateful utterances targeting a group be the object of a specific limit to free speech in order to protect interests such as the rights of others or democracy? In a state whose Constitution answers this question in the affirmative, forbidding denial—e.g., of the Holocaust—is

---

1. Some of the thoughts developed in this chapter were presented in a talk entitled "Hate Lie: Holocaust Denial in Comparative Law" that was delivered at the Hate Speech Regulation Conference, held at the Cardozo School of Law (New York City) in November 2005; and subsequently in a talk entitled "The Psychology of Denial" delivered at the 7th Biennial Conference of the International Association of Genocide Scholars held in Sarajevo in July 2007. On both occasions, I was able to benefit from many illuminating comments made by the other participants. I am also grateful to James Weinstein for having read a first draft of this chapter. Of course, all errors remain mine.

2. Argello v. City of Lincoln, 143 F.3d 1152, 1153 (8th Cir. 1998) *quoted in* Jonathan D. Varat, *Deception and the First Amendment: a Central, Complex and somewhat Curious Relationship*, 53 UCLA L. REV. 1107, 1112 n. 11 (2006).

3. For the origin of this sentence—written in 1905—and a critique of it, *see* Lawrence L. Langer, *Moralizing and Demoralizing the Holocaust*, *in* USING AND ABUSING THE HOLOCAUST 114–15 (Indiana University Press, 2006). Langer states: "The caution about paying attention to the lessons of history originates in the dubious dual premise that history has lessons to teach and that individuals and nations respond to them in ways that prove beneficial to mankind." *Id.*

unproblematic if this expression is seen as being insulting to the Jews, or as one that rids National Socialism of its crimes. I shall now introduce a distinction drawn by German authors.[4] What we call "denial of a crime against humanity" actually covers at least two kinds of expression. "Aggravated" or "qualified" denial (*qualifizierte Auschwitzleugnung*) explicitly targets a group of individuals. This is, for instance, the usual accusation expressed by deniers that "the Jews" invented the hoax of the Holocaust to exploit Germany. Another example could be the claim that "the alleged genocide from 1915 is Armenian propaganda." This kind of expression must be distinguished from "mere" or "bare" denial (*einfache Auschwitzleugnung*). In the latter case, no explicit accusation against a group is expressed. Denial of the crime, or of an essential component of it, stands alone. For example, the statement that "no gas chamber was used to kill human beings during World War II" is bare denial. Since my analysis in this chapter is based on an understanding of denial as a false statement of fact, in this inquiry, I shall exclude all kinds of speech that share some characteristics with denial but that are based more on opinion than assertions of facts, such as the justification, the approbation, or the glorification of a crime against humanity. I shall consider minimization only if it is quantitative, not qualitative.

Let us return to hate speech regulation. If a legal system allows such a limit on the freedom of expression, the case of aggravated denial does not present any particular difficulty: such speech is clearly hate speech. The case of bare denial is less clear-cut, since it does not involve overt hate speech. If such an expression is to be condemned in a legal system, must the bad faith of the speaker be proven? In other words, must the judge establish that the denier is aware that the crime he denies did actually take place (*mala fide* denier)? If, on the other hand, a denier is convinced that he is telling the truth (*bona fide* denier), should a judge discharge him? In short, is the proof of a "conscious lie" relevant in sentencing a denier? My main aim in this chapter is to answer this last question.

Such an inquiry necessitates the acceptance of a rather counterintuitive hypothesis, namely the very possibility of a *bona fide* denier. Therefore, the first part of this chapter will be devoted to the psychology of denial. Do deniers really believe in the truth of their statements, or are they lying? Do they intend to stir up hatred or merely establish the truth? I do not

---

4. *See, e.g.*, THOMAS WANDRES, DIE STRAFBARKEIT DES AUSCHWITZ-LEUGNENS 96–97 (Duncker & Humblot, 2000); and WINFRIED BRUGGER: BAN ON OR PROTECTION OF HATE SPEECH? SOME OBSERVATIONS BASED ON GERMAN AND AMERICAN LAW, 17 TUL. EUR. & CIV. L.F. 1, 15 (2002).

claim to master the skills in psychological science required for such an examination.[5] Furthermore, it appears to be difficult, if not impossible, to establish *in abstracto*—i.e., without any empirical data—the state of mind of a person and *a fortiori*, of a group of persons. Yet, despite these difficulties, I would like to make a few hypotheses concerning the psychology of denial. They shall serve as avenues for the subsequent legal analysis to be developed in the second part of this chapter.

1. A few "psychological" considerations

I shall distinguish two issues: one of hate and the other of bad faith. It seems plausible that an individual denying *mala fide* a crime against humanity is driven by hate, whereas a hypothetical *bona fide* denier is not. Nevertheless, it seems possible to dissociate these two issues and therefore form four hypotheses.

1.1 Bare Denial as a Hidden Racist Attack

In my first hypothesis, the denier limits his speech to a simple denial although he has more in mind. In legal systems that criminalize racist and denial speech, the evolution of such a discourse is characterized by "euphemization," a strategy to avoid legal sanctions. For instance, in France, since the introduction of the 1972 statute forbidding racist insults, Holocaust denial has been described as a rhetoric ersatz of anti-Semitism.[6]

This tactic aims at avoiding a sentence and not shocking public opinion with too explicit of a speech. An internal memo of the *Front National*, a French Far Right party, is illuminating:

> It is essential, while speaking publicly, to avoid crude speech. One can affirm the same thing in a measured language accepted by the public.

5. A professor of psychology, the former president of the International Association of Genocide Scholars, worked on this topic. *See* Israel Charny, *The Psychological Satisfaction of Denials of the Holocaust or Other Genocides by Non-Extremists or Bigots, and Even by Known Scholars*, IDEA, 6(1) (2001), *available at* http://www.ideajournal.com/articles.php?id=27 (distinguishing five "thinking defense mechanisms" by "innocent" deniers). *See also* WOLFGANG DE BOOR, WAHN UND WIRKLICHKEIT 62–67 (Beck 1997).

6. VALÉRIE IGOUNET, HISTOIRE DU NÉGATIONNISME EN FRANCE 160 (Seuil, 2000).

> In a certain caricature way, we could say "we need to arrange the return journey of Third World immigrants" instead of "Let's throw these bloody Arabs in the sea."[7]

To sum up, my first hypothesis is that the incrimination of simple denial aims at countering this strategy of a speech with a hidden meaning. The idea that Holocaust denial is a camouflaged form of anti-Semitism is the most widely shared view in the literature,[8] and one must admit that it is intuitively the most plausible. Later, I shall consider whether the law adopts the same view and treats these words as dissimulated hate speech.

1.2 Denial as a Way to Fame

There is another possible version of a *mala fide* denier. Professor Frederick Schauer proposes the following explanation as to why most American law review articles are prescriptive—as opposed to descriptive—and criticize judges for not having adopted a certain approach. He explains that "concluding that the Court was correct is not generally the way to fame, fortune, and tenure."[9] Certainly, the best way for a historian to achieve fame is to deliver a revised version of the past, one that is very different from that we thought we knew. Italian historian Costantini makes this point very clearly: "The easiest and surest way to make a name for oneself is to adopt a purely opposite approach: speaking badly of Garibaldi or singing the praises of Nero (two classical examples of revisionism). Revisionism is the typical vice of a historian seeking to advance his career."[10] Denial can be seen as an extreme form of revisionism, without a care for honest scientific methodology. Denial is certainly not the way to fortune or tenure—except, of course, in states having adopted denial as a national doctrine—but it is a high road to fame.

---

7. Document reported by Pierre-André Taguieff, *as quoted in* Igounet, *supra* note 6, at 526–27.

8. *See, e.g.*, ALEXANDER MENSDORF, IM NAMEN DER REPUBLIK, RECHTSEXTREMISMUS UND JUSTIZ IN ÖSTERREICH 7 (Löcker Verlag, 1990); Michel Rosenfeld, *Hate Speech in Constitutional Jurisprudence: a Comparative Analysis*, 24 CARDOZO L. REV. 1523, 1526 (2003).

9. Frederick Schauer, *The First Amendment as Ideology*, 33 WM. & MARY L. REV. 853, 863 (1992).

10. Claudio Costantini, *Revisionismo*, *in* LEZIONI SUL REVISIONISMO STORICO 54 (Cox 18 Books, 1999), *quoted in* Gianluca Braga, *La liberta di manifestazione del pensiero*, *in* INFORMAZIONE, POTERE, LIBERTA, A CURA DI MICHELE AINIS 107 (Torino: Giappichelli Editore, 2005).

Robert Faurisson may be a good example of this hypothesis. Who would have heard of him if he had remained as a teacher in a girls' school in the city of Vichy? Starting from the sixties, he tried to obtain celebrity, first with a delirious analysis of a poem by Arthur Rimbaud, then with an equally delirious study of the genocide committed during World War II. "With Faurisson, the search for scandal preceded the alleged search for the truth about the gas chambers and the genocide," writes a French historian.[11]

Here, we find ourselves on slippery ground. What begins as a conscious lie might end up being held as the truth. Furthermore, the adoption of denial in the aim of seeing one's name in the newspaper could be more or less unconscious from the beginning. This leads us to the hypotheses of "*bona fide*" deniers.

1.3 "Bona fide" Denial as Fanaticism: The Wishful Thinking of a Racist

A French Holocaust denier wrote that he did not understand "why R. Faurisson, if he is wrong, does not have the right to be mistaken, like any other historian and indeed any other man, as long as his good faith can barely be called into question."[12] In response to a letter from Faurisson, Olga Wormser-Migot, one of the first historians of the National Socialist concentration camps, expresses her disagreement with his denial of the gas chambers but describes him as "a man of good faith" and assures him that she "believes that [his] research is exempt of any motivation other than the historical truth."[13]

One shall distinguish between a "researcher" and an individual who denies a crime against humanity without any so-called "scientific" demonstration. In the first case, state denial aside, it seems difficult to obtain denial results after a real research. While one may be skeptical at the start of one's work, a serious and honest study should eventually clear any doubts. The story of Jean-Claude Pressac, a pharmacist who became a historian, is a good demonstration of this.

---

11. FLORENT BRAYARD, COMMENT L'IDÉE VINT À M. RASSINIER, NAISSANCE DU RÉVISIONNISME 442 (Fayard, 1996).

12. IGOUNET, *supra* note 6, at 273. Roques, the author of a denial PhD thesis, wrote this letter to Pierre Vidal-Naquet, a famous French historian and the author of indispensable works on Holocaust denial. *See* PIERRE VIDAL-NAQUET, ASSASSINS OF MEMORY (Jeffrey Mehlman trans., Columbia University Press, 1992).

13. I postulate that this quote is accurate, but I must mention that I found it in a denier's book: SERGE THION, VÉRITÉ HISTORIQUE OU VÉRITÉ POLITIQUE? 78 (La Vieille Taupe, 1980).

He was initially under the influence of Faurisson and doubted the existence of the gas chambers when he first went to Auschwitz. But he studied the existing documents and, unlike Faurisson, "let them speak" and acknowledged the reality of the mass assassination in the face of overwhelming evidence.[14]

But does the denier necessarily know that he is stating false facts? One can assume that his obstinacy with denial eventually leads him to believe in his thesis. Valérie Igounet writes that "the reaction of historians and intellectuals encourages [Faurisson] with the idea that he holds the truth."[15] According to the German Professor Günther Jakobs, "knowing oneself, with a few others, in opposition with the rest of the world does not mean that a denier is aware of the falseness of his statements. Such circumstances reinforce the fanatic's positions instead of making him doubt himself."[16] Describing Holocaust denial as "running amok against reality"[17] also implies perceiving it as a kind of "*bona fide* madness." Belgian historian Jean Stengers may have held this position with the most utter conviction. Stengers repeatedly upheld that he considered Robert Faurisson to be a "mad scientist" (*savant fou*).[18] To those who describe Faurisson as a dishonest fraud, Stengers replies that some of Faurisson's statements are so "outrageous" that they cannot be perceived as being dishonest. Instead, Faurisson should be described as a mad scientist, characterized by an "interpretative delirium" and a kind of obsessive madness that Stengers calls "fixed idea."[19] Recalling some of Faurisson's absurd statements, Stengers warns:

---

14. For the story of Pressac, *see* IGOUNET *supra* note 6, at 373–93. Pressac's pioneering works enabled a very significant step forward in the knowledge about concentration camps. *See* JEAN-CLAUDE PRESSAC, AUSCHWITZ. TECHNIQUE AND OPERATION OF THE GAS CHAMBERS (The Beate Klarsfeld Foundation, 1989).

15. IGOUNET, *supra* note 6, at 274.

16. Günther Jakobs, *Anmerkung*, JURISTISCHE RUNDSCHAU 344 (1997).

17. Martin Broszat, *Zur Kritik der Publizistik des antisemitischen Rechtsextremismu*, *in* AUS POLITIK UND ZEITGESCHICHTE, BEILAGE ZUR WOCHENZEITUNG DAS PARLAMENT, B 19/76, May 8th 1976, *quoted in* DOKUMENTATIONSARCHIV DES ÖSTERREICHISCHEN WIDERSTANDES, AMOKLAUF GEGEN DIE WIRKLICHKEIT, NS-VERBRECHEN UND "REVISIONISTISCHE" GESCHICHTSSCHREIBUNG (DöW, 1992).

18. Jean Stengers, *L'historien face à ses responsabilités*, 15 CAHIERS DE L'ÉCOLE DES SCIENCES PHILOSOPHIQUES ET RELIGIEUSES 19, 22-3 (Facultés universitaires de Saint-Louis, 1994) 19, 22–23 [hereinafter Stengers, "L'historien face à ses responsabilités"]; Jean Stengers, *Quelques libres propos sur "Faurisson, Roques et Cie,"* 12 CAHIERS-BIJDRAGEN 5, 23 (Centre de recherches et d'études historiques de la seconde guerre mondiale, 1989) [hereinafter Stengers, "Quelques libres propos"].

19. Stengers, "Quelques libres propos," *supra* note 18, at 23.

"Let there be no doubt: he believes in them."[20] Stengers underlines the absence of evidence from those who characterized Faurisson as a conscious liar,[21] but one can say the same of Stengers' own analysis. More precisely, it seems quite difficult to believe that a "scholar" denier, one willing to *prove* the "inexistence" of the genocide or the gas chambers, can possibly act in good faith. Nevertheless, the hypothesis of a *bona fide* denier deserves consideration.

Assuming that a denier can truly be mistaken, that he can state enormities *bona fide*, one difficult question arises: what could lead him to believe in the delirious interpretation of documents that he proposes? In order to analyze this hypothetical "*bona fide* denier," I shall use the concept of *wishful thinking*, a fallacy that adheres to the "I wish P were true, thus P is true" model. Freud distinguished between two kinds of expressions, which constitute two variants of wishful thinking.[22] *Illusion* is a belief that may be true or false, one that an individual holds because it satisfies one of his wishes. For example, the illustration of wishful thinking given by Joseph Gabel is an *Illusion*: emigrants routinely believe the regime they are fighting is close to its fall.[23] The second type of wishful thinking is delusion (*Wahnidee*). This is a false belief that is held because it satisfies a wish. "Despite overwhelming evidence that the belief is false, the agent continues to hold it because it satisfies some wish."[24]

If one considers that the denier is not really aware of the falsity of his affirmations, one can analyze his statements as a *Wahnidee*. The number of documents establishing the reality of the genocide committed during World War II is so overwhelming that one can expect the wish on which the delusion is based to be particularly strong and irrational. Maybe the desire to become famous can really blind the denier and lead him to put aside—*bona fide*—every document contradicting his thesis. A hateful ideology

---

20. Stengers, "L'historien face à ses responsabilités," *supra* note 18, at 22–23 n.6.

21. Stengers, "Quelques libres propos," *supra* note 18, at 23.

22. Sigmund Freud, *The Future of an Illusion*, *in* THE STANDARD EDITION OF THE COMPLETE PSYCHOLOGICAL WORK OF SIGMUND FREUD, VOL. 21, 30–32 (Hogarth Press, 1961). *See also* RAYMOND GEUSS, THE IDEA OF A CRITICAL THEORY: HABERMAS AND THE FRANKFURT SCHOOL 39 (1981).

23. JOSEPH GABEL, LA FAUSSE CONSCIENCE: ESSAI SUR LA REIFICATION III (1962).

24. Geuss, *supra* note 22, at 40. *See also* KARL JASPERS, ALLGEMEINE PSYCHOPATHOLOGIE 80 (6th ed., 1953).

seems, however, to be a more likely explanation.[25] In this way, the anti-Semite who is persuaded that Jews are manipulators will conclude "*bona fide*" that the latter fabricated the "hoax of the Holocaust." This hypothesis is compatible with the conclusions of two authors who surveyed a great deal of deniers' literature and carried out interviews with many of them:

> Although it is true that not all participants in the denial movement share the most extreme beliefs, we have found a subtle form of anti-semitism that crept into our interviews with them as "Some of my best friends are Jews, but. . .," or "I'm not anti-semitic but. . .," followed by a litany of all the things "the Jews" are doing. We contend there is a bias that drives deniers to seek and find what they are looking for, and to confirm what they already believe—the very core of pseudohistory."[26]

This could be true for several kinds of deniers: the "research" of the "scholar denier" is led by ideology and not by any scientific method,[27] the "denier on the street" believes in these theses because of his ideology.

> Unable to keep up with these laborious demonstrations, the average reader chooses according to his own prejudices ("I always believed Jews were cheaters.") The process would have no effect on an individual absolutely vaccinated against racism. But it can stir up and actualize a "pre-racist" tendency that is yet unconscious.[28]

So the denier's "good faith" could be a consequence of his racism. A few words about racism may complete this view. Perhaps we can define racist ideology with the Marxist concept of *false consciousness*, reworked by the

---

25. Another possibility would be an individual wishing so strongly that a crime against humanity did not occur that he really ends up believing that it did not. While I am open to many unrealistic hypotheses for the sake of inquiry, I cannot decently go so far as to consider the case of a humanistic *bona fide* denier.

26. Michael Shermer & Alex Grobman, Denying History: Who Says the Holocaust Never Happened and Why Do They Say It? 85 (2000); *see also id.* at 76, 87.

27. One could object that every historian is necessarily led by his ideology. But one must recognize that things are more serious when a fanatic anti-Semite works on the Holocaust or a fanatic anti-Black works on slavery, etc. Furthermore, we have seen that it is quite difficult to believe that a denier can keep on denying *bona fide* after carrying out research.

28. Joseph Gabel, Réflexions sur l'avenir des Juifs 136 (1987).

Frankfurt School and analyzed by Joseph Gabel, who describes it as an emotional attitude that prevents reasoning. Therefore, rational arguments have no effect on racism.[29] Adorno mentions

> numerous attempts to fight anti-Semitism by giving the "true facts"—attempts which are distinguished by their lack of success. What this theory has overlooked is the receptivity of many individuals to any hostile imagery of Jews, and the emotional resistance of these individuals to a less hostile and less stereotyped way of thinking.[30]

Because of this false consciousness, we can assume that an anti-Semite is, in this sense, "convinced" of the truth of denial theses. But we do not have to build such a construction to imagine a *bona fide* denier in the case of state denial.

1.4 The Repercussions of State Denial

If a state adopts denial as its national doctrine, a biased version of history is transmitted to the population through educational institutions. Individuals raised in this system are therefore denying *bona fide*. The state produces a population of *bona fide* deniers. Of course, those who engage in research based on sources other than the official historical narrative of their country should obtain results contrary to the national thesis. But we cannot imagine that every pupil would doubt what his history teacher teaches him: "The schoolboy *believes* his teachers and his schoolbooks."[31]

According to French historian Yves Ternon, when denial is adopted as a doctrine by a state where genocide took place, *bona fide* denial could also reach international scholars. Comparing Faurisson, a Holocaust denier, with Gilles Veinstein, a French scholar who refused to speak of "genocide" concerning the slaughters of Armenians in 1915, Ternon explains that "while the same techniques are used, if Veinstein, like Faurisson, attempts to sow doubt in the reader's mind by using the same line of argument, the motives are different. One should not draw a parallel between a neo-Nazi who denies the

29. *See* GABEL *supra* note 23, at 98–107.

30. THEODOR ADORNO ET AL., THE AUTHORITARIAN PERSONALITY 93 (1950), *quoted in* GABEL *supra* note 23, at 107.

31. LUDWIG WITTGENSTEIN, ON CERTAINTY § 263 (1969).

Jewish genocide to prepare the return of this monstrous political system and a researcher working in a scientific environment where he must humor those granting him access to his sources, and who feels constrained to adjust the historical truth, *insofar as he truly perceives it and is not misled by such an environment*."[32]

In summary, I have reached four possibilities. In my first hypothesis, an individual willingly uses denial as a diverted way of expressing hate speech. In the second case, the denier chooses denial as a way to get famous. In the third hypothesis, the racist opinions of an individual involve his acceptance of denial. In the fourth hypothesis, a national system of denial produces a real *bona fide* denial, at least in parts of the population educated in state schools. This can be summarized with the help of the following table:

	Hateful	*Not Hateful*
Mala Fide	1. Hidden hate speech	2. Way to fame
Bona Fide	3. Wishful thinking	4. Product of state denial

Once again, these are only hypotheses, some of which are more plausible than others. Furthermore, it is perfectly imaginable for an individual to switch from one pattern to another. For instance, an individual denying *mala fide* may evolve into a *bona fide* delirium. Another possibility is one of *radicalization*: an individual who first denies a crime on a "not-hateful-way-to-fame" basis could switch to a "hateful" one, as a result of the hostility provoked by his denial, a hostility that he attributes to "the Jews."[33]

Let us not forget either that "like all sociopolitical movements, Holocaust denial attracts a wide variety of individuals, each with different motives and intentions, loosely held together by a common set of beliefs and ideologies."[34]

---

32. Yves Ternon, Du négationnisme: Mémoire et tabou 49 (1999).

33. Some "pre-racist" tendencies may contribute to his crossing this line. *See* Gabel *supra* note 28 and accompanying text.

34. Shermer & Grobman, *supra* note 26, at 16. *See also* Pierre Vidal-Naquet, *Qui sont les assassins de la mémoire?* (1992), *in* Les Assassins de la Mémoire 206 (2005) *available at* www.anti-rev.org. Vidal-Naquet says: "Undoubtedly some of them are out-and-out cynical scoundrels, but some of them really believe in what they have to say. Most of them are anti-Semites, in the various accepted meanings of the term, but not all of them." *Id.*

There certainly are Nazis and fools among deniers.[35] Let us now turn to the legal aspect of the issue and find out if and how the law takes into account the denier's "psychology." I will distinguish two situations, depending on whether the denier is judged on the basis of a specific statute criminalizing denial or not.

2. Psychology of Denial Without a Specific Statute

2.1 Assessment of the Methodology

When there is no specific prohibition of denial in a legal system (or at least, not yet), it has occurred that a denier is sued on the basis of defamation[36] or his tort liability.[37] In such processes, good faith plays an important role since it allows the denier to escape a sentence.

But here, good faith does not simply mean believing in the truth of what one says. Believing in something and saying it without any verification does not mean acting *bona fide*. Many jurisdictions have imposed a verification test: one who states facts harming others must have done serious verifications.[38] As the French author of a dissertation on "the Lie and the Law" puts it: "Good faith is actually the absence of fault and the respect of an obligation of means in the objective search for truth."[39]

For example, the German Constitutional Court imposes a "duty of care" (*Sorgfaltspflicht*) for harmful statements. If this duty is done, speech is

35. There is, of course, a huge probability of being both. Consider, for instance, this statement made by an individual during his trial in France for having marked Jewish graves with swastikas, when asked about the reality of the destruction of Jews during World War II: "Someone will tell me that this is true, and another will tell me that it is a lie, so me . . . I don't know, I'm not that good in history." LIBÉRATION, September 12, 2007. *See also* Winfried Platzgummer, *Die strafrechtliche Bekämpfung des Neonazismus, in Österreich*, ÖSTERREICHISCHE JURISTEN-ZEITUNG 762 n. 114 (1994) (arguing that a Nazi-era joke might be justified for some neo-Nazis: "Blessed are the half-educated, for theirs is the Third Reich." The sentence alludes to the 8th Beatitude: "Blessed are they that suffer persecution for justice' sake, for theirs is the kingdom of heaven.").

36. In Germany, the law of defamation is still used against denial along with the specific section of the criminal code targeting it.

37. For instance, Sections 1382 of the French and Belgian Civil Codes state: "Any act whatever of man, which causes damage to another, obliges the one by whose fault it occurred, to compensate it."

38. *See, e.g.,* Cass. crim. January 3, 1970, bull. crim. n. 7.

39. YVES MAYAUD, LE MENSONGE EN DROIT PÉNAL: ESSAI D'UNE THÉORIE GÉNÉRALE 430 (1976).

protected, even though its falsity may reveal itself afterward.[40] This is not dissimilar to the Supreme Court of the United States' actual malice test for the defamation of public figures: the expression can be punished if made "with knowledge that the statement was false or with reckless disregard as to whether or not it was true."[41] Although the burden of proof is not the same—it falls on the plaintiff in the United States and not on the defendant, i.e., the speaker, which is the case in every other legal system that I am aware of—the understanding of good faith is.

Nevertheless, if one wishes to include an American point of comparison concerning the judicial response to pseudo-scientific works, *New York Times v. Sullivan* is not the most appropriate instance. American courts have faced this issue much more often with the controversy surrounding the teaching in public schools of the so-called "creation science," followed by the "intelligent design" theory. By applying the endorsement test, that is, by determining "whether an objective observer, acquainted with the text, legislative history, and implementation of the statute, would perceive it as a state endorsement of [religion] in public schools,"[42] the courts did determine if these "theories" were scientific. This is particularly obvious in two cases, perhaps because the judges intended to give an important didactic aspect to their decisions. One of these concerns "creation science,"[43] and the other "intelligent design."[44] The judges have characterized these fake sciences in a very similar way to what Shermer and Grobman have referred to as "pseudohistory."[45] In *McLean*, Judge Overton explains that the "creationists' methods do not take data, weigh it against the opposing scientific data, and thereafter reach the conclusions . . .. Instead, they take the literal wording of the Book of Genesis and

---

40. *See, e.g.*, BverfG, November 10, 1998, 1 BvR 1531/96, p. 198.

41. New York Times v. Sullivan, 376 U.S. 254, 279–80 (1964). *See also* Hustler Magazine v. Falwell, 485 U.S. 46, 56 (1988).

42. Wallace v. Jaffree, 472 U.S. 38,73;76 (1985), *quoted in* Santa Fe Independent Sch. Dist. v. Doe, 530 U.S. 290, 308 (2000). The endorsement test was first implemented in County of Allegheny v. ACLU, 492 U.S. 573 (1989).

43. McLean v. Arkansas Bd. of Ed., 529 F. Supp. 1255 (E.D. Ark. 1982).

44. Kitzmiller v. Dover Area School Dist., 400 F. Supp. 2d 707, 205 Ed. Law Rep. 250 (2005).

45. Shermer & Grobman, *supra* note 26, at 2 (defining pseudohistory as "the rewriting of the past for present personal or political purposes"). *See also id.* at 85 (describing the very core of pseudohistory as "a bias that drives deniers to seek and find what they are looking for, and to confirm what they already believe.").

attempt to find scientific support for it."[46] This is indeed very similar to what judges observe when they face denial. For instance, in the sentence of Robert Faurisson in July 1981, the tribunal of Paris explained that his writings "tend to brush aside by principle every testimony reporting the existence of gas chambers and to deny them any convincing value . . ., in the same way, every written document is dismissed with a semantic analysis constantly oriented in the sense of denial; Mr. Faurisson admittedly states that 'only one testimony' would lead him to reconsider his thesis, but this concession to 'scientific doubt' actually seems to target, in its author's mind, an impossible proof (*probatio diabolica*). . . ."[47]

This technique of examining methods is used when the author of a work with a historical appearance is sued for defamation or civil liability. This therefore happens when a judge is confronted with "scholarly deniers" in such trials. The judge does not try to establish whether the denier really believes in the results he presents (which would be quite difficult) but rather if he obtained these results after an objective and serious research.

In France, like in the United States, judges were targets of criticism for having determined whether a work could be deemed "scientific."[48] Nevertheless, it seems to me that there is no reason to blame them. First, nothing *forbids* them from doing so. When Jay Wexler blames a judge for having established that creationism is not a science, he deals with the *advisability* to do so, not with legality.[49] Furthermore, the judge can, and must, determine whether creationism is scientific in order to apply the endorsement test. If "intelligent design" and "creation science" are scientific, there is no reason to think that a reasonable observer would perceive their teaching in public schools as the endorsement of a religion. A supporter of such a judicial agnosticism is Justice Antonin Scalia. According to him, if a parliament expresses the view that "creation science" is indeed a science, then the courts must defer to this view. Almost the entirety of Scalia's dissenting

46. McLean v. Arkansas Bd. of Ed., 529 F. Supp at 1269.

47. T.G.I. Paris, July 8, 1981, Recueil Dalloz, Jurisprudence, 1982, p.59.

48. *See* Jay D. Wexler, *Kitzmiller and the "Is it science?" question*, 5 FIRST AMEND. L. REV. 90, 93 (2006); Jean-Pierre Azéma *in* Azéma/Kiejman, *L'histoire au tribunal*, 102 LE DÉBAT 48 (1998).

49. *See* Wexler *supra* note 48, at 97.

opinion in *Edwards v. Aguillard* is based upon this choice.[50] But even Scalia recognized that if "creation science" is no more than a presentation of the Book of Genesis, without any scientific evidence, its teaching in public schools is unconstitutional.[51] This supports what the judges ultimately did in *McLean* and in *Kitzmiller*, basing their decisions on multiple documents and expert testimonies.

The criticisms of those who argue that judges must not "tell history" are also unfounded. Courts do not judge what the historical truth is. They systematically begin their decisions in such cases by insisting that they do not intend to do so. What judges do give is a *discours de la méthode*: they examine the methodology used by the author of a work having at least a historical appearance. Two things are important here. First, their inquiry serves as a defense for the prosecuted "historian." If serious methods are used, the author will get the benefit of good faith and escape a sentence for defamation in French law. In Germany, the respect of a minimum of scientific approach will enable the author to benefit from the specific protection that the Constitution holds for scientific (and artistic) expressions, thus making it more difficult for an author to be convicted.[52]

Second, the judicial examination of the methods is not that problematic. One can hardly maintain that it is a difficult task to differentiate between a "method" leading to results denying the existence of gas chambers and the methods used by historians. Let us recall the warning of the French historian Antoine Prost: "Eliminating the issue of the method with the easy and false assertion that every method is as good as the other, repeating complacently that history is not a science and that the historian's subjectivity cannot be transcended, developing fashionable themes about history as literature—all this means renouncing the establishment of truths."[53]

With this examination of the method used by the denier, judges have objectified the concept of good faith. It is quite impossible for a judge to find out what a denier really thinks. But if the judge notices that the denier constantly excludes every source or document opposed to his thesis, he can

---

50. Edwards v. Aguillard, 482 U.S. 578, 621–26 (1987) (Scalia, dissenting).

51. *Id.* at 629.

52. For further analysis, *see* Thomas Hochmann, *Les limites à la liberté de l'« historien » en France et en Allemagne*, 69–70 DROIT ET SOCIÉTÉ 527 (2008).

53. Antoine Prost, *Histoire, vérités, méthodes: Des structures argumentatives de l'histoire*, 92 LE DÉBAT 127, 140 (1996).

conclude his bad faith. For a "not-pretending-to-be-a-scholar" denier, the solution would not be any different. It would also be difficult for him to prove that he respected any "duty of care" before stating that the gas chambers did not exist. The norms regulating defamation and civil liability do not oblige the telling of the truth, but there is a duty of a minimum of objective verification before expressing harmful statements.

2.2 Other Techniques: Inferring Bad Faith

An inference is a conclusion that a judge (or jury) may draw from the proof of certain facts. I mention in this section two elements that could lead to such a conclusion about a denier's bad faith. The reader should bear in mind that the cases this section relies on are quite uncommon: one is based on an odd statute that did not survive the case, and the other finds its origin in a denier suing a scholar for having described him as such.

1. Common Knowledge

To avoid a fastidious examination of the pseudo-arguments of deniers, many jurisdictions have taken judicial notice of the Holocaust, in that the Holocaust was "common knowledge."[54] Common knowledge (*notoriété* in French, *Offenkundigkeit* in German) is a legal concept that a judge applies to a fact that is considered to be true by a large part of the population on the basis of accessible and trustworthy sources.[55] In addition to not having to prove the existence of the fact, does common knowledge of a fact allow inferring the

---

54. For instance, the European Commission of Human Rights: X versus Federal Republic of Germany, Eur. Comm'n H.R., July 16, 1982, Req. No. 9235/81, 29 D.R. 194 (203). Idem in decisions *Ochensberger* (Dec. 2, 1994), *Rebhandl* (Jan. 16, 1996) and *Honsik* (Oct. 18, 1995). In Austria: OGH (Supreme Court), Dec. 10, 1993, 15 Os 1/93, and OGH, Jan. 13, 1999, 13 Os 169/98. In Germany: BGHSt (Criminal Supreme Court) 40, 97; 5 Str 485/01 (April 10, 2002); BverfG (German Constitutional Court), June 9, 1992, in NJW 1993, 917.

55. See for Germany: PETRA BUSCHHORN, RECHTSPROBLEME DER OFFENKUNDIGKEIT VON TATSACHEN IM STRAFVERFAHREN, WESEN UND BEGRIFF – VEREINBARKEIT MIT DEN TRAGENDEN VERFAHRENSMAXIMEN DES BEWEISRECHTS (Frankfurt/Main: Peter Lang, 1997); LOTHAR FEUERPEIL, DER BEWEISABLEHNUNGSGRUND DER OFFENKUNDIGKEIT GEMÄSS § 244 ABS. 3 SATZ 2, 1. VAR. STPO (Pfaffenweiler: Centaurus-Verlagsgesellschaft, 1987); ROLAND BRUTZER, OFFENKUNDIGKEIT, WESEN UND WERT DES BEGRIFFS IM STRAFRECHT (1973); for France: JACQUES DUPICHOT, LA NOTORIÉTÉ, CETTE INCONNUE (1971); for the United States: FED. R. EVID. 201(B).

bad faith of the one denying it? If a fact is common knowledge, individuals probably are indeed aware of it.

One of Ernst Zündel's trials in Canada confirms this. A German citizen taking part in the elaboration and the diffusion of racist and denial books—notably *Did Six Million Really Die?*–Zündel was prosecuted in Canada in 1983 on the basis of a False New Law aimed at "[e]veryone who wilfully publishes a statement, tale or news that he knows is false and that causes or is likely to cause injury or mischief to a public interest."[56] Prosecutors had thus to prove, on the one hand, the falsity of the book and, on the other hand, that Zündel knew it was false. To achieve the former, the prosecutors' representative intended to use survivors' and experts' testimonies. As for the intentional element, he wanted to convince the jury that "Zündel's belief that the Holocaust never happened was so "unreasonable," so much beyond the scope of normal public opinion, that he must have known it was false."[57] And therefore, he put forward a judicial notice motion, asking the judge to declare the Holocaust "as a matter within the common knowledge of each and every person."[58] The judge, however, despite having admitted that "there exists wide and highly regarded opinion that the Holocaust did occur," refused to take judicial notice of it "in light of the circumstances of this particular trial." Otherwise, this would not "[provide] the defence and accused with full answer and defence."[59]

The judge thus refused to take judicial notice of the Holocaust and consider it as a fact of common knowledge because he wanted to guarantee a fair trial, i.e., allow Zündel to attempt to prove that he was convinced of the truth of his allegations. *A contrario,* this seems to mean that common knowledge of the Holocaust could involve an inference of the denier's bad faith.[60]

2. The Denier's Racism

Another useful clue for determining the denier's bad faith can be his racism. This is strongly represented in one of the most famous trials involving denial,

---

56. Canada Criminal Code, Section 185.

57. Robert A. Kahn, Holocaust Denial and the Law: a Comparative Study 39 (2004).

58. *Id.* at 39 (quoting Griffith, the prosecutors' representative).

59. *Id.* at 40–41 (quoting Judge Locke).

60. *See* Klaus Miebach & Jürgen Schäfer, Münchener Kommentar zum Strafgesetzbuch § 130, Rn. 81 (2005).

the *Irving v. Penguin and Lipstadt* case.[61] British denier David Irving sued Deborah Lipstadt and her publisher for libel because she described him in her book as a Holocaust denier, a partisan of Hitler who had resorted to the distortion of facts and the manipulation of documents in order to serve his own purpose of exonerating Hitler.[62] The defendants sought to establish that these allegations were *justified*, i.e., that they were substantially true. Thus, they had to prove mainly two things. On the one hand, they sought to establish that David Irving had misrepresented the historical evidence: that no objective, fair-minded historian could come to Irving's conclusion. On the other hand, they had to show that these misrepresentations were *deliberate*. As the judge notes: "Irving rightly stresses that the Defendants have accused him of deliberately perverting the evidence. For their part the Defendants recognize that it is incumbent on them to establish... that the misrepresentation and falsification were motivated by Irving's ideological beliefs or prejudices."[63]

Therefore, the mental state of the denier was one of the issues at stake.[64] The defendants accused Irving of being a *mala fide* denier. After the judge found that Irving had misrepresented the evidence, Irving claimed that "such misrepresentation was innocent in the sense that it arose through simple mistake or misapprehension,"[65] i.e., that his denial was made *bona fide*. In order to determine Irving's motivation, the judge explained that he would take into account a variety of "circumstances from which inferences as to [the] motivation may be drawn."[66] Interestingly, these circumstances include, among other things, the nature of Irving's historical misrepresentations[67]

61. The judgment rendered by Judge Gray on April 11, 2000 was published as THE IRVING JUDGMENT (2000) [hereinafter Irving v. Lipstadt, § (section number)].

62. *See* Irving v. Lipstadt, § 2.15.

63. *See id.* at § 13.4.

64. Also insisting on this point, Lawrence McNamara, *History, Memory and Judgment: Holocaust Denial: The History Wars and Law's Problem with the Past*, 26 SYDNEY L. REV. 353 (2004). McNamara exaggerates a little when he seems to see this judicial study of the denier's intent as a characteristic of *any* libel trial. In order for the question of intent to be raised before the judge, it is also necessary for the defamatory meaning to involve an accusation of *deliberate* falsification, and for the defendant to choose the defense of justification.

65. Irving v. Lipstadt, § 13.138.

66. *Id.* at § 13.139.

67. In this inquiry, the judge applies a logic that is contrary to (and more intuitive than) the one defended by Stengers. *See* Stengers, "L'historien face à ses responsabilités," *supra*

and the evidence of his political or ideological beliefs. Although no allegation of racism was leveled by Lipstadt against Irving in her book, the defendants did indeed adduce evidence in support of such allegations because, "if true, they support the case that Irving has been guilty of deliberately falsifying the historical record for racist reasons of his own."[68]

Shortly before the end of the proceedings, one could have feared that the judge would regard racism as an obstacle to the "deliberate" aspect of Irving's misrepresentations. In one of the last dialogues of the trial, Judge Gray seemed indeed to infer the good faith of the denier from his racism, in a way that is similar to my "wishful thinking" hypothesis concerning the denier's psychology:

> Judge Gray: "If somebody is anti-Semitic. . . and extremist, he is perfectly capable of being, as it were, honestly anti-semitic and honestly extremist in the sense that he is holding those views and expressing those views because they are, indeed, his views."
> Rampton (Lipstadt's counsel): "What more would a historian who is an anti-Semite want to do in exculpation of Hitler. . . then to deny the Holocaust?"
> Judge Gray: "Yes, but he might believe what he is saying. That is the point. That is why it is important."[69]

Nevertheless, the judge eventually ruled the opposite way.[70] On the basis of the evidences adduced by the defendants—speeches, interviews,

---

note 18 and accompanying text. Whereas Stengers wrote, in substance, that some of Faurisson's statements were so outrageous that the crazy French denier must certainly have believed in them, Judge Gray observes that some of Irving's "mistakes and misconceptions" are so egregious that they appear "by their nature unlikely to have been innocent." Irving v. Lipstadt, §§ 13.143–13.144.

68. *Id.* at § 9.1.

69. DON GUTTENPLAN, THE HOLOCAUST ON TRIAL: HISTORY, JUSTICE AND THE DAVID IRVING LIBEL CASE 262 (2001).

70. The *bona fide* racism was recognized as a legal justification in Vienna in 1882, where Franz Holubek was prosecuted for incitement against Jews. At his trial, he insisted on his good faith, having read *Der Talmudjude*, an anti-Semitic book written by August Rohling. The court discharged him on this basis. *See* JACOB KATZ, FROM PREJUDICE TO DESTRUCTION: ANTI-SEMITISM, 1700–1933, 285 (1980).

writings, etc.—the judge found that Irving was an anti-Semite[71] and a racist.[72] Furthermore, Judge Gray explained that it appeared to him "that some legitimate light is or may be cast on Irving's motivation by an examination of those groups and individuals with whom he associates."[73] On the basis of the evidence adduced by the defendants, the judge found that Irving associated with the international leaders of Holocaust denial, accurately described by the judge as right-wing extremists, most, if not all, of them being neo-Nazis, racists, and anti-Semites. "I also have no doubt that Irving was aware of their political view," the judge added. "His association with such individuals indicates in my judgment that Irving shares many of their political beliefs."[74]

All of this led the judge to the conclusion that the

> picture of Irving which emerges from the evidence of his extra-curricular activities reveals him to be a right-wing pro-Nazi polemicist. In [Judge Gray's] view the Defendants have established that Irving has a political agenda. It is one which, it is legitimate to infer, disposes him, where he deems it necessary, to manipulate the historical record in order to make it conform with his political beliefs.[75]

Therefore, Irving's political beliefs played an important role in the determination of his motivation. They formed one of the clues enabling the judge to draw the inference that "for the most part the falsification of the historical record was deliberate and that Irving was motivated by a desire to present events in a manner consistent with his own ideological beliefs even if that involved distortion and manipulation of historical evidence."[76]

The denier's racism and/or anti-Semitism thus seem to be a clue to enabling the inference of the denier's bad faith. In a trial similar to the one in London, Robert Faurisson sued Robert Badinter because Badinter had characterized the denier as a falsifier, or more precisely, stated that he had Faurisson sentenced as such during his last trial as a lawyer before he became minister of justice. Many of the witnesses for Badinter insisted on Faurisson's

---

71. Irving v. Lipstadt, § 13.105.

72. *Id.* at §13.107.

73. *Id.* at §13.110.

74. *Id.* at §13.115.

75. *Id.* at §13.162.

76. *Id.* at §13.163.

anti-Semitism,[77] with this same idea that a denier moved by hate denies *mala fide*, i.e., is a "falsifier."[78] The denier's hate supports the inference that the denier consciously manipulated the evidence. The "wishful thinking hypothesis" does not therefore seem likely to obtain the favor of judges in cases where the issue of good or bad faith is relevant.

In summary, in such trials, where the denier's good faith could lead him to win the trial, judges seem to have always excluded this justification. They analyze the denier's work and notice his lack of objectivity or scientific rigor. Furthermore, it seems that the denier's hateful ideology, be it on its own or along with other clues, could allow the inference of the denier's bad faith. Finally, one can assume that common knowledge of a crime against humanity could lead a trier of fact to infer the denier's bad faith.

3. Explicit Prohibition of Denial and the Denier's Intent

Since the nineties, several European legal systems have adopted a new criminal offense: the denial of a crime against humanity (in most cases, only of the genocide perpetrated by National Socialists and their accomplices). Except in cases of strict liability, a criminal offense usually requires the realization of a material element and an intentional one. What does the latter consist of? Would the (hypothetical) *bona fide* denier commit the denial offense?

One thing must be clear before starting the inquiry. My aim here is not to argue whether "the consciousness of the lie" should or should not be part of the offense, but rather to examine whether the existing statutes do require such a state of mind. I intend to show that, in all but one case, they do not.

To begin with, the history of the appearance of these statutes seems to correspond to the first hypothesis of my introductory "psychological considerations." Lawmakers seem to regard denial as a trick that individuals willing to express hateful ideas have found in order to avoid any legal sanction. When an individual is prosecuted for something he said, jurisdictions are

77. The testimonies and the judgment of the tribunal of Paris, rendered on May 21, 2007 in favor of Robert Badinter, were published by his lawyer. *See* BERNARD JOUANNEAU, LA JUSTICE ET L'HISTOIRE FACE AU NÉGATIONNISME: AU COEUR D'UN PROCÈS (2008).

78. The judgment does not really deal with this question, since the issue was whether a precise judgment rendered in 1981 did in fact describe Faurisson as a falsifier and not whether Faurisson was a falsifier.

not tied up by the literal meaning of the words. They examine the speech at issue in its context in order to determine if it has the forbidden meaning. For example, while one can freely criticize the policy of the state of Israel, a tribunal will apply a hate speech statute to an individual who substitutes the word "Zionist" for "Jew" in order to express what the judge understands as an anti-Semitic attack.[79]

But tribunals cannot go too far with such interpretations and sometimes refuse to sentence "mere" denial. It thus seemed to several legislators that Holocaust denial had become a camouflaged anti-Semitic speech enabling its authors to avoid legal sentences. Several European parliaments adopted an explicit statute to counter this strategy.

The German example is quite telling. In 1994, the Federal Court of Justice overruled the sentence of a Far-Right leader Günter Deckert, stating that the mere denial of mass murders in gas chambers—without an explicit identification with Nazi ideology or a direct attack aimed at the Jews—did not allow any sentence on the basis of the section of the criminal code targeting incitement to hatred. The court of appeal had not sufficiently explained why mere denial was an attack toward human dignity, this being one of the constitutive elements of this offense.[80] The Federal Court of Justice did not acquit Deckert, but its ruling was depicted that way in the media.[81] This provoked an uproar in Germany and abroad, and the scandal erupted when the retrial court issued its judgment, describing Deckert as a "strong-willed and intelligent man for whom this claim was a thing of the heart."[82] These events led the parliament to pass a statute explicitly criminalizing "bare" Holocaust denial.[83] In Austria, a similar event—the release of neo-Nazi Walter Ochensberger—led the parliament to pass a specific prohibition of Holocaust denial in 1992.[84]

---

79. *See, e.g.*, Cass. crim. October 24, 1995, D. 1996, 666; *see also* FRANCK COHEN, LA DIFFICILE INSERTION DE LA LÉGISLATION PÉNALE SUR LA LUTTE CONTRE LE RACISME DANS LA LOI SUR LA PRESSE 140 (Diss. iur. Paris 1, 2003).

80. BGHSt 40, 97 (Mar. 15, 1994).

81. *See* Günter Bertram, *Entrüstungsstürme im Medienzeitalter-der BGH und die "Auschwitzlüge"*, NJW 1994, 2002 et seq.

82. LG Mannheim, June 22, 1994, NJW 1994, 2494; *see* Günter Bertram, *Noch einmal: Die "Auschwitzlüge" -Anmerkungen zum Urteil der 6. Großen Strafkammer des LG Mannheim vom 22. 6. 1994,* NJW 1994, 2397 et seq.

83. On the *Deckert* case, *see* WANDRES, *supra* note 4, at 116–18; KAHN, *supra* note 57, at 70–77.

84. *See* Brigitte Bailer-Galanda, *Die österreichische Rechtslage und der "Revisionismus" in* WAHRHEIT UND "AUSCHWITZLÜGE", ZUR BEKÄMPFUNG "REVISIONISTISCHER"

Many European high courts have expressed their understanding that the "aim" of the statutes forbidding denial was to sentence hidden hate speech. In Belgium, the constitutional court had to decide on an action against such a statute and was quite explicit. "The law does not mention such intentions [rehabilitating a criminal ideology which is hostile to democracy, offending deeply one or several categories of human beings] as a constitutive feature of the offense it introduces, but it appears from the preparatory works that the lawmaker did not do it because of the extreme difficulty of proof, notably because of the use of scientific-like expressions."[85]

The Paris Court of Appeal[86] also ruled that the prohibition of Holocaust denial had an antiracism goal, and that denial "spreads ideas tending to rehabilitate the Nazi ideology and politics of racial discrimination," which was confirmed by the high court.[87] The same court also ruled that "denial of crimes against humanity appears to be one of the strongest kinds of racial defamation against the Jews and incitement to their hatred."[88]

Criminalization of denial is equated to the criminalization of racism in the legislators' and the courts' minds. The archetype[89] of the denier that the legislator is thinking of corresponds to the first hypothesis I described at the beginning of this chapter: Holocaust denial as a camouflaged anti-Semitic attack. More precisely, the archetype of a denier can be seen as a modification of the archetype of the author of hate speech. Thus, anti-Holocaust denial statutes do not see the hypothetical individual as denying because he really thinks no genocide took place. These statutes target hidden racism and therefore seem to assume that the real significance of denial is racism, that it may lead to the same consequences justifying the prohibition of racism. Thus, the commission of the denial offense would not require any demonstration of bad faith; the very consciousness of committing the forbidden acts would be sufficient.

PROPAGANDA 221–23 (B. Bailer-Galanda, Wolfgang Benz & Wolfgang Neugebauer eds., 1995) 221–23; Mensdorf, *supra* note 8, at 18.

85. Cour d'Arbitrage, July 12, 1996, no. 45/96, J.T., 1997.

86. CA Paris, Dec. 9, 1992, Légipresse 1993, no. 103, III, 90.

87. Cass. crim., Dec. 20, 1994, Bull. crim. No. 424.

88. CA Paris, Dec. 16, 1998, *Garaudy*, Légipresse 1999, no. 159, III, 30.

89. On the archetype imagined by the designer of a rule, *see* Frederick Schauer, *Public Figures*, 25 WM. & MARY L. REV. 905, 913–14 (1983/1984) (stating that "[t]he designer of a rule invariably imagines a particular circumstance or set of circumstances toward which the rule is directed.").

The German Federal Court of Justice ruled unequivocally in 2002 that in a Holocaust denial case,

> in order to determine the intention of the accused, one cannot consider the possibility of him denying the indubitable historical fact of the extermination at Auschwitz because of a revisionist blindness. In section 130(3) of the Criminal Code, the lawmaker targeted precisely those fixed in their views. Therefore, the conscious contestation of the Holocaust is sufficient to determine the intentional denial in the sense of the offense. A "conscious lie" is not required.[90]

Such clear ruling cannot be found in every legal system forbidding denial, but the wording of the statutes does not raise any doubt: nowhere—as far as I am aware and apart from an exceptional case studied below—do the statutes require any specific intent by the denier. Some German authors assert that the word "leugnen" used in Section 130(3) of the Criminal Code implies an awareness of falsity, but I can find no support to this assertion in any dictionary.[91] Herbert Schaller, a regular lawyer of Holocaust deniers and neo-Nazis in Austria, made the same point during the Holocaust Denial Conference in Tehran.[92] He did find help in the dictionary, but in a rather curious way: the only argument he gives in support of this affirmation is a definition of the verb "lügen" (to lie)! Unfortunately for Schaller, "to deny" and "to lie" are not synonyms. Unlike the latter, the former does not imply an awareness of falsity.

---

90. BGHSt 47, 278 (April 10, 2002); NJW 2002, 2115. *See also* the case note of ANDREAS STEGBAUER, JURISTISCHE RUNDSCHAU 74 (2003).

91. THEODOR LENCKNER & DETLEV STERNBERG-LIEBEN, STRAFGESETZBUCH KOMMENTAR § 130 Rn. 20, (Adolf Schönke & Horst Schröder eds., 2006). Lenckner & Sternberg-Lieben chose one very particular definition among the three provided by the *Duden* dictionary (*Duden, Das grosse Wörterbuch der deutschen Sprache*, Vol. 4), exemplified only with negative phrases such as "I cannot deny that I am fine." Much more adapted are the other definitions, applying to the denial of a fact, or of the existence of God, where there is no mention of any bad faith or "akrasia" (acting against one's better judgment, i.e., "*wider besseres Wissen*"). I cannot imagine that any native German speaker would agree intuitively that "*leugnen*" implies an awareness of falsity. *See also* Michael Köhler, *Zur Frage der Strafbarkeit des Leugnens von Völkermordtaten*, NJW 1995, 2390: "*leugnen*, i.e. also the *bona fide* contestation of a fact."

92. The text of his speech is available at http://revurevi.net/Teheran/Schallerde.pdf. *See* pages 10–11.

The denier's state of mind therefore seems to be irrelevant. Does this present any legal difficulty? When the Human Rights Committee of the United Nations verified the conformity of the French statute forbidding Holocaust denial with the International Covenant on Civil and Political Rights,[93] many of the judges seemed to attach much importance to the denier's intent. The committee upheld the sentence of Robert Faurisson but expressed its doubts of the statute's conformity with the covenant read *in abstracto* and insisted that its decision concerned the statute as applied by French courts to Robert Faurisson. The problem with the Gayssot Law, as judges Evatt and Kretzmer explained, is that it seems "to prohibit publication of *bona fide* research" and that it does "not link liability to the intent of the author, nor to the tendency of the publication to incite to anti-Semitism."[94]

Among the several individual opinions attached to this committee's decision, only the one written by Judge Prafulla Chandra Bhagwati is clearly in favor of the conformity of the French statute with the covenant. According to this judge, Holocaust denial necessarily results in the encouragement of anti-Semitism: the "necessary consequence and fall-out" of Holocaust denial is, "in the context of the situation prevailing in Europe, [the] promotion and strengthening of anti-Semitic feelings."[95] Such was the opinion defended by France in its observations to the committee. In this regard, another judge criticizes the decision of the French legislator as an usurpation of competence:

> The assumption, in the provisions of the Act, that the denial is necessarily anti-Semitic or incites anti-Semitism is a Parliamentary or legislative judgment and is not a matter left to adjudication or judgment by the Courts. For this reason, the Act would appear, in principle, to put in jeopardy the right of any person accused of a breach of the Act to be tried by an independent Court.[96]

Judge Lallah observed, nevertheless, that in the case of Faurisson, French courts did examine whether the allegations tended to raise anti-Semitic

---

93. Human Rights Committee, December 16 1996; Faurisson v. France, CCPR/C/58/D/550/1993 (1996).

94. Faurisson v. France, CCPR/C/58/D/550/1993 para. D (9) (1996) (citing individual opinion by Elizabeth Evatt and David Kretzmer, co-signed by Eckart Klein concurring).

95. *Id.* at para. F (Prafulla Chandra Bhagwati, concurring).

96. *Id.* at para. E (7) (Rajsoomer Lallah, concurring).

tendencies. In this regard, French courts "appear to have, quite properly, arrogated back to themselves the power to decide a question which the Legislature had purported to decide by a legislative judgment."

These criticisms of the Gayssot Law *in abstracto* make two errors. First, they mention the denier's intent along with the consequences of the expression. Second, one cannot reproach a legislator for having associated a kind of speech with certain consequences. I shall begin by dealing shortly with this second point.

3.1 Legislative Discretion

It is possible for one to have doubts concerning the relevance of Judge Lallah's criticisms: the legislator is perfectly competent to consider that a certain act has evil consequences and therefore to decide to regulate or forbid it, even if these consequences are not certain.[97] Limits to free speech are ascriptive, as opposed to descriptive.[98] This point is particularly apparent in the case of obscenity, when legislators associate obscene expressions with depravation of youth or other harmful consequences. For instance, the Supreme Court of the United States ruled that "[n]othing in the Constitution prohibits a State from reaching such a conclusion and acting on it legislatively simply because there is no conclusive evidence or empirical data."[99] The German Constitutional Court ruled very similarly that "in such a scientifically unresolved situation, the lawmaker may estimate the dangers and risks and decide whether to adopt a measure or not."[100]

Of course, under the First Amendment—except in cases of "less protected expression"—the likelihood of the harmful consequence of the speech must be

---

97. *See* LEONARD WAYNE SUMNER, THE HATEFUL AND THE OBSCENE: STUDIES IN THE LIMITS OF FREE EXPRESSION 78–80 (2004); *see also* Frederick Schauer, *Is it Better to be Safe than Sorry? Free Speech and the Precautionary Principle*, 36 PEPP. L. REV. 301, 303–04 (2009); Winfried Hassemer, *Darf es Straftaten geben, die ein strafrechtliches Rechtsgut nicht in Mitleidenschaft ziehen?*, *in* DIE RECHTSGUTSTHEORIE 61 (Roland Hefendehl, Andrew von Hirsch & Wolfgang Wohlers eds., 2003).

98. *See* Frederick Schauer, *Speech, Behaviour and the Interdependence of Fact and Value*, *in* FREEDOM OF SPEECH AND INCITEMENT AGAINST DEMOCRACY 56–61 (David Kretzmer & Francine Kershman Hazan eds., 2000); H.L.A Hart, *The Ascription of Responsibility and Rights*, *in* ESSAYS ON LOGIC AND LANGUAGE 145–66 (Antony Flew ed., 1951).

99. Paris Adult Theatre v. Slaton, 413 U.S. 49, 63 (1973).

100. Josephine Mutzenbacher Decision, BVerfGE 83, 130 (141–42) (1990).

left to the trier of fact according to the "clear and present danger test."[101] But in other legal systems, the lawmaker is entitled to ascribe some consequences to a class of expressions.[102] Such a choice made by a legislator can, to a certain extent, be examined using a kind of "rational basis test" by the organ verifying the conformity with a superior norm of a norm restricting a right.[103] For example, the European Court of Human Rights checks whether an interference with freedom of expression pursues a "legitimate aim" and whether the reasons adduced by the national authorities to justify it are "relevant and sufficient."[104] The Canadian Supreme Court verifies the existence of a rational basis between the restriction and the feared harms.[105] Note that the organs applying the norm do not have to verify the correctness of the legislator's choice. For example, once the legislator has decided that it should be written on cigarette packages that tobacco endangers health, the judges enforcing this norm will not have to verify that "smoking kills" in all cases, and this has nothing to do with their "independence." Actually, contrary to what Judge Lallah stated, the French jurisdictions did not "[come] to the conclusion that [Faurisson's] statements propagated ideas tending to revive Nazi doctrine and. . . to raise or strengthen anti-semitic tendencies."[106] They only established that Faurisson's words had the meaning targeted by the Gayssot Law.

This is so because the prohibition of denial differs from other norms regulating expression, where the targeted speech is defined by its direct or indirect consequences, such as libel (harming someone's reputation) or incitement to violence. This brings us to the second point, relating to the distinction between the speaker's intent and the speech's consequences.

---

101. *See* William E. Lee, *Manipulating Legislative Facts: the Supreme Court and the First Amendment*, 72 TULANE L. REV. 1261 (1998).

102. This different treatment of the relationship between an expression and its consequences may be one of the greatest "exceptional" features of the American understanding of freedom of expression. *See* Thomas Hochmann, *L'exceptionnelle protection de la liberté d'expression aux Etats-Unis*, *in* L'EXCEPTIONNALISME AMÉRICAIN ET LES DROITS DE L'HOMME 178–81 (Ludovic Hennebel & Arnaud Van Waenyenberge eds., 2009).

103. Such a verification usually respects the margin of assessment of the political rule maker. See, for instance, the decision of the French Constitutional Court (*Conseil constitutionnel*), January 15, 1975, Rec. p. 19. *See also* Detlev Sternberg-Lieben, *Rechtsgut, Verhältnismässigkeit und die Freiheit des Strafgesetzgebers*, *in* DIE RECHTSGUTSTHEORIE 78 (Roland Hefendehl, Andrew von Hirsch & Wolfgang Wohlers eds., 2003).

104. *See, e.g.*, Jersild v. Denmark, [1994] 19 EHRR 1, para. 31.

105. *See, e.g.*, RJR-MacDonald Inc. c. Canada, [1995] 3 S.C.R. 199, § 154. On pornography, *see R. v. Butler*, [1992] 1 S.C.R. 452, § 108.

106. *See* Faurisson v. France, *supra* note 93 (individual opinion by Lallah, para. 7).

3.2 Intent and Consequences

The importance allocated to the denier's intent by the Human Rights Committee is widely shared in legal literature, where many scholars argue that only a *mala fide* or a hateful denier can be sentenced under such statutes.[107] This belief seems to be in accordance with something that Hans Kelsen criticized a century ago and that he called the "Dogma of Intent" (*Willensdogma*),[108] namely, the belief that an individual can be punished only for an act that he intended.

This, nevertheless, would be the case only if a legal norm ordered it to be so. One cannot accurately describe the existing legal order if one is led by absolute moral principles. Describing what the law should be, armed with moral and philosophical tools, is not a task to be neglected. But it becomes a mistake if one confuses this ideal world with the law in its existing form. In order to validate the Dogma of Intent, it is therefore necessary to look for a norm that implements it in the legal system. I claim that such a quest would not be successful within the regulation of the denial of crimes against humanity, at least, not in the legal systems that I have mentioned until now.

1. Some Distinctions

A dog might be able to distinguish between being stumbled over and being kicked[109]—even if this is not an undisputed statement among American legal scholars[110] and even if, from a moral point of view, opinions differ on the

---

107. For an example of a French perspective, *see* Bernard Beignier, *De la langue perfide, délivre moi. . ., Réflexions sur la loi du 13 juillet 1990 dite "loi Gayssot," in* POUVOIR ET LIBERTÉ, ETUDES OFFERTES À JACQUES MOURGEON 525-6 (1998); Sevane Garibian, *Taking Denial Seriously: Genocide Denial and Freedom of Speech in French Law*, 9 CARDOZO J. CONFLICT RESOL. 479, 484 (2008). The majority of the German authors thinks that bad faith is required. *See, e.g.*, KLAUS MIEBACH & JÜRGEN SCHÄFER, *supra* note 60, at § 130, Rn. 81; Lenckner & Sternberg-Lieben, *supra* note 91, at § 130, Rn. 20; THOMAS FISCHER, STRAFGESETZBUCH UND NEBENGESETZE § 130, Rn. 42–44 (56th ed., 2009). The strongest defense of this view was recently offered by Gerd Geilen, *Unvorsätzliche "Auschwitzlüge?" Bemerkungen zu § 130 Abs. 3 StGB, in* STRAFRECHT ZWISCHEN SYSTEM UND TELOS, FESTSCHRIFT FÜR ROLF DIETRICH HERZBERG ZUM SIEBZIGSTEN GEBURTSTAG AM 14. FEBRUAR 2008, 593 et. seq. (Holm Putzke et al. eds., 2008).

108. HANS KELSEN, HAUPTPROBLEME DER STAATSRECHTSLEHRE ENTWICKELT AUS DER LEHRE VOM RECHTSSÄTZE 133 (Scientia Verlag 2nd ed. 1984) (1911).

109. OLIVER WENDELL HOLMES, JR., THE COMMON LAW 3 (Macmillan & Co, 1882).

110. *See* Frederick Schauer, *Intentions, Conventions, and the First Amendment: the Case of Cross-Burning*, 55 SUP. CT. REV. 197 (2003) (arguing that with this claim, "Justice Holmes demonstrated his limited knowledge of the canine world.").

existence of a difference between an intentional or unintentional harm.[111] But as far as the legal limits of free speech are involved, the speaker's intent is not determinative unless the statute requires it to be so. Furthermore, one should note that Oliver Wendell Holmes, whose dog aphorism is often quoted as an argument by proponents of the necessity of psychological blameworthiness for criminal liability, wrote this sentence while explaining that ancient law was founded on vengeance. But he never made the mistake of arguing that modern criminal law always requires the agent to intend the harmful consequences of his act:

> when we are dealing with that part of the law which aims more directly than any other at establishing standards of conduct, we should expect there more than elsewhere to find that the tests of liability are external, and independent of the degree of evil in the particular person's motive or intentions.[112]

Furthermore, one should recall that the intent to express something is by no means equivalent to the intent to provoke certain consequences through this expression. As John Searle explained, a speaker's "representing intention is not the same as his communication intention. Communicating is a matter of producing certain effects on one's hearers, but one can intend to represent something without caring at all about the effects on one's hearers."[113] Therefore, the Dogma of Intent splits into two variants: the idea that one cannot be punished for an act unless he wanted to accomplish this act; and the idea that one cannot be punished for an act unless he wanted to provoke the consequences of this act. When applied to the denial of crimes against humanity, this distinction covers two kinds of intentions that are often merged[114] but, as the first part of this chapter has showed, can nevertheless

111. *See, e.g.*, RONALD DWORKIN, FREEDOM'S LAW, THE MORAL READING OF THE AMERICAN CONSTITUTION 255–56 (1996) (arguing that intentional harm is generally more serious than nonintentional (or merely expected) harm, and that the later, but not the former, should be covered by academic freedom); Michael Gorr, *Should the Law Distinguish between Intention and (Mere) Foresight?*, 2 LEGAL THEORY 359 (1996) (arguing that the distinction between the intended and the mere foreseen consequences of an act does not underwrite a difference in moral or legal culpability).

112. HOLMES, *supra* note 109, at 50.

113. JOHN R. SEARLE, INTENTIONALITY, AN ESSAY IN THE PHILOSOPHY OF MIND 165 (1983).

114. *See R. v. Keegstra* [1990] 3 S.C.R. 697, § 125 (stating that, "only rarely will one who intends to promote hatred be acting in good faith or upon honest belief.").

be conceptually isolated into hate (i.e., intent to harm) and bad faith (i.e., awareness of the falsity of the statement).[115]

With this in mind, it is interesting to distinguish between two types of norms restricting free expression. The first category resembles what German criminal law scholars would call *Erfolgsdelikt* and their French peers—*infraction matérielle*; the second one is similar to *Tätigkeitsdelikt/infraction formelle*.[116] Let me call the first category *"consequential" speech regulations* and describe these as norms encompassing the consequences provoked by an expression as an element of the offense. A good example of such a norm is libel, defined as a statement of fact harming someone's reputation. The second category is shaped by *"substantial" speech regulations*, which permit the punishment of certain expressions or significations with regard for their substance and not for their consequences. Most of the statutes targeting denial of crimes against humanity belong to this second category.

2. Looking for a Normative Support for the Dogma of Intent

We can now begin the inquiry: can the Dogma of Intent find any normative support in the legal systems studied in this chapter? In many legal systems, it is possible for one to find a norm providing that "[t]here is no crime in the absence of an intent to commit it."[117] This means that a criminal offense must contain—besides its *actus reus*—a mental element: the *mens rea*. This mental component should not be perceived as tantamount to the one required by the proponents of the Dogma of Intent.

---

115. For a jurisdictional distinction between bad faith and intent to harm, see the Supreme Court's distinction between "actual malice" in the common law sense of intent to harm (ill will), and "actual malice" as understood in the constitutional law of defamation, namely as bad faith (awareness of falsity): Garrison v. Louisiana, 379 U.S. 64, 70–75 (1964); Henry v. Collins, 380 U.S. 356 (1965); Greenbelt Coop. Publishing Ass'n v. Bresler, 398 U.S. 6, 9–11 (1970); Masson v. New Yorker Magazine, Inc., 501 U.S. 496, 510 (1991). *See also* Frederick Schauer, *supra* note 89, at 907 n. 15.

116. *See, e.g.*, Johanna Schulenburg, *Dogmatische Zusammenhänge von Rechtsgut, Deliktsstruktur und objektiver Zurechnung*, *in* DIE RECHTSGUTSTHEORIE 244 (Roland Hefendehl, Andrew von Hirsch & Wolfgang Wohlers eds., 2003); ROGER MERLE AND ANDRÉ VITU, TRAITÉ DE DROIT CRIMINEL § 648–53 (Vol. 1 1997)

117. *See* § 121-3 of the French Criminal Code. *See also* § 15 of the German Criminal Code (stating that, "[o]nly intentional conduct is punishable, unless the law expressly provides punishment for negligent conduct."). *See also* Model Penal Code §2.02 (stating, "a person is not guilty of an offense unless he acted purposely, knowingly, recklessly or negligently, as the law may require, with respect to each material element of the offense.").

3. "Substantial" speech regulations

For a "substantial" speech regulation, such as most of the anti-denial statutes, the second variant of the Dogma of Intent—the intent to provoke some consequence through the expression—can immediately be excluded, since such consequences are not part of the definition of the offense. Of course, the legislator deciding to forbid denial does so by considering some consequences it thinks this speech has or could have (harming a group of persons, threatening democracy, etc.). However, in most cases, the norm itself does not make these consequences an element of the offense. It is therefore irrelevant what the "motives" of the lawmaker may have been, what "interest" it wished to protect; the effects produced by the forbidden expression are not a condition of the commission of the offense. The requirement that the denier be hateful and aim at harming a group of people thus has no basis, since the *mens rea*, in a criminal offense, is related to the *actus reus*.

Now, how does the judge determine this *actus reus* in the concretization of a speech regulation? The judge—or the jury—will try to establish how an "ordinary" listener would have understood the utterance in its context. In communication, the "utterer's meaning" (Grice) is decisive, but for legal adjudication, it is not—what counts is how the utterance was likely to be understood. *Actus reus* is committed if the utterance is likely to be understood by a reasonable ordinary listener as bearing the meaning forbidden by the offense. Here, once again, Searle can help us with his distinction between saying something and meaning it on the one hand, and saying it without meaning it on the other. Searle explains:

> When I say something and mean it, my utterance has conditions of satisfaction in a way that it does not have any such conditions if I say it without meaning it. If I say "Es regnet" as a way of practicing German pronunciation, then the fact that the sun is shining when I utter this sentence is irrelevant. But if I say "Es regnet" and mean it, then the fact that the sun is shining is relevant, and it becomes relevant because saying something and meaning it is a matter of saying it with the conditions of satisfaction intentionally imposed on the utterance.[118]

When I gave, at the beginning of this chapter, an example of bare denial, I wrote: "no gas chamber was used to kill human beings during World War II."

---

118. Searle, *supra* note 113, at 169.

The occurrence of such a sentence, given the present context, cannot reasonably be interpreted as denying the Holocaust. In this sense, a Paris Tribunal could rule that the bare exposition of the deniers' theses does not constitute an offense according to the Gayssot Law, as long as the text does not show an endorsement of them.[119]

The *actus reus* of a "substantial" speech regulation is committed if the utterance can reasonably be interpreted in its context as carrying the forbidden meaning. As a result, the *mens rea* can only be the intent to express an utterance likely to be understood as having the forbidden meaning. To put it differently, the *mens rea* in a "substantial" speech regulation is the consciousness that one's words are likely to be interpreted as meaning something that is forbidden, like—in some legal systems—denying the Holocaust. Once again, such a consciousness will be established based on the standard of the reasonable ordinary man; as Holmes put it: "[t]he test of foresight is not what this very criminal foresaw, but what a man of reasonable prudence would have foreseen."[120] Such a requirement is, of course, very easy to meet and would be inferred from the content and context of the expression. An individual expressing a statement that can be reasonably interpreted as denying the Holocaust can be reasonably thought to have foreseen that his statement was likely to be understood that way. So much for the *mens rea*.

A rare situation where the author of such an expression could escape a sentence because of a lack of intention would then amount to the excuse of a factual mistake. This would be the case, for instance, of an individual having written that approximately "100 persons died in Auschwitz" but able to prove that he inadvertently forget four zeros. Of course, here again, the context of the appearance of the expression plays a major role in determining the reality of the mistake.

In June 1997, the French Court of Cassation stated that the outrageous (*outrancière*) minimization of the number of deaths corresponds to a denial offense "if made *mala fide*."[121] This led some scholars to argue that the Gayssot Law requires in every case proof of the bad faith of the denier.[122] I think this

---

119. Tribunal de Grande Instance de Paris, 17ch., October 22, 1996, *Ministère public c/Delcroix*, LÉGIPRESSE 1997, III, 26.

120. HOLMES, *supra* note 109, at 54.

121. Cass crim., June 17, 1997, Dalloz 1998, Jurisprudence, 50, case note Jean-Philippe Feldman. Contrary to similar statutes in other countries, the French statute does not explicitly mention the "minimization" of the Holocaust but only its "contestation."

122. *See* Beignier, *supra* note 107, at 525–26; Garibian, *supra* note 107, at 484.

is inaccurate for the reasons stated above. The only question worth asking is whether the bad faith of someone not formally denying but quantitatively minimizing the Holocaust must be proven under French law.

According to the first commentator of this decision, an "outrageous" minimization is inevitably made *mala fide*.[123] This may be true for practical purposes, but if one accepts the hypothesis of a *bona fide* denier, one can also imagine an individual minimizing the Holocaust in an outrageous but nevertheless *bona fide* manner. A minimization does not have to be stated *mala fide* to be outrageous, i.e., grossly exaggerated. Certainly, the word "outrageous" appears in the definition of the American tort of *intentional* infliction of emotional distress. But the "outrageous" feature of this tort is external to its author, as it clearly appears from the methodology given by the Restatement of Torts in order to determine if a conduct is "outrageous" or not: "Generally, the case is one in which the recitation of the facts to an average member of the community would arouse his resentment against the actor, and lead him to exclaim, 'Outrageous!'"[124] The question as to whether a minimization of the Holocaust is "outrageous" is different from that of the speaker's state of mind.

There are thus two ways of understanding the French court's mention of the bad faith of an individual grossly minimizing the Holocaust. First, the court may have intended to insist on the fact that minimization is actionable under the Gayssot Law only when it amounts to a contestation of the Holocaust. The reference to bad faith would then be useless and could be ignored. I mentioned earlier that while enforcing speech regulation statutes, judges interpret words in their context in order to determine if they have the targeted signification. Of course, this is also true of anti-denial statutes; for example, the French Court of Cassation ruled that contesting the existence of crimes against humanity enters the anti-denial statute even if it is presented in a disguised way, with insinuation.[125] This means that an expression that the judge interprets as a contestation of the Holocaust is actionable under the statute.

A second way of understanding this mention of bad faith is that it expresses a judicial will to require a supplementary element, one that is not foreseen in the statute, namely the proof of bad faith, but only in the case of minimization. Such a requirement should then be understood as a tool to

---

123. Feldman, *supra* note 121, at 52.

124. Restatement (Second) of Torts § 46, comment d (1965).

125. Cass. crim., September 12, 2000, DROIT PÉNAL 18 (2001).

restrict the limit to free speech, similar to the actual malice requirement of the Supreme Court of the United States' decision, *New York Times v. Sullivan*.[126]

This issue is nevertheless of limited interest. When confronted with such cases, judges will have to determine whether the speaker's minimization of the Holocaust qualifies as a contestation. After which, if they feel constrained to investigate whether the author of the speech acted *mala fide*, they will certainly have no difficulty in doing so, based on the methods presented in the previous section of this chapter. The true issue in such cases, the one mandated by the French anti-denial statute, is whether minimization amounts to contestation.

4. "Consequential" speech regulations

As far as consequential speech regulation is concerned, the two variants of the "Dogma of Intent" seem to merge: the forbidden act being defined by its consequences, the intent to commit the act would then amount to the intent to produce the consequences. Does this mean that, in any of the legal systems studied, the author of a libel must have been led by an intent to harm someone's reputation? Clearly not, for the same reasons as those brought forward concerning "substantial" speech regulations. The meaning and the effects of the utterance are determined by the judge or the jury, who tries to establish what an ordinary reasonable individual would have thought of the utterance taken in its context. The "speaker's intent" is not in any way determinative. The speaker must only be found "aware" that his speech was likely to have certain consequences, and such a conclusion will mostly follow from the examination under the "ordinary man" standard.

There are a few instances where some hypothetical consequences of denial are specified within the statute—for example, in Germany, denying "in a manner capable of disturbing the public peace"—but once again, this is independent of the denier's intent. The German judge will only have to establish whether the utterance in its context bears the meaning targeted by the statute and whether this speech is capable of "disturbing the public peace."[127] Nothing requires the judge to establish whether the denier intended

126. New York Times Co. v. Sullivan, 376 U.S. 254 (1964).

127. This requirement presents little difficulty in the adjudication of denial cases in Germany. An analysis of the public peace clause would go beyond the scope of this chapter. I can only refer to the leading article on this topic: Thomas Fischer, *Die Eignung, den öffentlichen Frieden zu stören*, 8 NStZ 159 (1988). *See also* the Introduction of this volume, *supra*, at xxii.

to provoke hatred or to disturb the public peace. The judge must interpret the utterance of the case from the point of view of a "reasonable listener," a task that is independent of what the speaker intended to mean and one that has nothing to do with the reason why the speaker expressed it nor with the consequences he intended to provoke with this expression.

5. Result: Irrelevance of the speaker's intent

The law cannot look inside minds. For example, it cannot forbid racist opinions but only their expression under certain circumstances. Returning to the *Front National*'s internal note that I mentioned at the beginning, the prohibition of incitement to racial violence does not prevent individuals from thinking "we must throw these bloody Arabs in the sea"; it merely forbids people from saying it publicly. If this is done, the expression can be condemned, with disregard for the motives of the speaker. The intentional element of such criminal offenses lies in the intention of saying what one said—not in the reasons that led to this choice—coupled with a bare awareness that the utterance was likely to be understood as being "meant," as defined by Searle.[128] Since the utterance at issue is interpreted by referring to the standard of the ordinary man, the speaker's awareness that it could be understood in this way rarely presents any difficulty.

What matters to the judge is whether the expression, taken as a whole, bears the signification targeted in the norm. Once we understand this, it is easy to dissociate the speech from the intent of the speaker.[129] The "reader/listener response" is decisive. A text regarded as a work of fiction by its author can be deemed defamatory if the judge considers that its fictional status is unclear to the "reasonable" reader.[130] For the same reasons, the "I was joking" justification (*animus jocandi*) is not always successful.[131] "Consequential" speech regulations are designed to punish and/or prevent the (feared) harmful effects of

---

128. *See supra* text accompanying note 118.

129. *See* Larry A. Alexander, *Free Speech and Speaker's Intent*, 12 CONST. COMMENTARY 21 (1995).

130. *See, e.g.*, Lindon et al. v. France, Eur. Court of HR, October 22, 2007; *see also Esra*, BVerfG (German Constitutional Court) June 13, 2007, 1 BvR 1783/05. *See also* Eric Barendt, *Defamation and Fiction, in* LAW AND LITERATURE 483–84. (Michael Freeman & Andrew D. E. Lewis eds., 1999).

131. For an example of French law, *see* Cass. Crim., November 4, 1997, DROIT PÉNAL (1998), comm. 33, case note Michel Veron (incitement to hatred meant as a joke); for Canadian law, *see* R. v. Buzzanga and Durocher, (1979) 49 C.C.C. (2d) 369, 376 (C.A. Ont.) (hate pamphlet meant ironically).

a speech. These effects can occur without such intent by the speaker. Words that are not intended to stir up hatred (for example, words uttered as a joke) can be seen by a judge as likely to stir up hatred (if, for example, according to the judge, it was not obvious that the utterance was not to be taken seriously). Therefore, there is no logical obligation to associate the liability with a specific *mens rea* of the speaker. In the absence of a legal norm requiring such intent, the prosecution does not have to prove that the author of an utterance interpreted as denial was moved by hate or acted *mala fide*.

6. *The Possibility of Making an Extra Requirement*

Of course, this does not mean that the lawmaker cannot choose to require such a specific moral element. This is not a constitutional obligation but rather the result of a comparative harm calculus recognizing the risk of error and the "chilling effect,"[132] namely the concern that a liability without a qualified *mens rea* would lead to self-censorship. Thus, in the United States, for example, the *New York Times v. Sullivan*[133] decision requires that the speaker be aware of the falsity of his allegations in order to offer greater protection of speech and not because such a requirement would be an essential component of the offense of libel.[134]

In Canada, Section 319(2) of the Criminal Code targets "Everyone who, by communicating statements, other than in private conversation, *willfully* promotes hatred against any identifiable group." The word "willfully" was discussed at length in the "somewhat incongruous" *Buzzanga* case, where "the appellants identif[ied] with French-speaking Canadians against whom they [were] alleged to have willfully promoted hatred."[135] Buzzanga and Durocher wrote and distributed a pamphlet promoting hatred against "French-Canadians" in order, or so they testified, to demonstrate the prejudice directed toward this group,

---

132. *See* Frederick Schauer, *Fear, Risk and the First Amendment: Unraveling the "Chilling Effect,"* 58 B. U. L. Rev. 685 (1978); *see also* Harry Kalven, Jr., *The Reasonable Man and the First Amendment: Hill, Butts, and Walker,* Sup. Ct. Rev. 267, 304–05 (1967).

133. New York Times Co. v. Sullivan, 376 U.S. 254, 279–80 (1964).

134. *See* Larry Alexander, *Incitement and Freedom of Speech, in* Freedom of Speech and Incitement against Democracy 108 (David Kretzmer & Francine Kershman Hazan eds., 2000). *See also* Gorr, *supra* note 111 (arguing that despite the absence of a difference in moral or legal culpability between intended and merely expected harm, there may be consequentialist reasons for imposing greater liability in the case of intended harms than in the case of merely foreseen harm (side effects)).

135. R. v. Buzzanga and Durocher, *supra* note 131, at para. 3.

"to show the things that were being said so that intelligent people could see how ridiculous they were."[136] The first judge convicted them nevertheless. The Ontario Court of Appeal noticed that in the absence of any specification concerning the mental element of a crime, the general *mens rea* "is either the intentional or reckless bringing about of the result which the law, in creating the offense, seeks to prevent."[137] So the insertion of the word "willfully" in 319(2) must mean something more: this section is limited to the "intentional promotion of hatred,"[138] which means that the conscious purpose of the agent must be the promotion of hatred, or that he foresees that the promotion of hatred is a substantially certain consequence of his act.[139] In a nutshell, the difference between the mental component in 319(1) and 319(2), according to the court, resides in the exclusion of recklessness in the latter, i.e., in the degree of the agent's certainty concerning the consequences of his act.[140]

Nevertheless, the court errs when it indicates the methodology to be followed in establishing this mental element:

> Where the prosecution, in order to establish the accused's guilt of the offense charged, is required to prove that he intended to bring about a particular consequence or foresaw a particular consequence, the question to be determined is what was in the mind of this particular accused, and the necessary intent or foresight must be brought home to him subjectively. . . . The purpose of this process, however, is to determine what the particular accused intended, not to fix him with the intention that a reasonable person might be assumed to have in the circumstances, where doubt exists as to the actual intention of the accused.[141]

This is a mistake because even when the norm requires establishing that the agent "intended" a particular consequence; this does not mean that the trier of fact must establish any real psychological event. The only person who

136. *Id.* at para. 16.

137. *Id.* at para. 32.

138. *Id.* at para. 33. This paragraph is quoted and approved by the Canadian Supreme Court in R. v. Keegstra, *supra* note 114, at §§115–116.

139. R. v. Buzzanga and Durocher, *supra* note 131, at para. 46.

140. For a similar distinction between "oblique intention" and "recklessness" in American law, *see* Dan W. Morkel, *On the Distinction between Recklessness and Conscious Negligence*, 30 AM. J. COMP. L. 325 (1982).

141. R. v. Buzzanga and Durocher, supra note 131, at paras. 50 and 52.

might be expected to inquire with some chance of success what an individual "intended" is the very individual himself, explains Kelsen.[142] But in a legal system, the application of a norm cannot only depend on the addressee of this norm. When a norm requires a mental element such as "willfulness," the trier of fact is not asked about a real psychic process—something he is not able to discover—rather about some external facts allowing him to infer this mental component.[143] Such an inference cannot be made other than by referring to the standard of the reasonable man, with regard for the particular circumstances of the case. Accordingly, the wording of the following South African statute corresponds much more to the reality of judicial work, by targeting the publication of "words based on one or more of the prohibited grounds, against any person, *that could reasonably be construed to demonstrate a clear intention* to be hurtful, be harmful or to incite harm, promote or propagate hatred (emphasis added)."[144]

To put it differently, the object of inquiry is not any psychological event occurring inside the agent's mind but what a man of reasonable prudence would have "intended" in the same circumstances. The legislator is free to make this extra requirement but it does not have a constitutional obligation to do so in any of the legal systems I am aware of, and it did not choose to do so in most legal systems that have a specific prohibition of denial. Contrary to this, one should note that in Austria, Section 3h of the constitutional law against National Socialist activities (*Verbotsgesetz*)—forbidding the denial of Nazi crimes—is the only disposition of this law that does not require establishing an intention to support the Nazi ideology.[145] In fact, I am aware of only one statute containing such an extra requirement about the denier's intent.

The Swiss anti-denial statute[146] shows two particularities compared to most of the other European statutes concerning denial. Indeed, it forbids denial, gross minimization or justification of any crime against humanity,

---

142. Kelsen, *supra* note 108, at 156–57.

143. *Id.* at 157.

144. Promotion of Equality and Prevention of Unfair Discrimination Act § 10 (2000).

145. *See* Christian Bertel, *Die Betätigung im nationalsozialistischen Sinn*, *in* FESTSCHRIFT FÜR WINFRIED PLATZGUMMER 126 (Helmut Fuchs & Wolfgang Brandstetter eds., 1995).

146. § 261 bis (4) Criminal Code (stating that "[h]e who, publicly, . . . belittles or discriminates in a way which affects the human dignity of a person or a group of persons because of their race, their ethnic belonging to their religion or who, for the same reason, denies, grossly minimizes or tries to justify a genocide or other crime against humanity").

whereas most other statutes are limited to the Holocaust. Furthermore, it requires the proof of intent to attack a group of persons; intent to harm is part of the offense.[147]

As far as the Holocaust is concerned, jurisdictions have always found that the element of intent was fulfilled.[148] Swiss judges seem to deduce bad faith from the common knowledge of the Holocaust, and from bad faith, they infer the intent to harm. In short, the required intent depends on the awareness that the denied crime took place. This has led to an interesting series of cases involving state denial.

In a 2001 case, a tribunal conducted a real inquiry on the good faith of Turkish citizens denying the Armenian genocide. It concluded that they did not intend to vilify an ethnic group but to defend the national point of view they had been raised in. A criminal denier "must be conscious that the facts he denies happened," which is unlikely for the Turkish defendants because of "the strong national orientation of the Turkish school system." This judgement thus seems to release *bona fide* deniers, recognizing the existence of such denial when this doctrine is adopted by a State.[149]

However, more recently in March 2007, a tribunal of Lausanne sentenced Dogu Perinçek, a Turkish nationalist politician, after his declarations that the Armenian genocide was an "international lie." The judge observed that Perinçek held a PhD in law and that he was aware of the arguments of his contradictors but had merely decided to brush them aside. "[He] cannot claim or even believe in the non-existence of the Armenian genocide." The judge concluded that Perinçek's statements clearly appeared to have racist and nationalist motives.[150] The appeal jurisdiction and the Federal Tribunal upheld the sentence of Perinçek.[151]

---

147. *See* MARCEL ALEXANDER NIGGLI, RASSENDISKRIMINIERUNG, EIN KOMMENTAR ZU ART. 261 BIS STGB UND ART. 171C MSTG 325–57 (1996).

148. *See, e.g.*, Federal Tribunal, Mar. 22, 2000, 6S. 719/1999, *available at* http://www.ediekr.admin.ch/php/idetails.php?id=2000-11.

149. Karaman Fikri und Konsorten, Tribunal of Berne, Sept. 14, 2001, *available at* http://www.armenian.ch. The association's appeal was rejected on formal grounds, a decision upheld by the Federal Tribunal in 2002.

150. Dogu Perincek, Tribunal de Police de Lausanne, Mar, 9, 2007, p.13, *available at* http://www.armenian.ch.

151. Federal Tribunal, Dec. 12, 2007, 6B_398/2007/rod. *See also* the recent sentence of another Turkish nationalist: Federal Tribunal, Sept. 16, 2010, 6B_297/2010.

These two judgments reached opposing solutions because of the determination of the mental state of the denier.[152] The judges took into account the education level of the deniers to determine if they could act *bona fide*: the accused were uneducated persons in the first case, whereas in the second case, the defendant was a doctor of law describing himself as "a cultured person having very good historical knowledge."

4. Conclusion

The issue of the good or bad faith of a denier—i.e., the question of his awareness of the falsity of his assertions—is relevant to some extent in trials not involving a specific anti-denial statute. On the other hand, when a judge has to decide on the basis of such a statute, the issue of the good or bad faith does not matter in most cases. Actually, requiring proof of the denier's knowledge that the crime he denies took place would imply that the statute targets the denier because he is *lying*. This mistake may be derived partly from the common statement that denial laws establish an "official truth,"[153] or from the misleading German term *Auschwitzlüge* (Auschwitz Lie) used to describe Holocaust denial. Such statutes do not protect "the truth." For instance, exaggerating the number of victims cannot be sentenced, based on these statutes.[154]

This does not mean that the subjective side of the denier should be completely ignored. A requirement of bad faith or hateful intent could be enacted

152. Perhaps the official recognition of the Armenian genocide by the Swiss parliament in December 2003 also played a role. In the 2001 judgment, the tribunal underlined that there was no official position of Switzerland on this issue, whereas the 2007 judgment refers, among other things, to this official recognition to conclude that the Armenian genocide is an averred historical fact.

153. *See, e.g.*, Lyrissa Barnett Lidsky, *Where's the Harm?: Free Speech and the Regulation of Lies*, 65 WASH. & LEE L. REV. 1091, 1099 (2008) (stating that, "by punishing Holocaust denial, a State attempts to establish an official Truth.").

154. The judge may sentence the exaggeration of the number of victims if he determines that it was an indirect way of denying the crime itself. For example, in 1980, French tribunals sentenced the author of the following utterance for incitement to hatred: "Under the Third Reich, six million Jews were gassed, or so the Jews state. I do not contest this and I would not question it either regardless of whether the Jews asserted the figure of 60 or 600 million. I am not able to produce any evidence for or against it." The court interpreted this statement as casting doubt on the reality of the Holocaust, and suggesting to the reader that he had been fooled. Cass. crim., IFRIG, June 2, 1980, no. 79.91.581.

in order to offer greater protection of speech. Almost none of the legal systems that prohibit a form of denial have taken up such an option. One should also keep in mind that even with such a requirement, the trier of fact will not inquire into the denier's mind but infer his intent from external circumstances, based on the standard of the "reasonable man."

Furthermore, bad faith and hateful intent, which are useless in the determination of guilt, may actually play a role in the fixing of sentences. In the 1998 condemnation of the denier Roger Garaudy,[155] the Paris Court of Appeal quoted several passages from his book and concluded—without questioning the possibility of good faith—that these elements established the denial offense. However, later in its ruling, while sentencing the accused, the court mentioned the bad faith of the accused and his intellectual dishonesty. The state of mind of the denier can thus be considered during sentencing, as an observation of the widespread moral presupposition that a lie deserves a harsher punishment than a mistake.[156] The French Court of Cassation often reminds tribunals that they may only take into account the motives of the accused during sentencing.[157]

I began this chapter with fortune-tellers. While I do not claim to be able to read into the future, I would nevertheless like to venture a prediction. If the extension of the sanction of various kinds of denial follows its own path—as the European framework decision against racism and xenophobia targeting "aggravated" denial of all "crimes of genocide, crimes against humanity and war crimes" indicate—there are good reasons to think that it will be accompanied by a similar amplification of the fear of stifling free speech and free research. In order to accommodate the different values at stake, a solution may be found in the area of the intentional element of the offense. The framework decision does not seem to ignore this when it mentions "intentional conduct" and adds that Member States may choose to punish only "abusive" conduct. Similarly, the 2003 Additional Protocol on the

---

155. Paris Court of Appeal, Dec. 16, 1998, *Légipresse,* 159-III, 30–34.

156. *See* Lenckner & Sternberg-Lieben, *supra* note 91, at n. 28 (arguing that a *bona fide* denier should receive a milder punishment than a *mala fide* denier); *see* Geilen, *supra* note 107, at 599. But see—before the introduction of a specific prohibition of denial in German law—the German judgment refusing to reduce the sentence in the case of an apparently *"bona fide"* Holocaust denier: BGH, NJW 1995, 340, *overruling* Mannheim, *supra* note 82, at 2498.

157. *See, e.g.,* Cass. crim., Sept. 3 1996, bull. no. 311. *See also* Mikaël Benillouche, *La subjectivisation de l'élément moral de l'infraction: plaidoyer pour une nouvelle théorie de la culpabilité,* 3 REV. SC. CRIM. 529, 535 (2005).

Convention on Cybercrime allows State Parties to require that the denial "is committed with the intent to incite hatred, discrimination or violence."[158]

Once again, there is no legal obligation to consider the intent and the motives of the denier. However, making such a requirement may be a good means—just like in Switzerland—of limiting the scope of the offense, especially if the lawmaker is less confident that any "denial or grossly trivializing" of any "crimes of genocide, crimes against humanity or war crimes" is susceptible of provoking the evil consequences the lawmaker wishes to avoid.

158. Council of Europe (2003), Additional Protocol to the Convention on Cybercrime, Concerning the Criminalisation of Acts of a Racist and Xenophobic Nature Committed through Computer Systems, Article 6(2) *available at* http://conventions.coe.int/Treaty/en/Treaties/Html/189.htm. Ukraine, Lithuania, and Montenegro declared that they would make use of this extra requirement.

Index